AF689344

Labour Law in Hong Kong

Labour Law in Hong Kong

Second Edition

Ng Sek Hong

This book was originally published as a monograph in the International Encyclopaedia of Laws/Labour Law and Industrial Relations.

General Editors: Roger Blanpain, Frank Hendrickx

Wolters Kluwer
Law & Business

Published by:
Kluwer Law International
PO Box 316
2400 AH Alphen aan den Rijn
The Netherlands
Website: www.kluwerlaw.com

Sold and distributed in North, Central and South America by:
Aspen Publishers, Inc.
7201 McKinney Circle
Frederick, MD 21704
United States of America
Email: customer.service@aspenpublishers.com

Sold and distributed in all other countries by:
Turpin Distribution Services Ltd.
Stratton Business Park
Pegasus Drive, Biggleswade
Bedfordshire SG18 8TQ
United Kingdom
Email: kluwerlaw@turpin-distribution.com

Printed on acid-free paper

ISBN 978-90-411-6011-9

This title is available on www.kluwerlawonline.com

Printed and Bound by CPI Group (UK) Ltd, Croydon, CR0 4YY.

The Author

Dr Ng Sek Hong is Reader in the School of Business at the University of Hong Kong. He attended the London School of Economics and Political Science of the University of London for an MSc degree in industrial relations and later, also for his PhD specializing in the field of industrial sociology. He teaches and has published several books and a number of articles in the area of employment and labour study, industrial relations and human resources.

The Author

Table of Contents

Table of Contents

General Introduction

Chapter 1. Geography

1. Hong Kong is situated on the southern coast of China at the entry to the Pearl River delta (also known as the Canton delta or the Zhujiang delta) in the Guangdong province. Occupying about 1104 square kilometres in area, it consists of three parts:

- a tip of the mainland adjoining China and 235 islands and covering 976 square kilometres, or 92 per cent of the total land area of Hong Kong;
- the Kowloon Peninsula connecting to the New Territories and facing Hong Kong Island; and
- Hong Kong Island.

2. The island, together with its adjacent islets, covers an area of 81 square kilometres. It has been the administrative, financial and banking centre of the territory. Kowloon, on the other hand, accommodates a variety of retail, trading and commercial activities. It also serves as the focal point of the territory's cross-border transport in housing the railway terminus and the ocean terminal. Since 1998 a new international airport has been commissioned in place of the now defunct Kai Tak airport. It is situated on the main outlying island, Lantao, at the Chek Lap Kok area and has now gained a reputation as one of the world's leading airports. In the early postwar decades, much of the industrial and residential space was clustered on the Kowloon Peninsula, especially around the Kwun Tong and Cheung Sha Wan areas. Today, however, it is no longer so concentrated, with a high proportion of the territory's housing estates and workplaces decanted to a fringe of suburban new townships developed in the New Territories since the 1970s, including Tsuen Wan, Kwai Chung, Tuen Mun, Shatin, Tai Po, Yuen Long and Fanling.

3. During the 19th century a series of three unequal treaties made between Britain and China led to the formation of the present territory of Hong Kong. There were:

- the Treaty of Nanking concluding the Opium War, signed in 1842 and ratified in 1843, under which Hong Kong Island was ceded in perpetuity to Britain;
- the Convention of Peking in 1860 under which the southern part of the Kowloon Peninsula and Stonecutter Island were ceded in perpetuity to Britain; and

– the Convention of 1898 under which the New Territories were leased to Britain for 99 years from 1 July 1898.

4. The abrogation of all unequal treaties made with China before the Treaty of Versailles ending the First World War implied the recovery of Chinese jurisdiction over the whole of Hong Kong. This has been the consistent view taken by the post-imperial Chinese government in spite of its administration under British rule. The political status of Hong Kong hence remained equivocal until the expiry of the lease of the New Territories became imminent as it drew close to the year 1997. After a two-year negotiation process, a Sino-British agreement was reached between the two governments in September 1984. As a sequel, a Sino-British Joint Declaration was ratified in 1985; it restored Hong Kong to Chinese sovereignty from 1 July 1997 and guaranteed the status quo of the Hong Kong capitalist system for 50 years.

5. The population of the whole territory is very dense by international standards of comparison. It registered a total of 7.1739 million at the end of 2012 with a population density of 6,620 persons per square kilometres and a sex ratio of 869 males per 1000 females. This figure compared with a total of 6.1491 million at the end of 1994 and 5.3975 million in 1984.

Chapter 2. Cultural Composition: A Hybrid Post-industrial Society in Transition?

6. The population is preponderantly Chinese, comprising 94 per cent of the total. The overwhelming majority was locally born but an increasing number of legal migrants have arrived from mainland China under the 'one-way permit scheme' which has a daily quota of 150. These arrivals numbered 54,600 in 2012. Most Chinese have their roots in the adjacent and largest southern province of China, Guangdong (i.e. Kwantung). Those speaking Cantonese form the largest community (since it originates from Canton, or Guangzhou as the provincial capital of Guangdong), followed next by the ethnic groups speaking the Siyi (i.e. Sze Yap) and the Chaozhou (i.e. Chiu Chow) dialects. The remaining part of the Chinese community originates from other parts of Guangdong as well as other Chinese provinces such as Kiangsu and Chekiang.

7. The non-Chinese who are not locally born are considered in general as an expatriate population who can, however, be localized by obtaining citizenship (which is tantamount to the right of permanent residence) provided that they have been continuously domiciled in Hong Kong for at least seven years. Previously, this expatriate community used to comprise predominantly 'Westerners' who were either British members of the civil service or 'expatriate' staff dispatched by multinationals from their headquarters in home countries such as Americans, Germans, French, Dutch, Australians, Canadians, Portuguese, plus pockets of Asians including Japanese, Singaporeans, Malaysians and Indonesians.

8. However, such a profile of the non-native population has recently been modified conspicuously as a result of the importation of guest migrant workers introduced to the territory to help alleviate its heavily strained labour supply, stemming in the late 1980s from both sustained economic growth and the territory's demographic stagnation as its population matured and started to age steadily.

9. Mirroring the effects of this compounding factor is the emergence of the Philippines and now, Indonesia, on the top of the league table of the home countries of visiting expatriates in Hong Kong, inasmuch as it has become the largest supplier of foreign domestic helpers in the territory (these domestic helpers and household maids help to relieve many middle-class housewives from domestic chores, thereby enabling the latter to enter or remain in the full-time salaried labour market). In the second place is the Philippines. Contributing to such an ethnic mix of the imported workforce staying now in Hong Kong are, in addition, Thais, Koreans, mainland Chinese, as well as Indians and East Europeans.

10. The transnational and multicultural spectrum featuring the cosmopolitan nature of the Hong Kong population has been made even more complex by a two way stampede of (a) herds of Hong Kong people emigrating to such host societies as Canada, Australia, USA and Singapore since the mid-1980s, in the wake of the political uncertainty looming over the 1997 transfer of sovereignty provided under the Sino-British Joint Declaration of 1985 and (b) a creeping and increasing number of these emigrants who, after their 'naturalization' in the host society, have returned to Hong Kong for work and business. Their status – whether deemed to be local or otherwise, as Hong Kong people overseas – has always been viewed as problematic and ambiguous, even for the public authorities in Hong Kong, China or Britain.

11. Reflecting its cosmopolitan character, Hong Kong has adopted English and Chinese as its two official languages. Such a linguistic dualism has been endorsed in the two 'benchmark' official documents enshrining the governance of Hong Kong after 1997. They are the Sino-British Joint Declaration of 1985 on the Future of Hong Kong and the Basic Law promulgated by the Chinese government as the mini constitution for the Hong Kong Special Administrative Region (SAR).

12. Before 1997 and its reintegration with China, Hong Kong as a highly internationalized city port was accustomed to the use of English as the principal language in both the public and private sectors. However, Chinese has now assumed parity with English as the standard medium of government now that Hong Kong has become an SAR of China, although English continues to be more popular in the field of business and commerce.

Besides English the Cantonese dialect has always been the most common spoken medium within the local (Chinese) community. However, Putonghua (Mandarin) has since the 1997 handover has become increasingly popular as the official spoken version of Chinese. In spite of the diversity between different spoken dialects, Chinese characters are common in their written form, thereby providing a unified means of communication in the use of Chinese.

Chapter 3. Political System

13. Prior to July 1997 Hong Kong was a British overseas dependent territory administered by the Hong Kong government headed by the Governor as the representative of the Queen of the United Kingdom reigning over Hong Kong. The Governor owed his authority to the Letters Patent which established the basic framework of the administration. This document, alongside the Royal Instructions, had the virtual effect of prescribing the constitution of Hong Kong during its pre-1997 colonial days. Hong Kong reverted back to China on 1 July 1997 and has since become an SAR of the People's Republic of China (PRC). In place of the Letters Patent and Royal Instructions, the Basic Law which China promulgated earlier came into effect simultaneously to become the constitutional instrument prescribing the (capitalist) socio-political system for Hong Kong.

14. The Basic Law prescribes a wide latitude of local self-governing autonomy for the Hong Kong SAR. However, the prerogative of dealing with its defence and foreign affairs belongs to the central government. The SAR is able to exercise executive, legislative and independent judicial power, including that of final adjudication. Its executive authorities and legislature are be composed of permanent residents of Hong Kong. The SAR is to continue as a free port, a separate customs territory and an international financial centre and may, on its own, using the name 'Hong Kong, China', maintain and develop relations and conclude and implement agreements with foreign states and regions, and international organizations in the appropriate fields, including economics, trade, the financial and monetary, shipping, communications, tourism, cultural and sports fields.

15. The Basic Law creates the office of the Chief Executive as the head of the Hong Kong SAR. He also heads the government of the Hong Kong SAR. In this capacity, he is responsible for implementing the Basic Law, signing bills (proposed legislation) and budgets passed by the Legislative Council, promulgating laws, making decisions on government policies and issuing executive orders. He is assisted by the Executive Council in policy-making. The Chief Executive is selected by election by a broadly representative local Election Committee appointed by the central government. The Chief Executive thus elected is appointed by the Central People's Congress in Beijing.

16. The Executive Council can be viewed as the *de facto* Cabinet for the Chief Executive in assisting him in policy-making. The Chief Executive in Council is the competent authority, for example, for introducing bills to the Legislative Council, making subsidiary legislation or dissolving the Legislative Council. This organ also determines appeals, petitions and objections under those ordinances which confer a statutory right of appeal. Members of the Executive Council are appointed by the Chief Executive and drawn from among the principal officials of the SAR government, Members of the Legislative Council and prominent personalities in the community.

By virtue of the Basic Law, the Legislative Council is the law-making assembly for the SAR. It is in this connection the competent authority to enact laws, approve the Annual Budget, control public expenditure and monitor the performance of the government by putting forward questions on matters of public interest and summoning persons concerned to testify or give evidence. It is also vested with the prerogative to impeach the Chief Executive (if initiated jointly by one-fourth of its members), as well as to endorse the appointment and removal of the judges of the Court of Final Appeal and the Chief Judge of the High Court. It has always been possible for the government and executive authority to introduce before the Legislative Council legislative and public funding proposals. However, members in the Council can move to propose independent legal enactment by way of presenting before the Council Private Members Bills. Nevertheless, pursuance of such an initiative requires the prior consent of the Chief Executive.

17. Other than enacting legislation, the Parliament-equivalent Council holds two major debates every year when it is in session: one which is comprehensive in coverage dealing with the entire platform of government policies which follows the Chief Executive's annual policy address; and the other is the budget debate on financial and economic affairs in the SAR as a sequel to the annual budget presented by the Financial Secretary in March and which he moves before the Legislative Council as the Appropriation Bill.

18. While in session, members of the Council may question the government on the rationale, implications and problems relating to public policy issues and official decisions. They either seek information on such issues or ask for official explanations and actions on them. Members may in this process request either oral or written answers to the questions, and may put forward supplementary questions for the purpose of elucidating an answer already given. However, since 1997 it has been more a common practice for the SAR legislature to summon the responsible government official or private person to appear before the Council to provide oral explanations and give evidence, if necessary, on matters of concern to public interest.

19. The Council normally meets in public every Wednesday. Following the pre-1997 practice, the Chief Executive occasionally addresses or answers questions from its members at a special meeting. The post-1997 Legislative Council appears to be able to sustain the transparency of its sessions previously maintained by its predecessor, inasmuch as all Legislative Council sittings and most meetings of its bill committees, subcommittees and panels are open to the public.

§1. Composition of the Legislative Council and Legislative Process

20. The law-enacting organ, the Legislative Council, elects its President from among its members. Altogether there are 70 members constituting the Council, comprising 35 members returned by geographical constituencies through direct elections and the other half of the membership returned by functional constituencies. The functional constituencies were designated by the pre-1997 government essentially by virtue of occupational criteria to articulate the specific interest of a given economic, social or professional group. Previously, unofficial members were appointed by the Governor under British rule but under the 1995 electoral arrangement, all appointed unofficial seats were rescinded, as sanctioned under the Sino-British Joint Declaration. However, in addition to the 21 functional constituencies which already existed 9 new functional constituencies basically reflecting the occupational and workplace (in addition to the residential) affiliation of the members were created, so that the entire working population was enfranchised with a second 'ticket' enabling them to vote to return a candidate from each of these nine industrial groupings of (a) primary production, power and construction; (b) textiles and garments; (c) manufacturing; (d) import and export; (e) wholesale and retail; (f) hotels and catering; (g) transport and communications; (h) financing, insurance, real estate and business services; and (i) community, social and personal services. Five new constitutencies were each added to both of these two franchise categories in the fifth term of the Legislative Council for the period between 1 October 2008 and 30 September 2012.

21. The post-1997 SAR legislature has inherited its pattern of composition from that of the colonial government at the eve of the transfer of sovereignity. However, those members returned by geographical constituencies are no longer a hybrid mix of those elected directly and those elected indirectly by an election committee comprising all elected district board members at the 'local government' level. Instead-,all of the 30 members in the division of 'geographical constituencies' were directly elected. This number is now raised to 35. At present, the SAR legislature is in its sixth term of office, from 2012 to 2016. The term of office of these Legislative Council members is hence four years, as prescribed by the Basic Law and the Legislative Council Ordinance. The composition of the Council has been evolved from its first term through the changes to its present formula of composition shown in Table 1.

Table 1 Composition of the Hong Kong Legislative Council

	First term	*Second term*	*Third term*	*Fourth term*	*Fifth term*
Membership	*(1998–2000)*	*(2000–2004)*	*(2004–2008)*	*(2008–2012)*	*(2012–2016)*
(a) elected by geographical constituencies through direct elections	20	24	30	30	35
(b) elected by functional constituencies	30	30	30	30	35
(c) elected by an election committee	10	6	–	–	–
Total	60	60	60	60	70

22. Geographical constituency elections are held on the basis of universal suffrage. For the fifth term of the Legislative Council, the Hong Kong SAR is divided into five geographical constituencies, each having five to nine seats. The list voting system operating under the largest remainder formula, which is a form of proportional representation voting system, is adopted. Under this system, candidates contest the election in the form of lists. Each list may consist of any number of candidates up to the number of seats in the relevant constituency. An elector is entitled to cast one vote for a list in the constituency in which he is registered. The seats for the constituency are distributed among the lists according to the number of votes obtained by the respective lists.

Any permanent resident of the Hong Kong SAR who is a Chinese citizen with no right of abode in any foreign country may stand for election in any geographical constituency, provided that he or she is a registered elector on the Final Register, has attained the age of 21, and has ordinarily resided in Hong Kong for the preceding three years.

23. For the fifth term of the Legislative Council, the functional constituencies listed are: (a) Heung Yee Kuk; (b) agriculture and fisheries; (c) insurance; (d) transport; (e) education; (f) legal; (g) accountancy; (h) medical; (i) health services; (j) engineering; (k) architectural, surveying and planning; (l) labour; (m) social welfare; (n) real estate and construction; (o) tourism; (p) commercial (first); (q) commercial (second); (r) industrial (first); (s) industrial (second); (t) finance; (u) financial services; (v) sports, performing arts, culture and publication; (w) import and export; (x) textiles and garment; (y) wholesale and retail; (z) information technology; (aa) catering; and (bb) District Council (first); (cc) District Council (second) and (dd) textiles and garments. The labour functional constituency returns three Legislative Council members, the District Council (second) constituency is provided with four seats, while the other 27 functional constituencies return one member each.

Functional constituencies which represent professional groups have electorates based on membership of professions with well-established and recognized qualifications, including statutory qualifications. Each individual member has one vote. The electorates of functional constituencies representing economic or social groups are generally made up of the business and employment units as well as corporate members of major organizations representative of the relevant sectors. Each corporate member appoints an authorized representative to cast the vote on its behalf in an election.

24. The legislative process in the Hong Kong SAR is still in large measure analogous with the parliamentary procedures in the United Kingdom. The first reading of the bill is moved in most instances by the government and is by and large ceremonial, entailing ‘nothing more than the formal citation of the title of the bill’, and is often introduced by with a brief official speech explaining the intent and main coverage of the bill. The second reading debate is usually resumed in the next or the next but one session. If there are no substantial objections or problems the bill will be immediately referred to the committee stage. Otherwise, the bill will be debated at this second reading session. If the debate turns out to be controversial, the second reading session may be adjourned to allow consideration for amendments.

25. The committee stage that follows the second is normally convened in committee of the whole Council. The Secretary for Justice, heading the Legal Department, proposed various amendments so as to streamline the proposed draft legislation as well as to incorporate amendments stemming from the debate. The Secretary for Justice then reports to the Council that the committee stage has been completed and recommends the third reading of the bill, normally as a procedural ritual. After the proceedings in the law-making assembly, the Chief Executive signifies his assent, which is announced next in the government gazette. By virtue of the Chief Executive's assent, a bill becomes an ordinance without being subject to approval from the central government.

26. The SAR Legislative Council emulates by and large its pre-1997 predecessor in structure and carries under its auspices a number of standing committees. These include:

- the Finance Committee which scrutinizes public expenditure, assisted by two sub-committees, the Public Works sub-Committee and the Establishment Sub-Committee;
- the House Committee;
- the Public Accounts Committee;
- the Committee on Members' Interests; and
- the Committee on Rules of Procedure.

27. The Finance Committee examines public expenditure, both at special meetings held in March to screen the budgetary draft estimates prepared by the Financial Secretary for the subsequent year as well as at regular meetings, between October and July, to consider proposals for supplementary provisions of funds for public expenditure outside the budget. These meetings are held in public. Under the umbrella of the Finance Committee, the Establishment Subcommittee examines and makes recommendations to the Finance Committee on the government's proposals for the creation, redeployment and deletion of directorate posts, and for changes to the structure of grades and ranks in the civil service. In parallel, the Public Works Sub-Committee examines and makes recommendations to the Finance Committee on the government's expenditure proposals under the Capital Works Reserve Fund for projects in the Public Works Programme and building projects carried out by or on behalf of subvented organizations.

28. The House Committee, whose sitting excludes the President of the Legislative Council, performs the in-house role of coordinating within a coherent framework of an overall integrated agenda all business of the Council and of its committees, including reports on subsidiary legislation tabled in the Council; questions that members intended to put to the government; motions and bills to be debated; and any other matters of public concern.

The House Committee may constitute under its auspices a bills committee to consider the principles and general merits of a bill submitted to it for scrutiny. A bills committee hence constituted may also consider the detailed provisions and amendments relevant to the bill. It usually tables a report before the Council and is dissolved on the passage of the bill or when the House Committee so decides. Besides, the House Committee may also appoint subcommittees to consider items of existing subsidiary legislation tabled in Council. Like the bills committees, these subcommittees on subsidiary legislation also become defunct upon the enactment of the subsidiary legislative item.

29. The Public Accounts Committee plays the role of ensuring that public expenditure has not been incurred for purposes other than those for which these funds have been designated and that the spending has been cost-effective and free from defaults and malpractices. In this connection, the Director of Audit submits two reports to the Legislative Council each year: one relating to value-for-money audits (in April) and the other pertaining to the audit of the government's annual statements of accounts (in November).

30. The Committee on Members' Interests investigates the arrangements for the compilation, maintenance and accessibility of the Register of Members' Interests. Its purview also includes matters pertaining to the declaration of interests by Council members as well as their ethics of conduct, and providing guidelines on and making recommendations thereof relating to their interests in the capacity as representatives in the law-making assembly.

31. The Committee on Rules of Procedure is responsible for reviewing the Rules of Procedure of the Legislative Council and its committees, and proposing to the Council henceforth such amendments of changes as are deemed necessary.

32. In a fashion almost reminiscent of the committee system of the American Congress in the United States, the Legislative Council has created a constellation of 18 panels to examine the government's policies and each specializes in a specific policy area of public administration. The functional areas which these panels cater to include (a) administration of justice and legal services; (b) constitutional affairs; (c) economic services; (d) education; (e) environmental affairs; (f) financial affairs; (g) health services; (h) home affairs; (i) housing; (j) information policy; (k) planning, lands and works; (l) manpower; (m) public service; (n) recreation and culture; (o) security; (p) trade and industry; (q) transport; and (r) welfare services. These panels may in turn each appoint their own sub-committees.

33. The Legislative Council may appoint, on an *ad hoc* basis, Select Committees to consider and deliberate any specific matters or bills. These Select Committees are to report back to the Council which may debate on the report of findings by the Committees.

34. Besides, the Council may set up an investigation committee under Rule 49B (2A) of the Rules of Procedure to enable the council to probe a motion of censure against a Council member for misconduct and to make recommendations on the motion as to whether to disqualify the member concerned.

35. The Legislative Council is vested with its own administrative autonomy under the auspices of a Council Commission. The Commission's main function is to provide support and services for the Legislative Council through the Council's Secretariat. The Commission has the authority to employ staff of the Secretariat and oversee its work, to determine the organization and administration of support services and facilities, and to formulate policies for the effective performance of the Secretariat in support of the Legislative Council.

36. The Legislative Council also furnishes the public with a grievance redress mechanism *vis-à-vis* any legislation, government policies and actions adverse to their interest. The Council members work by a roster of weekly duties to receive complaints and representations. Apart from this, they attend 'ward duty' at the Public Complaints Office to meet and offer advice to complaints from the public.

§2. Legal and Judical System

37. The legal system of the Hong Kong SAR has retained its hitherto pre-1997 character which has evolved essentially from the heritage of the British system. However, because of the change of sovereignty, the apex arrangement of the judicial structure needed to be reconstituted. Under the pre-1997 system, appeals from the decisions of the highest court (Court of Appeal) in the territory were heard in the Judicial Committee of the Privy Council in London. However, as Hong Kong becomes reintegrated with China as its SAR, the power of final judgment now resides locally, in the Court of Final Appeal. Appeal cases are no longer actionable in the British jurisdiction. Otherwise, the entire judicial system has remained intact as it was before 1997, with the High Court in the first tier, followed at the next level by the district court, coupled by a spectrum of specialized courts in parallel, including the labour tribunal, the small claims tribunal, the obscene articles tribunal, the coroner's court and the lands tribunal (which are equivalent to the district court), and the magistracy and juvenile court at the lowest tier.

38. By virtue of the Sino-British Joint Declaration and the Basic Law, the English fashioned common law and rules of equity have continued to be in force in Hong Kong, governing the conduct of judicial proceedings and decisions.

39. The Court of Final Appeal is at the apex of the judicial system, headed by the Chief Justice. The Court is to be constituted of five judges in its sitting. They can be drawn from a pool of three permanent judges, a panel of five non-permanent local judges and ten non-permanent judges sourced from other common law jurisdictions. The Chief Justice is assisted by the Judiciary Administrator in the administration of the judiciary.

40. Below the Court of Final Appeal is the High Court, comprising the Court of Appeal and Court of First Instance. Staffing the High Court are the Chief Judge of the High Court, 10 Justices of Appeal and 32 Judges of the Court of First Instance. The Court of Appeal hears all appeals from the decision of the Court of First Instance and the District Court. The Court of First Instance has unlimited jurisdiction on all civil and criminal cases.

41. At one tier lower is the District Court, staffed by the Chief District Judge, together with one Principal Family Court Judge and 34 judges. The District Court has prerogative of decision on criminal cases but subject to a maximum power of giving sentence of seven years' imprisonment. It can hear civil claims up to a ceiling of one million dollars, as well as cases of employee compensation, equal opportunity breaches and matrimonial disputes and stamp duty appeals.

42. At the bottom tier is the magistracy, staffed by the Chief Magistrate, 4 principal magistrates and 59 permanent magistrates and 10 special magistrates, who are able to hear only criminal cases. The ceiling of their sentencing power is two years' imprisonment and a fine of a hundred thousand dollars.

§3. Local Government

43. Before 1982 the structure of the local government emanating from the various piecemeal reform measures preceding the 1981 White Paper on District Administration (which documents a wholesome blueprint of local administrative reforms in a domain which has virtually been left in a vacuum state prior to the 1970s and 1980s) has been a hybrid pattern which was fragmented and cumbersome, involving an array of overlapping institutions like the City District Office, City District Committee, the Urban Council, the District Management Committee, the Area Committee, the New Territories Administration and the Heung Yee Kuk as the rural consultative council in the New Territories.

44. The benchmark institutional arrangement laid down under the 1981 White Paper to consolidate the above pluralistic organs was hence a harmonized two-tier local government structure comprising the district boards and district management committees, created in each of the 18 local administrative districts in 1982. Concomitantly, the District Boards Ordinance has made the district boards statutory bodies, since April 1982 in the New Territories and October 1982 in the urban areas, to perform the representative role of a local assembly for public consultation and participation in the administration of the districts. The district board system has been inherited almost entirely by the SAR government after 1997. However, following the 1998 review of the structure and functions of district organizations, the system has been endorsed and enhanced, as indicative in the re-labelling of the district boards as district councils.

The district council's agenda is hence to advise the government on a wide range of matters affecting the interests or well-being of the people living and working in the district. In this capacity, each district council operates a 'meet-the-public' scheme under which residents in the district may meet board members, as representatives of their local constituency, to articulate their views and grievances concerning the governance of their district. Reciprocally, the scheme also enables the Council members to collect public views on local matters and region-wide issues, to be ploughed back to the government to help improve the provision and quality of various public services. Besides, the Councils carry out minor works projects and community involvement schemes.

The bulk of the District Council members are elected on the basis of 18 local constituencies, totalling 412 who are serving a four-year term commencing January 2012. In addition, there is still a segment of 68 appointed members, alongside a fraction of 27 *ex officio* members (by virtue of their incumbency as chairmen of the rural committees in the New Territories).

45. Concordant to the council in each district, there is a district management committee presided over *ex officio* by the District Officer and on which the key departments providing essential services in the district are also represented. This official committee liaises closely with the district council on the administration of public services at the local municipal level, not only to coordinate the provision of these services but also to ensure that the district's needs are effectively met. It also enables the departments represented to consult, co-ordinate and collaborate with each other to optimize the value of their services provided to the public.

46. Still constituting part of the local government machinery is a fringe of ancillary consultative organs, notably the area committees and mutual aid committees. The latter are building-based resident organizations, established to improve the security, cleanliness and general management of multi-storey buildings. On the other hand, the area committees have been, since November 1994, rationalized to assume a more refined and specific role to (a) assist in the organization of community activities and government campaigns; (b) advise on issues of a localized nature in the area; and (c) encourage residents' participation in district affairs. There are at present 63 area committees.

47. The executive arm of the local government is part of the civil service, which is the district office, headed by the District Officer and belonging to the Home Affairs Department. The geographical jurisdiction of the district office corresponds to that of the district council (of which there are altogether nine in the urban sector of the territory and another nine in the New Territories, making up altogether 18 districts). The district offices serve as the government's focal points of liaison with the grassroots populace, both the local communities and their voluntary organizations. They have been, in particular, instrumental in explaining government policies and ameliorating misunderstandings and conflicts between the government and ordinary citizens and their households. Parallel to the District Office is a series of district-specific regional offices operated by those government departments whose nature of work has made it imperative for them to devolve their services to the locality – including, notably, the Police, the Social Welfare Department, the Labour Department, the Food and Environmental Hygiene Department and the Leisure and Cultural Services Department, etc.

48. The revamped structure of representative government in Hong Kong since the series of electoral reforms in 1980 which crystallized on the eve of the 1997 dateline of political handover is a three-tier system in its governance framework. Intervening between the central government-cum-legislative and executive councils on top and the district administration at the locality is an intermediate level of regional jurisdiction, with power more or less analogous to a municipal authority's. The arrangement is, however, dualistic, because the urban sector (namely, including Hong Kong Island and Kowloon Peninsula) has been always covered, since the pre-war years, by the Urban Council and its executive adjunct, the Urban Services Department; yet the New Territories 'domain' was not configurated in an analogous fashion until the creation of the Regional Council, in April 1986, as the statutory municipal authority for the New Territories. It is supported, as in the parallel case of the Urban Council, by the Regional Services Department of the civil service.

49. However, such a three-tier system in representative government was considered to be too cumbersome by the post-1997 SAR government. The view was, as articulated in the findings of the Review of District Organizations conducted in June–July 1998, that there were a proliferation of representative assemblies and that the two Councils at the municipal level were duplicating the roles of the district councils and hence could be deemed redundant and be abolished. As a sequel to the Provision of Municipal Services (Reorganization) Ordinance enacted at the end of 1999, the Provisional Urban Council and the Provisional Regional Council were dissolved. In their place, the SAR government erected a new structure for the delivery of municipal services in January 2000, as the jurisdiction of the two defunct municipal councils was transferred to the administration and other newly created statutory bodies.

50. The above exercise of structural rationalization led to the inception of two new government departments, namely, (a) the Food and Environmental Hygiene Department which monitors, regulate and maintains standards in the areas of food safety and environmental hygiene; and (b) the Leisure and Culture Services Department (within the domain of the Home Affairs Bureau) for the provision of leisure and cultural services, management of cultural facilities and the provision of arts and culture, sport and recreation.

In addition, a Liquor Licensing Board was created to assume the former functions of the two municipal councils in considering applications for and granting of liquor licences. Concomitantly, a Licensing Appeals Board was appointed at an upper tier to hear appeals against decisions on licensing of food and environmental hygiene as well as leisure matters. At the same time, the membership of the Sports Development Board and the Arts Development Council was enhanced. And a high-level advisory body, the Culture and Heritage Commission was established in April 2000 to advise the government on the policies and funding priorities for arts and culture, with a view to the provision of more focused strategic planning and better coordination in the funding and delivery of arts and cultural activities.

§4. The Electoral System under Representative Government Reforms and Development

51. The electoral system has been advanced and revamped several times in the process of its evolution since the beginning of representative government reforms in the early 1980s. In place of the pre-1982 territory-wide and monistic constituency that primarily served the Urban Council election, a geographical network of 18 district-specific constituencies has been instituted, and later inherited by the post-1997 SAR government. Each of these 18 geographical constituencies had the dualistic mandate, before 2000, of returning its deputies on the district board and the Urban Council/ Regional Council. The latter function, of course, has been rescinded following the dissolution of the two municipal councils in 2000.

The notion and demarcation of the geographical constituencies have been, however, compounded further by the electoral arrangement for direct election to the Legislative Council introduced since the mid-1990s. Prior to 1997, there were, in parallel to the 'district board' constituencies, nine geographical constituencies demarcated for the territory returning 20 directly elected members in the Legislative Council in the 1995 election. However, the boundaries and number of these geographical constituencies were substantially revised for the direct elections held after 1997 for administration. As a sequel, there are now consolidated for the entire territory altogether five geographical constituencies each returning five to nine directly elected members to the SAR Legislative Council.

52. A concordant structure of 'functional constituency' and the institution of an election committee vested with the role of indirect election to the Legislative Council add greater complexity to the electoral system.

Each functional constituency represents an economic, social, or professional/ occupational sector which is substantial and important to the Hong Kong SAR. These functional constituencies, almost analogous to the designation of occupationally denominated deputies in the law-making assembly, have been listed above.

53. Direct election to the legislature is based upon universal suffrage which has been instituted here since the electoral reforms commenced in the 1980s. It is defined to include now everyone who is a Hong Kong permanent resident or has ordinarily resided in Hong Kong for the preceding seven years. The age floor for enrolling in the franchise was formerly stipulated at 21, but is has now been lowered to 18. In the year 2012, of those who were enfranchised under the above criterion, a total of 3.47 million had registered themselves as electors with the official register.

The electoral franchise for the functional constituencies is, as the label implies, functionally or occupationally differentiated. The electorates for those constituencies representing the professional/occupational groups are based upon membership of profession with well-established and recognized qualifications, including statutory qualifications. Concomitantly, the electorates of functional constituencies representing economic or social groups are generally made up of corporate members of major organizations representative of the relevant sectors. Each corporate member appoints an authorized representative to cast the vote on its behalf in an election. For the fifth term of the Legislative Council (2012-2016), 35 members were returned by direct election based upon the geographical constituencies and an equal number of 35 was elected by the functional constituencies. The earlier practice of indirect election by an election committee was rescinded.

54. The policing of electoral activities in the territory belongs to the jurisdiction of an independent yet officially appointed agency called the Boundary and Election Commission created by virtue of the 1993 Boundary and Election Commission Ordinance. The Commission, now retitled as the Electoral Affairs Commission, is vested with the statutory authority to review the geographical constituency boundaries for the Legislative Council as well as the district council elections. It also advises the Chief Executive on instituting regulations on practical arrangements for the various elections and handle complaints pertaining to their conduct. The Commission, comprising three members headed by the High Court judge, is now also the competent agency for overseeing the conduct of elections, scrutinizing the procedures for these elections and arrangements to register the electors. In other words, it serves as the principal supervisory organ for prescribing the 'rules of the game' for the range of electoral activities and exercises in Hong Kong. It has, *inter alia*, redrawn the geographical boundaries for the relevant constituencies pertaining to the respective elections for the Legislative Council ; introduced a set of subsidiary legislation for voter registration and electoral procedures and published a code of guidelines to help regularize a variety of election-related activities.

55. A complementary agency specializing in the role of registering eligible voters in the franchise is now the Registration and Electoral Office which is also the secretariat and executive arm serving the Election Affairs Commission, responsible for implementing and administering the decisions of the Commission.

§5. The Consultative System of Advisory Boards and Committees

56. In addition to the two-tier popularly elected assemblies now enshrined as a result of the political and electoral reforms, it has been a celebrated tradition, as inherited from the pre-1997 government and the British colonial legacies, for the incumbent SAR administration to consult the relevant interested groups and professional/technocratic specialists on various aspects of public policy formulation and implementation through an extensive and informed network of advisory boards and committees. These advisory organs, either statutory or non-statutory, are instrumental in giving pertinent advice on various socio-political and technical issues to the government secretariat at the central level or specifically, to the head of a government department. Statutory bodies like the Hospital Authority are enpowered to exercise their legal prerogative in performing their functions within their purview of jurisdiction.

57. Membership of these advisory boards and committees includes both *ex officio* as well as unofficial incumbents who can, in turn, be either elected or appointed. In the case of the Labour Advisory Board, for instance, it has been the practice since its reforms in the 1980s for almost all workers' representatives to be selected by way of election among and by the registered trade unions in Hong Kong, while their employer counterparts are, on the other hand, nominated by the major trade, industrial and employer organizations in the territory.

58. At present, it has been estimated that as many as 5,100 members of the public are sitting on a total of about 460 such advisory committees and consultative bodies. Where these boards/agencies appear to proliferate, it has always been the intent and policy of the government to scale down their number in order to streamline and rationalize the structure of these adjunct bodies.

§6. The Civil Service: The Executive Functionary

59. The executive division of the Hong Kong SAR government is organized, in emulation of its pre-1997 predecessor, into both policy bureaux and departments. The policy bureaux, more or less equivalent to ministries, collectively form the government secretariat acting, in an implicit sense, like the cabinet of the Chief Executive at the central level of the government. There are currently twelve policy bureaux, each headed by a Secretary (also known as Director) of Bureau. At the apex of the administration, below the Chief Executive are the Chief Secretary for Administration, the Financial Secretary and the Secretary for Justice. The incumbents in these offices are politically appointed principal officials who are directly responsible to the Chief Executive and accountable to him for matters within the scope of their portfolios. They are also *ex officio* members of the Executive Council.

The Chief Secretary for Administration is the leading principal official of the SAR government and heads the government secretariat. She assists the Chief Executive in supervising the policy bureaux and performs a key role in coordinating their functions and activities (especially where the boundaries of their jurisdiction overlap) and ensuring harmonized decisions in policy formulation and implementation of the SAR government. The Chief Secretary's portfolio also covers specific priority areas of the Chief Executive's policy agenda, and is responsible for forging a closer and more effective working relationship between the executive arm of the government and the Legislative Council, as well as for drawing up the government's legislative programme. She also deputizes in this capacity for the Chief Executive in his absence.

The Financial Secretary oversees policy formulation and implementation in the domain of financial, monetary, economic, trade and employment matters. He chairs the Exchange Fund Advisory Committee, and the Economic and Employment Council. The Financial Secretary is hence responsible for the fiscal and economic policies of government. He is, in performing this role, the official who presents before the Legislative Council each year the public budget, which details the government's annual estimates of revenue and expenditure for the next financial year and outlines the official outlook and policy on economic development. As prescribed under the Public Financial Ordinance, he is responsible for moving the adoption of the Appropriation Bill in the Council, which empowers the government to spend and collect public revenue in accordance with the budgetary proposal for the subsequent financial year.

Under these policy bureaux are a total of 56 departments and agencies whose heads are responsible to the bureau secretaries for the direction of their departments and the efficient implementation of approved government policy formulated centrally at the government secretariat by the bureau secretaries.

60. The civil service provides the staff for all the bureaux secretariats and the government departments under their purview. As at 31 December 2012 , the strength of the service was 159,700 , with nearly 99 per cent of this number being locally recruited officers. Public service employment is now responsible for the hiring in Hong Kong of 4.2 per cent of the territory's workforce and it has been the purported policy of the SAR government to continue slimming down the size of the public sector to streamline the large civil service bureaucracy. The Civil Service Bureau of the government secretariat is the competent agency responsible for the management of the civil service and its human resources. The Bureau, in this capacity, deals with such matters as pay and conditions of service, appointments, staff management, manpower planning, training discipline and industrial relations (staff–management relations) in the civil service. Public sector people management is mandated by the three instruments of (a) the Public Service (Administration) Order; (b) the Public Service (Disciplinary) Regulations; and (c) the Civil Service Regulations. There is, in addition, a public yet independent agency which is the Public Service Commission which scrutinizes and advises the government on recruitment, promotion and appointment decisions covering the middle and upper levels of the civil service hierarchy.

Besides, the government also consults, on matter pertaining to civil service pay and conditions of service, a three-tiered structure of advisory organ: (a) the Standing Committee on Directorate Salaries and Conditions of Service; (b) the Standing Committee on Disciplined Services Salaries and Conditions of Service; and (c) the Standing Commission on Civil Service Salaries and Conditions of Service.

61. A creeping and yet large-scale process of major civil service reforms has been in progress as a sequel to a landmark consultative document published in 1999 on public sector reforms. These changes were conspicuous in the domains of:

– entry and exit – whereby a new entry system and terms of appointment for new recruits have been instituted since June 2000 so as to enhance the flexibility of the appointment system in the government and replace the existing pension system with a new provident fund scheme for new recruits. In parallel, staff reduction exercises (including rounds of voluntary retirement schemes) introduced in 2002 and 2003 covering 232 staff grades and a management-initiated retirement scheme tailored for directorate grade public servants led to the reduction of the size of the civil service to around 160,000 by 2006-07. In the year 2011–12, the civil service registered a staff wastage of 3.7 per cent.

Remuneration – modernizing the management of and improving the civil service pay adjustment mechanism in order to offer sufficient incentives to attract, retain and motivate staff of a suitable calibre so as to provide the public with an effective, efficient and high quality service. The policy norms are to enshrine 'a fair deal at work' for both the public sector employee and the public as the service-user, in addition to achieving 'broad comparability' between civil service and private sector pay;

- conduct and discipline – establishing the Secretariat on Civil Service Discipline to centrally process disciplinary cases as well as streamlining the long-drawn bureaucratic procedures in handling disciplinary cases. Greater autonomy is also devolved to the bureau and departmental level for human resource management and supervision. Besides, a Civil Service Integrity Entrenchment Programme has been launched jointly by the Civil Service Bureau and the Independent Commission Against Corruption in order to promote and enhance awareness within the public sector the culture of civil servants' integrity; and
- training and development – enhancing and expanding such activities so as to support implementation of the reform initiatives and make them sustainable. In particular, a three-year training and development programme was launched between 2001 and 2004 to focus on three main themes, namely, training of staff affected by the voluntary retirement exercise, training to equip staff with the requisite skills and knowledge to implement and civil service reform initiatives and promoting a continuous learning culture in the civil service. As part of the reform fixture, the Civil Service Training and Development Institute (CSTDI) was incorporated into the Civil Service Bureau in the interest of achieving greater efficiency and economies of scale. The CSTDI focuses on four core service areas: senior executive development, national studies programmes (held and conducted at the lead Mainland Universities and training institutes, like the National School of Administration, Tsinghua University, China Foreign Affairs University and Peking University), consultancy services in human resources management and propagation of best practices in people management, and the promotion of a culture of continuous learning in the civil service.

62. As provided by the Sino-British Joint Declaration on the Future of Hong Kong and prescribed by the Basic Law, Hong Kong does not have independent jurisdiction in dealing with its foreign affairs, which belongs to the prerogative of the central government at Beijing. However, Hong Kong may participate in inter national and regional organizations of mutual cooperation and conclude external agreements provided that (a) these activities are not pursued at the level of independent nation state; (b) the consent of the central government has been obtained; and (c) Hong Kong's participation status is legitimated and covered by the label as 'Hong Kong, China'. By the year 2004, the SAR government had concluded, in this capacity, more than ten international agreements with foreign states and regions on matters such as customs cooperation, cooperation in information technology and avoidance of double taxation (see Basic Law, Article 151). The post-1997 government has also concluded, with authorization of the Central People's government, 79 bilateral agreements with foreign states – comprising 37 on air services, 13 on visa abolition, three on readmission of persons, 24 on reciprocal judicial assistance, one on investment promotion and protection, and one on avoidance of double taxation. Up to now, Hong Kong has been able to submit itself to the application of 200 multilateral conventions, of which only 75 instruments have been ratified and applied to the mainland. During the year 2011–12, the SAR government concluded 16 bilateral agreements with foreign states. They covered areas like free trade, avoidance of double taxation, visa abolition, mutual legal assistance in criminal matters and transfer of sentenced persons. A multilateral convention, the Protocol on Preparedness, Response and Co-operation to Pollution Incidents by Hazardous and Notorious Substances 2000 was applied to the SAR in 2012.

In the year 2012, representatives of the Hong Kong SAR government participated as members of the PRC delegation more than 90 times in international conferences limited to nation states, including those organized by the World Intellectual Property Organization, the World Health Organization and the International Civil Aviation Organization. The Hong Kong SAR also participated, using the name 'Hong Kong, China', more than 1,600 times in intergovernmental conferences not limited to nation states, including those organized by the Asia-Pacific Economic Cooperation, the Pacific Economic Cooperation Council, the World Trade Organization, the World Customs Organization and the World Customs Organization.

At the end of the year 2012, a total of 120 foreign states maintained an official presence in Hong Kong, including 58 consulates general and 64 consulates. Besides, international agencies and organizations like the Bank for International Settlements, the European Union, the United Nations High Commissioner for Refugees, the International Monetary Fund, the International Finance Corporation and the World Bank have established offices in Hong Kong.

63. The Basic Law prescribes at its Article 13 that the central government is the competent authority for dealing with and handling the foreign affairs of the SAR. In this context, for the exercise of such a prerogative, the Ministry of Foreign Affairs of the PRC stations an agency in Hong Kong and since 1997 an office, the Commissioner of the Ministry of Foreign Affairs (MFA Office), has been established in the SAR to oversee the foreign and external affairs of Hong Kong.

The Hong Kong SAR government has liaised closely with the MFA Office in the following areas:

(a) participation in international organizations and conferences – for instance, obtaining the Central People's Government's approval for Hong Kong SAR government officials to participate as members of the PRC delegation in international conferences limited to states (Basic Law Article 152);
(b) negotiation and conclusion of international agreements with foreign states and regions – for example, obtaining the CPG's specific authorization for the negotiation and conclusion of Air Services Agreements with foreign states in accordance with the relevant provisions of the Basic law (Basic Law Article 133); and
(c) matters relating to the establishment of consular missions in the Hong Kong SAR – the establishment of foreign consular and other official or semi-official

missions is a matter for the MFA Office (Basic Law Article 157). The Hong Kong SAR government is responsible for the day-to-day management of the consular corps, such as the issue of consular identity cards, actual provision of privileges and immunities and ensuring the security of consular premises.

Chapter 4. Economic and Social Environment

§1. Population and Employment Statistics

64. The demographic structure of Hong Kong is historically affected by the continuous influx, except at intermittent intervals, of refugees from China and other parts of East Asia, especially Vietnam. Towards the end of the last century, the terrain was compounded by the factor of the territory's political uncertainty due to the impending changeover of its sovereignty from the British to Chinese scheduled for July, 1997. A local psychology of insecurity and anxiety has hence emerged since the mid-1980s as a sequel to the 1985 Sino-British Joint Declaration. The neurosis which prevailed touched off successive waves of large-scale emigration of Hong Kong people abroad – either to resettle permanently overseas or to secure a right of abode with a foreign passport in such popular countries of destination as Canada, Australia, the USA, Singapore and the UK. As the status and political fluidity of Hong Kong became increasingly clear and settled as an SAR of China, the emigration tide subsided and ebbed, accompanied, instead, by the return flow of those people who had earlier emigrated. In the year 2004, for instance, the estimated size of emigration away from Hong Kong dropped to a low level of 9,800. Recently, in the year 2012, this has receded further to 7,600, mostly destined for the United States, Austalia and Canada. The reversal of people moving away from Hong Kong engenders an inflationary pull in the territory's population growth. However, this profile has been modified by (i) the arrival of new immigrants from the Mainland, (ii) the influx of tourists from the north and (iii) creeping signs of a growth again of outward emigration flow due to the increasingly congested and polluted environment of Hong Kong.

65. Since the closing of the decade in the 1970s, Hong Kong has been afflicted by the problem of having to serve as a port of first asylum for refugees from Vietnam, who were preponderantly political in nature during the earlier periods but have become increasingly economically motivated thereafter. At the end of 1979, there were over 50,000 Vietnamese refugees in Hong Kong awaiting resettlement in host countries elsewhere. This number since then began to subside to 11,896 in 1984. However, the size of the Vietnamese population staying in Hong Kong is a variable affected by the number arriving (which has dwindled significantly) as well as those resettled and later repatriated back to Vietnam following an agreement reached between the British and Vietnamese governments in 1991 on the orderly repatriation from Hong Kong of its Vietnamese migrants not identified as (political) refugees. (This arrangement was a sequel to the Comprehensive Plan of Action, CPA, endorsed internationally at the general conference held in 1989, and providing that only those Vietnamese migrants screened and classified as refugees under the terms of the 1951 United Nations Convention and 1967 Protocol were eligible for resettlement. Such an instrument required by implication the mandatory return of these who were not classified as refugees back to Vietnam.) A substantial number of people have since been repatriated to Vietnam under this arrangement jointly administered by the Hong Kong government and the United Nations High Commissioner for Refugees (UNHCR). During the year 1994, a group of 5,581 persons were returned voluntarily to Vietnam while since 1989, altogether a total of 44,194 Vietnamese migrants have been sent back either voluntarily or by mandatory repatriation arrangements. In the same year 1994, there were only 363 illegal arrivals in Hong Kong from Vietnam, while 7,443 Vietnamese stranded here in the territory were either settled overseas or repatriated

At the end of 2000, 97 Vietnamese refugees and 116 Vietnamese migrants remained in Hong Kong. This was after the resettlement of more than 143,000 Vietnamese refugees in other countries, the repatriation of more than 67,000 Vietnamese refugees/migrants in 2000. Since the late 1970s Hong Kong had absorbed, by the year 2000, some 16,000 Indo-Chinese people. With the formal conclusion of the internationally agreed Comprehensive Plan of Action and because of the changed circumstances in Vietnam, Hong Kong was able to end its status and policy as a port of first asylum for Vietnamese with effect from 9 January 1998. By implication, any unauthorized arrivals of Vietnamese after this date were to be treated in the same way as illegal immigrants from elsewhere, and they were to be repatriated as soon as possible. On 22 February 2000 the Hong Kong SAR announced a Widened Local Resettlement Scheme to allow some 1400 Vietnamese refugees and eligible Vietnamese migrants to apply for settlement in Hong Kong. This scheme enabled, as a corollary, the SAR government to close the last refugee centre in Hong Kong, and in the world, on 1 June 2000. The closure of the centre also signifies the conclusion of Hong Kong's commitment to and its work on the Vietnamese programme which lasted for a quarter of a century.

There was, in addition, another category of illegal arrivals of people from Vietnam. They were the ex-China Vietnamese who had settled in the mainland before arriving in Hong Kong illegally. Predominantly ethnic Chinese, they fled Vietnam in the early 1980s. Having obtained asylum on the mainland, they are considered to have no further claim for refugee status or resettlement in other countries. In Hong Kong, the official policy is to repatriate them to the mainland, where they are assumed to have already enjoyed adequate protection.

66. At the same time, legal immigration from mainland China under the one-way permit admission arrangement and a daily quota of 150 (upgraded from a previous ceiling of 105 in 1995) rose to level of 57,530 in the year 2000 and to 38,100 in 2004. This figure stood at a level of 54,600 in 2012. The bulk of this intake has been for reasons of family reunification.

67. Controversies have clouded the eligibility to stay in Hong Kong of those mainland Chinese born of Hong Kong citizens whose birthplace was, however, outside Hong Kong. Although Article 24(2)(3) of the Basic Law prescribes that these people shall be deemed as Hong Kong permanent residents and enjoy right of abode, tussles developed between the SAR government and the claimants for such status over the interpretation of the Basic Law provision around the turn of the decade, leading to a wave of litigation which resulted in a ruling by the Court of Final Appeal on 29 January 1999 against the government's administrative practice which limited such entries within the framework of the Certificate of Entitlement Scheme. The Scheme stipulated that a person's status as a permanent resident of

Hong Kong, as prescribed by Article 24(2)(3) of the Basic Law could be established only by his holding a valid travel document (i.e. a one way permit) with a valid certificate of entitlement affixed to it. This accorded with the Immigration Ordinance which declared that in order for a person to claim right of abode by birth in Hong Kong, at least one of his parents had to be a Chinese citizen who had such a right at the time of his birth. However, the 'time-of-birth' requirement, as well as a concomitant requirement that the claimant has to be subject to the exit approval prescribed by Article 22(4) of the Basic Law, were both interpreted by the Court of Final Appeal as 'unconstitutional' in contravention of the Basic Law.

Afflicted by the fear that the liberal interpretation by the Court of Final Appeal would touch off a stampede of mainland arrivals claiming their right of abode by birth (a survey by the Census and Statistic Department suggested that because of such a judicial decision, an estimated 1.6 million persons in the mainland would become eligible for such a right), the SAR administration submitted the contested and equivocal provisions of the Basic Law in this controversy to the State Council of the central government and sought an authoritative interpretation from the Standing Committee of the National People's Congress on the disputed provisions of the Basic Law. The National People Congress Standing Committee gave an interpretation on 26 June 1999 which upheld the position of the SAR administration and rescinded the earlier judgment by the Court of Final Appeal in Hong Kong.

The interpretation clarified that persons born of Hong Kong residents in the mainland were eligible for right of abode in Hong Kong only if, at the time of their birth, at least one of their parents had such a right under Article 24(2)(1) or Article 24(2)(2) of the Basic Law. Furthermore, the eligible person had to apply for exit approval from the mainland authorities before coming to Hong Kong for settlement. The Court of Final Appeal subsequently endorsed the interpretation as the benchmark ruling in its decision on a court case in December 1999, thereby ending the constitutional controversy on the subject of 'right of abode'.

The above Basic Law interpretation by the National People's Congress, the first of its kind since the SAR regime commenced in 1997, was widely castigated by the liberal sector of the Hong Kong community as an undue exercise of patent intervention by the central government into the internal affairs of Hong Kong, over which the SAR was supposed, as purported by the Basic Law, to enjoy a high level of autonomy.

68. Although illegal immigration in the past, chiefly from the mainland, has been a crucial factor affecting the growth of population and its fluctuations, this movement has by and large been placed under control through the cross-border cooperation of the immigration authorities in both Hong Kong and the mainland. The tide of influx seems to have subsided substantially now. For instance, the annual number of illegal immigrants arrested has declined sizably from a daily average of 103 in 1993 to a comparable average of 86 a day in 1994. The total daily average arrest figure further declined to 23 for the year 2000, a 30 per cent drop compared with 33 in 1999. The entry of illegal immigrants lessened to a plateau of ten daily arrests for 2003 and eight daily arrests of mainland illegal immigrants for 2004.

During the year 2012, 1,286 illegal immigrants from the Mainland were apprehended, or 21 per cent less than in 2011. In the same year, 342 illegal immigrants from Vietnam were arrested, or 22 per cent more than that of the previous year. At the same time, 414 non-ethnic Chineese illegal immigrants were arrested, or 56 per cent more than the preceding year.

Most illegal immigrants, including those from other parts of Asia like India, Pakistan and Thailand or even Eastern Europe who have stayed beyond the period permitted by their visas, were largely attracted by the relatively good pay they were able to gain from working, even illegally, in Hong Kong. Both illegal immigrants working in Hong Kong and their employers are liable to heavy penalties if apprehended in the workplace, such as at building and construction sites. They are invariably repatriated back to their home countries.

69. Indicative of the improving and high living standard in the local population, life expectancy at birth in the 1990s and after the turn of the century has improved. In 1980 it was 70.71 years for men and 76.78 for women but in 1994 the comparable level was 75.4 for men and 81.0 for women. The life expectancy statistics rose further in 2004, to 78.6 for men and 84.6 for women. In the year 2012, life expectancy for males was 80.6 years and 86.3 years for females. This pattern has shown increasing convergence with the 'ageing' or 'maturing' demographic structure in other highly industrialized societies such as Japan, Europe and North America. Correspondingly, the rate of infant mortality, declining from 8.8 per thousand live births in 1984 to 4.9 in 1994, 2.5 in 2004, and now further down to 1.5 per thousand in 2012, was also low by international standards as indicative of socio-economic advances in society. An important ramification, together with the effects of sustained decline in birth rate (to 12 per thousand in 1994 and 7.2 per thousand in 2004 and 1.2 per thousand in 2012) has been a conspicuous drop in the dependency ratio, from 449 per thousand in 1984 to 404 per thousand in 1994 and further to 370 per thousand in 2004. It receded to a level of 335 per thousand in 2012. In the meantime, the rate of natural increase of the population has declined concomitantly, from 9.6 to 7.0 per thousand during the ten-year period since 1984. When compounded by the migration movement in and out of the territory, the population grew at an average annual rate of 0.8 per cent over the five-year period 1999–2004. The growth rate dropped to 0.7 per cent during the period 2007-2012.

The decline in population growth has in turn given rise to a slowdown in the growth of the territory's labour force, which helps explain the problem of labour shortage as it developed and afflicted the economy around the turn of the decade in the late 1980s and early 1990s.

70. The population of the territory, as estimated in 2004, was about 6.89 million (6,895,500). This figure represents an increase of 0.7 per cent compared to that estimated a year earlier, in 2003. The population now grew to a size of 7,173,900 in 2112, representing an increase of 0.9 per cent compared with that of the previous year. At the same time, the size of the SAR's labour force rose to a level of 3.79 million in the year of 2012, which represented an increase of 2.2 per cent over that of 2011. The sex composition of this labour force was still biased towards men, with 52.1 per cent males and 47.9 per cent females.

71. Hong Kong has scarcely any natural resources. However, it has the advantages of an excellent deep-water harbour, a well-built infrastructure of highways, telecommunications, financial services and external transport system and a hard-working, enterprising and adaptable local population. Education is now comprehensive for the first nine years, while senior secondary education is generally available for anyone who is willing and able. Post-secondary education at the tertiary level has grown on a conspicuous scale since the late 1980s, first with the creation of a third university and subsequently the conversion of the polytechnics into degree-giving universities. Altogether there are now eight universities and institutes within the network of tertiary institutions subvented wholly or partially by the officially sponsored University Grants Committee (UGC). Outside the UGC funding framework, there are 10 degree-awarding tertiary institutions, including the Hong Kong Academy for Performing Arts, the Open University of Hong Kong, the privately administered Hong Kong Shue Yan University and Chu Hai College of Higher Education, alongside the Hang Seng Management College,Tung Wah College, the Caritas Institute of Higher Education, the Centennial College, the Technological and Higher Education Institute of Hong Kong and the Vocational Council. Besides, there are other providers of sub-degree qualifications. The number of post-secondary institutions totalled altogether 30.

72. In the year 2004, for instance, 397,500 children were enrolled in government and aided primary schools and 414,300 children in government and aid secondary schools. Concomitantly, 14,500 first-year first-degree places were available in universities funded by the UGC, covering about 18 per cent of the 17–20 age group. Another 39 per cent of young people belonging to the same age cohort had access to other local higher education opportunities (for example, sub-degree programmes and vocational training) or went to universities overseas. These numbers together yielded an overall post-secondary participation rate of 57 per cent for the 17–20 age group in the academic year 2004–5, representing a sizable increase from the comparable level of 30 per cent in the academic year 2000–1.

73. In the year 1994, about 1.2 million students, or 20 per cent of the local population, were enrolled in full-time education attending 2,200 institutions staffed by 57,000 teachers and supervised by the Education Department. At the turn of the century, in the year 2000, about 1.29 million students, or 19 per cent of the population were enrolled in full-time education. In spite of the mild fluctuation in the number of young people attending full-time education, there has been a noticeable upgrading in the level of education background of the local population, indicative of a relatively well developed and improving infrastructure of education and manpower training in Hong Kong. The Vocational Training Council (VTC) has hitherto been the statutory agency and competent authority for coordinating official policies and activities in the area of technical education and vocational training. However, this function has been gradually detached from the VTC and placed, instead, with the

Education and Manpower Bureau[1] of the central administration within a holistic framework of steering education and manpower policies for the territory, especially with a view to building and enhancing an integrative infrastructure of human resources for Hong Kong as a knowledge-based economy. Emanating from the rising problem of technological unemployment due to those workers displaced and made redundant because of either their skill obsolescence or industrial restructuring, the government has since 1993 created an Employment Retraining Board catering for the retraining, skill-recycling and renewed employability of those workers retrenched and displaced principally because of a rapidly shrinking manufacturing sector in the territory.

In spite of a popular global trend of deregulating the labour markets, there has been, as attested by the experiences of the industrially advanced economies, growing intervention by national governments to institutionalize the skill markets by way of competency validation and certification. Hong Kong appears to be emulating such a trend in its labour market development as the administration has been keen to sponsor the gestation of an economy-wide 'qualification framework'.

74. In 2004, the SAR government adopted in principle the establishment of a seven-level cross-sectoral qualification framework (QF) and its associated quality assurance mechanism. The QF system, provided by the Accreditation of Academic and Vocational Qualification Ordinance, prescribes and endorses qualifications of academic, vocational and continued education which it supports. A host of agencies, known as the Industry Training Advisory Committees (ITACs), have been created to develop competency-based qualifications for various industries. By 2012, there were eighteen industries having established these industry-specific bodies for instituting and advancing their QF. These industries represented about 45 per cent of the general labour force. Such bodies are each responsible for preparing an inventory of Specification of Competency Standards (SCS) for the industry concerned. The code stipulates the skills, knowledge and competency level expected for the relevant jobs in the industry and defines the career path of progression in each ocupation. It also provides the basis for the design of the requisite training programmes. They are also instrumental for shaping the activities and policies in a variety of human resource functions like performance appraisal, recruitment, training and career development.

Quality assurance and assessment of the competency qualifications recognized under the QF, however, belong to the jurisdiction of the Hong Kong Council for Accreditation of Academic and Vocational Qualifications. 'Lead' universities like the University of Hong Kong, the Chinese University of Hong Kong and the University of Science and Technology are self-accrediting. For the dissemination of information in this domain, a web-based data-base is provided by the Qualifications Register which lists an array of qualifications and the learning progammes leading to their attainment recognized under the QF.

---

1. The Education and Manpower Bureau has been re-organized and now re-titled as the Education Bureau since 2007 when its labour and employment activities, generically labelled as the 'Manpower' portfolio, were hived off and merged with an associated portfolio of social welfare and public security to constitute a newly created Labour and Welfare Bureau.

The introduction of the QF system is envisaged to provide more diversified career ladders, enhance the quality and vocational applicability of education and training programmes and activities, bestow wider recognition on the skills, knowledge and experience of workers and promote lifelong learning. These labour market institutionalization measures will, it is hoped, contribute to the upgrading of the quality of the economy's manpower and second, help sustain Hong Kong's competitive power in the global economy.

75. Notwithstanding the above developments, the statutory body of the Vocational Training Council (VTC) continues to be the mainstream organ vested with the function of coordinating official policies and activities in the area of vocational education and technical training. However, there are growing signs that the VTC's prerogative in policy formulation will be eclipsed and usurped increasingly by the Education Bureau (EDB) of the government secretariat at the nerve-centre of the SAR administration. The EDB, headed by the Secretary for Education, oversees the entry domain of educational affairs in Hong Kong. Its jurisdiction covers the formulation and review of the SAR's education policy, securing funds and resources from the government budget to pursue these policies and steering the effective implementation of all educational programmes within an integrated framework of its governance. Given such developments, the VTC has been emasculated and relegated to a provider of vocational training and technical education at a number of institutes of vocational education (IVE) and skill centres, alongside a self-funded continuing professional development centre which it operates. The number of IVEs now proliferates, including the Technological and Higher Education Institute of Hong Kong, the Institute of Professional Education and Knowledge, the School for Higher and Professional Education, the Hong Kong Institute of Vocational Education, the Hong Kong Design Institute, the Hospitability Industry Training and Development Centre, the Chinese Cuisine Training Institute, the Maritime Services Training Institute and the Youth College.

There are growing clues to suggest that the establishment is anxious to harmonize the SAR's educational system more closely with that of Mainland China. This is symptomatic, for instance, in the re-structuring of a three-year curriculum among local universities into a four-year one, which is the Mainland model. The second incident was a government attempt to institute the teaching of moral and national education as a mandatory subject in primary and secondary schools. This policy move was widely received by the public with apprehension. Resentment grew among parents and teachers that such a subject was intended to nurture amd enhance the level of national consciousness and identification with the PRC among children and youths in Hong Kong. The situation was made worse by the publication by the officially sponsored National Education Services Centre in 2012 of a teaching guide titled *The China Model Handbook*. In a place where the ethos of individual freedom of thought and expression had taken root under the former British administration, its appearance precipitated a prevalent disquiet on the suspected nature of this book as an instrument of brain-washing. As a sequel, the SAR government rescinded its decision on the introduction of this subject. The guide was also shelved subsequently. This episode in the autumn of 2012 gives hints as to the fragile basis upon which the legitimacy of the SAR government is grounded.

Emanating from the rising problem of technological unemployment due to those workers displaced and made redundant because of either their skill obsolescence or industrial restructuring (old manufacturing activities either migrating northwards across the boarder to mainland China or running down, while new industries, chiefly at the tertiary level, are emerging and growing), the government has since 1993 created an employee retraining board to cater to the retraining, skill-recycling and renewed employability of those workers unemployed and displaced principally because of a rapidly shrinking manufacturing sector in the territory.

§2. Industrial, Business Restructuring and Economic Diversification

76. Before the volatile years of the late 1990s and early 2000s, the Hong Kong economy had achieved for almost two decades a sustained process of economic growth. For instance, the average annual growth rate during the ten-year period between 1981 and 1991 registered a level of 4.5 per cent a year. Such a record of economic performance has given Hong Kong a renowned image as one of the more successful newly industrialized economies (NIEs) in East Asia.

In the mid-1990s the growth momentum remained relatively steady. During the year 1994, the territory's gross domestic product (GDP) rose by 5.5 per cent in real terms, compared with a corresponding growth rate of 5.8 per cent in 1993. However, in spite of a secular trend of sustained growth, the economy was caught twice in the 'doldrums' of recession.The first time was shortly after the 1997 hand-over in July, stemming from the monetary and financial upheavals of East Asia. The second down-turn was in the aftermath of the collapse of the American property and stock markets in 2008 which emasculated the nation's banking system and triggered a global recession. The growth of the economy after the turn of the decade into the 2010s has been uneven. In the year of 2011, it registered a modest growth of almost 5 per cent (exactly 4.9 per cent). Yet it subsided to 1.4 per cent in the following year, because of a less hospitable environment for exports, notably due to the prolonged recession in Europe.

The development of the Hong Kong economy has been a cyclical and market-led process, in contrast to the planned state intervention in most other new Asian economies. Historically, Hong Kong does not lack experience with the 'drama' of industrial restructuring. Hong Kong emerged as an entrepôt when colonized by Britain in 1841. It traded largely in maritime and mercantile activities backed by an infrastructure of shipping and other harbour services/port facilities. The pre-war economy was commercial in nature, and it remained essentially a city port after the Second World War until the 'watershed' year of 1949. The Chinese civil war and the subsequent liberation of China touched off the massive escape of Chinese capital, alongside the industrial knowhow and technical manpower brought to Hong Kong by people seeking asylum in the territory. Further aided by the huge influx of refugees, who served as a cheap labour pool of unskilled and semi-skilled workers, Hong Kong was able to industrialize rapidly. This was Hong Kong's first experience of economic restructuring. In this context, the dual imperative of market forces and escalating political upheaval on the mainland quickly converted its entrepôt-based commercial into an industrial one. Hong Kong became a low-cost offshore base for foreign capital and a haven for subcontracting workshops which, largely home based, thrived on relatively cheap labour to produce manufactured or semi-manufactured products for exports to overseas markets, including Europe and America.

77. This period of post-war industrialization in Hong Kong also witnessed a process of decommercialization. Hong Kong's traditional mix of commercial and mercantile activities began to recede as China entered a period of political turmoil because of the civil war. This decommercialization process was accelerated further by the trade embargo levied upon China by the United Nations during the 1950s in the aftermath of the Korean War. The trade sanction almost halted the previously huge flow of goods between the mainland and the rest of the world which was handled through Hong Kong's port. However, Hong Kong's subsequent economic success has built upon, in part, the infrastructure inherited from this tradition of entrepôt activities. Its resources, such as an efficient and stable banking system, an effective network of domestic and international telephone services, a stable and competent civil service bureaucracy, a web of established retail outlets and public transport support, and a low taxation regime, have all contributed to Hong Kong's competitive advantage in global trade and commerce. At the micro level, Hong Kong also witnessed a concomitant phenomenon of business adjustments among enterprises in the private sector. At the beginning, many of these private business realignments appeared as *ad hoc* endeavours, fragmented and piecemeal. However, eventually, as the economy began to mature into an industrial city with an established manufacturing base, business adjustments at enterprises happened in a more structured and organized fashion. These activities tended to take on a more systematic appearance, coined in strategic terms and labelled widely in the 1960s and 1970s as 'diversification'. Many of the British *hongs* (noble houses) extended beyond their traditional portfolio as trading conglomerates and started to branch into real estate development, retail sales, restaurants and catering, and later, telecommunications.

78. At the same time, there also emerged an agenda of nurturing Hong Kong's young economy to move upstream into a more competitive 'realm' of diversified economic activities and enhanced productivity, rather than staying at the 'Third World' stage of relying upon low-tiered manufacturing in textile and clothing and other light labour-intensive industries. A blueprint laying out a variety of strategic possibilities as to how the economy could be diversified and its business be reformed and enhanced was detailed in the report by the 1979 Advisory Committee on the Diversification of the Economy, a high-level and essentially *ad hoc* consultative organ appointed to advise the government on the policy strategy of steering Hong Kong's economic development after the turn of the decade. A key imperative envisaged by the 1979 Diversification Committee affecting Hong Kong's future business activities and their configuration was technology (especially due to computerization), application of micro-electronics, and numerical control devices. At the workplace level automation for both production and office work has been increasing. This policy document also canvassed for a more interventionist government in order to help support the industrial development of the territory, through various measures of discretionary leverage such as by way of applying monetary policy instruments, enhancing its provision on manpower education and training, as well as engaging in an array of new infrastructural building activities (notably, the planned commissioning of a new airport to be sited at Chek Lap Kok on Lantao Island).

79. The report of the 1979 Diversification Committee therefore advocated a fairly drastic, if not novel, departure of the government from its once almost sacrosanct economic philosophy of 'non-intervention' into the private sector. This official commission recommended that in order to facilitate the transfer of advanced technology, develop new industries, expand overseas markets and stimulate foreign investment, the government should adjust its policy stance to assume a more active and wholesome role in handling the frontiers and key factors for diversifying and upgrading the economy into a more sophisticated and versatile one. The essential areas where the government was advised to extend its scope of discretionary intervention pertain to:

(a) Hong Kong's economic relationship with China;
(b) land;
(c) financial facilities;
(d) education and training;
(e) industrial development;
(f) trade promotion and industrial investment programme;
(g) external commercial relations; and
(h) technical and social research.

Hong Kong experienced a second 'drama' of economic restructuring in the 1980s and 1990s, with lingering effects which have persisted until the present. Hong Kong's restructuring this time entails a reversal of the dual process of de-commercialization and industrialization which happened in the post-war years. Instead, the secular trend is towards the paired and reciprocal processes of deindustrialization and re-commercialization, as briefly documented below.

I. Recommercialization

80. In the mid-1980s, China launched a major initiative to modernize its huge command economy, steadily opening up its coastal areas and, later, its inland provinces by the hybrid logic of 'market socialism'. The reactivation of China's external trade relations with the West and other industrial nations belonging to bodies like the Organization for Economic Cooperation and Development (OECD) has stimulated a huge expansion of China's trading activities abroad. Hong Kong has been a key beneficiary of this China trade boom as the gateway to the mainland. Vested with an efficient infrastructure system of transport, telecommunications, and banking services, plus a stable government and convertible currency regime, Hong Kong has been recycled swiftly back to its commercial role as an entrepôt. It used to serve for China in this capacity before the Korean War embargo, levied in the early 1950s by the United Nations as a sanction against China. Across the historical divide, Hong Kong rediscovered its commercial role in the 1990s by trading largely as a modern business and financial centre. It now strives to excel as a city port in the provision of high value-adding 'service' activities, placing a premium on technology, modern hardware and human resources of a high quality. Instead of concentrating on such traditional maritime industries as shipbuilding and repairs, wharf and go-down storage, and waterfront stevedoring, as it did before the war, Hong Kong has advanced and diversified its core tertiary activities into new areas such as container port handling and trucking, air cargo transport, logistics, banking and telecommunications.

81. Hong Kong's restructuring drama around this time was punctuated by the rapid growth of its stock and share markets to become one of the largest financial markets in Asia. This has ushered in such globally important issues as corporate governance, performance and conformance, on the agendas of publicly listed companies. Globalized competition in the capital fund market exerts heavy pressure upon these listed companies to improve corporate performance in order to attract potential investors, inducing their managements to seek leverage in such cost-saving devices as 'downsizing', 'de-layering' or 'de-bureaucratization'. Indeed, there has been a noticeable drift towards the recasualization of labour hiring as a lever against high costs and for enhancing performance, efficiency and productivity of a business unit. The advent of a global propensity for corporate businesses to fragment their huge and stable workforce is also increasingly felt in Hong Kong. However, it is debatable as whether such workplace reforms pursued at the expense of destabilizing the labour force and employment system are essential in order to lift an enterprise's performance. Moreover, the zeal with which these downsizing measures and hiving away a stable workforce are pursued by these enterprises is hardly commensurate with the new ethos of people management propagated under the human resource perspective.

II. Deindustrialization

82. Parallel to recommericalization has been another attrition process, which curtails in both absolute and relative dimensions Hong Kong's role as an industrial base of manufacturing activities. Deindustrialization occurred due to migration of factories away from Hong Kong in the 1990s, in a process that again arose from the China factor. Paradoxically, this was also due to mainland China's industrial take-off. The PRC, in its reform euphoria since the mid-1980s, has liberalized admission of foreign and overseas investment. It also provides a lucrative outlet for Hong Kong capital with an expanded market, a supply of cheap labour, and production goods. Hence, it has afforded this city economy with a low-cost 'hinterland' (of cheap land and labour) to which the latter's manufacturing activities could be decanted and relocated. The migration *en masse* of factories across the border, pushed away from Hong Kong due to the spiralling pressures of acute land and labour shortages as well as escalating production costs (of land and labour prices), led to a dramatic 'withering away' of Hong Kong's manufacturing production sector. The deindustrialization process has drastically curtailed the size (again, in both absolute and relative terms) of Hong Kong's industrial employment, causing a sizable group of middle-aged and redundant blue-collar workers to leave their workplaces and become jobless. Many of them, impoverished by skill obsolescence, have had difficulty finding other employment in spite of zealous retraining assistance provided by the government via the Employment Re-training Board.

The mass relocation of Hong Kong factories northwards to the mainland is a classic illustration of how assembly-line production processes can be divided and become housed in dispersed locations, by virtue of business decisions which are primarily cost induced. Such hiving off exercises are probably explicable by the large hinterland now accessible to Hong Kong capital after its political liberalization, and in part by the functional and structural flexibility enjoyed by Hong Kong enterprises.

§3. The Labour Force (and Immigration)

83. The social history of Hong Kong can be described as a process mirroring its demographic history inundated by migration and its population movement. Tides of migration influx have, in reflection of the socio-political stability in China and other parts of the East Asian region, contributed to the periodic and sometimes 'explosive' expansion of the territory's population.

84. From the beginning of its early colonial days, the development of maritime trades and commerce in Hong Kong was able to offer urban settlers moving out of China significant attractions of economic opportunities. Migration from China was hence responsible for a steady growth in Hong Kong's population from 32,983 (31,463 being Chinese) in 1851 to 878,947 (859,425 being Chinese) in 1931. Later, Sino-Japanese hostilities towards the end of the 1930s triggered a massive influx of Chinese refugees, the stampede of which raised the size of the population to an estimated level of 1.6 million at the outbreak of the Second World War.

85. There was, however, an interlude, of a temporary drop in the territory's population during the war years when Hong Kong fell under Japanese Occupation. Yet it recovered quickly during the immediate post-war years of rehabilitation, rising from about 600,000 in 1945 to reach a new level of 1.8 million by the end of 1947.

86. Phenomenal growth in the local population then followed, in the aftermath of the 1949 civil war in China, its liberation and the 1950 Korea War. The ripple effects of economic dislocation and political turmoil in the mainland sparked off successive flocks of refugees. The inflow between September 1945 and December 1949 into Hong Kong reached an unprecedented scale of 1.2 million people. The population grew sharply from 600,000 in 1945 to over 2 million in 1951, registering an average increase of 39.4 per cent each year during this period. Although the exodus subsided as a result of strict controls imposed by both the Chinese and Hong

Kong governments on refugee movement, the local population continued to grow endogenously because of its natural increase, whose rate rose to almost 30 per thousand in the population in 1955 and stayed at that high level throughout the 1960s.

87. The migration tide of the 1950s coincided with and helped sustain the industrial 'take-off' of the economy in the subsequent decade following the Korean War. While trade stagnation arising from the United Nation's embargo imposed against China during this period probably provided the primary impetus in having touched off the process of industrial development, it was due to the effects of this immigrant movement that the subsequent 'transformation' of Hong Kong into an industrial centre was able to come about successfully. Migration from Guangzhou (Canton), Shanghai and other Chinese cities engendered the transfer to Hong Kong of capital, technological knowhow and managerial expertise, entrepreneurship and most important of all, manpower and general skills in strong demand by the new industries, especially at the semi-skilled level, since the bulk of them were labour-intensive. Noticeably, cotton spinning was one of such key industries imported from China during this period; later it became Hong Kong's industrial base which branched off into other lines of the textile industry, such as garment-making for which Hong Kong has become a world leading exporter since the 1970s. Other industries having also emerged during the 1950s and 1960s included artificial flowers, wigs (which had withered away, however, towards the end of the 1970s), as well as metal work and machine shops, plastics and more recently, electronics, toys and watches.

88. These manufacturing activities have hitherto given Hong Kong industry a structural bias towards export-oriented production and labour-intensive technology. A corollary to this industrial structure has been the mass employment, until recently, of semi-skilled operatives in factories with manual dexterity yet whose skills could normally be acquired after a few weeks' training. During the 1950s and 1960s the refugee population (who became subsequently the first-generation of 'post-war' settlers in Hong Kong) supplied the territory with a ready manpower pool from which semi-skilled or unskilled labour could be recruited at relatively inexpensive wage prices to enable these labour-intensive industries to develop and compete favourably in the export world market.

89. The labour force of this earlier generation has been characteristically described as a mass of individualistic, pragmatic and conservative workers featuring the so-called 'refugee mentality'. Obsessed with a psychology of trouble aversion and a creed for economic security, these industrially disaffected workers were collectively docile, non-recalcitrant and reluctant to organize themselves into trade unions to challenge their employers. Instead, they were willing to lay themselves open to the whim of the 'free' market forces and to adapt to the latter passively through the unorganized practice of individual hiring and haggling in the workplace. Paradoxically, the relative absence of union organization on the shop floor and of other institutional forms of labour market regulation (notably, without any territory-wide statutory minimum wage nor industry-wide collective bargaining arrangements), against a background of a hard-working, and politically inhibited, migrant workforce, was considered the prime mover of Hong Kong's economic growth. Even a world renowned economist acknowledged, more than forty years ago, the apparent material advantages that the sovereignty of the market seemed to have bestowed upon Hong Kong:

> In these circumstances it seems likely that the policy of laying as little restraint as possible on the profit-seeking entrepreneur will have conduced to a greater reduction in unemployment and rise in real wages than a policy that brought some immediate relief and protection to the wage earner in his working life, but by regulations that impede enterprise.[2]

90. In retrospect, to give an interpretation of Hong Kong's success in its early-days industrial history of the 1950s through the early 1970s, it is clear that the character of its labour force, which was acquiescent, non-articulate and predominantly 'refugee', played a significant role in making possible the 'bounty' of a prudent trade-off to advance economic efficiency and the territory's commonwealth at the price of 'compressed' distributive justice in society.

91. Migration from China was drastically curtailed as a result of a stringent curfew installed at the border since the early 1960s. An offshoot has been the subsequent consolidation of the territory's manpower supply, especially at the blue-collar industrial level, as the inflow of people from China was contained. When the territory's birth rate began to slow down at the turn of the 1970s, demographic stagnation began to emerge because of such a moderation in the natural growth rate of the population. However, from 1979 onwards, this demographic equilibrium was once again upset, under the dual impact of (a) the resurgence of the immigrant stampede from China and (b) shipments of Vietnamese refugees, on boats, seeking transient asylum in Hong Kong.

92. Coinciding with the inflow of Vietnamese refugees in the late 1970s was the renewed pressure of immigrant movements from China. The bulk of the Chinese immigrants arriving during this period were illegal entrants without proper official documentation, but who otherwise aspired to the lifestyle and material affluence in Hong Kong. The government's 'touch-base' policy (which granted *de facto* rights of stay to those illegal entrants once they had touched base in reaching the urban metropolitan areas of the territory) would have tolerated such arrivals successfully reaching the urban areas to settle within the territory. However, the policy was repealed at the beginning the 1980s, thereby stemming an important source of non-authorized migration and labour supply to the territory. In spite of strict border control by both the Chinese and Hong Kong governments, the lucrative labour market in Hong Kong still proves sufficiently attractive to draw pockets of illegal immigrants from the Mainland, especially for work on building and construction sites.

---

2. E. H. Phelps-Brown, 'The Hong Kong Economy: Achievements and Prospects', in Keith Hopkins (ed.), *Hong Kong: The Industrial Colony*, Hong Kong: Oxford University Press.

93. Compounding the fluidity of the local labour force and contributing to its transient character has been an internal process of socio-demographic metamorphosis which emanates from the 1997 syndrome. The impending 'change-over' of sovereignty has triggered off a sustained exodus of emigrants from Hong Kong during the thirteen years of its political transition. Such an emigration crisis not only engendered the immediate problem of 'brain drain' of professional and managerial personnel away from Hong Kong but also precipitated the subsequent issue of the 'returning emigrants', and the detrimental impact of the skill outflow upon the pace of localization (as a sequel to decolonization) in the territory's professional and managerial echelons. Paradoxically, the manpower and skill gaps left by the 'brain drain' episode have, in part, been met by the 'internationalization' of the labour market in the upper crust of the professional/managerial occupations. These shifts in the working population have yielded a 'hybrid' feature of diversified types embracing the committed, semi-committed and non-committed in the labour force. They included: (a) emigrants on the move; (b) prospective emigrants planning to move; (c) 'commuting' emigrants who shuttle between destinations (d) 'returning' emigrants; those locals in Hong Kong who are able to advance socially upwards on a 'fast lane' because of the openings left vacant by the emigrants; (f) those locals already in possession of overseas passports without the need to leave Hong Kong to fulfil the 'residential' requirements; (g) those who are not attracted by the idea of emigration and opt to maintain their present Hong Kong citizenship status and identity, in spite of 1997 political transition; (h) expatriates who are pulled by the widened opportunities available in Hong Kong, because of the gaps caused to localization of professional and managerial jobs by the present emigration outflow, and (i) the inflow of immigrants arriving recently from China.[3]

94. The character of the Hong Kong labour force has also been made more pluralistic because of the admission of foreign guest workers into the local labour market as a sequel to the government's policy adjustments in the 1970s and 1980s. The pre-1997 government adopted a liberal admission policy, yet confined largely to the apex of the territory's manpower structure, which was applied to those 'expatriate' employees who possessed skills, knowledge or experience of value which were not yet readily available in Hong Kong. However, it was steadfast in not admitting any foreign guest workers at the lower reach of the manpower hierarchy – largely to protect the employment interests of local workers. This policy of an embargo placed on the entry of guest workers was partially liberalized in 1973, when overseas workers, largely from the Philippines, were admitted and allowed to work as domestic maids for Hong Kong households.

95. The embargo was liberalized further in the late 1980s, when the government approved the recruitment of about 15,000 workers from overseas, including technicians, craftsmen, supervisors and experienced operatives to work in Hong Kong

3. Ng Sek-hong and Cheng Soo-may, 'The Affluent Migrants as a "Class Phenomenon: The Hong Kong Case"', in Lau Siu-kai, Lee Ming-Kwan, Wan Po-san and Wong Siu-lun (eds.), *Inequalities and Development: Social Stratification in Chinese Societies*, Hong Kong: Hong Kong Institute of Asia-Pacific Studies, The Chinese University of Hong Kong, 1994.

for a two-year contract. These intakes were later consolidated in 1992 into an integrated General Scheme of Labour Importation, oriented chiefly to regulate the entry of guest migrant workers of general skill's and essentially intended to supplement the domestic labour force in those sectors beset by incessant and sustained labour shortage. The General Scheme hence expanded the scale of labour importation, yet subject to a ceiling of 25,000 in total at any given time. There was a parallel intake during this period of imported construction workers designated specifically for the new airport and associated infrastructural building projects, also subject to a quota limit of not more than 27,000.

96. Adding to the above mix, the government instituted in the early and mid-1990s a special intake of 'professional' personnel recruited from the mainland, catering essentially to the graduate employment market and intended to support the growing Sino-Hong Kong trade and economic relations. The initial batch of intake was subject to a quota of a thousand recruits.

97. The decision of the government to lift the ban on the entry of foreign workers of general and lower skills, and to allow their admission into Hong Kong, can be viewed as a policy measure of deregulating the local labour market at the fringe of the economy's manpower hierarchy, in order to add flexibility and help alleviate labour shortage and workplace bottlenecks. However, such a deregulatory policy decision coincided with a creeping problem of structural and technological unemployment generated by the northward migration of Hong Kong's manufacturing industry across the border. An apprehensive labour movement perceived these intakes of foreign workers as intrinsically perverting the job interests of those displaced from the factory who were encountering difficulties in their transfer to the newer service trades. In the highly politicized context of the transitional period before 1997, this adjusted policy of liberalizing control on migrant workers offered a politically aspiring labour movement a powerful case for labour protest. Its 'crusade' appealed immensely to a parochial (and 'protectionist') psychology of the 'grassroots' electorate.

98. Organized labour levied a stream of agitational protests against a politically neurotic administration. However, its vociferous demand upon the latter to rescind such a policy of labour importation also antagonized the business lobby groups, which have been keen lobbyists for labour importation. Labour unions' agitation against labour importation peaked in the summer of 1995 in the wake of a visible growth of unemployment, coupled with a slowdown of the economy. Labour's offensive coerced a reluctant administration to review and announce the suspension of the General Labour Importation Scheme in September that year. Conceding that the imported hires could be competing with local workers, the government agreed to phase out the core scheme, the General Labour Importation Scheme. However, to address likely labour supply gaps at the fringe, a safety valve alternative was substituted, known as the Supplementary Labour Scheme, in place of the General Scheme. Prolonged haggling followed between labour and capital, alongside the government, on the precise intake size allowed under the 'stop-gap' Supplementary Scheme and it was settled eventually at the level of 2,000.

99. The controversies clouding the policy debate about labour importation climaxed again shortly after the SAR government assumed office. The Chief Executive (equivalent to the Governor in the pre-SAR government) articulated a pro-business stance on this issue in his first annual policy address in October 1997. Citing the case of foreign domestic helpers, he argued that imported workers could perform to contribute to Hong Kong's well-being; for example, foreign domestic helpers had helped to alleviate the laborious chores of family work in many households and hence opened up career opportunities to tens of thousands of Hong Kong women. The Chief Executive announced a planned intake of migrant guest workers in a large batch at the semi-skilled and unskilled levels (specifically deployed for the construction works envisaged under his housing programme and infrastructural building agenda) and again alienated a labour movement anxious to champion the interests of working-people. Yet an imminent confrontation was averted because of the Asian currency upheavals, which triggered Hong Kong's economic downturn and an upsurge in unemployment. The gloomy prospects of a sluggish and redundancy-prone employment market coerced the SAR government, now purged of its earlier optimism, into deciding to freeze its previously announced plan to liberalize the entry of guest imported labour to work on building and construction sites.

100. As the economy showed signs of a steady recovery in 2005, there was a resumed dialogue between the government and the business sector about recruiting a large batch of foreign guest workers – this time for the garment and clothing industry – in order to assist and support its revival as a key base for nurturing the reindustrialization of Hong Kong. Protracted hard bargaining is still in process between capital and organized labour in prescribing a workable formula to stipulate a mandatory yet reasonable ratio between local workers and their foreign counterparts at the workplace level so as to regulate entry and protect the job interests of the domestic labour force in the industry. However, up to the present, such a plan of importing garment-making guest workers has still not yet materialized. As it appears, haggling between the two sides of industry in the Labour Advisory Board is caught in an impasse and may have given precedence to the importation of talents from the Mainland in the upper tiers of the labour market.

101. Today, the pluralistic mixed-bag of foreign guest workers in Hong Kong is made up of the following 'streams':

(a) foreign domestic helpers (FDHs), whose population reached a level of 218,430 at the end of 2004, an increase of 0.7 per cent compared with the number of 216,863 in 2003. About 54.8 per cent of these foreign maids were recruited from the Philippines and 41.2 per cent from Indonesia;
(b) the Supplementary Labour Scheme, as governed by the dual principles that:
   - local workers be given priority in filling job vacancies available in the job market; and
   - only employers genuinely unable to recruit local workers to fill their job vacancies be allowed to import workers. Each application to recruit foreign workers at the technician level or below has to satisfy three conditions

(tests) before being vetted by the Labour Advisory Board for the government's approval. These qualifying conditions include: advertising in newspapers, a four-week process of job-matching by the Labour Department, and a tailor-made retraining course for workers;

(c) the Admission Scheme for Mainland Talents and Professionals: introduced in 2003 to replace an older scheme, this programme aligns the conditions for admitting mainland people for employment with those applicable to foreigners. It purports to attract talented people and professionals from the mainland to work in Hong Kong for meeting local manpower needs and enhancing Hong Kong's competitiveness in the global market;

(d) admission of mainland students graduated from University Grants Com mittee (UGC)-funded institutions in Hong Kong, which admits mainland students who have graduated from UGC-funded institutions since 1990 for employment, provided that (i) they possess special skills, knowledge or experience of value to and not readily available in Hong Kong; and (ii) they are employed on a salary broadly commensurate with the market level. The rationale of this scheme is to enable Mainland students having completed a full-time programme to enter Hong Kong for employment in order to help enhance its competitiveness in the global economy;

(e) admission of skilled persons who can enter Hong Kong without having a prior offer of employment from outside Hong Kong, under 'A Quality Migrant Admission Scheme' which was launched in 2006;

(f) entry of investors from outside Hong Kong with capital not less than a stipulated amount but who are not expected to commence any business locally; this scheme is entitled 'The Capital Investment Entrant Scheme';

(g) admission of professionals from outside Hong Kong, who are able to furnish Hong Kong with special skills and provide training to local people in areas of competencies which the SAR lacks. They are given citizenship after a period of residence of seven years. This has been a long practised policy which was inherited from the previous British administration; and

(h) grant of permission for non-local students who graduated fom a locally accredited full-time degree curriculum to remain in Hong Kong for one year for employment.

§4. SOCIAL AND CULTURAL VALUES

102. The class structure in Hong Kong is conspicuous for its fluidity, given its nature as a young society relatively open to social mobility. Although the Confucian notion of social order used to envisage traditional Chinese society as stratified into four layers (in descending order of the scholar officials, peasants, artisans and merchants), such a social hierarchy seems to have left few or no imprints in Hong Kong. Indeed, a class structure has hardly crystallized in Hong Kong, possibly also because of its vastly 'migrant' background. Instead, given the transient nature of such a background, the most cherished assumption here has been the imagery that the individual can attain self-excellence and status in society by striving hard to obtain and accumulate wealth. There is a widespread belief in the efficacy of the 'cash nexus' and the work ethos of self-reliance and economic betterment is a commonplace.

103. However, within the family domain, vestiges of the Chinese tradition of familism and deferential values are still to a large extent conserved and identifiable. Yet, there are growing signs of emasculation of these normative assumptions, once firmly rooted in Chinese custom and practices. First, this is in part due to the rapid growth of economic affluence, as this urbanized post-industrial society becomes increasingly exposed to Western cultural influences such as the inculcated values of individualism and instrumentalism. The second reason is the structural process, probably also symptomatic of the 'late urbanism' syndrome, whereby the traditional three-generation extended family is steadily phased out and replaced by the conjugal family pattern.

104. Hong Kong society has shifted and evolved hastily during the 13-year transition period since 1984 and thereafter as an SAR able to conserve itself as a capitalist economic system within the PRC which mandates the governance principle of 'one country, two systems'. Paradoxically, contrary to the Joint Declaration prescription to conserve the status quo of Hong Kong society, it is precisely the status quo itself which has been altered due to dramatic changes in lifestyle, restructuring of the economy and businesses, internal socio-political agitation and strife, persistence of external influences, institutional adjustments such as in the educational system and shifts in the mood of the leadership in the central government.

105. One of the noticeable shifts in Hong Kong society is its more affluent lifestyle made possible by three factors: (a) the availability of mass consumption goods at inexpensive prices; (b) the sustained advances in real wage levels for almost three decades – the 1960s, 1970s and 1980s – thanks to the economy's growth in income and productivity; and (c) the fading away of the refugee mentality as the native-born children of immigrant parents aspire to a better quality of life.

106. Over the last few decades, Hong Kong's occupational structure has shifted from blue-collar workers – predominantly refugees – to a much larger proportion of white-collar workers such as professional, managerial and service workers. As a result, Hong Kong, like many other highly urbanized industrial societies, has gained a large middle class. However, the remaining members of the working class are trapped in a state of relative poverty because of their age and low obsolete (industrial) skills. Also constituting part of the labouring class are the imported 'guest workers' and recent immigrants arriving from mainland China. Typically, they are unlettered, inarticulate, docile and vulnerable to workplace exploitation.

107. The rise of the middle class has resulted in the parallel growth of the retail industry, spearheaded first by the highly popular Japanese department stores and recently, by the chain fashion stores. The retail, restaurant and hospitality industries, while advancing in closer pace with trends in consumption patterns, have also become more vulnerable and sensitive to the economy's well-being and people's level of purchasing power and propensity to consume. This sensitivity – manifested visibly in the slump-ridden 1990s and early 2000s – betrays the volatility of Hong Kong's consumer-oriented service activities which can be triggered by a decline in the territory's external trade and export performance if its competitiveness weakens in the region, or worldwide, which may lead to an economic downturn.

108. The high usage of pagers and mobile telephones, fax transmission and, more recently, electronic networking has nutured an ideology of 'technological determinism', which is characteristic of post-industrial societies. At the same time, what has been labelled as a value system of the'Hong Kong ethos'. has been sustained by a creed for economic opportunities, career success and excellence, as well as indulgence in the cash nexus among the local people. What are emphasized and exalted are also instrumental values which sanctify competition, individualism and egalitarianism. Ironically, those located within an amorphous central class betray little signs of a solidaristic class consciousness. Even when they combine and associate, such as by joining trade unions or professional bodies, their purpose is often merely to take advantage of the concessionary goods and consumer services offered to members, or to upgrade their skill knowledge and competency and occupational status to enhance their pay and career-advancement prospects, by attending, for example, union organized extra-mural classes.

109. There are two other distinct features of the central class. The first is an investment creed of its members to procure either real estate properties or stock and shares in the capital market. Such a propensity has in part been stimulated by Hong Kong's rapid expansion of its monetary, financial and capital institutions and aggravated by the inflation spiral in the early 1990s. The second is the development of an electoral culture under systematic official cultivation and sponsorship by a British administration anxious to institute a governance infrastructure of popular rule on the eve of its withdrawal. Yet Hong Kong lacks a commensurate culture of political participation at the grassroots level – thanks to its colonial legacy and a passive captivity of its people due to a sustained psychology of political apathy in which its earlier refugee generations had been trapped. Since the 1960s, however, the permissive nature of a non-coercive, non-authoritarian administration led by the British ordained civil service has afforded Hong Kong a hybrid political culture on which it has prided itself. Under this permissive culture, its people have allegedly 'ample freedoms' (personal freedoms, economic freedom and employment/occupational freedom, etc.), yet lack any proven experiences in the practice of democracy – the embryonic brewing of which did not commence until the electoral reforms of the 1980s.

110. The economic system of Hong Kong has been anchored essentially in the notion of a market economy of 'free enterprise'. Such a concept is in turn founded on the twin principles of (a) private ownership of property and (b) the freedom of individuals to enter and engage in equal and mutual contracts at their own free will and risks, both in business as well as at work. Here, it has been perforce a cornerstone assumption that people are free to work, to employ, to sell and to purchase as they choose. These basic freedoms have been reiterated and enshrined in the Basic Law as the quasi-constitution for Hong Kong as an SAR of China. Moreover, as individuals, they are also able to retain the bulk of the fruits of their labour in gainful economic activities, inasmuch as personal income (salary) tax is kept relatively low (subject to a standard rate of 17 per cent). And the same approach applies to profit taxes as well.

111. Hong Kong is and has always been a free port, having very few tariffs on imports and is almost entirely permissive with regard to the free movement of capital and money. For these attributes it has earned the reputation of being one of the world's most celebrated bastions of 'free-wheeling' capitalism – being rated consistently on the international league table as the world's freest economy during recent years by the Heritage Foundation. Within this framework, the government, either before or after 1997, has painstakingly followed a neo-*laissez-faire* policy (labelled otherwise as a policy of positive non-intervention or of intervention by selective discretion by neither restricting nor favouring systematically any particular sector or line of economic activity). It does not offer a subsidy to any industry, or tax concessions to foreign capital which invests locally. Instead, the tradition has always been an almost minimal provision of regulations upon the private sector. Typically, most essential services of public utilities including power supply, telephone and bus services are run by private enterprises assigned by the government under officially regulated franchise arrangements. Their profits are governed by a 'scheme of controls' to protect public interests against monopolistic or oligopolistic domination. However, in line with a global trend of deregulation, these 'closed' industries are being opened up steadily to allow the entry of more competitive players. It was only recently that a territory-wide statutory minimum wage was introduced, as the government and the business sector eventually yielded to the vociferous demands waged by organized labour for such an institutional safeguard against depressant low pay.

112. The local currency has been pegged to and linked with the American dollar in exchange value so as to sustain local confidence since October 1983 during the volatile years of hectic negotiation between China and Britain on the future of Hong Kong in the early 1980s. In fact, the Hong Kong dollar has always been backed fully by the official reserve of foreign exchange. Concomitantly, the role of stabilizing the Hong Kong dollar via the day-to-day intervention into the money market with a mix of monetary policy instruments is performed by the Monetary Authority (established in 1992), which functions like a quasi-central bank or the US Federal Reserve. However, a wholehearted and actively conducted monetary policy is by comparison still feeble. Nor is the government committed to applying the budgetary lever of fiscal intervention with any rigour, given its ardent faith in a self-regulating economy. In essence, the logic of long-term adjustments for the economy is built into its nature of relative freedom from any institutional rigidities. The following exposition on Hong Kong's experiences is exemplary:

> The level of unemployment rose and, as a result, the level of real wages fell. This kind of automatic adjustment in cost and prices in times of recession is the main theme of the classical macroeconomic model ... In Hong Kong, the government has long insisted that the economy fits well into the classical model, using the popular argument that it is a self-regulating one with a high degree of wage/price flexibility. It is claimed that the Hong Kong economy responds quickly to a recession in the form of a decrease in real wages followed by a decrease in prices. As most of Hong Kong's manufactured goods are for export, the fall in prices will make those products more competitive in the overseas markets. In this way, exports and manufacturing output can be stimulated through an essentially automatic mechanism. At the same time, falling prices increase the real cash balance of consumers and consumption will in turn be stimulated, setting in motion the economy's recovery from recession. ... Such an emphasis upon the economy's natural adjustment process apparently persisted until the latest recession, which began in late 1997.[4]

113. The global recession of 1973–75 afflicted Hong Kong by depressing both real wages and prices; it was followed by a rapid rise in economic activity during the ensuing years 1975–77. Exports, in particular, recovered and have expanded speedily since 1976, coupled with a sharp increase in private consumption thereafter. These spurts in trading activities gave rise to double-digit growth of the economy subsequently in the period of 1976–78.

114. In retrospect, two decades of almost uninterrupted prosperity have elevated Hong Kong to an affluent state of relative job abundance, with little pressure from the problems of urban unemployment and associated poverty. The resilience of the economy has nurtured another 'Asian miracle' in miniature, sustained by an average annual growth rate of 4.5 per cent achieved in real terms for the period from 1987 to 1991. Even in the early 1990s, amidst an impasse of political and constitutional reforms, there were still ample advances in both local consumption and investment demands, coupled with a modest growth in domestic exports and the continued buoyant performance of re-exports activities largely due to the factor of booming China trade. Annual inflation subsided from 12 per cent in 1991 to less than 10 per cent (9.5 per cent) in 1992, and the economy was able to register 5 per cent growth for the year 1992.

115. However, the economy began to betray signs of fatigue from the mid-1990s onwards. Unemployment, hardly a problem during previous decades, showed a trend of creeping growth which alarmed an apprehensive labour movement and later, the government. The unemployment level escalated to almost 3.5 per cent by the mid-1990s, when the number of jobless exceeded 100,000. The inflation syndrome of cost spirals, due to the strained supply of land and labour, alongside production bottlenecks, caused Hong Kong's manufacturing businesses to re-locate

4. Edward K.Y. Chen, 'Economic Setting', in Ng Sek Hong and David G. Lethbridge (eds.), *The Business Environment in Hong Kong*, Hong Kong: Oxford University Press, 4th edition, 2000, pp. 19 and 41.

their production plants across the border to the mainland hinterland. The drain of factories to the north created 'an army' of industrially unemployed and underemployed, comprising the middle-aged and older workers, skilled and semi-skilled.

116. Between 1994 and 1995, with unemployment on the rise, there began a slowdown in economic growth, accompanied by the stagnation of the real estate property market, a slump in retail trade and the restaurant and catering industry (because of a cutback in consumer spending). What compounded Hong Kong's adjustment problems in moving into the realm of a 'high quality, high productivity, and high value adding' service-oriented economy was the complex issue of how business could conserve its versatility and vitality when its cost efficiencies and competitive niche were being eroded amid political uncertainties of the impending handover.

117. The main indicators of Hong Kong's advance towards a post-industrial city-economy is attested by two factors: the relative share of the secondary and tertiary sectors in contributing to Hong Kong's GDP; and the relative share of these principal sectors in hiring and employing its aggregate workforce. The manufacturing sector's percentage share in the employed workforce declined from 47 per cent in 1971 to 41 per cent in 1981, to 28 per cent in 1991, to 16 per cent in 1995 and to 13.2 per cent in 2007. Such a share receded further to a level of around 11 per cent in 2012. Its contribution to the economy's GDP also dropped steadily from 31 per cent in 1970 to 21 per cent in 1982, to 16.7 per cent in 1990, and again to less than 16 per cent in 1994 and 8.8 per cent in 2006. This fraction went down further to a meagre level of 2 per cent in 2011. By contrast, the service sector's percentage share in the aggregate labour force increased from 41 per cent in 1971 to 47 per cent in 1981, in 63 per cent in 1991, and further to 80 per cent in 1995 and 86.6 per cent in 2007. This share now rose to 88.4 per cent in 2012. Concomitantly, there has been a parallel and sustained increase in its contribution to the economy's GDP, from 60 per cent in 1970, to 65 per cent in 1992, to 69.4 per cent in 1990, and again to more than 80 per cent in 1994 and 91.2 per cent in 2006, now reaching 93 per cent in 2011.

118. The economy's industrial restructuring has also given rise to the reconfiguration of its skill mix, now consolidated into a knowledge-based occupational structure increasingly predominated by white-collar employment. Noticeable is the proliferation and subsequent consolidation of service-oriented jobs such as sales, services, clerical, and associated workers. The relative share of professional and managerial workers in the employed workforce advanced from 10.4 per cent in 1987 to 13.6 per cent in 1991 and 34.2 per cent in 2005, whilst that of clerical workers also increased from 17.3 per cent in 1987 to 19.7 per cent in 1991 but receded to 16.4 per cent in 2005, of sales and service workers from 28 per cent in 1987 to 31 per cent in 1991 yet declining to 16.1 per cent in 2005. Correspondingly, there has been a decrease from 42.9 per cent in 1987 to 35 per cent in 1991 and 14.8 per cent in 2005 of those who were engaged in manufacturing activities.

119. Paradoxically, the sizeable drop in the number of industrial jobs appearing in Hong Kong's official statistics is attributable to the rapid strengthening of the economic links between Hong Kong and the mainland. It has been argued that Hong Kong's industry has not withered away but has actually expanded in securing a cheaper production base beyond the border. According to estimates, factories owned by Hong Kong capital are at present responsible for hiring about four to five million workers on the Mainland. This number would correct the view that the secondary sector of manufacturing and production activities has been on the retreat in Hong Kong.

120. The economy faded shortly after the mid-year changeover of sovereignty from Britain to China in 1997. Actually, the pessimism about a labour market trapped in the doldrums of an oversupply was arrested for a brief interval before and after the July political handover. Unemployment statistics fell to an almost negligible 2.5 per cent of the general labour force. For a short time, optimism revived and prevailed. Amid the post-handover euphoria, the Chief Executive announced his intention of resuming the intake of foreign workers in large batches for the building and construction trades.

121. Nevertheless, later in the year the trauma of the Asian financial upheaval began to shock Hong Kong and its basically fragile economy, now predominated by service industries and trades. The crisis touched off a syndrome of business pessimism, precipitating after the collapse of a leading Japanese department store, Yaohan, a sustained wave of company insolvencies and closures, corporate downsizing and de-layering, staff cutbacks, lay-offs and redundancies. Stop-gap measures, like practices of short-hour working and pay freezes, became widespread. The labour market was trapped in a state of glut again.

122. In the following year 1998, there was a sequence of business failures affecting an increasing number of retail stores, restaurants, real estate property agencies, and investment houses. Even the stevedoring trade (largely dealing with container port handling activities) attempted to cope with the onset of a lean period by cutting back its workforce. Alongside episodes of retrenchment, other corporate employers were also reputed to make free recourse to austerity measures like converting permanent posts into part-time or temporary supernumerary hiring, hiving off non-core work, using external subcontracting agencies by outsourcing, as well as rationalizing and consolidating pay packages, and declaring pay pauses and even wage cuts, in addition to instituting performance pay and cut-back in training outlays. Many smaller shops fared even worse. In battling for survival, they lost the ability to pay wages. To cope, many short-circuited the Employment Ordinance by introducing short-hours, job-sharing and extended unpaid holidays. Unemployment figures rose steadily, reaching a new height of 6.3 per cent near the middle of 1999.

123. However, with the advent of the 'new economy' and an associated euphoria about the information technology industries arriving at Hong Kong around the turn of the millennium, the economy began to recover. This upturn helped arrest unemployment levels and the year 2000 showed promising signs of an economy revitalized in the aftermath of the East Asian financial upheavals. The unemployment rate fell from 5.6 per cent in the first quarter of the year 2000 to 4.4 per cent in the fourth quarter of the same year. However, this trend was soon halted by a second wave of economic adversity, caused by an almost global emasculation of the 'bubble economy' sustained by over-expanded information technology industries. The second downturn once again triggered an upsurge of unemployed workers, reaching 4.5 per cent in the first half of the year 2001. Hong Kong was beset by high level of unemployment throughout 2001, reaching 5.3 per cent in the third quarter and 6.1 per cent in the fourth quarter. High unemployment persisted into the year 2002, attaining a height of 7.8 per cent by mid-year. However, it began to show signs of abating in the latter half of that year, as the economy appeared to pick up, largely due to improved performance in the export sector. The unemployment level subsided to 7.6 per cent in August 2002.

124. At its peak, unemployment affected almost every sector of the Hong Kong economy. Particularly vulnerable were manufacturing industries, distributive trades (wholesale and retail services), catering, building and construction, transport and financial servicing. And the effects of corporate downsizing and lay-offs spread to the upper segment of the occupational hierarchy. There were visible increases in unemployment rates among elitist groups such as managers, administrators and professionals in the upper echelons of society.

125. The SAR government, apprehensive about high unemployment rates, responded by announcing a budget that promised both tax cuts and enlarged public spending in an effort to stimulate the economy and assist the needy. It pledged further funding to provide skill and vocational retraining, plus an enhanced job placement service. However, such measures were not enough and the government seemed to have no imaginative ideas for dealing with the widespread unemployment problem and the need of the unemployed. The official package was piecemeal and fragmentary and it fell short of wholesome levers such as subsidies for employers taking on the unemployed and insurance to provide for workers losing their jobs and suffering a sudden loss of income.

126. However, as unemployment escalated each time due to the incidence of these crises, the government, reacting in a typically *ad hoc* fashion, appeared to have adopted an increasingly heavy dosage of intervention into the labour market. Such a drift to using public levers was demonstrated, for instance, in the high profile agenda articulated by the SAR government in coping with the 'doldrums' caused by the 'SARS' virus epidemic in the earlier half of the year 2003. Again, economic adversity due to the territory-wide stagnation of business and economic activities, essentially as a result of the people's aversion to visiting public places for shopping, leisure and even patronizing the restaurants, and the virtual halting of the tourist trade, pushed the unemployment level to a new height of 8.8 per cent for the month of July 2003. Graduate unemployment was especially pronounced, and the job bidding among these young novice entrants into the full-time labour market depressed further the general wage level to new 'lows'.

127. The official package of public measures for addressing the 'unemployment' agenda proliferated. These included, *inter alia*, creating jobs (yet mostly of a peripheral and temporary nature), enhanced job placement services and assistance provided by the Labour Department, expanded facilities for education, vocational education, skill upgrading, training and retraining for those unemployed and waiting for employment and re-employment, as well as loans granted as petty capital to assist those self-employed to start as entrepreneurs in small businesses. However, as noted earlier, these public dosages are essentially fragmented, of a 'stop-gap' nature and devoid of a long-term strategy for labour protection against the vicissitudes of a volatile economy. Apart from making available public assistance to the unemployed within the existent social security framework, the administration has been steadfast in denying any proposal to make a standing fund of unemployment subsidy/assistance available to those deprived of a job and in need. Equally docile has been the labour movement in articulating the needs of the labouring masses. And the trade unions were patently disappointed when their quest for a minimum wage law to uplift the low paid workers (like those working for cleaning subcontractors on outsourcing tasks hived off by corporate employers) from their doldrums was denied again by the SAR government . In place of granting these marginal workers a better deal at work in the form of enacting a statutory wage floor, the Chief Executive in his October 2006 annual policy address merely made an official pledge to monitor sectoral low pay by way of a suasive and voluntary practice via sponsoring a 'Wage Protection Movement' – i.e. persuading and encouraging employers in these sectors to peg their pay in line to the median wage level for regular full-time employees in these trades.

Chapter 5. The Political Status of Hong Kong

128. Hong Kong was restored from British rule to China and reunified with its motherland in July 1997. Because of the institutional and political diversity between the two, Hong Kong has been able to conserve its capitalist economy as an SAR of the PRC, and enjoys a high degree of self-governing autonomy.

129. The above 'landmark' political shift emanated largely from the problematic future status of Hong Kong because of the impending expiry of the lease of the New Territories and the northern part of the Kowloon Peninsula from China to Britain by the dateline of 1997. In order to settle the looming impasse, China and the United Kingdom entered into diplomatic negotiations in 1982 and concluded an agreement on Hong Kong upon the expiry of the New Territories lease. The accord, formally known as the 'Joint Declaration of the Government of the United Kingdom of Great Britain and Northern Ireland and the Government of the People's Republic of China on the Question of Hong Kong' was to restore this territory presently under the British administration to China with effect from 1 July 1997 as an SAR of the latter. The Hong Kong SAR, directly answerable and accessible to the Central People's government in Beijing, has been able to 'enjoy a high degree of autonomy, except in foreign and defence affairs'. Concomitantly, its pre-1997 social and economic systems, including a latitude of rights and freedoms, its people's lifestyle, private property and ownership of enterprises, etc. are preserved – as by virtue of the Basic Law essentially drafted in Hong Kong and promulgated subsequently by China's National People's Congress in 1990. The Basic Law guaranteed that these systems and policies will remain unchanged for 50 years. The Sino-British accord was ratified in the following year, in 1985, by the two nations which also registered the agreement with the United Nations on 13 June 1985 – thus 'confirming their acceptance of its internationally binding nature'.

130. At the same time, political and electoral reforms were introduced in Hong Kong under official sponsorship by the pre-SAR government which sought to 'democratize' the hitherto colonial administration by creating, through gradual phrases, a British-fashioned system of representative government. These measures entail, *inter alia*, the enlargement of the electoral franchise as well as the eventual transformation, by steps, of the officially appointed law-making Legislative Council into a popularly elected assembly based largely upon western parliamentary principles. Election to the Legislative Council was initiated in 1985 on a partial and experimental basis through a dualistic constituency arrangement – as noted earlier, one being the 'functional constituency' and the other 'geographical' constituency.

131. These reforms were continued after 1997 by the SAR government, as prescribed by the Joint Declaration and the Basic Law which provided a skeleton timetable on how these reform measures were to proceed.

132. In the light of the momentous implications of the transfer of sovereignty and Hong Kong's reversion back to China by the political dateline of July 1997, it is important to survey briefly these implications for the territory in evolving its governance system, labour conditions and labour law and industrial relations during the thirteen-year period of political transition and these sixteen years of Hong Kong as an SAR belonging to China.

Chapter 6. The Political Prescription for Hong Kong: The Model of 'One Country, Two Systems'

133. Under the 1984 Sino-British Joint Declaration, Hong Kong has been able to maintain its present properties and social fabric as a capitalist city economy, as also prescribed by the Basic Law – the mini-constitution which China promulgated for Hong Kong. Politically, it has also been transformed into a self-administering territory which owes its sovereign allegiance now to China upon the ending of British rule in 1997. Capital and labour, as well as their mutual relationship, are preserved as they were before, given China's guarantee written into the Basic Law for safeguarding private property, ownership of enterprises, the legitimate right of inheritance and foreign investment, as well as the freedoms of the person, of speech, of the press, of assembly, of association, of strike and of choice of occupation, etc.[5]

134. The implication of the above political formula of China's 'one country, two systems' model is obvious.[6] Such a socio-political prescription is intended to permit, *inter alia*, the institutional continuities of Hong Kong's present social arrangements, in spite of the 1997 transfer of sovereignty and as a sequel to its reunification with China. In this context, several features are worth noting in charting the evolution and the future of labour and industrial relations system in this territory.

135. It is envisaged that labour law in Hong Kong will continue to perform its 'primary' function of limiting 'the range of the worker's duty of obedience and [enlarging] the range of his freedom',[7] inasmuch as the territory is to be maintained as a capitalist economy giving scope to waged employment, which implies the notion of both 'a power to command and a duty to obey'.[8] The paradoxical relationship between the manager and the managed is likely to continue to feature in the average workplace in Hong Kong, even now that the SAR owes its governance mandate to a sovereign state which is nominally 'socialist' in character. (Socialism is withering and becoming nominal at best in many aspects inside China now that it has been modernized by the recent process of economic reforms – entailing endeavours which purport to transform the nation into a modern industrialized nation state of 'market socialism'.)

136. Theoretically speaking, the nexus of a 'labour–management relationship', as well as the principal intention of labour law (which is to regulate and restrain

5. See 'Joint Declaration on the Question Hong Kong', clause 3(5). In other words, under such a novel formula of 'one country, two systems', Hong Kong is destined to persist as a highly autonomous SAR of China. In this capacity, it is envisaged to continue playing its renowned role 'as a bastion of free-wheeling capitalism' for at least 50 years after the 1997 changeover, within the sovereign domain of a socialist nation.
6. Deng Xiaoping, *Building Socialism with Chinese Characteristics*, Beijing: Foreign Language Press, 1985, p. 31.
7. Paul Davis and Mark Freedland, *Kahn-Freund's Labour and the Law*, London: Stevens and Sons, 1983, p. 18.
8. Otto Kahn-Freund, *Labour and Law*, London: Stevens and Sons, 1972, p. 5.

both the power of management and the power of organized labour), are equally applicable to the capitalist system, the socialist system of production, or even a hybrid system of 'market socialism'.

137. However, it has become increasingly fashionable, in the currency of a 'corporatist' perspective on industrial society and its politics, for labour law to canvass a critical and occasionally hostile stance towards workers' combinations and their industrial actions. This has inspired a relatively conservative interpretation of labour law in popularizing the restraining importance of restrictive regulation. Such a strategy of restriction therefore contributes generically to the 'reducing of trade union power in collective bargaining and in the day-to-day conduct of industrial relations', as well as an increase in the strength of managerial control in industrial relations.[9] By such an approach, 'legalism' as the core prescription of labour law is hence considered to be inhibiting or limiting. This is because it sees the law as a regulatory or even coercive instrument of enhancing discipline in industrial relations and in so doing, as a means of promoting higher efficiency and productivity in the performance of the economy.[10]

138. In Hong Kong the labour law infrastructure since the late 1960s can be described, on the whole, as reformist while fundamentally retaining its native character of 'permissiveness'. The reform strategy, emanating essentially from the British model, extends from a previous stance of 'non-intervention' and is now poised to use the law where it thinks 'fit exceptionally to do so, for example, in the extension of recognized terms and conditions of employment and … in the expansion of individual employment and even on collective issues'.[11]

139. To the administration, the choice between the continuation of a moderate reformist approach on the one hand and the shift towards a more restrictive and disciplined orientation on the other may pose a formidable dilemma for the authorship of labour law in Hong Kong. The contradiction is apparent since the administrative-cum-legal framework in Hong Kong after 1997 is to all intents and purposes to 'support and preserve capitalism', whilst its socialist motherland is also in the process of metamorphosis to evolve a new realm of 'market socialism', which recognizes a liberalized latitude of market-oriented 'capitalist' operations. The key question for the labour and employment agenda for the Hong Kong SAR administration is whether these contradictions can be sufficiently reconciled and addressed by the prescription of 'one country, two systems'.

140. The logic of the market has continued to reign for the 17 years since Hong Kong was reintegrated with China in this young industrial society which is

---

9. John Clark and Lord Wedderburn, 'Modern Labour Law: Problems, Functions and Policies', in Lord Weddeburn *et al.*, *Labour Law and Industrial Relations: Building on Kahn-Freund*, Oxford: Clarendon Press, 1983, pp. 128 and 131.
10. *Ibid.*, p. 131.
11. John Clark and Lord Wedderburn, 'Modern Labour Law: Problems, Functions and Policies', in Lord Wedderburn *et al.*, *Labour Law and Industrial Relations: Building on Kahn-Freund*, Oxford: Clarendon Press, 1983, p. 127.

likely to become increasingly cosmopolitan, pluralist and sophisticated, both industrially as well as socially. In addition to the Sino-British safeguards as furnished by the 1985 Joint Declaration, it has been made clear that the Chinese government will (i) pursue the policy of 'one country, two systems';[12] and (ii) enable the Hong Kong legislative body, in line with the principles of the Basic Law, to 'make specific laws in light of the development of the region's situation'.[13] To the extent that labour and capital here are likely to sustain their mutual relationship of 'antagonistic cooperation', it may be said that the 'market' imperative and the socio-political implications of 'pluralism' for sectional interest representation will significantly shape the territory's labour legislation beyond 1997 in the SAR era. Two recent issues of a labour–capital duel are exemplary:

(i) a High Court ruling which excludes items like 'commission' and 'tips' from the scope of basic wages in the latter definition (yet this judical decision was later revised by an amendment to the Employment Ordinance which redefined the scope of wages to include 'commission' and 'tips' of a regular nature); and
(ii) the SAR government's policy decision to promote an essentially voluntary pay movement to help uplift the low wage conditions of the low paid marginal workers, and its steadfast reluctance to enact a minimum wages law for Hong Kong. Such a policy prescription was, however, rescinded when the government, imposing a fragile consensus upon labour and capital, was able to usher on to the statute book an officially mandated minimum wage level for the general labour force.

12. *Beijing Review*, vol. 29, no. 2, 13 January 1986, p. 6.
13. *Ibid.*

Chapter 7. Labour Law

§1. Definitions and Notions

141. Labour law is that part of law which deals with persons (including both private individuals as well as legal persons) in their capacity as either employees or employers. By its nature, it is hence concerned with work and the work situation as well as the relationships arising therefrom. Where British-based common law prevails, the notion of subordination has been a key criterion for determining whether or not an employment relationship exists. The cardinal test, by implication, is hence to ascertain whether or not a person works under the command, authority and control of the employers. Where the work is not carried out in a position of subordination, it is not likely that an employment relationship will be established and recognized at law, as in the instance of the self-employed. However, it has been generally accepted that even salaried professionals (such as doctors, lawyers and accountants) are also subject to a degree of subordination to their superiors in the workplace, in spite of the large amount of job autonomy and self-discretion they normally enjoy.

142. The above idea notwithstanding, it has to be noted that in Hong Kong the competent authority to rule upon the existence or otherwise of an employment relationship is the judiciary, at the level of the Labour Tribunal or the higher courts above it. This has remained the case in spite of the change of government in 1997 when Hong Kong reverted back to China as its SAR.

143. By virtue of the 'one country, two systems' political formula, Hong Kong has been able to retain its pre-1997 legal system which is attributable essentially to its British heritage. Labour law offers no exception as it comprises two principal components: (i) common law and (ii) statute law. Common law is that part of the law of England formulated, developed and interpreted by the common law courts based upon the common customs of the country and has remained largely unwritten. In parallel, statute law is law enacted by the legislature, laid down in Acts of Parliament (as in the United Kingdom) or Ordinance of the Legislative Council (as in Hong Kong). Like the British situation, there has been a gradual process of expansion in statutory labour law, especially where common law has been found inadequate to protect the interests and rights of parties involved in employment.

144. Labour law is generally conceived to serve the purpose of governing the relationship between the employer and the employee who carries out his/her work in a subordinate position under a labour contract, whether express or implied. However, the scope of application for statutory labour law is confined in general to the private sector and does not cover, following again the British practice, the civil service. In this connection, employees of the government are excluded form the exigencies of any statutory enactments by virtue of the Interpretation and General Clauses Ordinance.

145. As in other industrial societies, labour law in Hong Kong is concerned with both the individual and collective aspects of employment or labour–management relations. After 1997, the 'market' imperative has continued to dominate, enabling sectional interests to be articulated on a platform of representative government in shaping the gestation of labour legislation in the SAR. That the territory's entire legal system is to be conserved intact after and in spite of the political changeover has been made explicit by the 1984 Sino-British Joint Declaration. After the establishment of the Hong Kong SAR, the laws previously in force in Hong Kong (i.e. the common law, rules of equities, ordinances, subordinate legislation and customary law) were maintained, save for any that contravened the Basic Law and subject to any amendment by the Hong Kong SAR legislation.[14]

§2. Individual Labour Law

146. Individual labour law is that part of labour law which governs and regulates the individual employment relationship between the employer and the employed. The rights and obligations prescribed for either party are often mutual, as arising from the contract of employment. Pertinent issues in the purview of individual labour law are concerned with:

- the categorization of employees who can be classified into such major groupings as manual workers, non-manual workers, seamen, apprentices and overseas employees, etc.;
- the properties of the individual contract of employment: in terms of such aspects as the categories; form and content, as well as the legal capacity of individuals to conclude such agreements;
- the notion of a lawfully employable person;
- the rights and duties of the employer and the employee in the course of and arising from employment;
- statutory modifications of the above rights and freedom, also such statutes of an imperative nature as the anti-corruption law and bill of rights legislation;
- annual leave, holidays, rest days and work hours;
- wages and remuneration and protection there of;
- protection, benefits and other rules pertaining to the employee's temporary incapacity to work for reasons such as illness, accidents at work and maternity confinement;
- job security, associated with issues such as lay-off; retrenchment and severance payment; long service payment and termination of the contract of employment;
- protection against anti-union discrimination;
- covenants of non-competition;
- settlement of individual (grievance) disputes; and

14. Joint Declaration of the Government of the United Kingdom of Great Britain and Northern Ireland and the Government of the People's Republic of China on the Question of Hong Kong, 1984, Annex I, Section II.

- other statutory provisions relating to specific aspects and conditions of employment.

§3. Collective Labour Law

147. Collective labour law is concerned with the regulation of collective labour relations, which can be those between employers and employees, as well as those among employees themselves. The essential ingredients constituting collective labour law are:

- trade union rights and regulation;
- employees' unions and employers' associations and their membership, organization and rules governing their internal government, etc.;
- collective bargaining;
- the law of industrial conflict: strikes, lock-outs, etc.;
- the law governing the settlement of collective labour–management disputes;
- industrial safety; and
- manpower planning.

§4. Legal Nature

148. Labour law in Hong Kong can be described in general as 'imperative' in nature. In other words, it is not permissible to deviate from legal standards or rules even if the employee has agreed to waive his/her legal entitlement or part thereof by way of either individual or collective acts of 'contracting out'. Of course, such a prohibition on 'contracting out' arrangements does not preclude the possibility of improvement on the minimum statutory conditions being incorporated into the terms and conditions of the individual labour contracts, or provided in collective agreements.

149. Contraventions of the relevant statutory provisions in labour law pertaining to the individual contracts of employment are actionable in most cases upon complaints initiated by the afflicted party. The normal time limit allowed for litigation in the Labour Tribunal is six months, but otherwise is six years in the District Court.

150. Criminal sanctions, however, are attached to those provisions in the labour law that define such aspects as (i) the employability of persons and the employer's obligation to document such information at the workplace; (ii) protection of the workers as regards work hours of young persons in industry, rest days, statutory holidays, paid annual leave, minimum age of employment, wages, maternity protection, anti-union discrimination, severance pay, industrial safety and health, compensation for work injuries and disease, and rights to apprentice training. On the other hand, official sanctions are not involved in that part of the labour law dealing with the inception and dissolution of the individual labour contracts.

151. In determining claims for severance pay and damages for wrongful dismissals in court, it has been customary to place the onus of proof generally upon the employer. However, if legal sanctions are involved, the statutory obligations incumbent upon and implied for the parties have to be interpreted restrictively. This often means that the benefit of the doubt belongs to the accused by English common law.

152. Labour law, generally regarded as consistent with the public interest, is also applicable to expatriate workers in Hong Kong.

§5. Categories of Employees

153. Previously, in Hong Kong employees were legally classified into two principal categories, manual and non-manual workers. While collective labour law has always been applicable in common to both groups, it has been discriminatory in the application of individual labour law inasmuch as it used to cover all manual employees but only those non-manual employees whose monthly earnings did not exceed a prescribed income ceiling.

154. However, the above differential treatment in applying individual labour law to all manual and a prescribed segment of non-manual workers has now been rescinded. Following an amendment to the Employment Ordinance in the early 1990s, all non-manual employees have been now placed under the protective purview of the Ordinance and their legal entitlements are no longer subject to the monthly ceiling for income or earnings which the Ordinance used to stipulate.

Chapter 8. The Historical Background of the Labour Movement (1850–2012)

§1. Origins of Hong Kong (1850–1911)

155. The history of Hong Kong can be traced back to its early days of colonization in the 19th century, when the imperial Chinese government ceded this territory to Britain after its defeat in the Opium Wars.

156. Its history is hence associated with the infamous opium trade, starting in the mid-18th century and involving such European franchised traders as the British East India Company, which exported to China this 'commodity' in exchange first for its tea and silk but later, for its silver and bullion. When the Chinese government banned the opium trade in 1799, tensions began to brew between the imperial authority in the mainland and the British who were engaged in the profitable but illegal trade and who used the island of Hong Kong as a shipping post.

157. The tension escalated into open hostilities in 1840, after the gallant endeavour of a senior Chinese official to suppress the opium trade, burning chests of opium which he had seized in Guangzhou (Canton). The First Opium War erupted, lasting from 1840 to 1842. Hong Kong was ceded in 1842 by China, defeated, to Britain under the Treaty of Nanking – the first of a series which China has hitherto considered derogatory and labelled as the 'unequal treaties'.

158. The Second Anglo-Chinese War (1856–8) broke out because of disputes over the interpretation of the earlier treaty and the boarding of a British vessel (the *Arrow*) by the Chinese in search of suspected pirates. The 1858 Treaty of Tianjin (Tientsin), which concluded the Second Anglo-Chinese War (otherwise also known as the Arrow War), vested the British with the privilege of diplomatic representation in China and later, the Convention of Peking extended the ceded territory of Hong Kong with the addition of the Kowloon Peninsula and the Stonecutters Island. In 1898, another convention in Peking resulted in the lease of the New Territories and northern Kowloon Peninsula to the British for 99 years, up to 1997.

159. In 1845, the population of Hong Kong registered a size of 23,817 in number including 595 Europeans. The 1850s saw the first major wave of refugee influx as a sequel to the Tai Ping Rebellion and attendant upheavals in China. By 1861 the population was estimated to be 165,000; it grew to 300,000 by 1901; and to 878,947 by 1931 (comprising 859,425 Chinese).

160. Hong Kong trade unions in the early days were largely hangovers from the traditional pre-industrial Chinese craft guilds, many of which were organized on the basis of particularistic ties like clanship and common dialects. Their activities were marked by elaborate rituals and concerned in many instances with the maintenance of control over a specific trade in a locality – by organizing both the employers and the workmen in fraternities. Family clans and friendly societies, parochial and based upon kinship ties, the region or dialect, were also active. Secret societies, notably the Triad Societies (whose members were originally committed to the overthrow of the reign of the Manchu Dynasty viewed as a foreign regime), flourished. Menaced by the criminal activities of these secret societies, Hong Kong passed an ordinance in 1845 in an attempt to control them, followed later by the enactment of the 1887 Triad and Unlawful Societies Ordinance, and in 1911 of the Societies Ordinance (no. 47). This latter piece of legislation has hitherto required that all societies in the territory, including guilds and labour organizations, be registered or officially exempted.

§2. Industrial and Socio-political Unrest (1911–1927)

161. Manchu rule in China came to an end in 1911 when the last emperor was deposed in Peking, virtually bringing the imperial era to a conclusion in its history. Three years after the 1911 Revolution trade unions were banned on the Chinese mainland. For this reason Hong Kong was to evolve later into a strategic foothold for sheltering and nurturing the mainland labour movement in its subsequent process of gestation and development.

162. In Hong Kong, the 1911 schedule of exempted societies under the Societies Ordinance comprised altogether two general merchant associations, 34 master guilds (with three including a mixed membership of both the workmen and employers). When the schedule was last published in 1919, it had grown to a list including 35 workmen's guilds. In the same year, the May Fourth Movement erupted on the mainland, when students demonstrated in Peking (Beijing) on 4 May against a proposal in the Versailles Conference to hand over the former German concession, Shangtung, to the Japanese. This disadvantaged treatment at the Versailles Conference, then concluding the First World War, provoked simultaneously a tide of unrest in Hong Kong, including students' and workers' demonstrations, riots and strikes. In the wake of this agitation, the Chinese Engineers Institute, a Hong Kong union organizing 9,000 mechanics, waged a successful strike which secured from the employers significant wage increases. These industrial actions had the important effects of encouraging the formation of new industrial unions throughout southern China. Further strikes were also touched off in Hong Kong.

163. The 1911 Societies Ordinance was soon replaced by a new one passed in 1920, which abandoned the earlier principle of registration and instead, outlawed the Triad Society and its associated rituals. Although not intended for curbing union activity, the revamped legislation on societies did give the Governor in Council the power to ban any society deemed to be injurious to law and order in Hong Kong.

164. When Dr Sun Yat-Sen, the founder of the Republic and the Nationalist Party (the Kuomintang) took rein of the government in 1921, he repealed the previously restrictive regime of Chinese laws against trade unions and actively sought the support and allegiance of the working mass. At the same time, the Communist Party was established in China, having its own Labour Secretariat for organizing the new industrial unions. In 1922, seamen in Hong Kong organized by the Chinese

Seamen's Union came out on strike, followed by sympathetic actions waged by 12 other unions in demonstration of their 'working class solidarity'. Life in Hong Kong was paralysed by its first general strike, involving a total of 120,000 strikers and settled later virtually on the seamen's terms. As a sequel, the Seamen's Union became the vanguard in the emerging Hong Kong labour movement led by the Hong Kong Federation of Labour which, comprising 70 member unions, listed the 'struggle against imperialism and capitalism' as its key mission. By 1924, the Nationalists were collaborating with the Communists, combining together to form a united front which helped ferment labour unrest in the Colony, where it was observed: 'The unions, which had developed out of societies like the Triad rather than the craft guilds, took on more and more a leftist complexion and became frankly revolutionary, nationalistic and anti-foreign.'

165. Evidently, union leadership during this period was political in nature, hardly involving the grassroots participation of the rank-and-file members which it purported to represent. For these echelons in the labour movement, the search for economic improvement was frequently subordinated to the wider political aims of revolutionary nationalism.

166. On 19 June 1925 began the historically legendary chapter of the General Strike-Boycott in Hong Kong and Canton, which almost extinguished the economy of the colony as a trading port. The industrial episode was largely politically inspired, fuelled by the tussle between the two parties forming the coalition Chinese government housed in Canton and that between this fragile coalition government and the colonial administration in Hong Kong. When the more conservative Nationalist faction gained and consolidated power in Canton, the British and Chinese authorities got together to negotiate a joint settlement of the General Strike-Boycott on 'double-tenth' (10 October 1926). The General Strike collapsed and the Hong Kong government, baffled by this experience, subsequently introduced a coercive law controlling illegal strikes in the colony.

167. In 1927 Shanghai saw once again a major split and the beginning of bitter rivalry between the Nationalists and Communists. Thereafter, the unions were purged of their newly acquired political power, becoming emasculated and covert or otherwise subordinate to the Nationalists. The colonial authorities in Hong Kong also acted and in 1927, the Illegal strikes and Lock-outs Ordinance was enacted, outlawing strikes and lock-outs designed to coerce the government or against any trade or industry other than those in which the strikers were engaged. The same law also disallowed the foreign control of any Hong Kong unions, and prohibited the use of union funds for any political purposes.

§3. The Depression Era (1928–1945)

168. The ensuing years 1928–1945 were marked by a relative absence of industrial unrest and union action, when seven labour associations/trade unions were outlawed and banned. Several factors helped explain union inactivity and the low agitational level. ,First, the worldwide depression witnessed massive unemployment and labour surplus – a phenomenon which also afflicted Hong Kong. Second, the 1925–6 Hong Kong–Canton General Strike-Boycott had impoverished the union movement both in money and popularity. Third, labour legislation which both China and Hong Kong introduced had led to visible curbs on union activities in both the mainland and the colony. Fourth, waves of upheavals within China, coupled with a prevalent feeling of job insecurity among workers, created a conducive condition for the criminal infiltration of the Triad Societies into areas traditionally belonging to the labour movement. In this gloomy context, criminal gangs, rather than unions, began to control a widening segment of the unskilled labour market, while the surviving Hong Kong unions became little more than friendly societies, or welfare fraternities, yet lacking an agenda to improve the collective well-being of the labouring mass.

169. The union movement revived briefly its activities during the period 1938–41. The revival was partly inspired by the temporary reunion of the Communists and the Nationalists in face of the imminent threat of Japanese aggression (which commenced in 1937) and in part under the sponsorship of the colonial administration anxious to foster the development of 'responsible and pragmatic' trade unionism in the colony modelled after the mother-country's system in Britain. According to police estimates in the late 1930s, there were about 300 associations in Hong Kong, including 84 labour unions with 44,000 members, plus a fringe of another 89 clubs and quasi-labour unions enrolling some 7,000 members.

170. In 1941 the Japanese occupied Hong Kong, and its unions and their activities came to halt.

§4. Postwar Industrial Relations

171. After the Japanese Occupation (1941–5) during the Second World War, the British authority resumed its administration in Hong Kong. Since 1941, the territory's population had declined consistently, down to an estimated size of merely 500,000 to 600,000 in 1945. The subsequent years of 1946–9 witnessed fierce fighting in China, as the long and bitter tussle between the Nationalists and Communists resumed, escalating into a full-scale civil war which caused widespread social dislocation and upheavals in the mainland. During this four-year period as many as 1,285,000 refugees were believed to have entered Hong Kong seeking asylum. The 1949 Communist victory and liberation of China led to a stampede of incoming refugees. However, this tide receded later, especially in the face of the strict control upon population movement introduced gradually by the new people's government in the mainland.

172. Before 1941, the colony had always had a high proportion of migrant male workers who shuttled between their home villages in the neighbouring province, Kwantung (Guandong) and their workplace of employment in Hong Kong. The 1921 census, for instance, showed the males outnumbering the females by three to two, while the 1931 census indicated a ratio of 5.5 men for every woman engaged in the manufacturing industry. However, since the 1950s Hong Kong has become a less transient place for the commuting Chinese workmen and instead, it has been home and host for a refugee population now identifying themselves with the territory in terms of both home-building and gainful employment.

§5. A Divided Labour Movement

173. During the Chinese Civil War of 1945–9, the adversaries, the Communist and Nationalist parties, were each striving to win popular grassroots support not only on the mainland but also in Hong Kong. The Communists moved vigorously to organize the colony's workers in all the key sectors of the economy, noticeably in the docks, public utilities, textiles, transport and shipping industries. In contrast, the Nationalists in their own bases nurtured a network of competing unions in the same industries – visibly in their strongholds which were located in the restaurant and other service industries.

174. The contest for popular support between the rival factions at the 'grassroots' level on the shopfloor, coupled with a shortage of skills experienced during the postwar reconstruction process, as well as rapid inflation because of bottlenecks and strain in resource supply, coalesced in breeding a creeping growth in industrial unrest during the period 1946–50. In the wake of these confrontational pressures, the Chinese Engineers Institute, the biggest craft union at that time in Hong Kong, called a cross-industry strike of the trade in 1947. It lasted for 27 days, affecting more than 10,000 mechanics spread across numerous establishments, both private and in the civil service. In 1949 the inflation syndrome (in part a spill-over from the mainland inflation crisis) touched off, in succession, a stream of wage demands and trade disputes in the large public utilities and British enterprises – climaxing in the famous Hong Kong Tramway Dispute in 1949. In the next year, 1950, a benchmark case involving arbitration (the sole case of private sector labour arbitration in Hong Kong's industrial history up to the present) occurred over the wage dispute in the Dairy Farm Co. The award of HK$30 per month was adopted not only in the Dairy Farm itself but also by other major Western establishments in Hong Kong, with the blessing of the unions' consent. The settlement of this dispute and the extension of its terms to other industries helped end a period of intensive industrial haggling and strife centred upon the wage issue, which had a strong politico-ideological flavour. Noticeable in this period was the industrial strength and militancy of certain unions which were, however, political in nature. Evidently, their industrial successes had been instrumental for the consolidation of their power, their poular appeal and influence in the labour force. Concomitantly, active wage bargaining and negotiation in this period had prompted and inspired the inception of the Employers' Federation of Hong Kong, in 1947, out of the labour sub-committee of the General Chamber of Commerce. This organization was to a large extent made possible by the sponsorship by the major Western employers – that principal group of employers affected mostly by these agitational demands.

175. The organized power of the labour unions prompted and induced the Hong Kong government to introduce, in 1948, statutory procedures for the compulsory registration of trade unions under the new enactment, the Trade Unions and Trade Disputes Ordinance. In the following year, 1949, the two rival trade union centres, the left-wing communist-leaning Hong Kong Federation of Trade Unions (FTU) and the right-wing pro-Nationalist Hong Kong and Kolwoon Trades Union Council (TUC), were formed and registered under the Societies Ordinance. Both union centres opted not to register under the new trade union registration law of 1948 which placed a restriction upon trade union federations formed across industry and seeking affiliations overseas. The labour movement in Hong Kong has hitherto been split along this line of ideological cleavages although since the 1990s there have been growing signs of mutual rapprochement and working dialogue between these two once polarized union centres.

§6. Industrialization and Trade Unions

176. After experiencing a postwar period of fairly intensive industrial haggling and strife in the late 1940s and early 1950s, Hong Kong entered a period of relative industrial peace and stability which coincided with its process of economic take-off due to industralization. Compared to a large number of highly industrialized or new industralized economies (NIEs), the territory has enjoyed a low level of industrial conflict, if measured in terms of the dual criteria of 'working days lost' and number of disputes.

177. The advent of industrial peace that characterized the 1950s and 1960s reflected, in part, the domestic scene of political developments in China. Its liberation in 1949 and Britain's subsequent recognition of the People's Republic served to clear the air, leading to visible changes in the strategy of the left-wing trade unions in the Hong Kong. The FTU was hence observed in 1953 to have 'taken little interest in the wages and conditions of service of the members of its affiliated unions, its main emphasis being on such welfare projects as medical and unemployment benefits and the provision of schools'. Coupled with and contributing to growing political stability in the colony was a subsided rate of inflation (partly because of the earlier influx of the mainland refugees, which helped alleviate much of the postwar tightness of skill supply in the labour market). In parallel, it appears that sustained economic growth in this period had enabled 'the majority of employers' to grant 'wage increases unilaterally, pre-empting demands coming from the workforce'. At the same time, the approach of employers towards the trade unions in the two rival political divisions was far from being coherent. Within the public utilities, for instance, most managements extended recognition to the relatively docile right-wing unions in preference to their left-wing counterparts. This was a posture probably reminiscent of these employers' embattled experience in and around the time of the episode of the 1949 Tramway Strike. On the other hand, the major dockyards maintained a consistent dialogue with the left-wing communist unions, in a manner almost tantamount to the practice of informal union recognition.

178. The period which ensued, 1967 to 1974, was marked in general by an increase in the number of stoppages (yet of shorter duration); these were initiated more by spontaneous shopfloor protests than trade union orchestrated struggles as it was in the earlier years. In general, the rise in the number of strikes was explicable in terms of three main factors: first, an increase in the cost of living (manifested in such incidents as the Kowloon riots of 1966); second, the contraction or closure of many small and medium-sized plants (due to the rapid pace of industrial development and giving rise to a variety of discord and conflict over issues such as arrears of wages, prolonged lay-off and redundancy compensation, etc.); third, growing workers' awareness of their employment rights – at a time when economic, social and education standards had improved and the scope of the employee's statutory rights was extended and upgraded under the officially sponsored labour reform programme supported by conspicuous improvements in labour legislation.

179. Pragmatic accommodation with the need for stability and growth was perhaps an important factor that helped explain the restrained posture and low profile of open political activity on the part of the left-wing unions in Hong Kong during this period. Apparently, such a strategy was deemed to be in harmony with China's economic interest and policy. The exception to the above moderate stance was probably the labour militancy articulated in the 1967 civil disturbance, which was largely inspired by the Cultural Revolution that spilled over from China. At the height of the disturbance, there was embattled confrontation between the 'antiauthority' struggle committees and the Hong Kong administration climaxing in police raids on the offices of the left-wing unions and other pro-China organizations in search of weapons, explosives and other offensive materials. A number of vanguard agitators, including several union officials were arrested and prosecuted on criminal charges. An immediate ramification of this 'radical' challenge was to cast a general stigma on the whole labour movement, and the unionized population declined considerably, from 171,620 to 165,579 in 1967. In particular, the left-wing Hong Kong Federation of Trade Unions shrank in size, from 96,735 to 95,408 in its declared strength. However, the setback was brief and the left-wing union groups have since then made a rapid recovery – notably in the mid-1970s, when China commenced its 'open door' policy in building and strengthening its diplomatic standing in the international community.

180. Worldwide recession in 1974 ushered a downturn in the territory's economic conditions – resulting in large-scale retrenchment, short-time working and wage cuts in some industries. Strikes were, in this context, fewer and man-days lost were lower in number. However, economic recovery from 1976 onwards did not appear to have touched off any significant and immediate rise in the level of industrial unrest. One plausible reason was the relative shortage of labour that had developed, inducing many employers to voluntarily adjust wages ahead of anticipated requests in order to retain their employees. Such a state of relative industrial peace could also be linked to the emerging body of newly introduced or improved legal norms prescribing such security arrangements as severance pay, and instituting such judicial machinery as the Labour Tribunal for determining claims which arose from workplace grievances and might otherwise lead to industrial unrest if left unattended and allowed to escalate.

181. During this period, the trade unions, including both the left-wing and right-wing ones, continued their activities in recruiting, bidding for and conserving their membership. For instance, keen competition erupted between two veteran unions, the left-wing Hong Kong and Kowloon Spinning, Weaving and Dyeing Trade Workers' General Union and the right-wing Cotton Industry Workers' General Union, when the outbreak of two major redundancy disputes in the textile industry served the focal point for their active intervention. In the transport sector, the left-wing Union of the Godown and Wharf Workers had been consistently active in the wharf-based stevedoring and container port trade.

182. A sizable proportion of the labour–management conflicts that occurred in the late 1970s emanated from and affected the construction and engineering work carried out for the newly commissioned Mass Transit Railway system that mobilized, at the height of its construction project, more than 20,000 workmen. In most of these work-site disputes, the embattled workers typically sought intervention from either the two left-wing unions (the Hong Kong and Kowloon Cement and Concrete Construction Trade Workers Union and the Hong Kong Bricklaying and Construction Union) or a third, which was a politically independent union.

183. In spite of such union presence in industrial conflict, this post-recession period witnessed the resurgence of spontaneous stoppages and shopfloor actions. While these labour protests involved varying degrees of worker militancy, and assumed diversified forms including sit-ins, go-slows, strikes, plant occupations and sieges of management, there were symptoms of a growing readiness on the part of the workers – now younger, more educated and articulate – to initiate independent industrial action without or in advance of union consent or advice. Such a drift towards grassroots autonomy in the workplace has created considerable pressure constraining the unions to demonstrate their capability of protecting the workers in industrial conflict and sustaining their solidarity with the workforce. Concomitant with this devolution to the workplace of the workers' and their work-groups' power was the evident increase in the proportion of job security issues (pertaining to, for instance, lay-offs, retrenchment, redundancy and employer insolvency), *vis-à-vis* pay discords, in causing industrial conflicts. The pattern of these conflicts apparently demonstrates a consistent shift towards the preponderance of smaller and short stoppages.

184. The union militancy that once featured the posture of the left-wing union organizations in the civil upheavals of the late 1960s had by and large subsided towards the turn of the decade into the 1970s. Probably mirroring the new mood of reformism in China, pragmatism and an accommodating attitude towards capitalism instead characterized increasingly the industrial approach of the left-wing unions. This was evident in the conciliatory orientation they adopted towards industrial conflict, as well as the anxiety they displayed again in seeking to secure recognition from the major employers, notably in the large-scale enterprises belonging to the key utility industries. There were also growing signs to suggest that these unions would modify their traditional policy of non-participation in the tripartite institutions of labour–management–government dialogue. The Hong Kong Federation of Trade Unions (FTU) ended its earlier boycott of the Labour Advisory Board election in the late 1970s. Concomitantly, it has also become a more articulate and confident spokesman for workers' interests on employment and associated public policy issues such as industrial safety, housing, transport, taxation and elimination of poverty and narrowing of income and wealth inequalities in society.

185. The apparent integration increasingly achieved by the left-wing unions with the establishment and its institutions was, however, accompanied by a rising level of militancy shown by the politically independent or neutral unions during this period under review. Notable in this connection were the civil service unions, when the public sector in the late 1970s provided the main arena for their agitation, involving essentially economic issues in pay relativity disputes. The growing number of emulative pay demands levelled against the government by these staff unions representing the sectional interests of different grades in the civil service, and the attendant waves of industrial actions or threats of them, led to the official appointment of a public body, the Standing Commission of Civil Service Salaries and Conditions of Service, in 1979, to review the pay and structure of government employees in a service-wide appraisal exercise.

186. In the mid-1980s, the local trade unions began to discover steadily a new political role in acting as spokesmen for labour's interests under the officially sponsored development of representative government. As a sequel to these political reforms, the labour sector is now designated as a functional constituency – to be represented by the registered trade unions to elect their deputies for three seats in the progressively liberalized Legislative Council. Correspondingly, the unions as well as other non-union quasi-labour organizations have also been coopted into the consultative machinery which China appointed in the late 1980s, notably to assist in drafting the Basic Law and advising the Chinese authorities on Hong Kong affairs.

187. With the withering away of Taiwan's influence within Hong Kong, the right-wing Hong Kong and Kowloon Trades Union Council (TUC) has withdrawn increasingly from the labour arena as the second leading trade centre. Concomitantly, while the mainland and Taiwan are steadily building a dialogue across the Straits, the polarization between the old adversaries the Hong Kong Federation of Trade Unions (FTU) and the Trades Union Council has waned, with growing signs of their mutual rapprochement. However, the labour movement remains fragmented in spite of the dilution of the left-wing versus right-wing polemics. Organized labour in the 1990s drifted back to a politico-ideologically split union movement in which confrontation centred upon, this time, upon the polarized stance between the veteran pro-China vanguard organization, the Hong Kong Federation of Trade Unions (FTU), and the newly constituted, yet popular, third union centre allied to the Democratic Party, the Hong Kong Confederation of Trade Unions (CTU).

188. As Hong Kong evolves into a post-industrial society of late urbanism, it is worth noting a propensity for its trade unions to develop and evolve into 'community unionism' as a new form of 'third sector' organization. The explanation for such a potential development is several-fold. First, trade unions in Hong Kong have been free from the constraint of the collective bargaining institution and its bureaucratic implications. Second, the political reforms sponsored by the government, both before and after 1997, led to a process of democratization and growing mass participation in election activities. Trade unions in Hong Kong are encouraged by the shifting political context of electoral advances to evolve a strategic role of organizing the grassroots neighbourhood community in support of either their own nominated candidates or in partnership with the formal political parties to bid for seats in the Legislative Council by direct election. In addition, some trade unions in Hong Kong are equipped (as workers' self-organizations) to perform an 'agency' role of penetrating the neighbourhood community for mutual assistance and insurance. Besides, due to the changing labour market and the subsequent growth of the self-employed, seasonal workers and part-time employees, and those employed in other forms of atypical employment arising from the employers' creed of flexibility in the labour market (in other words, a drift towards re-casualization), the workplace has become less of a 'bastion' for labour unions to enlist and organize their membership. Instead, the unions are now paying equal attention to the residential community for sustaining a dialogue and liaising with their members.

The above approach is also consistent with the legacy of Hong Kong unions, which have never been strong at the workplace level. Given such feebleness, some 'vanguard' unions and labour bodies now act as the spokesperson of workers across all trades in the neighbourhood regarding employment, wages and labour market issues. The labour grievances which some unions articulate are even generic and not specific to employment affairs, pertaining to housing, transport, general price level and cost of living, pollution and environment, as well as associated ecological issues which can affect the wage-earners' well-being as employees or self-employed. The agenda for those unions is to cater to the 'working life' betterment of the people, whether they are workplace or neighbourhood-based. They also lobby extensively for official leverage against the industrial vicissitudes of 'post-industrial urbanism', in the capacity as labour's pressure groups belonging to the 'third sector' domain at a time when these agencies are expected to have a widened scope in Hong Kong.

189. There is hence a potential for trade unions in Hong Kong, which were largely either industry, occupation or workplace oriented, to restructure themselves and perform the role of community unions in response to the socio-industrial challenges of post-industrialism and late urbanism. The future unions assuming such a community role can be located within the 'third sector', outside the state and private business domains, as well as outside the conventional ambit of any specific trades, industries or occupations.

There are still problems associated with attempts to create a union-focused community outside the occupation. If unionization were to be based upon organization of the neighbourhood community, these community unions would lack a collective awareness due to a lack of common occupational interest and identity. Instead, they could be fragmented and proliferate, each as an 'enclave' of a localized working people's combination. These 'combines' are occupationally and industrially mixed, and are pluralistic, yet isolated and segregated spatially from each other. For this reason, the model of a 'community union' as a 'third sector' agency will be open to problems of internal organization and integration because it lacks the workplace 'nexus' of conventional unionism. Hence, it is premature to predict whether this form of 'community unionism' will in future prevail within the Hong Kong labour movement. It may take years for it to crystallize into a shape which can eclipse the 'mainstream' union tradition as an effective alternative of worker organization in the 'postindustrial' age.

Chapter 9. The Role of the Government: Abstention versus Intervention

§1. The Philosophy of Government

190. In Britain, the traditional philosophy of the government towards labour and industry has been one of non-intervention or abstention by the state. The governing principle is for it to 'hold the ring' enabling the employer and the employee to negotiate with each other as the direct participants in the employment arena. Although gradually modified by an increasing degree of state intervention in the postwar drift of the 'welfare state' approach and later, under the counter-union policy prescription of the Conservative government led by Margaret Thatcher, the 'voluntaristic' theme still predominates as the primary tenet in shaping the conduct of British industrial relations,.The Labour government which came to power in the first decade of the twenty-first century under Tony Blair steered a middle 'third way' approach towards domestic politics in rope-dancing between capital in business and organized labour.

191. 'Voluntarism' as a principle of labour administration that cherishes the permissiveness of the industrial relations system (without being subject to the rigour of a highly interventionist framework of legal regulation) has been inherited to a large extent by the pre-1997 government in Hong Kong, given its historical and institutional linkages with Britain. This heritage has persisted into the post-1997 SAR era, constitutionally guaranteed by the Basic Law which prescribes the continuation of the status quo and the applicability of the British common law system. Indeed, the administration's ideology here, both before and after Hong Kong's reversion to China, is its almost doctrinal adherence to the stance of sustaining a 'free market' economy, which it has always believed as fundamental to the well-being of Hong Kong. However, such freedom is not totally unqualified since it is circumscribed by the government's readiness to legislate or regulate by administrative discretion in areas deemed necessary or where it is considered to contribute to the public community's collective betterment. It has been cherished in Hong Kong as a sacrosanct policy of 'positive non-intervention', as exemplified by a senior government official and a leading proponent of such a philosophy in the following terms:

> It is preferable to describe our attitude to the economy as one of positive non-interventionism: this involves taking the view that, in the great majority of circumstances it is futile and damaging to the growth rate of the economy for attempts to be made to plan the allocation of resources available to the private sector. ... We do not assume that constraints and ground rules necessary for competition to work can always be taken for granted ... we have actually enshrined a framework of constraints and ground rules in the law.[15]

15. Sir Philip Haddon-Cave (formerly Chief Secretary, Hong Kong Government), 'The Marketing of Some Aspects of Public Policy in Hong Kong', in David Lethbridge (ed.), *The Business Environment in Hong Kong*, Hong Kong: Oxford University Press, 2nd edn, 1984, p. xiv.

§2. GOVERNMENT INSTITUTIONS

192. The Labour Department of the Hong Kong SAR government is responsible for labour administration in the SAR. Headed by the Commissioner for Labour, the Department is the competent official agency which administers labour legislation and deals with employment and industrial relations matters in the private sector. In 1994, the Registry of Trade Unions (formerly an independent government department responsible for registering trade unions in Hong Kong, including both employers' and employees' organizations) was integrated into the Labour Department and has become part of the latter's establishment thereafter. Other official and judicial agencies whose functions are relevant to the labour field include:

- the Labour and Welfare Bureau of the Government Secretariat, which is the policy bureau in the government secretariat responsible for overseeing and coordinating, *inter alia*, the work of the Labour Department and Social Welfare Department in the sphere of labour and employment, social welfare and security;
- the Civil Service Bureau, which is a service bureau of the Government Secretariat responsible for human resource management and maintaining staff relations in the civil service;
- the Labour Advisory Board, which is non-statutory yet is the principal advisory/consultative body, tripartite in composition, to the government on the formulation of labour policies and legislation;
- the Labour Tribunal, which is equivalent to a labour court or the industrial tribunal in Britain with judicial jurisdiction to determine and settle, via simplified procedures, claims arising from the individual contract of employment (that is, individual 'rights disputes');
- the Vocational Training Council, which is the statutory advisory body to the government on manpower training policies, with administrative authority to organize and promote industrial training via its complex of industrial training boards, as well as to run an array of technical institutes and institutes for vocational education;
- the Occupational Safety and Health Council, which is a statutory body responsible for the promotion of occupational health and industrial safety in workplace by way of education and training; funded by a levy imposed on the premium of all employees' compensation insurance policies in Hong Kong;
- the Employee Retraining Board, which is a statutory agency, at the beginning funded by a levy on the payroll of the imported foreign workers (this is no longer the case), with the responsibility to retrain workers dislocated and displaced from industry in the shrinking manufacturing sector due to the economy's restructuring process;
- the Equal Opportunity Commission, which is a statutory body responsible for promoting and steering human rights pertaining to equal opportunity at and outside the workplace, and vested with administrative power for administering and enforcing the existing four pieces of anti-discrimination legislation in Hong Kong (viz. the Sex Discrimination, Disability Discrimination, Family Status Discrimination and the Race Discrimination Ordinances).

193. Generally speaking, it is the Labour and Welfare Bureau of the government secretariat, advised by the Labour Department, which in most cases institutes the relevant procedures in initiating new labour legislation. Drafting instructions are issued subsequently to the Department of Justice (formerly the Legal Department during the pre-1997 administration) which is responsible for the ensuing task of technical authorship. It is normal practice, however, for the Labour Department to submit beforehand the relevant legislative proposal to the Labour Advisory Board for consultation and securing a tripartite consensus on the proposed legislation. The consultative process also normally includes circulating the draft legislation to the relevant trade unions and employers' associations prior to its introduction before the Executive and Legislative Councils.

194. It is permissible, in principle, for members of the Legislative Council to initiate new legislation or legislative amendments by way of Private Members' Bill. This mode has been practised in the pre-1997 era in moving amendments to improve provisions of the Employment Ordinance on severance pay and maternity protection. Such an ability of the Council members have, however, become more circumscribed in the SAR government, chiefly because it requires the prior consent of the Chief Executive before the legislative proceedings can commence.

195. To administer the complex of labour legislation and to carry out and promote the official policies in the diverse functions of labour administration, the Labour Department has evolved a fairly well-established organizational structure comprising altogether eight clusters of functions, each headed by an assistant commissioner for labour or equivalent (viz. areas of employment services, labour relations, employees' rights and benefits, policy support and strategic planning, occupational safety, occupational safety support services, occupational health and medicine promotion and occupational health and medicine clinical services). Each assistant commissioner, answerable to a Deputy Commissioner for Labour and in turn the Commissioner for Labour, is responsible for the work of several divisions and sub-agencies within his/her jurisdiction. These are detailed in the organizational chart in Figure 1.

Figure 1 Organization Structure of the Labour Department (as at 31 December 2007)

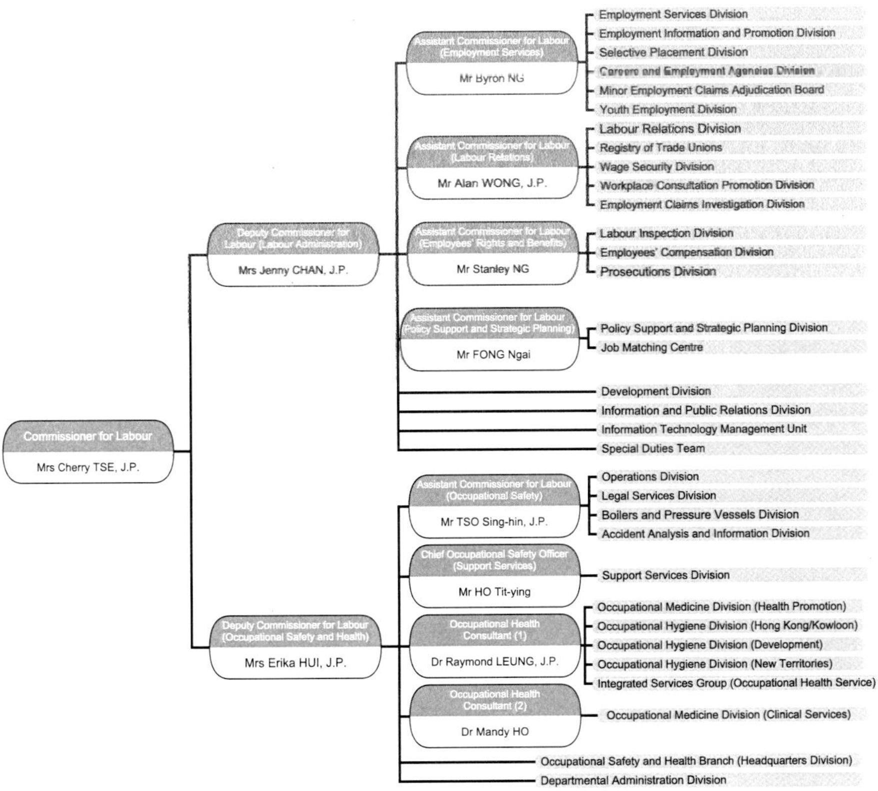

Source: Labour Department, *Annual Report 2007*, Hong Kong, Labour Department, SAR government, 2008, p. 48.

Chapter 10. Sources of Labour Law

§1. International Sources

196. Instruments promulgated by the International Labour Organization (ILO) on labour standards, legislation, policy and practices have been a major factor influencing or even shaping labour law in Hong Kong. It has been the declared intention of the government, both before and after 1997, to adopt as far as practical, the labour standards set by the ILO.

197. The status of Hong Kong in the ILO, by virtue of it dependency upon the United Kingdom up to 1997 and thereafter upon China after its reversion to the latter as its SAR, is not that of a full Member State but a 'non-metropolitan territory'. As such, Hong Kong is represented on the ILO under the official auspices of the United Kingdom and subsequently, China, after the 1997 sovereignty transfer. In this context, Hong Kong has continued to participate in the ILO after 1997 in the same status as before, except now it owes its representation on this UN international agency to the People's Republic of China.

198. By virtue of the ILO constitution and governance procedures, Hong Kong does not ratify any conventions which the ILO promulgates. Instead, declarations in respect of Hong Kong on the application of any conventions are made by China on Hong Kong's behalf after full consultation between the two governments. In making declaration for Hong Kong, the convention can be:

(i) applied without modification, entailing full acceptance by the administration of every provision contained in the convention;
(ii) applied with modification, implying acceptance not of all but of some selected provisions in the convention;
(iii) one on which decision is reserved, when the convention cannot be accepted for the time being since its major parts cannot be implemented and applied by legislative or administrative measures; or
(iv) deemed inapplicable, to the extent that the convention's subject-matter is not relevant to Hong Kong because of geographical, political, physical reasons or other inherent constraints.

199. A Member Sate is required under the ILO Constitution to report measures taken to implement in its non-metropolitan territory(ies) those conventions it has itself ratified, at intervals of once every two years. In this connection, prior to 1997, the government of the United Kingdom reported on behalf of Hong Kong on all the conventions ratified by the UK (except those which have been declared inapplicable to Hong Kong) as well as those conventions which it has not yet ratified should these be called by the ILO. However, now as a SAR of China having a high level of self-governing autonomy, Hong Kong is able to apply any ILO conventions and report, via China, biannually on their application independent of the status of their ratification by the People's Republic.

200. As at the end of the year 2012, the number of ILO conventions applied to Hong Kong, with or without modification, was 41.

201. In formulating its labour policy and the gestation of its labour law, Hong Kong also draws reference and inspirations from other international instruments, like the International Covenant on Economic, Social and Cultural Rights and the International Covenant on Civil and Political Rights.

§2. Natonal Sources

I. Legislation

202. The major source of labour law is legislation enacted as statutes by the legislature, the Legislative Council in the Hong Kong SAR. Attached to the principal ordinance is its subsidiary legislation, as in the form of 'regulations' or 'orders' made under the relevant ordinance. The competent authority for making such a subsidiary body of legal rules rests with the Chief Executive in Council (i.e. the Chief Executive acting upon the advice of the Executive Council), often based upon recommendations made by such agencies as specified under the enabling clauses of the relevant ordinance (for instance, the judiciary, the Department of Justice, the Labour Department, etc.)

This form of subsidiary enactment has become more common now in Hong Kong.

203. Important items of labour legislation now adopted in Hong Kong include the following:

- industrial relations:
  - Labour Relations Ordinance, chapter 55;
  - Trade Union Ordinance, chapter 332;
  - Public Order Ordinance; chapter; and
  - Labour Tribunal Ordinance, chapter 25;
- employment conditions:
  - Employment Ordinance, chapter 57;
  - Trade Boards Ordinance, chapter 63;
  - Protection of Wages on Insolvency Ordinance, chapter;
  - Contracts for Employment Outside Hong Kong Ordinance, chapter;
  - Employment of Young Persons and Children at Sea Ordinance, chapter; and
  - Immigration Ordinance, chapter 115;
  - Minimum Wage Ordinance, Chapter;
- workmen's compensation:
  - Employees' Compensation Ordinance, chapter 282; and
  - Pneumoconiosis (Compensation) Ordinance, chapter 360.
- industrial health and safety:
  - Factories and Industrial Undertakings Ordinance, chapter 59;
  - Air Pollution Control Ordinance, chapter;

Boilers and Pressure Receives Ordinance, chapter;
Radiation Ordinance, chapter 303; and
Gas-holders Examination Ordinance, chapter 54.

– manpower and industrial training:

Apprenticeship Ordinance, chapter 47
Industrial Training (Construction Industry) Ordinance, chapter 317;
Industrial Training (Clothing Industry) Ordinance, chapter 318;
Vocational Training Council Ordinance, chapter; and
Employee Re-training Ordinance, chapter;

– civil and human rights:

Sex Discrimination Ordinance, chapter;
Disability Discrimination Ordinance, chapter;
Family Status Discrimination Ordinance, chapter; and
Personal Data (Privacy) Ordinance.

II. Reference to the British Model

204. A common characteristic of law-making by the legislature in Hong Kong has been to draw reference to the British legal system. Such an institutional heritage has persisted and continued intact after 1997, in spite of the sovereignty transfer.

205. However, it has not been a case of wholesale transplanting the British model to Hong Kong in its entirety. Instead, the British model which Hong Kong emulates has been adapted here with a measure of discretion, especially tailored to suit the local culture and environment.

206. Apart from benchmarking against the British system, there have been references in legislative initiatives and authorship drawn against comparable labour statutes which other countries have adopted, such as those of the neighbouring states of Singapore, Malaysia and Sri Lanka (formerly Ceylon) or other British Commonwealth states, the United States or other Member States of the European Union. The policy norm has been for the Hong Kong SAR to maintain a level of labour standards broadly equivalent to those of neighbouring countries with similar economic development as well as social and cultural background, by way of continuous improvements to labour legislation and administrative measures.

III. Common Law

207. In addition to the labour statutes locally enacted, the English common law and rules of equity are also applicable generally to Hong Kong. It was also a constitutional principle, up to 1957, that English Acts of Parliament could be invoked in Hong Kong. However, no incidents of this nature ever happened during the reign of British rule.

208. The traditional British approach in labour and industrial relations is noticeable for its reliance upon the 'voluntary' rather than the 'legislative' philosophy. In the past, there was an absence of vigorous legislative intervention in the field of industrial relations – with the statutory codes aimed at prescribing a minimum of rights and leaving considerable freedom, collective and individual, for the parties to the employment relationship. Understandably, common law principles were hence important in Britain for the regulation of individual labour contracts and to a lesser extent that of collective industrial relations. Although this situation has been progressively modified with the introduction of growing items of, first, protective (under the Labour government) and later, regulatory (under the Conservative Thatcher government) labour legislation. The exigencies of common law are still reminiscent – either in shaping certain ingredients of the enacted statutes themselves or in judicial decisions over various labour relations issues heard in courts.

209. Given the strong affinity once mutual between the British and Hong Kong legal systems, it is natural for common law to have played, and be expected to continue playing beyond the territory's 1997 reversion back to China, an important role in shaping labour law and regulating employment relationships in Hong Kong.

IV. Labour Tribunal and Other Courts of Law

210. Besides, an important aspect of labour law lies in the judicial decisions made by the Labour Tribunal and other courts of law in applying and interpreting it. The Labour Tribunal was created by the Labour Tribunal Ordinance of 1972 to provide a simple and inexpensive judicial mechanism for determining individual claims for monetary awards under the individual employment contracts or which arise from disputed statutory rights of employment. The Tribunal constitutes part of the judiciary and its cases are heard by a career judge, the Presiding Officer. However, the competent jurisdiction of the Labour Tribunal is limited to dealing with individual disputes over rights. For this reason, it cannot intervene in the settlement of disputes of interest.

211. There is the availability of appeal to the courts at higher levels from the decisions of the tribunal, as based upon points of law. It is permissible to do so first in the District Court (which is competent for both civil and criminal proceedings, with a career judge sitting alone without a jury); from thence to the High Court and the Court of Appeal (composed of three high court judges sitting together). The ultimate recourse was, up to 1997, to the Judicial Committee of the Privy Council in London but this procedure has been rescinded and replaced by Hong Kong's own Court of Final Appeal created since 1997 because of the constitutional detachment of its judicial system from the British one.

V. Custom and Practice

212. Custom and practice, in particular those emanating from Chinese tradition, standards and norms, have always been an important influence affecting the emergent features of labour law in Hong Kong. Generally speaking, the Hong Kong government prior to 1997 and its post-handover successor have exercised reasonable prudence in tailoring local statutes, rules and other administrative measures to the cultural specificities of this essentially Chinese community. Otherwise, introduction of foreign prescriptions and practices could prove so alien that they might work perversely to the detriment of society's welfare and its heritage. Typical examples which illustrate this consideration are the appointment of a number of Chinese festivals as statutory holidays in the Employment Ordinance, the designation of the lunar year-end bonus as the thirteenth month's pay in the same legislation and the legal recognition of mixed employer–employee combinations as a legal form of trade union eligible for registration – which are handovers from the prewar system of traditional Chinese guilds.

213. The role of custom and practice may also be recognized by the court when deciding upon cases of employment and industrial relations matters. However, where conflict in application exists, it may be generally said that statutory rules tend to prevail and take precedence over custom and practice. For this reason, it is normally impossible for the parties to contract out of their legal obligations and rights prescribed by statutes. In other words, neither party can waive his/her entitlement by invoking custom and practice as a defence. However, they represent an important factor as a supplement (not as a substitute) to the existing labour legislation, especially in areas of ambiguity left unspecified by the statutory provisions. Indeed, at common law, custom and practices may be construed to constitute an acceptable term for the purpose of formulating an employment contract.

VI. Collective Bargaining

214. Parties to a collective agreement may establish their mutually acceptable body of governing norms and standards of employment on a voluntary and collective basis. However, in line with the British practice, the terms of a collective agreement are not legally enforceable unless they have been, *a priori*, incorporated expressly into the individual contract of employment. Moreover, the effects of any part of a collective agreement are only applicable in scope to those employees and employers who are parties to it and cannot be extended to other outside parties. Since the practice of collective bargaining is not widespread in Hong Kong and is limited mainly to the public sector and a few large private enterprises, collective bargaining has so far played a feeble and inconspicuous role in structuring labour law in Hong Kong.

Chapter 11. The Language

§1. Official Language

215. Hong Kong is a cosmopolitan and highly industrialized city, whose population can be described as multicultural and pluralist in ethnic background, including Chinese, British and a variety of other nationals. These diverse ethnic groups, however, do not each cluster into mutually segregated communities. Instead, there have always been a considerable degree of common interest and mutual interaction across the racial divide. The assimilation of non-Chinese into Hong Kong society has never appeared problematic.

216. In the past, English used to be the sole official language. As a result of a popular movement in the early 1970s propagating the Chinese language, the government has adopted the use of Chinese as an official language alongside English. It has since then been active in promoting the use of Chinese in both its administrative domain as well as in legal courts, epitomized by the enactment, in 1974, of the Official Languages Ordinance, chapter 5. An increasing number of official meetings and functions are now bilingual including, among others, the proceedings of the Legislative Council, the District Boards and the Labour Advisory Board. In parallel, the proceedings of the Labour Tribunal are generally conducted in Chinese as other courts of law are also moving, where practicable, consistently in the direction of 'bilingualism'.

217. In addition, information guides and explanatory pamphlets on labour law are published by the Labour Department in both English as well as Chinese.

218. In spite of the transfer of sovereignty and Hong Kong's reversion to China, the use of English has persisted in importance as an instrument of communication, especially given the cosmopolitan character of Hong Kong as an international city and a knowledge-based postindustrial economy.

§2. Language Used in the Enterprise

219. The local community in Hong Kong is predominantly Chinese-speaking in day to day life although a significant component, notably the younger and better educated white-collar workers, is bilingual using both Chinese and English.

220. The common language used at the workplace is Chinese, both for spoken and written purposes, and its use at the grassroots level is essential if management is to maintain effective communication with the rank-and-file workers, most of whom are conversant in Chinese only. Conversely, since English is widely acknowledged as the international language of business, white-collar workers in the commercial, professional and service sectors have, by tradition, relied upon English as the principal medium for written communication, supplemented by Chinese (or Cantonese, which is the dialect of the Guangdong Province in Southern China), although Mandarin, or Putonghua, which is the official spoken medium, has increased in popularity now that Hong Kong has been reunified with China.

Part I. Individual Employment Relations

Chapter 1. Definitions and Concepts

§1. The Different Categories of Employee

221. There exists no standard nomenclature whereby the labour force in Hong Kong can be readily differentiated into different categories of employee. However, a number of broad groupings can be distinguished with reference to a variety of different criteria. Three principal sources of distinction are identifiable: (i) legal; (ii) administrative; and (iii) customary. Each will be discussed in turn.

I. Legal Sources/Statutory Sources

222. Before 1990, there was a statutory distinction made between the basic categories of manual and non-manual workers by virtue of the Employment Ordinance which, enacted since 1968, is the principal item of legislation governing contracts and conditions of employment.

223. The Ordinance used to differentiate between manual and non-manual categories of employees in its scope of application. Its coverage, besides including all manual workers, was limited to those non-manual employees whose monthly earnings did not exceed a stipulated ceiling reviewed and subject to periodic adjustment by the government in order to harmonize it with the economy's level of inflation. However, an explicit and full legal definition of these two basic employment categories was absent in the statute book itself. Instead, the interpretation was purposively left open, so that the court was able to rule on individual cases. This treatment was also probably explicable by the ambiguities inherent in their boundary, which could defy prior attempts to draw a clear and precise line between the two.

224. However, in recognition of the shifting composition of the occupational structure, now comprising an increasing proportion of professional, managerial, technical and service white-collar workers, as well as the 'equity' argument that the higher income earning white-collar workers also need the protective shield of the Employment Ordinance (rather than relying totally upon common law for the interpretation of their individual labour contracts), the administration decided to rationalize the Employment Ordinance by amending it in 1990 to rescind its notional reference to the traditional 'manual versus non-manual' divide. Such a distinction has since then been withdrawn from the territory's statute book. It follows that now both the manual workman and the non-manual staff member are to be treated on equal legal footing without any discrimination.

225. There are other special categories of employees identified by the Employment Ordinance and other associated pieces of labour legislation. Each of these is briefly introduced as follows.

A. Apprentices

226. The Apprenticeship Ordinance was introduced in Hong Kong in 1976 apparently in cognizance of the economy's demand for a growing variety of trade skills in industry generated by the fast pace of industrialization during the 1960s and early 1970s. Concomitantly, it was also a public policy objective to assist young people in entering industrial employment by equipping them with proper and relevant training through an internship. The legislation is hence aimed at promoting apprentice training and to regulate such a process to ensure its conformity with modern standards of training.

227. The scope of the apprentice law is, however, not universal in its application to every trade or occupation at all skill levels in the manpower economy. Instead, it is specific to those designated trades or occupations which are gazetted by the government. In principle, such a designation under the prerogative of the Chief Executive can take place any time, thereby steadily augmenting the coverage of the Ordinance. Examples of trades and occupations hence designated include vehicle mechanic, vehicle electrician, electrical fitter, lift mechanic, machinist, electrician, instrument mechanic, fitter, plumber, bamboo scaffolder, carpenter, joiner, and hotel cook.

228. The Apprenticeship Ordinance, in addition, lays down the general rule whereby the employer in a designated trade can only employ a young person if the recruitment and employment afterwards are governed by a valid contract of apprenticeship or if the young recruit is already qualified with a competent certificate of completion of his apprenticeship. Under this legislation, a young person to be engaged as an apprentice in the designated trade is aged over 14 and under 19. The contract of apprenticeship, or the indenture, has to be registered with the Vocational Training Council, or else exemptions from compulsory registration has to be sought from the authority. In general, such exemptions are tenable where the young person has already completed a major part of the apprenticeship before the trade was designated under the law.

229. For apprentices, the duration of their indentures in these designated trades is mandatory, as prescribed by the Council at the time of designation. Generally speaking, the tenure of indenture is for a standard period of at least three years, although it can be varied at the authority's discretion. To prevent unethical acts of raiding or poaching of apprentices by other employers, the law makes it a punishable offence for a person to induce a registered apprentice to terminate his contract of apprenticeship prematurely or to employ a registered apprentice notwithstanding the knowledge that he is bound by a contract to another employer. Upon the expiry of the indenture deed and completion of apprenticeship, the employer is legally obliged to issue a certificate of completion to the graduate apprentice, and endorsed by the Vocational Training Council as a qualifying credential attesting to his/her skill competence.

230. To ensure that the apprentice is able to receive adequate training, the employer is under a legal duty to provide appropriate on-the-job training and experience according to the standards prescribed by the Council. A concomitant duty, also legally prescribed, is for the employer to sponsor and release the apprentice, yet without affecting his/her pay, to attend for related complementary technical education at a technical institute. In parallel, the technical institutes, administered officially by the Vocational Training Council, are legally obliged to accord priority to these candidates in their enrolment and admission into the courses. The Vocational Training Council maintains an inspectorate which is empowered to enter and inspect any workplace where an apprentice or young person is believed to be employed. For this purpose, an employer engaging a registered apprentice is required to maintain the appropriate records and returns and to report to the Council at half-yearly intervals on the work performed, progress made and overtime worked by the apprentice and any absence from work or from the prescribed technical course.

B. Workers Engaged Overseas outside Hong Kong

231. This category of workers is protected by the Contracts for Employment Outside Hong Kong Ordinance, retitled from its predecessor, the Contracts for Overseas Employment Ordinance, in the 1990s. The law was also amended in this exercise to extend its scope to cover not only the manual workers hired from Hong Kong for overseas work but also those non-manual workers in employment outside Hong Kong, provided that their monthly wages do not exceed a stipulated earning ceiling level.

232. The Ordinance makes it mandatory for each of the workers specified hence in this category to enter into a contract with the relevant employer, to be attested by the Commissioner for Labour. The Commissioner's endorsement is to ensure its conformity with a number of standards which are laid down in the corresponding International Labour Conventions. Hence, this legislation aims to protect these employees against any undesirable acts of the foreign employers in causing possible abuses to and exploiting employees while working abroad.

233. For this reason, the Commissioner for Labour will only give his/her consent upon ascertaining that the worker concerned accepts the agreement of his/her own free will and with a full understanding of the contract's content – and also that he/she has been medically examined at the employer's expense and found fit to work. The contract, necessarily in writing and endorsed by both parties (the employer can, however, be represented by a fully authorized agent) prior to the employee's departure, has to be supported by a guarantor or by a bond furnished by a person who is a permanent resident in Hong Kong. The minimum age for the employee to enter into such a contract is 18.

234. In addition, such a contract has to specify certain basic rights and obligations of the parties covering such aspects as the place and nature of employment, the manner of wage advancement and its repayment; hours of work and holidays; duration of and dissolution of the contract; provision for food, lodging, medical care and workmen's compensation; the employer's duty to pay for the employee's home visits as well as his/her repatriation from the place of employment (including his/her dependants, if applicable); safety precaution for the arrival of the employee and the availability of facilities enabling the employee to send remittances to Hong Kong.

235. It is not permissible for the employer to transfer the employee, without the latter's free consent, to another employer. In the instance of such a transfer, the endorsement of the appropriate authority in the host country has also to be obtained. Repatriation of the worker and his/her dependants should occur normally within three months after the contract expires. Even if both parties agree to renew the contract, it is still necessary for a home visit to be arranged at the employer's expense, if the worker has been separate from his/her dependants for more than 18 months.

C. Seamen

236. As a maritime port and entrêpot in its history, Hong Kong's seafaring trade has always constituted an important source of employment for its local workforce. However, the size of the merchant navy in recent years has been shrinking steadily – partly because of ebbing entry into the trade due to the competitive pull of land employment and in part as a consequence of automation in the container industry and growing availability of alternative maritime personnel from other Asian sources – which may have curtailed the industry's demand for local seafarers.

237. The Hong Kong SAR now has its own independent registry for shipping responsible for enforcing the international standards prescribed by the International Maritime Organization and under the auspices of various International Labour Conventions instruments.

238. Recruitment into the merchant navy in Hong Kong by shipowners is regulated and supervised by the Seamen's Recruitment Office and the Mercantile Marine Office, according to the provisions laid down under the Merchant Shipping (Seafarers) Ordinance. In 1994 the active number of seafarers in Hong Kong registered with the Seamen Recruitment Office has already subsided to a meagre level of 2,600 compared to a much larger number of almost 100,000 local seamen hired in the heyday of the industry in the 1960s and the 1970s.

239. The unprecedented slump in the scale of the territory's merchant navy is sufficiently alarming to cause a concerted effort mounted recently by both the administration and the Hong Kong Shipowners' Association to cater for the enhanced and organized training of manpower for the industry. A notable endeavour in this connection is probably epitomized by the creation of the Merchant Navy Training Board within the umbrella framework of the Vocational Training Council – together with the opening of a modern and well-equipped Seamen's Training Centre operated by the Council. The Training Centre now provides training courses for both the new entrants as well as the in-service seafarers, while the Marine Department is responsible for the related roles of monitoring training leading to maritime qualifications as well as examining candidates for certification of the latter's competency. For grooming the upper echelon of the merchant navy, the Sea-going Training Incentive Scheme was launched in 2004. The training scheme, intended to meet the maritime industry's increasing demand for local qualified personnel with sea-going experience, provides financial incentives to young entrants aspiring to become shore-based professionals in the maritime trade and to do so by taking up sea-going training as cadets. By the end of 2012, altogether 231 cadets had been enrolled for the training programme.

D. Children and Young Workers

240. As is common in other industrialized nations, young person and children are differentiated in Hong Kong as a special employee category placed under statutory protection with respect to working hours, safety and conditions of work in industrial and where applicable, also non-industrial workplaces.

241. In this context, the Employment Ordinance proscribes, by virtue of its subsidiary legislation (i.e. the Employment Regulations), the hiring of any child labour under the age of 15 in both industrial as well as non-industrial employment. However, subject to stringent requirements, children under 13 and 14 may be employed in non-industrial establishments (for example, in the entertainment industry like movie production).

242. However, for young persons aged between 15 and 17, their protective shield is limited to industrial employment, as provided under the Young Persons (Industry) Regulations of the Employment Ordinance, which is the subsidiary legislative instrument governing the weekly rest days, permissible overtime, night work and safety measures for young persons working in industry. Besides, young person below the age of 18 are prevented by law from being hired at any workplaces selling liquor.

II. Common Law Sources

243. There are, in addition, several categories of workers whose notional identity may have legal ramifications under common law principles. These workers proliferate as flexi-hiring has grown increasingly popular globally nowadays. Now labelled generically as atypical employment, the emergence and re-emergence of these categories actually epitomizes the recasualization of a sizable segment of the labour market as a syndrome of postindustrial competition among firms to cut and save on labour overheads. They include the following.

A. *Temporary or Casual Workers*

244. Virtually, a temporary or casual employee has all the general and specific rights and obligations of any other employee with respect to the various statutory benefits and protection that accrue to the employee under a 'continuous contract' – inasmuch as he/she has satisfied the general qualifying conditions on account of his/her length of service and the number of hours he/she works in each week. However, it is plausible to place a temporary worker on a fixed-term contract, as is now commonly done by employers, so that the contract is not a 'continuous' monthly and open-ended one. Such a contractual format hence enables the employer to circumvent the duties of providing for advance notice or wages in lieu otherwise payable were the contract a 'continuous' and open-ended one.

B. *Part-time Workers*

245. In principle, part-time employees are not reckoned as a distinctive and separate category of workers under the Employment Ordinance, the principal statute governing employment standards in Hong Kong. Like temporary or full-time employees, labour contracts are to be deemed at law to be 'continuous', provided that the general qualifying conditions governing 'continuous contracts' by the dual criteria of (i) length of service and (ii) weekly hours of work are met. These qualifying conditions were liberalized in the 1990s in order to extend the coverage of contractual 'continuity' over a larger number of part-time workers. However, for the bulk of part-time workers, a 'continuous contract' is absent as their work hour configuration does not meet these qualifying conditions. Although the Employment Ordinance still affords a part-time worker protection on wage security and against acts of anti-union discrimination, it has been considered desirable, especially by the labour movement, to amend the Employment Ordinance to bestow pro-rated statutory benefits upon part-time employees *vis-à-vis* their full-time counterparts engaged on a 'continuous' contract.

C. *Freelance Workers and the Self-employed*

246. A floating army of mobile worker crews was deployed in the manufacturing sector in the 1970s and early 1980s; they moved between industrial establishments upon the latter's call for their service. Under such arrangements, which evolved in Hong Kong industry when it reached its heyday about thirty to forty years ago, there was generally no regularized and formal wage relationship between these floating work groups and the firms. Hiring instead took the common form of labour subcontracting in what are popularly labelled as 'outsourcing' or 'externalization' arrangements, while remuneration was normally awarded on a job or a straight-line piece-work basis. The relevant contract between the firm and the work group was a contract for service which was specific to the project performed.It lapsed upon the completion of the work. These industrial work groups were hence more or less autonomous and self-managing, independent of the managerial prerogative of the host enterprises. However, a measure of continuity was implied in the nature of their relationships of mutual trust, since the crew could expect retention by the firm or at least, in the lean period, priority in re-engagement, should production recover afterwards. Thus, this system of labour subcontracting has enabled medium-sized and small manufacturing plants to vary their manpower size with a measure of flexibility in seasonal adjustment, thereby obviating the difficulty of having to retain a full-scale stable workforce during the lean seasons with excess capacity.

Analogous to the above earlier practice in industry is the augmented propensity today for firms to hive off their regular employees and convert them into contingent workers of self-employed status where flexi-hiring entails an advantage. These changes are known to have affected, almost wholesale, the stevedoring trade where the container truck drivers had been converted, since the late 1990s, from direct employ into self-employed workers.

247. However, inasmuch as these work crews operated under the roof of the host firm like other regular workers, a frequent question arose in the 1980s as to whether their members could in any conceivable manner be categorized as employees and if so, for whom. Up to the present, the Labour Tribunal seems to have accepted as a plausible defence by the host firm the claim that such a group was not in its direct employ but was engaged under a contract for services. However, it is equally problematic to place the onus of the employer's responsibility upon the leader of the worker crew, who could hardly be construed as a risk-taking entrepreneur or contractor *per se*. Instead, it has been normal for such a group leader to work simply as a member and receive his work-based share of the group's earnings; otherwise, he may be paid an extra bonus by the firm as the premium for the recruiting and supervisory services which he renders. Such ambiguity in ascertaining the relative status of the engaging firms, the mobile work group and its leader *vis-à-vis* each other mirrors the equivocal status of this type of workers as they may be deemed to fall outside the purview of the Employment Ordinance.

248. However, this practice of 'flexible' work group hiring in the industrial plants has seemed to wither away today – largely as a sequel to the massive relocation of factories away from Hong Kong across the border to mainland China because of lower labour and land costs there.

249. Nevertheless, there still exist in Hong Kong pockets of trades and industries where workers are engaged, either individually or collectively as a gang, for odd and casual jobs on a piece-work basis and are hence held to be self-employed on a basis analogous to the mobile work groups in factories as outlined above.

Trades where this type of quasi-hiring work arrangement can be found are stevedoring (notably, container port trucking), building and construction, taxi driving and a few traditional craft industries. Moreover, such practices have been adopted by an increasing number of corporate employers as they are downsizing their establishments, hiving off the peripheral departments and outsourcing the jobs to the laid off employees as independent agents.

250. Generally speaking, the distinction between a 'contract of service' on one hand and a 'contract for services' on the other is the key to determining whether any *bona fide* employment relations exist – that is, if the worker involved is an employee or is held to be self-employed.

D. Others (Company Directors and Partners, etc.)

251. A company director who concludes a labour or service contract with his company is held generally to be an employee of that company. However, a non-executive director without such a contract and not remunerated with a regular salary is not an employee.

252. A partner, on the other hand, is a self-employed person in business who is remunerated not on a salary but by taking a share of the profits. However, there can be 'salaried partners' – as in the case of professional associates engaged under a contract, like architects and lawyers in professional firms. Such persons, notwithstanding their nominal designations, are probably employees at law.

III. Customary Sources

253. According to traditional Chinese 'custom and practice' the employment status of workers can be classified in terms of the relative permanency of their engagement and their strength of commitment to the firm. Such a normative practice, popular among Chinese firms in the earlier days of Hong Kong's industrialization during the 1960s and 1970s, has elements and qualities closely analogous to the Japanese tradition of lifetime employment norms.

254. In Hong Kong, a common typology of three broad employment groups or categories, the *cheung-kung, cheung-saan-kun* and *saan-kung*, are hence identifiable by virtue of the degree of their permanency of employment. Literally, these labels refer respectively to a 'long-term (i.e. permanent) worker', 'long-term casual worker', and 'casual (i.e. temporary) worker'. Such a three-tier stratification has implications wider than merely suggesting the workers' differentials in job security and employment permanency. Associated criteria like skill differentials, methods of wage payment are relevant as well in affecting the location of the individual on this status continuum. And the individual's employment status is in turn a significant variable for determining the accrual of fringe benefits.

255. Workers and staff members belonging to the first tier, the *cheung-kung*, are relatively elitist. They are normally hired and paid on a monthly basis, being retained in the permanent core and as such, also being the last to be laid off or discharged. In a study of a glass factory in Hong Kong in the 1970s, a social anthropologist (Barbara E. Ward) noted that the skilled workmen commonly fell under this category of the permanent monthly employed and were awarded the 'staff' status – eligible for a variety of bonuses and fringe benefits covering such items as free and subsidized meals, living quarters and year-end bonus. By contrast, temporary casual workers were normally engaged on a daily or piece-rated basis. As such, they were generally unskilled or of lesser skill – enjoying fewer fringe benefits, less security, fewer chances of promotion and marginal in attachment to the firm *vis-à-vis* their permanent counterparts. This customary categorization by *kung* (i.e. worker) also affects the duration of a labour contract for the employee.

256. Decasualization of the labour market from the 1980s onwards, however, worked to emasculate the usage and legacy of the above customary typology of the *kungs*. As Hong Kong employers started importing and emulating the more enlightened arrangements of Western-style personnel management, many firms began to convert their piece-rate and daily-rate compensated casual workers into staff status by placing them on a monthly payroll. Such a shift towards permanent employment as the predominant form of hiring was assisted partly by the government's propagation of continuity of employment in the Employment Ordinance.

§2. The Individual Labour Contract

I. Different Categories of Labour Contract

257. The principal philosophy of the individual labour contract, or contract of employment, is derived from the British model of common law which assumes the legal enforceability of the individual contract of employment, supplemented by statutory legislation which provide a minimum 'floor of rights' for employees on the key contractual conditions. In the British legal tradition, such a notion of the individual contract of employment assumes that the employer and the employee are equal contracting partners, each with the freedom to enter into and dissolve the contract as well as to decide on and alter its terms. The employment contract is recognizable by the basic criterion of a symmetrical obligation of the parties to pay wages in exchange for the promise to work.

258. As a basic principle of individual labour law, it is important to distinguish between, on the one hand, a contract of employment which is tantamount to a contract of service and, on the other hand, a contract for services. This is characteristically considered in British common law more as a contract of business transaction than one of employment relationship. This tradition of distinction is inherited from the earlier British notion of the 'master and servant' relationship, in the legacy of which the modern notion of the employment contract is rooted. Indeed, the distinctive features of a contract of service, as *vis-à-vis* a contract for services, are probably better explained and represented by the actors of the master and the servant and their mutual relationship. Although such a usage has become castigated in modern times for its connotation of subservience and even servility, it remains imperative to conceptualize an employment relationship in terms of such a core notion of fidelity (that is, the 'master–servant' relationship) in order to differentiate it from a contract for services.

259. Given the background concept of the 'master–servant' relationship, it is fundamental to the contract of service for it to uphold (i) the prerogative (of the employer) to control and (ii) the parallel obligation (of the employee) to obey and be subordinate. Such a notion is now incorporated expressly into the relevant statute governing the contract of employment, namely, the Employment Ordinance (which emulates the UK Contract of Employment Act). The Ordinance defines such a contract as 'any agreement, whether in writing or oral, express or implied, whereby one person agrees to employ another and that other agrees to serve his employer as an employee' (section 2).

260. Conversely, no master–servant relationship arises out of a contract for services. Instead, a contract is deemed to be a contract for services where it provides that one party shall perform services for another so as to produce an agreed result but there shall be no right of control by the principal over the way in which it is to be done or performed by the other party as the agent. In such an instance, it has been usual for the common law to deem one party as the principal and the other party as an independent agent or contractor. In summary, the legal thinking behind the distinction is that an employee's work is an integral part of the employer's business, whereas an independent contractor merely renders services for, but is not integrated with, the employer's business.

II. Legal Test to Ascertain a Contract of Service

261. In real life there has still not yet evolved a conclusive set of criteria and rules, whether at law or otherwise, by which a distinction between these two kinds of 'service' contract can be determined explicitly – save that there appears to be a general acceptance of the basic principle as outlined in the above. Initially, the English courts have invoked the 'right to control' as the ultimate test. However, the more recent trend has been to accept more liberal criteria in interpreting and establishing a labour or employment contract. The reason is, conceivably, that in modern industry not all employers may be able, competent or willing to exercise detailed control or effective supervision over specialized labour. In this context of rapid techno-structural development in the workplace, other tests have developed, such as (i) the organizational test (that is, by asking whether the work performed would constitute an integral part of the business being organized by the employer); and (ii) the multiple test (that is, by examining all aspects of the employment relationship by weighing them in a comprehensive manner against an array of relevant criteria including the employer's power of selection, the payment of wages, granting of holidays, pensions and superannuation, the employee's liability to salary tax and the employer's power to suspend and dismiss, etc.)

262. In addition, what has been of growing eminence is a relatively recent notion, the entrepreneurial test, which is itself a composite test. The characteristic treatment under this approach is to examine the relationship from the assumption construed of a self-employed person in order to ascertain whether the person concerned is himself in business on his own, or otherwise. Such an exercise is likely to invoke asking such questions as whether the individual has provided his own equipment, and hired his own helpers, whether there has existed any degree of financial responsibility for investment and any degree of risk borne and whether there is any opportunity for profit from such activities in which he is engaged in such a capacity.

263. In spite of these developments, no single or constellation of tests has prevailed and proved invariably satisfactory. It is hence a pragmatic approach for the court to treat the distinction as a question of fact, to be determined by the evidence submitted in each individual case, based upon its own merits.

III. Duration of Contract

264. There are in general two types of labour contract according to the duration: a contract for an indefinite period, as distinct from a contract for a definite period or for precisely indicated work. In principle, the contract for a definite period ends when the period as agreed expires. By the same logic, a contract for precisely indicated work ends when the work is finished. Such a contract hence provides for a fixed duration of job tenure and either party who unilaterally and wrongfully breaks the contract before it expires is liable to indemnify the other party with damages amounting to the wages that would have accrued for the period between the time of breaking and the time of its expiry – subject to mitigation.

265. Conversely, a contract for an indefinite period is open-ended in its duration. The permissible duration is hence subject to the exigencies of statutory regulation as prescribed by the Employment Ordinance. The Ordinance prescribes the duration of the employment contract, unless where legally sanctioned deviations have been expressly agreed in advance by the parties. Generally speaking, the law has deemed, in the absence of express agreement to the contrary, that a contract of employment is a contract for one month, renewable from month to month, provided that it has become a 'continuous contract' by legal definition. However, such a presumption (that is, a 'continuous' contract of employment is deemed as a monthly one) under the Employment Ordinance can only be displaced under either of the following two conditions:

(i) where the contract is not, by its nature, a continuous contact; and
(ii) where there exists an express agreement that the contract, even if continuous, is not a monthly one.

266. These two conditions warrant a brief explanation. The notion of a 'continuous contract' is a key one describing a contract of employment under the Employment Ordinance, the First Schedule of which stipulates that where at any time, an employee has been engaged under a contact of employment during the period of four or more weeks preceding such time, he/she shall be deemed to have been in continuous employment during that period. In order to be reckoned as such, the individual needs to have worked at least 18 hours in the week; otherwise the time is not recognized as a week for the purpose of qualifying for the 'continuous contract'. However, it is technically permissible for these days or hours worked not to be consecutive in sequence; and they need not be worked under the same contract, so that they can be worked under separate daily contracts. In this connection, breaks such as those due to absence from work arising from illness or injury, statutory holidays, rest days or annual leave, lay-off, etc. will be reckoned as days of work for determining the 'continuity' of the contract which is, moreover, in no way broken by absence due to a strike or lock-out associated with industrial action (see Employment Ordinance, Chapter 57, First Schedule).

To remove the presumption at law under the Employment Ordinance that a contract is a monthly one where of its nature is continuous, there has to be an express and prior agreement between the parties to the contrary. In any case, it is not permissible for the agreed duration to be less than seven days. As a corollary, the law admits that any contract of employment, whether or not it is a 'continuous contract' may be for a period in excess of one month. However, unless evidenced in writing and signed by the parties concerned, it will still be deemed as a monthly contract renewable automatically from month to month if it is continuous by virtue of the length of service which has been worked.

IV. Statutory Limitations

267. The law has, however, placed certain statutory restrictions upon the above contractual freedom enjoyed by the private parties. A notable illustration is where an employment contract is entered into by a manual worker for a period of six months or more, it is deemed by the Employment Ordinance, by virtue of its Section 5(3), still to be a contract for one month renewable from month to month. It is understood that the spirit of such provisions, traced back to the Masters and Servants Ordinance which preceded the Employment Ordinance, is to protect the (vulnerable) employee from being bound inadvertently to a contract for an unduly long period. For this reason, its application is restricted to the manual workers and leaves the situation of the non-manual employees in an open-ended state. Generally speaking, it is up to the mutual consent of the parties to enter, in this latter instance, a contract of employment which can exceed six months, provided that it is evidenced in writing.

V. Probation Period

268. The Employment Ordinance does not expressly prescribe the need for a probation period and its duration, unless it is adopted by the parties in employment. However, it has been customary for a probation period, where it is agreed upon, to last for three months. Indeed, that section of the Ordinance governing the notice term for terminating a contract of employment on probation makes reference to a three-month probation period. Such a duration has hence become a normative practice.

VI. Form and Content

269. A contract of employment, by virtue of both the Employment Ordinance as well as the principle of English common law, need not be in writing. Instead, it is an instrument which can be either in writing or oral. Alternatively, it can be even partly written and partly oral. However, in order to avoid unnecessary misunderstanding or disputed interpretation of an otherwise vague, implied and non-specific contract, it has been the purported policy of the Labour Department to encourage the direct parties to enter into written contracts of employment. Employers, especially among the large-scale organizations, are also advised to codify the rules and regulations of the workplace in the form of an 'employee handbook' in order that their employees can be better informed of these requirements and expectations.

270. The Employment Ordinance, in addition, makes special rules governing the employer's obligations to disclose information about wages (Sections 44 to 46). It requires, in the first instance, every employer to inform each employee ,, before the latter enters employment and in a manner intelligible to him/ her, of his/her conditions as regards wages – including such aspects as the rate of wages, overtime and allowance, as well as the mode of calculation. There is a concomitant requirement for the employer to give information on subsequent changes in such conditions. During employment, if the employee submits an appropriate request in writing, the employer is obliged to deliver to the latter a written notice pertaining to these mattes. Failure to comply with these statutory duties is liable to constitute a criminal offence. As such, it is an 'absolute offence' and it is not necessary to prove an intention to break the law. Technically, it is sufficient to substantiate the charge by just establishing the fact that a contravention did take place.

VII. Conditions Necessary to Conclude a Valid Contract of Employment

271. Any agreement, whether oral or in writing, must embody certain basic prerequisites before it can be recognized as a proper contract of employment. Specifically, the basic conditions necessary to validate such a contract include:

- Two parties: there must be two parties to the contract, namely, the employer being one and the employee the other. Although the employee must be an individual, the employer can be an individual, a company, a firm or other corporate or legal person.

- Consideration: there must be 'consideration' for an agreement, basically in terms of the wages to be paid by the employer to the employee for work performance and vice versa, work to be performed by the employee to earn the wages payable from the employer.
- Capacity: both parties must have the recognized capacity to enter into the contract, with an intention that such an agreement will give rise to legally recognized rights and obligations which are enforceable upon the parties. 'Capacity to contract' is hence a basic property of the agreement whereby the parties must be persons whom the law admits as being competent to enter a contract of employment (or of apprenticeship, if deemed as such by the law). In this connection, the legal ability of certain categories of person to conclude a contract is worth noting as here below.

A. *Minors*

272. Every person who has reached the age of adulthood (which is 18), by virtue of the General and Interpretation Ordinance) can conclude a legally effective contract of employment. A minor or infant, however, can also enter such an employee contract or apprenticeship deed, provided that it is on the whole substantial for his benefits (for instance, the nature is to teach the minor, to enable him to be paid wages for labour or is of such a nature which is necessary to the minor). The test of a 'beneficial' character is, however, based upon the overall effects of the whole agreement, notwithstanding specific terms in the contract which are detrimental to his interest. Even where the contract may contain certain stipulations restricting the infant, the contract is still liable to be deemed as beneficial on the whole to the infant and enforceable in court. By virtue of various statutory regulations, the legal capacity of the infant to enter employment for certain trades and industries, as well as in certain circumstances, is expressly delimited or circumscribed. The most significant statutory limitations are the prohibition placed against child labour (for those who are aged 15 or younger) as well as the stringent control imposed upon young persons employed in industry.

Where the employer himself is an infant, his contractual capacity is valid only to the extent that the service thus rendered for him is necessary, as pertaining to his personal requirements.

In any case, it is possible for an invalid contract to become effective and binding upon a minor when attaining the age of 18, provided that he is ready to make a fresh promise, either expressly or implied, after due consideration in his newly acquired capacity to enter such a labour contract.

B. *Women*

273. In general, a woman enjoys in Hong Kong, without discrimination, the full legal capacity to conclude and dissolve her individual contract of employment. This has been the position achieved after previous statutory limitations which were aimed at protecting women labouring in industry have been liberalized in the currency of global-wide propagation to promote women's rights and advance gender equality. Such rights have been further advanced and vindicated by the enactment of the Sex Discrimination Ordinance in the 1990s.

C. *The Government*

274. By virtue of the General and Interpretation Ordinance, the government is not generally bound by any legislative provisions, including those pertaining to the field of employment and industrial relations, save where it is otherwise specified – as in the instance of the Employees' Compensation Ordinance, as well as the application of the anti-union discrimination protective clause of the Employment Ordinance. This notwithstanding, it is generally accepted that the government has full capacity to enter into a contract of employment. However, it has also been observed that such contracts do not in fact bind the government in the same way and to the same extent as a comparable instrument does outside the civil service. Specifically, the government is held to possess the prerogative to dismiss at will (that is, to do so at pleasure and without a need to give the cause) on the rationale that the government cannot bind itself as to incur the risk of fettering its future executive action, or that it is in the public interest that the public employee should hold office only at the will of the government.

Where there are the Civil Service Regulations and other government regulations purporting to govern the duration and other conditions of employment of the civil servants outside the ambit of the Employment Ordinance, their legal status appears to have remained obscure and dubious, rather than unequivocal. A solution suggested in addressing such ambiguities is to recognize the enforceability of these civil service rules in part as contractual, especially where these norms are held to be relevant and pertinent to the two parties and their relationship.

D. *Foreign Sovereign and Diplomatic Representatives*

275. These include public ministers such as ambassadors, envoys, ministers resident, *chargés d'affaire*, representatives of international organizations like the United Nations, International Labour Organization, World Trade Organization, as well as personnel belonging to the International Court of Justice. They are capable of concluding individual contracts of employment. However, they enjoy immunity from any suits or legal proceedings in respect of any liability for breach of contract they have concluded with their employees. Of course, it is possible for them to waive their 'diplomatic' privilege and submit themselves to the jurisdiction of the legal courts in Hong Kong.

However, the right of immunity is not reciprocal since the employee of such a foreign sovereign, or government or its diplomatic representative is liable to legal actions initiated against him by the latter. Nevertheless, it is held that the institution of legal actions by the diplomatic representative connotes a waiver from his/her immunity, thereby enabling the defendant employee to lodge a counter claim against the diplomat.

E. Insanity and Unsound Mind

276. A person suffering from mental disorder, or a drunkard, is held generally to be incapable of concluding or being bound by a contract of employment, unless his sanity has been proved.

VIII. Legal Objects and Purpose

277. The objects of the agreement which the parties enter into have to be lawful. Any individual contract of employment is illegal and void, if it contradicts the provisions of a statute or the rules of common law. For a contract to be deemed as void in this way, it is necessary that the consideration for it should be wholly illegal or such part of the consideration as pertaining to any specific clauses in the contract should be illegal. It follows that if any consideration is held as illegal, all the promises dependent upon that consideration are void. On the other hand, if the consideration is not entirely tainted with illegality, and should just a part of the multiple promises dependent upon it be illegal, the remaining legal promises may still be held to be valid in court.

278. In addition to the problem of contractual illegality due to a statutory breach, a contract can also be deemed illegal and invalid where its objects conflict with certain principles of public policy laid down under common law (consistency with public policy is essential insofar as it refers to the interest and well-being of society at large). Examples contrary to public policy and interest are labour contracts which are connected with or which encourage immorality and are hence null and void.

IX. Consent and Servile Contracts

279. There must be consent by the parties to the agreement. Forced labour in Hong Kong is outlawed and an individual labour contract can be concluded only if both parties agree voluntarily to enter such an instrument. Consent may be given expressly or tacitly. However, any violence or the threat of it, deceit, or error and prejudice perpetrated so as to induce the making of the agreement will render it invalid and void.

280. As a corollary to this general freedom of labour and contract, a labour contract which may involve or implicate the employee in enslavement is hence void, especially since it is also in breach of established public policy.

281. Therefore, it is not permissible for the parties to employment to attach to the labour contract any servile clauses or any elements suggesting servitude. By implication, a contract purporting to enable the employer to maintain an employee in his service to the total exclusion of all the jobs in the future can also be held invalid. In another context, it is also not permissible for the employer to transfer the services of an employee to another employer without the employee's consent (which has to be, if it is to be recognized, in the form of a new or renewed contract discharging the old obligations and creating new ones). The assignment by an employer of his rights and obligations under the existent labour contract to another one is not valid. This is because such an employer, without obtaining the prior consent of the employee, is committing an act which implies enslavement by assigning to another person what is basically the employee's duty to work. In fact, an assignment by the employee to another person of his wages or salary or his entitlement to them under the labour contract is not valid either, if it will have left the employee, the assignor himself, destitute.

Chapter 2. Rights and Duties of the Parties in the Course of Employment

§1. Introduction

282. Basic to the labour contract is an employment relationship which implies primarily, in 'market' terms, an exchange between wages paid and work done. Other than this basic element of economic exchange, an employment relationship also embodies an array of symmetrical rights and obligations for both parties. The duties for the parties to employment are pluralistic. For instance, these can be explicit, formal and mandatory as prescribed by statute, common law and administrative rules of the government, or informal and implied from custom and practice. Alternatively, it is also plausible to conceive certain duties of the parties on the voluntary basis of ethical or moral standards, as exalted and propagated by their proponents in the form of assuasive or advisory guidelines. An example of this nature is the *Code of Labour Relations Practices* published by the Labour Department. First published in 1976 and revised and updated periodically since then, this handbook is more or less a 'communiqué' of the official 'gospel' for promoting harmonious industrial relations in the private sector. The *Code*, however, was later retitled as the *Guide to Good People Management Practices*, symptomatic perhaps of the importance now attached to human resources management.

283. A brief narration of the mutual obligations incumbent upon the two parties of the employer and the employee when they enter into an individual contract of employment is hence in order, as in the following.

§2. Duty of Mutual Respect

284. Both the employer and the employee have a duty, legal as well as moral, to treat each other with appropriate respect and consideration. For instance, unlike the older days of master and servant relations, the employer can no longer treat his employee as an expendable chattel, or as an object without feelings and emotions. The individual labour contract is hence to entail the fundamentals of mutual trust and confidence.

§3. Duties of the Employee

I. Duty to Serve

285. By common law, it is a fundamental obligation of the employee to serve his employer faithfully and to work under his command, authority and control, provided that such control is lawful and reasonable (i.e. without any malicious intent). With the rise of modern management, this authority, which rested with the employer, has been epitomized in the notion of 'managerial prerogative'. In this connection, the Employment Ordinance confers statutory effects upon this principle, by stating that an employer can summarily dismiss his employee on disciplinary grounds if the latter wilfully disobeys a lawful and reasonable order.

286. Specifically, the employee is obliged to perform competently, using his reasonable skill and care, at the time agreed upon, in the place agreed upon and in the manner and conditions agreed upon. By common law interpretation, the employee has to keep to the working hours as agreed under his contract. Hence, by implication, under the Employment Ordinance, absence from work or unpunctuality are legitimate reasons for the employer to deduct wages payable to the employee, if the latter is employed and remunerated other than by way of 'piece-work'. Such a deduction is strictly limited, being proportionate to the period of time during which he was absent from work.

287. Normally, the employee can dispose of his time freely after working hours but there are instances where it is either part of the contract or a regulation of the workplace that he is not to undertake any extra work or if so, the employer's prior consent is necessary. However, such an obligation has become loosened now that atypical employment such as part-time working has emerged and is growing in the labour market. Except where the nature of the job is such that it involves attending a mobile workplace (as in the instance of 'outdoor' work), the work must be performed in the place agreed upon. A unilateral change in the place of work on the part of the employer, especially when the change involves a significant increase in the travelling distance for the employee, may be considered as a breach of the initial contract. Thus, the severance pay provisions of the Employment Ordinance used to prescribe as a valid condition constituting the dismissal of the employee 'by reason of redundancy' the relocation of the employer's undertaking across the Victoria Harbour of Hong Kong. However, since the installation of the cross-harbour tunnel facilities, such a cross-harbour provision has been rescinded in favour of a more liberal interpretation which pertains to any change of workplace which involves a long distance.

288. However, the general problem of job transfer is a more equivocal issue and can be so varied in nature that it makes any statutory regulations governing transfer impractical. In fact, to determine the validity of any work transfer in the context of its possible implications for remuneration, place of work, duties and skill requirement of the job, reference has to be made to the type and organization of the enterprise, the initial nature of the job which the employee performs, as well as the background (for instance arising from technological causes) and the repercussions of the transfer upon the individual employee in order to ascertain the suitability of the new job in terms of pay, rank, competence, responsibilities and other attributes.

289. The notion of 'managerial prerogative' seems to imply the authority of the employer enabling him to transfer and deploy his employee at his discretion, so long as the action is within legal and reasonable limits. However, the Labour Department advises the employer to giver the employee adequate advance notice of the transfer order. In parallel, as noted earlier, a duty is also incumbent upon the employer to inform his employee, in an intelligible manner, of all contingent changes in the employee's conditions, which includes the rate of wages, overtime rate and any allowance – whether calculated by the piece, job, hour, day, week or otherwise.

II. Duty to Respect Professional Secrets

290. It is generally understood under common law that an employee may not communicate or divulge, without the prior consent of his employer, any trade secrets learned in the course of employment or any confidential information about the employer's business (for instance, product design and methods of operations, etc.)

In some large-scale modern enterprises, such an employee duty is expressly incorporated within either the employment contract or the firm's in-house regulations. Virtually, violation of this obligation is generally considered as a breach of trust sufficiently serious to justify summary dismissal under the conditions which the Employment Ordinance specifies. This is because the employee:

(i) has committed misconduct, such conduct being inconsistent with the due and faithful discharge of his duties; and
(ii) is guilty of fraud or dishonesty (Employment Ordinance, Section 9).

Besides being subject to disciplinary actions, he is also liable to civil actions instituted by the employer for the recovery of damages. In the event of suspected commission of fraud, proceedings with penal implications are likely to follow as well.

III. Other Obligations

291. The employee is expected to perform and discharge his duties in his capacity as a normal employee – i.e. as a *bonus pater familias* and not as 'the best' possible employee. Both by common law and prescription of the Employment Ordinance, the employee is obliged to obey lawful and reasonable orders from his employer or his delegate. In the course of his performance, he cannot be habitually negligent in performing his duties, otherwise he is liable to summary dismissal. Other obligations of the employee, either normative or legal as prescribed by statutory or contractual obligations, or implied by common law, include:

(i) compliance with rules and regulations of the workplace;
(ii) time-keeping and acquisition of prior permission for absence and leave from work;
(iii) furnishing documentation on personal identity in order to authenticate one's status of employability;
(iv) provision of associated data on personal particulars to the employer for the purpose of personnel records within the purview of the Personal Data (Privacy) Ordinance;
(v) observation of the code on health and safety precautions;

(vi) no acceptance of gifts, bribes, commission or any such 'advantages' in respect of his work unless where the consent and knowledge of the employer are secured (for instance, tips that are open and customary, as in the restaurant, hotel and hospitality industries);
(vii) not working for a competitor of his employer in his spare time; and
(viii) maintenance in good condition of any of the enterprise's property (notably, equipment and tools) which is delegated to the employee's responsibility.

§4. Duties of the Employer

I. Duty to Employ the Worker

292. This fundamental duty entails the employer's obligation to provide work and pay wages. Apart from the temporary cessation of work during the period when the employee takes his rest day, statutory holiday, annual leave and sick leave, the employer is obliged to provide him with work pertaining to the individual contract of employment. However, the Employment Ordinance enables the employer to withhold temporarily the supply of work to the employee under the situation of (i) suspension of the employee on displinary ground and (ii) lay-off. Yet suspension normally should not last more than a fortnight unless criminal proceedings have been started in connection with the act for which the suspected employee is suspended. On the other hand, the employer may temporarily lay off his employees for short intervals not exceeding a total of 12 (normal working) days in any period of four consecutive weeks, for production reasons such as seasonality of activities due to market demands and unforeseen breakdown of plant. Although the employer is not obliged at law to give notice of lay-off, it has been reckoned as reasonable for the affected employees to be given advance notice, preferably not less than seven days, of such an impending lay-off.

II. Duty to Pay Wages

293. Parallel to the employer's duty to provide work is his legal obligation to pay his employees due wages in respect of work done or to be performed as prescribed by the contract of employment. According to the Employment Ordinance, wages are due at the end of a wage period (which is the period in respect of which wages are payable under a labour contract). These must be paid as soon as is practicable but in any case not later than seven days thereafter. Similarly wages and other sums due must be paid within seven days of the completion or termination of a contract of employment. Defaults of wage payment, if found willful and without reasonable excuse, will render the employer liable for a criminal offence. The same statute also censures and prevents an employer from entering, renewing or continuing a contract of employment unless with reasonable belief that he is able to pay wages as they become due. The implications are that as soon as the employer no longer believes in his ability to meet such payments, he is obliged at law to dissolve the contract. Otherwise, contravention of these statutory duties is also liable to prosecution. In extreme cases, the employee of an employer in default of wage payment can apply to court for the arrest of the employer, given that there are reasonable grounds to believe that the latter may abscond from Hong Kong in evasion of his duties to pay the outstanding wages.

III. Duty to Indemnify

294. The employer is generally obliged to cover any expenses that may be reasonably incurred by the employee in the performance of his labour contract. One obvious example is the usual right of the employee to claim reimbursement from the employer on travelling expenses incurred in pursuance of the employer's business. The employer's obligation is, however, more ambivalent should it also involve the commission by the employee of a wrongful act. However, at common law, the employer is held vicariously liable to compensate a third party for damages caused to the latter by his employee in the course of performing his duties. Moreover, it is presumably tenable for the employee to recover any personal loss he suffers, if the act was committed under his employer's order, or under the latter's authority and for the purpose of his business.

IV. Provision of Decent Working Conditions

295. The Factory and Industrial Undertakings Ordinance, together with its body of subsidiary legislation, as well as the Young Persons (Industry) Regulations of the Employment Ordinance, lays down the minimum standards of working conditions in industry. However, no corresponding set of statutes exists in the commercial and tertiary sectors. Other than legal norms, the *Code of Labour Relations Practice,* now the *Guide to Good People Management Practices* published by the Labour Department, exhorts employers to achieve higher workplace standards by making it safer, less hazardous to their health and more pleasant for all employees. These varied measures, if adopted, can hence contribute to reduced accident rates, increased efficiency and improved labour– management relations. To rationalize the workplace, employers are urged to:

(i) improve standards of 'housekeeping', including cleanliness, tidiness and general appearance of the workplace;
(ii) improve lighting, ventilation and temperature in the workplace;
(iii) reduce noise, dust, fumes and vapours in the workplace;
(iv) ensure that work is done as safely as possible;
(v) ensure that employees use protective equipment, observe the safety standards laid down by law and cooperate in safety measures;
(vi) reduce strain and monotony involved in work;
(vii) encourage employees and their representatives to cooperate in improving working conditions; and
(viii) provide for consultation with employees or their representatives on working conditions.

In addition, the employer cannot discriminate against an employee on the grounds of sex, disability, attending family duties, age and ethnicity,[16] or for belonging to any union or participating in its activities. He is also expected to allow employees the necessary time off in order for the latter to perform their civil duties, such as in auxiliary police and also to act as members of a jury at court. Depending on the circumstances, the employee may or may not be paid wages by the employer when he is absent from work without reasonable excuses and approval.

V. Reception of New Workers

296. Under the Employment Ordinance, an employer is obliged to inform an employee, before the latter commences his employment, of the conditions under which the employee is to be employed. These conditions, especially those of wages, have to be explained in an intelligible manner, either oral or in writing, to the employee.

Such an explanation needs to cover, *inter alia*, the rate of wages, overtime rate and any allowances calculated by the piece, job, hour, day, week or in any other way. Although not legally obliged, employers are encouraged by the *Code on Labour Relations Practices* (now know as the *Guide to Good People Management Practices*) to offer their new employees induction training which disseminate the basic sklls and knowledge for peromance. Subsequently, training aimed to serve to upgrade skills and inculcate competencies, as well as addressed to enhancing safety, is equally desirable. If available, a new employee should also be furnished with a copy of the firm's employee handbook briefing him on the details of its inventory of in-hour regulations and personnel practices.

VI. Duties in the Instance of Change in Conditions of Work

297. In general, the assumption of 'managerial prerogative' vests the employer with the right of deploying his employee, within reasonable and lawful ambits. However, if any reassignment implies or results in changes in his conditions of employment, it is a legal duty for the employee, as obliged by the Employment Ordinance, to notify the employee promptly of such changes. The disclosure of such information, either in writing or oral, has to be intelligible and given by the employer when the change in conditions is made.

298. The consent of the employee to these changes is necessary, while the notice period has to be reasonable, normally equivalent to that as required to dissolve the contract. Such advance notice is always useful or even imperative, since any major alterations to the terms of employment can be construed as implying the revoking of an existent labour contract and offering a new one.

16. A law censuring racial discrimination has now been enacted. However, age discrimination is not yet sanctioned by law.

VII. Obligation of an Employer to Keep Records

299. For the purpose of discharging his obligations pertaining to various statutory employment benefits prescribed by the Employment Ordinance, an employer has to maintain a record of annual leave, sick leave, maternity leave and duration of services for every employee. According to the Immigration Ordinance, it is also necessary for the employer to inspect and register the identity cards and other equivalent documents of employees for attesting to their employability. However, such a generic duty of the employer to keep records on individual employees has now been compounded and constrained by the simultaneous obligation of the employer to observe the confidentiality of the latters' individual data and to use them with discretion and their consent, as prescribed by the Privacy Ordinance (Personal Data) introduced in the mid-1990s.

300. Should any class of employer be considered by the authority as having an obligation to keep records in an appropriate form to facilitate the provision of information about wages, the Commissioner for Labour may publish such a requirement, specifying the class of employers and the format of such records in the Government Gazette, as empowered by the Employment Ordinance. However, such an authority has not been yet invoked by the Commissioner.

VIII. Other Responsibilities Due to the Employee

301. The employer is responsible for the safety of his employee and the latter's belongings in the course and at the place of employment which the employer owns or manages. These duties are prescribed by both the rules of common law as well as statutory provisions. By virtue of the principles of common law, the employer is liable to compensate the employee for injuries caused to his body as a result of his negligence. On the other hand, statutory codes have been introduced to regulate standards of industrial safety and accident prevention, as backed by penal sanctions. In this connection, the employer is legally obliged to report promptly any accidents occurring to the employee (within two days) to the Labour Department. The Employees' Compensation Ordinance also holds the employer liable to pay compensation to his employees for any incapacity, both temporary and permanent, which he suffers as a result of industrial injury or in specified cases, occupational disease which arises out of employment.

302. It is also useful to outline briefly the common law duty of the employer concerning the issue of negligence. The standard care incumbent upon the employer is the reasonable level of care which a prudent and average employer should take in all circumstances. The employer will hence be liable if he has not exercised sufficient care and failed to prevent something which was reasonably foreseeable. 'Reasonable care' is tested by such requirements as:

(i) that the employer is obliged to take positive steps to ensure the safety of his employees in the light of the knowledge which he has or ought to have;
(ii) where there is developing knowledge, that he must keep reasonably abreast with it and not be too slow in applying it;
(iii) that if he has a greater than average knowledge of the risk, he must take more than average precautions; and
(iv) that the employer must weigh and consider the risk against the effectiveness of the precautions needed to meet the risk, as well as their costs and inconvenience.

303. Negligence of the employer can be in whole or in part. An example of default of the latter nature is the case of contributory negligence – as attributable to both the employer and the employee himself, or even that of a third party.

IX. Intrinsic Nature of the Employer's Duty

304. The duty of the employer is an intrinsic one since it is not possible to nullify such responsibility by delegating this duty to an agent or someone else. Moreover, his duty is owed to each employee as an individual and not to them collectively. By implication, the employer is obliged to adopt greater precautions when dealing with inexperienced employees, or with new and untrained employees, or with young persons.

305. An employer can be vicariously responsible for the commission of a wrongful or tortious act by his employee in the course of employment that gives rise to injury or damage to a third party. This is because the employer authorizes the act and may have instigated or created the situation in which the employee commits the act, although the employee himself has, in his own capacity, to be liable as well. The key determinant for ascertaining the employer's liability rests upon whether or not the acts are committed by the employee in the course of and for the purpose of his employment. In this connection, the employer may be liable not only where he has expressly authorized the wrongful act but also where the employee performs it wrongfully under the auspices of his delegated prerogative and tacit consent. In more extreme cases, the employer might still be vicariously liable even where he has expressly prohibited the act, if it is demonstrated that the act has been done in the scope of employment and for the purpose of the employer's business.

306. The employer's vicarious liability may also arise where he has a responsibility which cannot be delegated by merely employing someone else to do the work. Actually, the notion of vicarious liability for contractors/subcontractors is not only restricted to common law duties but is also incumbent expressly upon the principal employer, in terms of certain statutory liabilities such as injury compensation as well as wage responsibility in the building and constriction trade.

307. Moreover, the employer can be held liable under statute for an act committed by his employee that is punishable at law by penal sanctions. For instance, under the Employment Ordinance, the employer is liable vicariously for unlawful acts of anti-union discrimination perpetrated by his agents or officers against his employees.

Chapter 3. Working Time, Rest Days, Annual Vacation and Holidays

§1. Working Time

I. Introduction

308. There are no general regulations, statutory or administrative, on the standard or normal hours of work in Hong Kong, except in the case of young persons employed in industry. However, the labour movement has become vociferous recently in canvassing for the introduction of legislation to regulate the standard work hours for the general workforce at large. But the government has been steadfast in refraining from legislating on work hours, in spite of a service-wide shift towards a five-day working week within the public sector – apparently intended to be pattern-setting and emulated by private sector employers on a voluntary basis. In response to lobbying by organized labour, the government has undertaken an investigatory study of standard hours recently. However, enactment in this area is not prospective in light of the vigorous opposition from business and its associations.

309. Prior to the turn of the century, legal prescription of work hours for protective purposes in industry was limited not only to young persons but extended to cover women workers as well. The Women and Young Persons (Industry) Regulations, incorporated into the mother ordinance of the Employment Ordinance since 1980 but now rescinded, provided for such legal norms as the length of work hours, rest days and overtime work which these workers are permitted to take up with their employers. Enforcement of this industrial code was by way of inspection at the workplace by members of a labour inspectorate of the Labour Department.

II. Employment of Young Persons in Industry

310. The Employment of Young Persons (Industry) Regulations, a set of subsidiary legislation administered by the Labour Department under the Employment Ordinance, place protective restrictions on the working hours of young persons aged between 15 and 18 who are employed in industry. The standard working hours permissible are stipulated at 8 hours a day and 48 hours a week. The daily work schedule has to be kept between 7 am and 7 pm and any overtime work is proscribed. The maximum period of employment, inclusive of the time allowed for meals and rest, is limited to ten hours a day. However, a measure of flexibility is provided by the Regulations, inasmuch as by mutual agreement between the employer and the young person he employs, the working hours of the latter may exceed 8 in a day or 48 in a week, provided that the total number of hours worked by the young person does not exceed 96 in any two consecutive weeks. This notwithstanding, the maximum period of employment in a day must remain ten hours.

Besides, the employer is obliged to provide the young person with a pause after every five hours of continuous work. Such a rest period cannot be less than half an hour, to enable him to take either a meal or rest. It is also mandatory for young persons engaged in industry to be given one rest day a week.

However, the Commissioner for Labour is empowered under the Employment Ordinance to grant special permission under or exemptions from any provisions regulating the employment of your persons in any industrial workplace subject to such conditions and for such periods as he may deem fit. For example, the Commissioner may grant permission for a young person aged 16 or above to be deployed for shift work between 7 pm and 11 pm and the likely prerequisite for approval is the provision at the workplace of a suitable room, free from any industrial process, which can be used for dining and resting purposes by these young person workers on shift work.

III. Night Work for Young Persons in Industry

311. By virtue of the Employment of Young Persons (Industry) Regulations, the employment of young persons for night work in industry is generally proscribed. As noted earlier, their permissible period of industrial employment is restricted to the hours between 7 am and 7 pm. Yet exemptions to the above prohibitions may be sought from the Commissioner for Labour, subject to meeting certain stringent conditions specified by the Commissioner at the time of granting the permission.

IV. Employment of Children

312. The Employment of Children Regulations, another set of subsidiary legislation attached to the Employment Ordinance, place an economy-wide prohibition on child labour. In this context, the minimum age of employment, mandatory for both the industrial and non-industrial sectors, has been stipulated at the age of 15. Nevertheless, the law has been designed to allow a reasonable measure of flexibility. Specifically, children aged 13 and 14 years may take up employment in non-industrial establishments, subject to the condition that they attend full-time schooling if they have not yet completed secondary year 3, as well as other associated requirements aimed at protecting their safety, health and welfare.

313. In parallel, the Dutiable Commodities (Liquor) Regulations also disallow juvenile below the age of 18 to work in any licensed premises and amusement houses which carry a liquor licence. This code is, however, administered by the Liquor Licensing Board and the Police Force.

V. Working Hours in General

314. There is no statutory restriction on the hours of work for adult workers aged 18 or above in all economic sectors. Work hours vary extensively inside the labour force between different industries and occupations: generally speaking, sales and service workers, as well as workers in the retail trades, restaurants and hotels serve the longest hours. Even white-collar workers in the financial and business service sector who used to work comparatively short hours have to stay up at night because of the globalization of the financial market. Compensation for overtime work is not fixed by law, either generally or specifically for any group of workers.

There has been, however, a recent upsurge of public concern for official regulation of standard hours for the general labour force, especially after the enactment of a statutory minimum wage law in 2011 as a lever against the vicissitudes of the low paid workers. However, the government is still oscillating on its policy stance on standard work hour legislation. Instead, it plays the role as a pattern-setter. As an employer, it spearheads the adoption and practice of a five-day working week among public sector employees in the civil service.

§2. Rest Days

I. In General

315. Part IV of the Employment Ordinance entitles all employees in Hong Kong to one rest day in every seven days – that is, almost tantamount to a weekly rest day. Young persons employed in industry are entitled to analogous rest day protection under the parallel and more vigorous instrument of the Young Persons (Industry) Regulations.

316. A rest day is defined by the Employment Ordinance as a 'continuous period of not less than 24 hours during which an employee is entitled to abstain from working for his employer'. To qualify for such weekly rest days, the employee must have a continuous contract of employment with his employer, by having completed at least four weeks' service. The law does not, however, stipulate whether or not rest days should be paid. Instead, pay for rest days depends upon the express or implied conditions in the respective contracts of employment. Its availability is, however, common among the monthly rated employees, whose wages are usually not deducted for rest day absence, while it is not unusual for piece-rated workers not to be paid for taking their rest days.

317. Rest days are to be assigned by the employer to employees and can occur on a regular basis (such as on a particular day of the week or on fixed days of the month). Alternatively, rest days can be assigned on a rotational basis, provided that these are taken at seven-day intervals. In case of the former, it is sufficient for the employer to inform his employee of a fixed and non-varied schedule. However, should the latter practice be adopted, the employer is legally obliged to inform his employees on the timing of the 'appointed rest days' during the month before it commences, either orally or in writing or by a roster showing a schedule of the appointed rest days.

318. Subject to the consent of the employee, an employer may substitute some other rest day for the original appointed rest day. In such cases he must appoint a substitute rest day either within the same month before the original rest day or within 30 days thereafter. In the event of a breakdown of machinery or plant or workplace demand or in any other unforeseeable emergency, the employer may summon the employee to return to work on the original rest day but he must, within 48 hours, notify the employee of when the substituted rest day has to be taken, in any case, within 30 days following the initial date.

Voluntary work on rest days is permissible in general. An employee may, on his own request and if his employer agrees, work on a rest day. Reciprocally, an employer may request an employee to work on a rest day, but this has to depend upon the free consent of the employee. Generally speaking, work on a rest day should be reckoned as overtime work and be remunerated accordingly.

The Employment Ordinance also nullifies certain attempts by the employer to induce or coerce his employee to work on rest days. For instance, under the legislation any condition in a contract of employment which makes the payment of an annual bonus (like a Chinese Lunar New Year bonus) conditional upon an employee agreeing to work on his rest day is declared void.

II. Rest Days for Young Persons Employed in Industry

319. All young persons under the age of 18 employed in industry must be given, by virtue of the Employment of Young Persons (Industry) Regulations, one rest day a week. Unlike the general provision in the Employment Ordinance itself, rest days taken by these young employees are mandatory and it is not permissible for them to waive their entitlement and choose to work on a rest day. Nor can a rest day initially assigned by the employer be moved to another day, unless with the prior consent of the Commissioner for Labour, which has to be obtained at least two days in advance.

III. Enforcement

320. An employer who, without reasonable excuse, fails to grant to an employee any rest days as required under the Employment Ordinance or fails to inform his employee of his rest day in the month before it commences, is guilty of an offence. The employer is also liable to prosecution if he requires, except in circumstance of emergency or with the employee's consent, such an employee to work on his rest day.

§3. Annual Leave

I. In General

321. Paid annual leave, a statutory employment benefit provided by the Employment Ordinance since 1979, cannot be waived privately and substituted by payment in lieu unless it exceeds ten days. Besides, such leave must contain an element of consecutivity.

322. The law entitles the employee to annual leave with pay after he has served under a continuous contract with his employer for 12 months. An employee's entitlement to paid annual leave increases progressively from 7 days to a maximum of 14 days, as given by his length of service as follows:

Year of service	*Annual leave entitlements*
1	7
2	7
3	8
4	9
5	10
6	11
7	12
8	13
9 or above	14

The time of annual leave, to be appointed by the employer after consulting the employees concerned or their representatives, must be notified in writing to the employees at least 14 days in advance, unless a shorter period has been mutually agreed upon.

As a rule, paid annual leave can be granted and taken in either of two alternative methods. There can be a period which is continuous and unbroken. Alternatively, a second option is to grant the employee a maximum of three days separately and the balance consecutively where his leave entitlement is less than ten days, while at least seven days consecutively where his leave entitlement exceeds a total of ten days. This latter arrangement is, however, practicable only subject to the request of the employee. Any rest day or statutory holiday falling within a period of annual leave will be deemed as annual leave and another rest day or holiday needs to be appointed.

II. Common Leave Year

323. It is permissible for an employer to elect any period of 12 consecutive months as the common leave year for all of his employees. In such instance, the employer is obliged to give a month's notice either to each of his employees in writing or by posting a notice in a conspicuous place in the place of employment. Where an employee has not served for 12 months in the common leave year, the employer should calculate his leave entitlement on a pro-rated basis and any fraction of a day computed should be reckoned as a full day for annual leave calculation.

III. Annual Leave Shutdown

324. An employer may elect to close down his business or part of it for the purpose of granting his employees paid annual leave. Rules of plant or business shutdown, however, differ from the general provisions as stated earlier, inasmuch as:

(i) a longer period of notice is required, making it necessary for one month's notice in writing to all employees affected. Such a notice listing the names of these employees must be exhibited in a conspicuous manner at the workplace;
(ii) every employee who is otherwise not eligible for annual leave because of insufficient length of continuous service, but who has to stop work due to the closure, shall be allowed these days involved as annual leave with pay as well. Such leave allowed has the same effect as that granted in respect of 12 months' employment under a continuous contract before the closure.

IV. Annual Leave Pay

325. After the employee has taken his annual leave, he must be paid the relevant annual leave pay on the nearest pay day that follows. The pay shall be equivalent to the wages (excluding overtime pay) that the employee could have earned if he had worked during the period of annual leave. The average daily wages earned during the period of 28 days preceding the leave should constitute the basis for calculating the annual leave pay, if the employee's wages are piece-rated or variable from day to day.

326. Payment in lieu of annual leave is proscribed except for any leave earned which exceeds ten days or in the circumstance of termination of employment. The employee about to leave his present employment is entitled to payment in lieu of any annual leave not yet taken in a leave year if he has completed 12 months' service (a leave year being any period of 12 months intervening between the day on which his employment commenced and an anniversary of such day). And an employer with less than 12 months' employment but having served three months or more in a 'leave year' is eligible to pro-rated pay in lieu of annual leave, provided that the contract is dissolved not for reason of summary dismissal due to his serious misconduct or default in performance.

V. Annual Leave Records

327. For the purpose of granting paid annual leave, the employer is obliged at law to maintain a record of:

(i) the day of commencement and termination of the employment of each employee;
(ii) all periods of annual leave taken by each employee;

(iii) all periods of closure of business or part thereof for the purpose of granting annual leave to the employees; and
(iv) all annual leave pay received by each employee.

VI. Failure to Grant Annual Leave

328. Failure on the part of the employer to grant paid annual leave to his/her employees is liable to constitute an offence punishable by criminal sanctions under the Employment Ordinance.

VII. Annual Leave Practice in the Private Sector

329. While the provision of paid annual leave is a statutory benefit introduced to the Hong Kong workplace on a territory-wide basis now for nearly thirty years, it has been a long existing practice, either by custom or contract, upheld as an employment norm in many industries and trades in the private sector. Examples include, for instance, the big trading companies, banks, insurance and other financial institutions and hotels. In these instances of private and voluntary practices, paid annual leave granted is always more generous and in excess of the legal norm, often entailing a leave period ranging from a fortnight to one month.

§4. Short Holidays

I. Statutory Holidays

330. Under the Employment Ordinance, all employees are entitled to 12 statutory holidays a year. These holidays are designated in the yearly calendar as follows:

(i) the first day of January;
(ii) the Chinese Lunar New Year's Day;
(iii) the second day of the Lunar New Year;
(iv) the third day of the Lunar New Year;
(v) Ching Ming Festival;
(vi) Labour Day, being the first day of May;
(vii) Tuen Ng (Dragon Boat) Festival;
(viii) the day following the Chinese Mid-Autumn Festival;
(ix) the Chung Yeung Festival;
(x) the Chinese Winter Solstice Festival or Christmas Day, as decided by the employer;
(xi) Hong Kong SAR Establishment Day, being the first day of July; and
(xii) the National Day, being the first day of October.

II. Statutory Holiday Pay

331. An employee having been employed under a continuous contract for not less than three months is entitled to the holiday pay. Holiday pay should be paid to the employee not later than the day on which he is next paid his wages after the statutory holiday.

III. Work on Statutory Holidays

332. It is possible to summon and retain an employee for work on a statutory holiday, provided that it is covered by 48 hours' prior notice and subject to the appointment of an alternative holiday within 60 days before or after the statutory holiday. If the employer and employee agree, a substituted holiday may be taken in lieu of the statutory or alternative holiday but it has to be made available within 30 days.

IV. Restriction on Pay in Lieu of Holiday

333. Taking the holiday is mandatory at law and it is not permissible for an employer to offer an employee simply pay in lieu of a holiday which has to be granted.

V. Other Public Holidays

334. In addition to Sundays, there are 17 general holidays in a year under the Holidays Ordinance, which pre-dates the more recent enactments on statutory holidays, rest days and annual leave within the purview of the Employment Ordinance. The Holidays Ordinance, in spite of its non-imperative nature, is widely adopted in the commerce, banking and service sectors where it sets the norm for scheduling holidays among the white-collar employees. The parallel operation of these two pieces of legislation governing holidays (namely, the Employment Ordinance and the Holidays Ordinance) gives rise to a dualistic system of holiday arrangement which warrants periodic review and mutual tailoring in order to harmonize the two statutes.

Chapter 4. Remuneration and Benefits

§1. Definition of Wages

335. Remuneration paid to the employee for work done is defined by the Employment Ordinance generically under the statutory notion of 'wages'. Wages as given under this legal definition are to consist of all remuneration, earnings or allowances, however designated or calculated, which are capable of being expressed in monetary terms and payable to an employee in respect of work done or to be done under his contract of employment. However, the following items are expressly excluded from the scope of its coverage:

(i) the value of any accommodation, education, food, fuel, light, medical care or water provided by the employer;
(ii) any contribution paid by the employer on his own account to any pension fund;
(iii) any travelling allowance or the value of any travelling concession;
(iv) any sum payable to the employee for defraying any special expense which he has incurred due to the nature of his employment;
(v) any gratuity payable on completion of a contract of employment; and
(vi) end of year payment, or annual bonus, or any proportion thereof, which is of a gratuitous nature and payable at the discretion of the employer; and
(vii) any commission, attendance allowance or attendance bonus which is of a gratuitous nature and is payable only at the discretion of the employer.

336. Therefore, 'wages' as defined include not only the basic wages, but also other associated allowances of a regular or recurrent nature, like costs of living allowance, overtime pay and allowance, attendance allowance, commission and performance bonus. Such a notion of wages is imperative for denominating an employee's (pay) entitlements to such statutory benefits as end of year payment, maternity leave pay, severance payment, long service payment, sickness allowance, holiday pay, annual leave pay and wages in lieu of notice. However, overtime pay is also reckoned for such purposes only inasmuch as it is of a constant nature or its monthly average over the past 12 months is not less than 20 per cent of the average monthly wages of the employee during the same period.

§2. Payment of Wages

337. A wage period is deemed by the enabling legislation, the Employment Ordinance, to recur at monthly intervals unless there was evidence to the contrary. A wage period as a notion is that interval in respect of which wages are payable to the employee. In spite of this legally prescribed norm, it is also a common practice for firms in such trades as building and construction to pay their employees by arrangements of more frequent and shorter intervals, say, for every week or every fortnight.

338. The law has been strenuous in regulating the payment and protection of wages. To begin with, it requires the payment of wages, which become legally due on the last day of the wage period, to be made as soon as practicable but in any case not later than seven days after its expiry. Secondly, in the event of completing a contract of employment, the wages and other sums due to the employee are also payable immediately at that point according to the law, whereby these payments must be effected as soon as practicable but in any case not later than seven days after they are due. Thirdly, upon terminating a contract of employment, all the sum due to the employee must also be paid as soon as is practicable and in any case not less than seven days after these are due. The law specifies such prompt payment to include normally, *inter alia*, such items as:

(i) the amount of wages earned for work done by the employee since the end of the preceding wage period;
(ii) any sum payable in the form of 'wages in lieu of notice' to other party; and
(iii) any other sum due in respect of employment and service rendered as statutory benefits, including severance pay, statutory holiday pay, sickness allowance, maternity leave pay, as well as the recovery of any non-statutory items such as refund of travelling expenses, bonus, gratuity and provident fund payments.

§3. Manner and Place of Payment of Wages

339. The Employment Ordinance prescribes, in addition, the manner and place of effecting wage payment whose scope has been listed above.

340. First, the Employment Ordinance stipulates that wages must be paid on a working day directly to the employee himself or to a person whom the employee has duly appointed as his agent. Such payment has to be effected in legal tender (i.e. cash). However, if the employee agrees, it is possible for wages to be paid by cheque, money order or postal order or directly to the employee's deposit account in a licensed bank.

341. The same ordinance also makes it mandatory for wage payments to be effected in the office or other place which is customarily used by the employer for the payment of wages or in any other place which the employer and the employee may mutually agree between themselves. The law, however, identifies clearly specific places, unless these are themselves the workplaces, where payment of wages is proscribed. Theses censored venues include:

(i) any place of amusement;
(ii) any place where totalizer or pari-mutual betting is conducted or where authorized cash sweeps are organized;
(iii) any place where intoxicating liquor or any dangerous drug is sold; and
(iv) any retail shop or store

342. In addition, employers are also prohibited from making a contract of employment conditional upon an employee's obligation to spend his wages according to designated ways or to specify persons with whom to spend them. In parallel, the employer may not, in any way, bind his employees to patronize any shops, stores, or other places which he has established for the sale of commodities to his employees. Although there is no law preventing an employer from giving an employee food, accommodation or other allowances or privileges in addition to wages, an employer is not allowed to give an employee any intoxicating liquor, dangerous drugs, or a cash sweep or betting ticket as remuneration for his service. (These legal restrictions basically emulate the parallel provisions in the Truck Acts in Britain.)

§4. Protection of Wages

I. General Legal Procedures

343. The basic obligation of the employer to pay wages is hence imperative. Failure of the employer to pay wages within seven days after they are due is a contravention of the relevant provision of the Employment Ordinance. An employer may need in these circumstances to pay interest on the outstanding amount of wages due to the employee. If wages are not paid within one month after they become due, such default can be deemed to imply so serious a breach of his contractual obligation that employees may treat it as a nullification of the contract and are hence entitled to claim wages in lieu of notice from the employer as in the instance of wrongful dismissal without proper notice. But an employee should inform his employer where he is exercising such rights under the Ordinance. If backed by reasonable doubts, these employees who are owed wages can apply to the court for a warrant for the arrest of an employer who is suspected to abscond from the territory in an attempt to evade wage payment.

II. Offences and Penalties

344. An employer who fails to pay wages to an employee when they become due is liable to prosecution and, upon conviction, to a fine of HK$200,000 and to imprisonment for one year.

An employer who fails to pay interest on the outstanding amount of wages to the employee is liable to prosecution and, upon conviction, to a fine of HK$10,000.

III. Business Insolvency

345. In the event of business insolvency, employees can approach the Legal Aid Department, normally upon referral by the Labour Department, for assistance to initiate legal actions in order to register and recover their claims for wages and other sums due in any subsequent bankruptcy or winding-up proceedings, often with 'preferential' rights *vis-à-vis* other creditors. However, these legal procedures for wage recovery are no longer required and have given way to a more simplified and streamlined system of remedial proceedings, as a sequel to the inception, in 1985, of a centrally administered statutory Protection of Wages in Insolvency Fund.

IV. Protection of Wages in Insolvency Fund

346. The surge of business failures in the early 1980s, when Hong Kong was adversely affected by global economic and trade recession, had precipitated widespread grassroots agitation by workers who were owed wages. This syndrome in turn induced an initially reluctant government to create a centrally administered security fund in order to provide a leverage of 'contingency' cover for wages owed to workers by employers who had become insolvent as a result of their business failures. The offshoot arising from an officially appointed Working Group on Problems Experienced by Workers of Companies in Receivership, and its subsequent recommendation was the inception of the Protection of Wages on Insolvency Fund to assist these workers in distress by way of wage advances from a central reserve. The Fund was started in April 1985, ratified by virtue the Protection of Wages on Insolvency Ordinance enacted in the same year. It has since been financed by an annual levy imposed upon companies as a surcharge on their business registration, as prescribed by the Business Registration Ordinance also amended in 1985 to make possible the new levy arrangement.

347. The 1985 legislation thus enables the Fund to pay arrears of wages to employees up to the preferential limit prescribed by both the Companies and Bankruptcy Ordinances – if their employers have lost the ability to pay wages outstanding because of their insolvency or business failures. Such payment, of an *ex gratia* nature intrinsically, may be authorized by the Commissioner for Labour, subject to the ability of the Protection of Wages on Insolvency Board to review his decision upon appeal. Official actions for such disbursement of wage arrears remission can be initiated either upon the submission of an application from the workers affected (provided that a bankruptcy petition or a winding-up petition has been presented against the employer or the firm), or directly by the Commissioner for Labour himself on his discretion, in the case of a small business employing fewer than 20 persons, provided that he is satisfied that:

(i) if the employer is a company, he is unable to pay his debts; or
(ii) if the employer is a person, and not a company, he has been in a bankruptcy state.

348. In essence, the Insolvency Fund helps provide employees in Hong Kong with a cushioning arrangement to tide over their wage security against an employer's default in payment. It enables them to recover wages owed to them while saving them that cumbersome experience of having to go through the often extended and tedious judicial process of liquidation for debt recovery (in particular, the debt cleared is often partial and not in its entirety). This measure hence helps avert the earlier agony of a prolonged waiting period which could have caused genuine hardship to these workers in distress because of lengthy court proceedings. However, the leverage amount available from the Fund to each worker in every claim is also subject to an officially stipulated ceiling. Moreover, what is afforded under such arrangements is basically a 'stop-gap' safety valve operated by the Fund, which can in turn recover the advanced payment from the liquidated assets of the default employer under the relevant legal proceedings. Consistent with the legal purview of the Companies and Bankruptcy Ordinances, the competent scope of the Fund's 'relief' cushion embraces all items of remuneration and earnings, including wages, statutory holiday pay, annual leave pay, end of year double pay, maternity leave pay and sickness allowance payable to the workers who are owed these payments.

§5. Wage Deduction

349. As noted earlier, it is generally not permissible under the law for an employer to deduct wages from his employee's entitlement except under conditions which the Employment Ordinance specifies. Legal deductions are only sanctioned by reason of absence (but only in direct proportion to the time of absence) or to compensate for damages caused to or loss of the employer's goods, equipment or property, yet subject to a limit of HK $800 or one quarter of the wages payable to the employee in every wage period. In addition, there are specified conditions under which wage deductions are allowed. Examples include, *inter alia*, those for:

(i) meals supplied by the employer at the employee's request, at a rate not exceeding the cost of the food;
(ii) residential accommodation provided by the employer, occupied by the employee and/or his family;
(iii) the recovery of any advance or overpayment of wages made by the employer to the employee, subject to a maximum of one-quarter of the wages payable in any wage period and not including interest charges;
(iv) the repayment of any loan advanced by the employer, if these deductions were endorsed by the employee in writing;
(v) contributions to be paid through the employer towards any medical benefit scheme, superannuation scheme, provident fund or thrift scheme which has been lawfully established;
(vi) requirement for such deductions as authorized by law such as to secure salary tax payment owed from the employee; and
(vii) other purposes made at the written request of the employee and with the written approval of the Commissioner for Labour.

350. It is also imperative that the total amount of wage deductions for the various reasons stated above, should not exceed the legally prescribed amount (that is, one half of the wages payable in that period) unless with the written approval of the Commissioner for Labour. This does not include those deductions which are due and proportionate to absence from work.

§6. Vicarious Wage Liability in the Building and Construction Industry

351. Such a statutory obligation incumbent upon the principal contractor in the building and construction industry has entered the statute book, the Employment Ordinance, since 1977, vesting the employees of the principal's subcontractors with a measure of wage security in the event of their employer's defaults in payment.

352. This section of the Ordinance basically invokes the notion of vicarious liability by holding any principal contractors, superior subcontractors or superior nominated subcontractors vicariously responsible for the wages owed to workers in any building works who are hired by their subcontractors. The latter's defaults of wage payment in a succession of notorious industrial disputes in the industry in the 1970s, perhaps symptomatic of the financial vulnerability of the building subcontractors , have caused the government to adopt such an innovative notion for wage protection though limiting its purview just to the building and construction trade.

353. As noted already earlier in the preceding chapter, it is useful to reiterate what the notion (of 'vicarious liability') implies in the context of both common law and statutory regulations in Hong Kong. It denotes a person's likely liability for:

(i) the acts of his servants (or direct employees, in the modern employment context) in the course of employment; –
(ii) the acts of the subcontractors or agents – if he is the principal. Such a principle defining the onus of extended responsibility is actually not entirely new in Hong Kong since it has been invoked also in governing cases of workmen's compensation under the Employees' Compensation Ordinance.

354. The wages claimable under the vicarious principle from the superior parties of the subcontractor in default are, however, limited to the first two months of the arrears of wages owed to the workmen. The law also requires the claimant to have been deployed wholly on work for the principal contractor or for the main nominated subcontractor. Moreover, the claim has to be initiated under a written notice from the employee to the principal contractor or the main nominated subcontractor concerned – to be served within 60 days of the date on which the wages become due.

355. The wages are hence payable by the principal contractor, or in conjunction with every superior subcontractor, either jointly or separately, within 30 days after the receipt of the notice. Any sums thus paid by the principal contractor constitute a debt due from the subcontractor to his principal contractor or superior subcontractor(s). As such, they are recoverable accordingly as a civil debt. It is also possible for the principal or superior subcontractor to claim contributions from his subcontractors who are vicariously liable for the onus of default of the subcontractor in debt. Again, such advanced payment is recoverable by way of deductions from any future proceeds which the principal has to disburse to the subcontractor in default.

§7. Wage Information

356. It has been already noted that an employer is obliged to inform each employee in an intelligible manner, before employment commences, of the conditions regarding wages under which he is to be employed. It is also worth reiterating other associated obligations of the employer to disclose wage information:

(i) if an employer receives a written request for such information from the employee before starting employment, it is his duty to furnish him immediately with such information in writing;
(ii) it is the employer's duty to inform his employee of any changes in wages and other conditions of employment, as well as entertain requests for such information from the employee; and
(iii) it is the employer's obligation to inform and clarify with the employee on such items as overtime and wage deductions at the time of payment of wages for the period concerned.

§8. Wage Standards

357. There was no statutory territory-wide miniumum wage law in Hong Kong until 2011. Before that, the Trade Boards Ordinance, enacted since 1948, provided a machinery for fixing sectoral minimum wages by means of a system of industry-specific trade boards on which both employers and workers in the trade investigated may be represented. However, this legislative instrument has remained on the statute book yet been dormant since its enactment. Besides, foreign domestic helpers as a category of guest workers in Hong Kong are protected by a minimum wage floor which is, however, enforced administratively by way of their two-year contract which has to be attested by the public authority.

358. The government, either before or after 1997, has always been lukewarm about introducing a territory-wide minimum wage law for protecting the general labour force against excessive low pay. It shares apparently the widespread employers' apprehension in the private sector that minimum wage legislation would entail 'unnecessary' and 'undesirable' intervention with the freedom of the private wage and employment market – supposedly a hallmark of the 'free-wheeling' capitalism which sustains Hong Kong's prosperity.

However, as a sequel to the recent waves of recession in the earlier half of this decade, the pathos of low wage conditions, afflicting such trades as catering, security guarding and employees of outsourcing agencies like cleaning has been exposed. In spite of vociferous lobby for a minimum wage legislation (alongside standard work hour regulation) articulated by organized labour on behalf of the industrially deprived, the SAR government sidestepped the issue by instituting, in 2006, a stop-gap measure of a voluntary. Wage Protection Movement in the low pay sectors on a two-year trial basis. However, due to the lukewarm attitude of the employers towards this campaign and persistent canvassing by the labour unions, the government eventually succeeded in wresting consent from the employers' associations and was able to promulgate a statutory minimum wage law in 2011.

Chapter 5. The Suspension of the Individual Labour Contract

§1. Introduction

359. The performance of the individual contract of employment may be suspended when both or either party to the contract cannot perform their respective obligations and pursue their duties temporarily. Such suspension from work can be due to factors independent of their will and competence to work, as the employee may be physically handicapped or incapacitated because of sickness, accident, maternity confinement or other forms of incapacity. Likewise, it may be impossible for the employer to provide work because of a business ebb or shortage of raw materials and produces goods – or even breakdown of office equipment, machines or the plant. Besides, it is also permissible for the employer to institute suspension actions on disciplinary grounds.

360. In Hong Kong, the employee is entitled to a variety of protection and rights in conserving his income and employment security in spite of and in the event of such suspension, or involuntary work pause. Of course, these provisions vary according to the nature of the issues, each of which will be briefly considered as follows.

§2. Work Accidents and Occupational Diseases

361. The Employee's Compensation Ordinance is the competent piece of legislation in Hong Kong governing employers' obligations in the event of accidents at work resulting in injuries, or certain specified occupational diseases afflicting the employee. This statue, renamed from the former Workmen's Compensation Ordinance first enacted in 1953, is largely adapted after a draft Workmen's Compensation (East and West Africa) Model Ordinance circulated to all British overseas dependent territories by the British Colonial Office in 1937.[17]

I. Application of the Employees' Compensation Ordinance

362. As a sequel to its 1980 amendment and extended scope, the law protects virtually all waged and salaried workers manual as well as non-manual, under the preview of the Ordinance. However, there remain specified categories in the workforce who do not fall under its jurisdiction. These include, *inter alia*, outworkers; members of the employer's family who also abide in his residence; as well as casual or intermittent workers (unless they are employed for the purposes of the employer's trade or business, or for the purposes of any game or recreation – provided that

17. The Model Ordinance emulated, in essence, the UK Workmen's Compensation Acts of 1897, 1906 and 1925. However, such a principle was abolished and superseded in 1946 in Britain by the National Insurance (Industrial Injuries) Act, itself inspired by Lord Beveridge. Hong Kong has adopted and continues to practise hence what is basically now a pre-Beveridge system.

they are engaged or paid through a club). Unlike the jurisdiction of most other important labour law, civil service employees are also covered by this Ordinance for their protection against industrial injuries and occupational diseases.

II. Employers' Liability under the Employees' Compensation Ordinance

363. Basically, the legal liability incumbent upon the employer as a sequel to an injury which his employee sustains in the course of and arising out of employment is two-fold. The first is his responsibility to pay compensation to the injured employee and the second is his duty to notify the Commissioner for Labour of the accident. In discharge of the latter obligation, the employer is legally required to inform the Labour Department, in the prescribed form, of any accident within seven days after it happens or is known to him. Should the accident be of a nature serious enough to cause the incapacity of the employee for more than three days, he is, in parallel, liable to compensate the injured employee for his incapacity and loss of wages and hence earning ability. However, he is absolved from such liability of compensation where:

(i) the injury is self inflicted;
(ii) the injury is caused by the employee's addiction to drugs or alcohol, resulting in serious and permanent incapacity; and
(iii) the injury is similar to any injury from where the employee has falsely represented to his employer that he was previously free.

III. Categories of Employee Compensation

364. There are two important notions in Hong Kong crucial in determining such injury compensation to the employee. The first is:

(i) that of making periodical payment, in a manner analogous to the regular payment of normal wages and salaries earned, to the injured employee in supporting him during his temporary incapacity and absence from work during the sick leave period; while the second is
(ii) that of paying a lump-sum in compensation payable to the injured employee himself in the event of permanent incapacity, either total or partial, in respect of the equivalent loss of his earning ability, or to the dependants of the deceased where the industrial accident/occupational disease has resulted in death.

365. Periodical payment, to be disbursed on the normal pay days, are at the rate of two-thirds of the difference between the injured employee's normal monthly earnings (i.e. those prior to the accident) and his monthly earnings after the accident (which would be literally 'nil' in the period of sick leave while recovering from his incapacity which is temporary).

366. On the other hand, compensation for permanent incapacity represents an indemnity payable to the injured person who is hence handicapped for the remaining part of his working life. For this reason, the amount awarded as compensation has to be mitigated by age. The same logic applies to the case of industrial injury resulting in death.

367. Before 1980, compensation for permanent total incapacity used to be fixed at the level equivalent to 48 months' earnings. Legislative amendments to the Ordinance, however, not only liberalized this ceiling of 48 months' earnings but also transformed this number into a variable geared to the following age grades:

Under 40 years	96 months' earnings
Over 40 years but under 56 years	72 months' earnings
Over 56 years	48 months' earnings

368. Correspondingly, compensation for partial permanent incapacity is normally payable in proportion to the relative degree of percentage loss of the injured employee's earning capacity attributable to the accident, as determined by a medical board according to the First Schedule to the Ordinance.

369. The age-specific formula of a sliding scale is applicable as well to fatal accidents, where the amount payable to the deceased's dependants also varies accordingly:

Under 40 years	84 months' earnings
Over 40 years but under 56 years	60 months' earnings
Over 56 years	36 months' earnings

370. Such an employer's obligation to pay the lump-sum indemnity is on top of any periodical payments that have been disbursed to the injured person's temporary incapacity. However, the employer may stop or reduce proportionately the periodical payments otherwise payable to an injured person who chooses, of his own free will, to return to work before the expiry of the sick leave period as medically recommended.

371. The Employees' Compensation Ordinance was amended and extended in 1994 to cover cases where the employee sustains injury from an accident encountered on his way to or from work in the event of inhospitable weather (specifically, as when a typhoon signal no. 8 or above, or a red or black rainstorm warning signal is issued).

IV. Procedures

372. Claims for employees' compensation in respect of injuries sustained by the employee as a result of accidents arising from and in the course of his employment are effective only within a 24-month period after the accident. Where a prima facie case exists, the Commissioner for Labour and his authorized officers may make a claim for compensation on behalf of the injured employee (or his dependants, in the case of fatal accidents).

Where an injury gives rise to a claim to employees' compensation, the injured employee and his employer may agree upon the settlement of the claim in writing to the extent that the agreed level is not less than that payable under the legislation. It is not permissible for the parties to contract out, either by reduction or relinquishment, of their statutory rights and obligations in anticipation of any accidents.[18] Within 21 days after its approval, the employer has to effect payment or becomes liable to a surcharge for delayed payment.

373. To provide the injured employee with a 'fall-back' of financial support in the event of the employer's or the insurer's defaults in discharging payment either of employee compensation or common law damages, the parallel legislation, the Employees' Compensation Assistance Ordinance, enables the employee to apply for a 'make-up' payment from a centrally administered official agency, the Employees' Compensation Assistance Fund which the Ordinance creates. The Fund is financed by a levy imposed on the premium of every employee compensation insurance policy issued by an insurer as from 1 July 1990 onwards.

374. Where the compensation case is contested by the parties (in particular, by the insurer) without reaching an agreement, the dispute has to be adjudicated by judicial proceedings at court. The court, moreover, is the competent authority with the jurisdiction to:

(i) determine the amount of compensation to be paid and its manner of allocation, as in fatal accidents, where the deceased employee leaves only dependants who are partially and not wholly dependent upon his earnings;
(ii) determine the sum, either by periodical payments or lump sum, payable by the employer to meet the costs of providing constant attention where this is necessary in order to enable an injured employee to perform the essential activities of life. Constant care payment is in addition to the compensation that accrues to the employee or his dependants; and
(iii) review the level of periodical payments upon application from either of the parties.

18. Although this may be acceptable under specified restrictive circumstances and given the authorization by the Commissioner for Labour where, for instance, an aged or physically handicapped workman is considered specially liable to meet with an accident or if a workman who wishes to be employed in any specified trade, industry or process is diagnosed as suffering from or possesses records of pneumoconiosis problems.

V. Vicarious Liability of the Principals

375. In industries and trades where contracting and subcontracting exist, such as in building and construction, the principal may be held liable to pay compensation to an employee engaged by his lower-tier contractor or subcontractor who sustains injury from an accident in the course and arising out of the execution of work undertaken by the principal. The principal is also required to give due notice of any such claim to the direct employer of the workman (i.e. his contractor or subcontractor) and in so doing, is entitled to recover the relevant indemnification from the latter. However, this does not preclude the injured employee from seeking and obtaining compensation from his direct employer rather than the principal.

VI. Medical Expenses, Prostheses and Surgical Appliances

376. An employer is obliged to meet the medical expenses and the cost of supplying, fitting and servicing within a ten-year period any relevant prosthesis and surgical appliance that is needed by an employee who has sustained an injury during and because of his work. The expenses of the prosthesis or surgical aids, subject to stipulated maxima for the initial outlay and subsequent repair or renewal, are payable by the employer upon due certification by a Medical Assessment Board.

377. Medical expenses are payable only within 24 months after the accident that gives rise to the injury, and are not otherwise payable if the employer has provided free and adequate medical treatment to the employee.

VII. Occupational Diseases

378. Where an employee contracts certain types of occupational diseases as listed in the schedule to the Employees' Compensate Ordinance, he is also entitled to the law's protection in the event of incapacity as a consequence of such illness. These include, broadly speaking, cases of:

(i) poisoning attributable to the use of handling of, or exposure to the fumes, dust or vapour of specified substances;
(ii) any pathological effect on health due to X-rays, radiating apparatus or radioactive substances; and
(iii) any cataract or ulceration of the eye due to exposure to molten glass or metal, glare from furnaces or exposure to tarry compounds or mineral oils, etc.

VIII. Pneumoconiosis (Compensation) Ordinance

379. Workmen in the construction and quarrying industries are susceptible to a type of occupational hazard causing damages to the lung or other respiratory organs due to sustained exposure to silica, asbestos and dust. In this connection, the Pneumoconiosis (Compensation) Ordinance was conceived in 1980. The enactment has, in addition, epitomized an unprecedented government departure from its hitherto principle of non-intervention into the private liability of workmen's compensation obligations at the workplace level, by creating a mandatory and officially administered central insurance scheme to finance the payment of compensation to employees or their dependants for incapacity sustained during their employment, provided that the cause is due to either of the two principal types of pneumoconiosis: silicosis and asbestosis.

380. The scheme is hence pioneering in Hong Kong in having instituted the innovative notion of industry-wide collective liability, by creating a central Pneumoconiosis Compensation Fund Board, with its members appointed by the Chief Executive (or the governor prior to 1997). However, the prerogative of prescribing the levy structure and specific rates of the levy rests with the Legislative Council, normally upon the advice given by the Fund Board.

381. The notion of a central insurance fund has emanated essentially from the official awareness of the technical difficulty in ascertaining which employer(s) and his workplace are responsible for causing the contracting of the disease, especially in view of the high mobility of job and place of work among building workers across different construction sites. This system was later extended to cover compensation for loss of the ability to hear due to and arising from work.

382. The procedures for processing this type of compensation are broadly comparable to those available in dealing with ordinary employee compensation cases. However, any such claim for compensation and medical expenses should be notified within 24 months after the date of incapacitation. The role of assessing the incapacity due to this type of disease again rests with the Pneumoconiosis Medical Board upon referral from the Labour Department.

383. Due to the possibility that more than a single employer is involved, the law prescribes that in order to calculate this type of indemnity the level of monthly earnings is to be determined by averaging them over a period of 12 months prior to the date of incapacity. The projected rate for an adult employee, moreover, is to apply if a person suffering from pneumoconiosis is younger than 18 years old, or that of a qualified craftsman if he is an apprentice. For a self-employed or unemployed person (who has been previously engaged in these works) earnings are to be construed from published statistics on the overall average daily wages that prevail for the government-funded construction and building projects. Payment for permanent incapacity may be effected by either of two modes at the recipient's choice. Should a lump sum payment be chosen, the indemnity will be so computed as to allow a built-in margin (which is also medially determined) for future deterioration. Otherwise, payment will be split into two separate instalments whereby the actual degree of deterioration is to be determined in a second assessment for computing the second instalment which occurs six years after the initial round of payment.

384. Settlement of pneumoconiosis compensation payable by the Central Fund Board is by way of certification by the Commissioner for Labour. However, such decisions may be reviewed by the Commissioner upon application from the parties and further appeal is permissible to the District Court, should the results of the review still be found unsatisfactory.

IX. Relationship with Civil Liability at Common Law

385. Injuries sustained by an employee may, or course, be associated with and give rise to a legal liability actionable in court against some other person as a third party. Under such circumstances the injured employee may institute, as concurrent with his statutory claim for employees' compensation, any judicial proceedings to recover damages from the third party. Nevertheless, it is normally necessary to deduct any awarded sum of civil damages thus successfully secured from the employees' compensation already paid by the employer, who may thus recover it as reimbursement.

386. If the injury is attributed to the negligence or other wrongful act of the employer, the injured employee may simultaneously seek from the employer employees' compensation as prescribed by statute as well as sue him for civil damages. Again, the awards obtained under these two separate claims are normally held to be mutually offsetting.

X. Compulsory Insurance

387. By virtue of the subsidiary legislation to the Employees' Compensation Ordinance on compulsory insurance, the Governor in Council of the pre-1997 government has declared it mandatory for every employer to take out insurance with an authorized insurer against the employer's liability under the Employees' Compensation Ordinance. This statutory practice has been sustained after the 1997 political handover.

XI. Suspension of Contract During Absence Due to Incapacity

388. Sick leave due to the incapacity of the employee as a result of industrial injury or occupational disease only serves to suspend the performance of his individual labour contract; it does not constitute any justifiable cause for dissolving the contract. Indeed, it is against the law for the employer to terminate the contract of service of an employee who is incapacitated under circumstances which entitle him to employees' compensation, until the latter has either been medically certified as fit to resume his work or the compensation for permanent incapacity, as determined by and after the relevant medical assessment, becomes payable. Violation by an employer of this legal proscription against any discharge of such a nature constitutes a punishable offence.

XII. Other Penal Sanctions

389. It is also a punishable offence under the Ordinance if an employer makes any deductions from the earnings of his employee in order to defray the cost of insurance against his liability to pay employees' compensation.

Failure on the part of the employer to notify the Commissioner for Labour of an accident occurring to his employee is also an offence, punishable by fines.

XIII. Seamen

390. The Employees' Compensation Ordinance is also applicable to the maritime industry, covering all ranks including the masters, seamen and apprentices provided that they are hired as crew members of a Hong Kong registered vessel. In the case of a foreign ship, the Ordinance may also apply to any crew members recruited in Hong Kong, inasmuch as the employer formally submits (or has agreed to submit) to the jurisdiction of the court in Hong Kong, whether or not the accident happens in Hong Kong waters.

XIV. Proposal for Reforms

391. Now that the statutory provisions on compulsory insurance have been brought into force, it may be consistent with the long-range policy objective of erecting a more equitable and efficient machinery of workmen's compensation in Hong Kong for it to evolve a territory-wide comprehensive scheme of central insurance to cover industrial accidents. The main rationale for advancing future reform in such a direction, it appears, is the argument that a centrally administered insurance scheme can be more cost-effective, and perhaps fairer and more efficient than private arrangements, so that it can contribute better to the accrual of actual compensation pay-out to victims and their families. Under the existing system, it appears that the private insurance industry has been able to squeeze and appropriate, as commission, a significant share of the funds disbursed by the employers as workmen's compensation. The implication is hence the possibility that such payment contributed by the employers could have benefited the injured employees more directly and to a greater extent were it not for the filtering effects of the 'intermediary' agencies of the insurers who tax both parties rather heavily in connection with workmen's compensation.

§3. Sickness Allowance

I. General Provisions

392. If an employee is absent from work because of sickness or accident outside work which temporarily prevents him from performing his contractual duty to work, he may not be paid any wages for the period of his incapacity. Nevertheless, if caused by a work accident, the absence is not reckoned as sickness and his stipendiary payment is safeguarded at law as periodical payment to indemnify the injured employee for his incapacity on a temporary basis. This notwithstanding, where the sickness is not caused by an industrial accident, the Employment Ordinance still entitles an employee to receive a stipendiary benefit during the period of his sick leave, at a stipulated rate of his normal pay as a sickness allowance.

393. The provision of sickness allowance is, however, not *ipso facto* but subject to the following conditions:

(i) that the employee must have worked continuously for his employer for a period of one month preceding the sickness causing his absence; and
(ii) that the sick leave is not less than four consecutive days. Paid sickness days are hence accumulated at the rate of two paid sickness days for each completed month of the employee's employment during the first 12 months of employment, four paid sickness days for each completed month of employment thereafter. Paid sickness days can be accumulated up to a ceiling of 120 days.

394. The paid sick leave granted has to be supported by a valid medical certificate, which has to be issued by a recognized medical authority (either under a recognized medical scheme operated by the employer, or a hospital, or a registered medical practitioner) specifying the number of days of absence as well as the nature of the sickness or injury causing the absence. Paid sick leave is differentiated into two categories depending upon the relative stringency of validation by the medical authority which the law prescribes.

395. The first category, with an upper limit of 36 days which can be accumulated by an employee, can be 'consumed' subject to a simple procedure that the sickness is supported by a medical certificate issued by a registered medical practitioner or a registered dentist. However, if the sick leave quota under the first category is used up and exhausted, an employee has to make recourse to the second category, where paid sick leave can be 'stored' up to a ceiling of 84 days. Yet the approval of paid sick leave in this latter category is governed by more stringent conditions, inasmuch as

(i) the sick leave has to be supported by a certificate issued by a hospital doctor or dentist; and
(ii) a brief record of the medical investigation into the case and the treatment hence prescribed has to be produced upon the request of the employer.

II. Level of Sickness Allowance

396. The statutory level of sick leave pay, legally labelled as sickness allowance, is prescribed at four-fifths of the employee's normal pay (excluding overtime), having been raised from the previous rate of two-thirds. The payment of such an allowance has to be made to the employee or his authorized agent not later than the day the employee is next paid his wages. However, where the employee is monthy salaried, the non-deduction of pay for the period of sick leave implies that the employee enjoys full pay already – at a rate more favourable than the legal floor of four-fifths.

III. Other Qualifications Attached to Sickness Allowance

397. There are, in addition, a number of specified exceptions under the Employment Ordinance exempting the employer from his obligation to pay sickness allowance. In this connection, sickness allowance is hence not payable if the unfitness for work is caused by the employee's own serious and willful misconduct – such as indulgence in drug-taking or other unlawful acts, or engaging in fights with malicious intent. Secondly, in order to preclude the accrual of double benefit, the employee may not receive sickness allowance if he is paid already on and for a statutory holiday. By the same token, if he is already entitled to compensation (i.e. periodical payment) under the Employees' Compensation Ordinance for temporary incapacity during the sick leave interval, he is not eligible for sickness allowance pay as well. In the third place, the employee can also lose his right to sickness allowance by failing to accept appropriate medical attention and advice available to him. Specifically, this means that (i) if the employee refuses, without any reasonable excuse, to submit himself for treatment by a company doctor under a recognized medial scheme organized by the employer, or (ii) where hospitalized, he disregards and denies the advice of the company doctor or of the hospital doctor. In either case, sickness allowance is not tenable.

IV. Record of Sickness Allowance

398. An employer is required to maintain a record detailing the entitlement to sickness days and sickness allowance for each of his employees. The entry in the record has to be endorsed by the individual employee within seven days of his return to work from paid sick leave. If an employer fails to maintain such a record, the employee shall be entitled to payment for whatever sick leave is not covered by the record, even if payment has in fact been effected already. An employee can inspect his own sickness allowance record and the Commissioner for Labour is also able to summon, either by written notice to the employer or by notice in the Gazette, any such employer records for a period up to two years preceding his notice.

V. Employment Protection

399. It is not permissible at law for an employer to dissolve the contract of employment of an employee on a paid sickness day, except in cases of summary dismissal due to the employee's serious misconduct. This provision hence confers a measure of security on the employment of the employee absent from work due to and during his sickness. An employer who violates such a clause commits an act of unlawful dismissal and is liable to recompense the employee with the following:

(i) wages in lieu of notice;
(ii) a further sum equivalent to seven days' pay; and
(iii) any sickness allowance to which the employee is entitled.

§4. Pregnancy and Maternity

I. In General

400. The case of a female employee who is incapacitated due to pregnancy and maternity can also apply for the temporary suspension of her contract of employment due to her confinement on maternity absence from work, as provided in Hong Kong under the Employment Ordinance.

401. To qualify for maternity leave, a female employee needs to have worked for the same employer under a 'continuous contract', provided that she has given notice of her pregnancy to the employer. To protect her because of childbirth, the law entitles the employee to a continuous period of ten weeks' maternity leave. However, if confinement occurs later than the expected date of confinement, she is eligible for a further period of leave equal to the number of days from the day after the expected date of confinement to the actual date of confinement. She may also enjoy an additional period of leave for not more than four weeks on the ground of illness or disability due to her pregnancy or confinement.

II. Employer's Consent and Giving Notice

402. Given the consent of her employer, a pregnant employee may commence her pre-natal leave from two to four weeks before the expected date of confinement. However, if the employee does not decide on the date, or fails to secure her employer's agreement, the employee's leave would begin four weeks immediately before the expected date of confinement and ends six weeks immediately after the actual date of confinement. If her natal confinement occurs before the scheduled maternity leave, her maternity leave would be deemed to commence on the date of confinement. In this case, the employee is obliged to give notice of the date of confinement and her intention to take her ten-week maternity leave to her employer within seven days of her confinement.

403. In addition, a female employee who intends to take any special extended maternity leave is also obliged to give her employer due notice to that effect. Unless it is required by the employer, it is not necessary for the employee on maternity leave to give notice of her intention to return work after confinement. But where required, such notice must not be less than eight days before she returns and shall state the date on which she returns to work as well as the date on which she was confined, unless the employer has been so notified previously.

III. Payment for Maternity Leave

404. An employee giving birth is eligible for paid maternity leave subject the following conditions:

(i) she has been employed under a continuous contract for not less than 40 weeks immediately before the commencement of her maternity leave;
(ii) she has given notice of pregnancy and her intention to take maternity leave to her employer after pregnancy has been confirmed, by presenting, for example, a medical certificate confirming her pregnancy to the employer; and
(iii) she has produced a medical certificate specifying the expected date of confinement if so required by her employer.

Maternity leave pay, stipulated by law at the level equivalent to four-fifths of the employee's normal wages, is payable for a period of ten weeks. Payment should be effected on the normal pay day of the employee. For an employee employed on piece rates or whose daily wages are variable, the maternity leave pay should be a sum equivalent to the average daily wages earned by her on the days she had worked during every complete wage period (the wage period should last not less than 28 days nor exceed 31 days).

IV. Medical Certification of Maternity Leave

405. A pregnant female employee who has given notice to her employer of her intended maternity leave may have to produce a medical certificate testifying her pregnancy or confinement as well as specifying the (expected) date of confinement. However, such an obligation applies only if so required by her employer. If summoned by the employer, the female employee who intends to take special extended maternity leave must also produce a medial certificate in evidence of the illness or disability arising out of her pregnancy or confinement. Under the law, only a registered medical practitioner or a registered midwife has the proper authority to issue such a medical certificate in evidence of pregnancy, confinement and the expected or actual date of confinement. By the same token, only a registered medical practitioner can issue the working mother with a certificate of illness or disability arising out of pregnancy or confinement.

V. Protection of Employment During Maternity Leave

406. The individual contract of employment remains in force and valid while being suspended as the employee takes her maternity lave. However, to provide express protection to the female employee in respect of her job tenure, the Employment Ordinance states specifically that maternity leave, whether paid or unpaid, does not in any way break the continuity of employment of a female employee with her present employer. Moreover, during the period between the date on which the pregnant employee gives notice of her intention to take maternity leave and the date on which she is due to return to work (upon the expiry of the leave), a contractual 'freeze' applies to the labour contract, prohibiting any act of the employer to terminate her service.

407. If a pregnant employee is dismissed by her employer before she has served a notice of pregnancy, she may serve such notice immediately after being informed of her dismissal. Under such circumstances, her employer must withdraw the dismissal or the notice of dismissal. However, it may be permissible for the employer to dismiss a pregnant employee where:

(i) the discharge is a case of summary dismissal due to the employee's serious misconduct; or
(ii) the employment is, as expressly agreed between the parties, on probation for a period of not more than 12 weeks and the dismissal is for reasons other than pregnancy.

408. Contravention of the above protective clause on job security during maternity leave is not only a punishable offence but also entitles the aggrieved female employee to a retributory payment if she is eligible, by virtue of the criteria mentioned earlier, to paid maternity leave. This payment is tantamount to what should have accrued to the working mother as the pay for her ten weeks' maternity leave entitlement. In addition, a sum of one month's pay equivalent is payable as payment in lieu of notice for dissolving the contract. Moreover, the employer is liable to prosecution and upon conviction to penalties of a fine attached not merely to acts of unlawful dismissal by the employer during the protected period of maternity leave but also to his defaults in failing to grant the female employee the appropriate maternity leave and the leave pay as well as such contingencies as expenses for medical examination, post-natal medical treatment, etc. As a sequel to an amendment to the Employment Ordinance in the 1990s, punitive legal sanctions have also been extended to prevent an employer from requiring a pregnant employee to handle heavy, hazardous or harmful work.

VI. Paternity Leave

409. There is in the pipeline a proposed enactment on paternity leave of three days, with payment at the minimal level of four-fifths of normal pay. By comparison, comparable benefits in the civil service are better, providing the working father with five days and full pay.

§5. Public and Auxilary Civil Service

410. In Hong Kong, the law is silent governing the provision of leave or otherwise to an employee when he has to suspend temporarily the performance of his labour contract because he is called upon to discharge his civic duties or public service during his normal working hours. Examples of these public duties are to serve as a juror; to participate in electoral activities; to serve as a member of the Executive Council, Legislative Council, or the District Council; to serve on the variety of officially appointed advisory/consultative committees; as well as to attend the training sessions and active duties for auxiliary civil or police services.

411. However, in the specific instance of jury service, the law is unequivocally clear in assigning priority to such a duty over that owed to the employer. This is because the Jury Ordinance makes explicit the legal censure of any employer who discriminates or attempts to discriminate against an employee for performing his duties as a juror (in which case, he is liable to summary prosecution under the Jury Ordinance, Laws of Hong Kong, Chapter 3, Section 33). It is hence obligatory for the employer to grant his employee the necessary leave enabling the latter to perform his juror duties when called to these services.

412. Nevertheless, for the above and other cases of absence from work for performing these varied public duties, the law does not make it an employer's duty to pay or provide a guaranteed income to the employee during the necessary interval of absence. Nevertheless, a Hong Kong citizen is normally paid a special allowance by the government when being called to perform jury duties or duties in the auxiliary,civil or police services.

413. As a general principle, the Employment Ordinance provides that if an employee is absent from work on a day by reason of law, mutual arrangement or the custom of the trade or business, he is deemed to be continuing in the employment of his employer, so that the day shall be reckoned to count as a day on which he has worked for the purpose of determining the continuity of his individual contract of employment.

§6. Annual Leave

414. Annual leave and its taking will not constitute a temporary suspension of the individual contract of employment. This would not break the continuity of employment. The statutory rules governing the scheduling of such vacation and its payment are provided under the Employment Ordinance as have been detailed in an earlier section in Chapter 3.

§7. Technical Disruption of Work and Other Economic Reasons

415. The Employment Ordinance contains 'lay-off' provisions which govern the temporary suspension of the performance of the labour contract due to the shortage or non-provision of work. The law, however, is neither overtly explicit nor unequivocal in specifying the conditions under which suspension or lay-off of such a nature can occur. Yet, at common law, these are in general taken to include 'lay-off' for reasons of loss or reduction in production, unforeseeable breakdown of plant, machinery or office equipment or comparable reasons where there is either express agreement between the parties or an implied condition of employment in the relevant establishment or industry. It has been construed by the Labour Department that the maximum duration of lay-off permissible is not to exceed a half of the total number of normal working days in any period of four consecutive weeks. Otherwise, it must not exceed a third of the total number of working days in any given period of 26 consecutive weeks. Should such a spell of non-provision of work go beyond the 'legally' admissible level, severance pay will become payable to the laid-off employee(s) since the relevant labour contract will have, by implication, been deemed to have been breached or frustrated by the employer. Conversely, the continuity of the individual contract of employment cannot be broken or in any way curtailed by lay-off, so long its duration is within the prescribed and permissible limits.

§8. Bad Weather

416. There are no specific clauses in the Employment Ordinance or any laws in Hong Kong governing the suspension of performance of the individual labour contract due to bad weather. Although Hong Kong is vulnerable to seasonal rainstorms and typhoons (whose gale force wind can cause widespread activity disruptions and property destruction), the law has opted not to prescribe any standard rules or procedures to cover work and the workplace under such emergency situations. Instead, the necessary contingencies are basically left to the mutual agreement between the employer and his employee, taking into account such factors as the nature of the employment and the individual employee's place of residence, the availability of transport, as well as other constraints.

417. However, in its advice offered to the public, the Labour Department encourages employers to reach an agreement in advance with their employees on the procedures governing work and their release from work on the approach of or during a typhoon or rainstorm (the Hong Kong Observatory has instituted a system of escalating signals of warning on the approach of a typhoon of a rainstorm). These voluntary rules are expected to include, *inter alia*, specifying the method of payment or non-payment of wages under various weather conditions. In the absence of any legal stipulations in dealing with work or non-work in inhospitable weather, employers are advised to release their employees, for their safety, at reasonable times, so as to enable them to reach their homes while public transport is still in service, except for those who have to engage themselves in essential or emergency duties.[19]

§9. Strike

418. The Employment Ordinance expressly provides that the continuity of the individual contract of employment cannot be construed to be broken due to any absence because of a strike (by the employees) or a lock-out (by their employer). Nevertheless, a day on which the employee is absent for these reasons shall not be deemed as a day worked or a day on which he has been provided with work. It may hence be construed, in this connection, that even if the industrial action does not impede directly or break the continuity of the labour contract, it may be yet deemed to do so if the employee fails to work for 18 hours or more in a calendar week because of the strike without advance notice to the employer.

§10. Suspension on Disciplinary Grounds

419. As already mentioned above in an earlier section, the employee may be suspended by the employer for disciplinary reasons, thereby precluding effectively the performance of the labour contract. Such suspension of an employee from work without dissolving the relevant contract can be justified when the employee has committed or is reasonably suspected of having committed some acts which would have entitled the employer to dismiss him summarily. However, the suspension may not last for a period beyond 14 days unless criminal proceedings have been initiated but not concluded within that period. In the latter situation, the suspension may be extended until the completion of such proceedings.

420. For suspension actions of a disciplinary nature to be initiated, an employer is not obliged to give advance notice of his decision before instituting it, nor to pay any wages in lieu of notice. Nor is he obliged to pay the suspended employee any wages, although there is nothing to prevent him from making an *ex gratia* payment if he wishes to do so.

§11. Agreement between the Employer and the Employee

421. It is generally permissible at law for the parties to the labour contract to agree mutually to suspend the performance of their contract for a certain period of time, as in the form of leave with or without pay. Such voluntary suspension of the individual's work duty by mutual consent may apply, *inter alia*, to enable employees to attend full-time courses of study in educational and training institutions, either overseas or local or to pay home visits to their native villages in mainland

19. Such a 'suasive' guideline on the desirable procedures is propagated annually by the Labour Department, via the mass media, in anticipation of the rainy and typhoon seasons.

China, etc. Normally, there is no responsibility incumbent upon the employer to pay the employee wages during such a 'leave' period. However, it has been common as a good personnel or human resource practice, and for advancing staff development and commitment to the organization, for the employer to grant 'full-pay' study leave in sponsoring his employee to pursue a course of study which may contribute to his business.

422. While taking such leave as endorsed by mutual consent, the employee is normally considered to continue in the employ of his employer without any break in 'continuity', similar to instances of statutory holiday, rest day, sick leave, maternity leave or annual leave taking.

Chapter 6. The End of the Individual Labour Contract

§1. Job Security in General

423. In Hong Kong, severance pay provisions, introduced since 1974 under the Employment Ordinance, have provided a measure of core safeguard to employees whose employment is adversely affected by redundancy or lay-off. Subsequently, the 1986 enactment of the long-service payment provisions entailed an improvement in enshrining an employee's employment security, entitling the discharged employees to such payment according to the dual factors of their age and length of service. However, the functional importance of the long-service payment has been eclipsed with the introduction of mandatory provident fund on an economy-wide basis for the working population at the beginning of this century to cover the income security of the retired persons.

424. Previously, an employer in Hong Kong was considered generally to enjoy an almost absolute prerogative to discharge his employee, provided that he respected the appropriate term of notice or the equivalent in terms of payment (i.e. wages in lieu, or WILON). Other than the above requirement, the employer was not obliged at law to justify the dismissal, since there was no provision on any legal redress or sanction otherwise made available under the notion of 'unfair dismissal'. However, as a sequel to an amendment to the Employment Ordinance in the 1990s, the notion of 'unreasonable dismissal' has been introduced to bestow upon an employee a measure of employment protection. An employee is entitled to claims for remedy against unreasonable dismissal if he is discharged other than for a valid reason as specified in the Ordinance, and provided that he has been in continuous employment for the same employer for a period of not less than 24 months. Correspondingly, the Labour Tribunal or any court of law has also become competent to order reinstatement of the discharged employee as a remedial measure.

§2. Freedom to Enter Into and Dissolve a Contract

425. To protect a manual worker who may have inadvertently submitted himself to an excessively long labour contract which may have otherwise implied a form of servitude, the Employment Ordinance deems his employment to be covered by a monthly contract renewable from month to month if such a contract should have been made voluntarily by the direct parties to last longer, for a period of six months or more. In the case of non-manual employment, the contract may theoretically extend for a period in excess of six months – but only where it can be so proved in writing and having been signed by the parties, otherwise it will still be treated as a monthly contract.

426. The rationale for the above legal presumptions rests with the international norm that it would have contradicted the principle of freedom of labour – a principle that Hong Kong has endorsed in applying the relevant International Labour Conventions nos. 29 and 105 on Forced Labour and the Abolition of Forced Labour

– that the employee should be prevented, for his protection, from binding himself under contract to serve the employer for all his life.

427. The implication has been, at common law, that the employee is capable of terminating an individual labour contract of indefinite duration with a period of notice and that any clause in the contract stating to the contrary could be deemed null and void. The situation may be more equivocal, however, in the case of a contract for a defined duration – like a contract concluded for a stated period until a specified retirement age which could contradict, given the presumption noted above, the general principle censuring a lifetime labour contract. The logic appears to be that while such a contract does not by its intent purport to bind the employee in perpetuity, it may effectively preclude the employee from exercising his freedom of labour – as in the instance of a professional soccer player who may enter a fixed-term career to last until his career is more or less run down, say, at the age of 35.

428. In this connection, it appears reasonable to assume that the length of the employee's working life expectancy should be taken into account in determining whether or not the duration of any labour contract is unduly prolonged and has inappropriately deprived the employee of his freedom of labour.

§3. Organizational or Ownership Changes

429. In the event of amalgamations, mergers, takeovers, sales, transfer and changeover in ownership of enterprises, etc. there is no automatic transfer of the individual employment relationship to the new employer. Although there is a general presumption that a labour contract applies by its intent only to the original parties and that any inter-employer transfer of the employed without the latter's consent is not lawful, a transfer of the employment relationship can be effected, together with the liabilities and obligations formerly incumbent on the old employer, if the acquirer, acting in the capacity of the new employer, offers to re-engage the serving employee(s), provided that the conditions offered for the re-engagement are no worse than those under the previous contract and that the employee is to continue to retain and enjoy his full seniority as if there were no break in the continuity of his employment. Of course, it is not mandatory upon the acquirer to take over the whole complement of the existing staff and workers. Should he decide not to inherit the onus of continued hiring, these employees will have to be discharged by their old employer (i.e. the transferer who relinquishes the enterprise) with the appropriate term of notice or payment in lieu of notice plus the full amount of severance pay due to the individual employee in accordance with his length of service.

§4. Seniority and Job Security

430. Collective agreements concluded by trade unions in the industrially advanced countries always cover, where they apply at the plant level, the relevant rules for lay-off and recall, generally based upon the employee's seniority in the trade or firm concerned. The norm tends to be the 'first-in-last-out' or reciprocally, the 'last-in-first-out' principle.

431. The explicit recognition of such a seniority rule for priority discrimination in a case of 'lay-off', retrenchment or collective discharge is, nevertheless, not widespread among Hong Kong enterprises. Yet the employee's legal entitlement to severance pay and the amount payable are closely associated with his length of service. There is, first, the qualifying criterion of at least two years' continuous service in order to be eligible for severance pay. In the second instance, for those employees thus qualified, the actual size of severance pay accruing to the individual again depends upon his history of service, calculated pro-rata at the rate of two-thirds of his last month's pay (or HK$15,000, whichever is less) of every reckonable year of service for the monthly rated employees or, in the case of the piece-rated, daily rated or other time-rated employees, a comparable rate of 18 days' pay.

432. The introduction of long service payment in the mid-1980s under the Employment Ordinance was also anchored in the equivalent notion of recognizing length of service as the principal variable for determining entitlement and the formula of payment. As its title makes it clear, the nature and rationale of such a statutory payment is to explicitly reward the employee's stable service and attachment to the enterprise – payable either because of resignation due to ill health or old age or upon discharge for reasons other than summary dismissal or retrenchment (as and when severance pay is normally claimable instead). Given such a spirit of legislation, the long-service payment provisions have been amended and improved since their first enactment to harmonize with a dualistic criterion of (i) length of service; and (ii) age, being a factor to adjust payment to the employee according to a sliding scale.

§5. Lifetime Commitment in Employment

433. Although at law the principle of freedom of labour ordains that a labour contract should not bind an employee to serve a single employer for his whole lifespan, the loyal commitment of the servant to his master or employer in permanency has been a cherished norm in pre-industrial societies and is still a common practice in Japanese enterprises, and in other successful cases of Asian or even Western management. Such loyalty in employment sanctifies a non-contractual bond of mutual trust between the parties (conceptually represented as the 'psychological contract') and is normally rewarded by the employer with promotion, status, pay increments, permanence of employment and other fringe benefits, such as long service or seniority bonuses, accommodation and educational subsidies, superannuation benefits and other welfare measures, often based upon 'seniority'.

434. In Hong Kong, many employers, notably in the civil service, comparable large corporate conglomerates as well as small traditional Chinese businesses, do place a strong value upon the loyalty and commitment of their employees. As noted in an earlier section, there has been a custom here in employment practice for firms to differentiate the employee's status according to whether he is a permanent worker, a permanent casual or a casual worker. In this connection, the relative permanency of job tenure varying between the employees is heavily geared to such differentials in employment status. Generally speaking, it is the norm for the permanent workers to be retained as the last group in the event of redundancy. Even where retrenchment is inevitable, it is not unusual for these permanent workers to be paid off with a comparatively generous package in terms of severance pay and other compensatory items.

435. However, in the advents of globalization and intensified competition today, the practice of flexi-hiring has also become increasingly popular in the Hong Kong labour market. Such developments have eroded the norm of permanent employment among large corporate employers, especially as their agendas of business restructuring to rationalize themselves into leaner and more competitive entities have led to cyclical waves of downsizing, delayering and lay-off of personnel. In this context, large-scale employing bureaucracies like Cathay Pacific Airways, Hong Kong Bank, the power plants and even the government have waived their commitment to permanent employment practices as their time-honoured strategy of stabilizing and motivating their work force. For instance, the government has now shifted to 'fixed-term' contract hiring of new recruits in place of permanent and pensionable employment, while Cathay Pacific has also commenced casual hiring of flight attendants on an hourly basis.

§6. General Ways of Dissolving an Individual Contract of Employment

436. At common law, a labour contract can come to an end lawfully under any of the following situations governing the dissolution of such a contract:

(a) upon the expiry of the period for which the contract for a definite period was concluded;
(b) upon the completion of the precisely indicated work for which the appropriate type of labour contract was concluded;
(c) upon the mutual consent by both parties to the contract, if it was concluded for an indefinite period or for a definite duration before its expiry;
(d) upon the death of the employee. However, the death of the employer does not invariably frustrate the employment contract, provided that the ownership of the business passes to a personal representative of the decreased employer and that his personal representative within four weeks after the death renews the employee's contract or re-engages him under a new contract (in writing) on terms not less favourable than the previous one. Otherwise, the employee of the deceased employer is to be treated as being terminated by reason of redundancy and is henceforth entitled to severance payment;
(e) as an Act of God (*force majeure*) which is an event independent of the will of both parties to the contract, and which puts one or both of them in such a position that it is impossible for them to carry out their contractual obligations,

partly or totally. If the impossibility of executing the contract is definitive, the contract will be terminated. The party who invokes the 'Act of God' justification will bear the onus of proof. Events which are acceptable as Acts of God must make the execution of the contract absolutely impossible;

(f) by frustration of contract, where the contract is terminated because of a change of circumstances such that performance of the contract has become unlawful (for instance, as contrary to public order) or physically impossible (as in the event of prolonged sickness) or such that the whole basis and object of the original contract has been destroyed. This means that the contract has come to an end, *de jure*.

§7. Dissolution by Serving a Term of Notice According to Statute

I. Continuous Contract

437. The notion of a 'continuous contract' is of key importance governing the individual contract of employment under the Employment Ordinance – itself a notion borrowed from the UK Contract of Employment Act of 1963. Just as legal entitlements of the employee to such benefits as rest days, statutory paid holidays, annual leave with pay, maternity leave and pay, sickness allowance, severance pay and long-service payment, etc., are conditional upon the employee having served the same employer continuously, the obligations of the two parties upon the dissolution of the contract are governed in a large measure by this important notion of a continuous contract.

438. A 'continuous' contract is a contract of employment which is able to satisfy the relevant qualifying conditions prescribed by the first Schedule to the Employment Ordinance. 'Continuity' is basically defined with reference to the minimum time period specified and the manner whereby employment is served during that period. Once such a criterion is satisfied, its 'continuous' property cannot be revoked even by express mutual agreement to the contrary. Specifically, an employee is deemed by the law to have been in continuous employment if he at any time has been in employment for four weeks or more next preceding such time. To define 'continuity' in the notion, each week (that is, a calendar week ending on a Saturday) must be one in which the employee has worked at least 18 hours. The manner of his wage calculation and payment is not a relevant determinant in this connection for reckoning 'continuity'.

439. If the employee would usually have worked but has been absent because of illness or injury, the day(s) concerned will be reckoned still as a day(s) worked for the definition of 'continuity', provided that any such incapacity lasting for more than 48 hours is evidenced by a medical certificate issued by a registered medical practitioner. By the same token, day(s) of absence shall also be counted as a (day) worked in the instance of statutory holidays, paid annual leave, rest days, or maternity leave. Where an employment relationship has been established to be a continuous one, its tenure is not to be broken by an absence on account of a strike in which the employee takes part or because of a lock-out by the employer. These days of absence will not be treated, however, as days worked for the purpose of determining the 'continuity' of employment.

II. Notice

440. Notice is the unilateral expression of the decision of either of the two parties, the employer or the employee, that he no longer considers himself to be bound by the existing contract after a given date. In other words, the party serving the notice indicates his desire to have the labour contract dissolved or terminated after the date concerned. The period that lapses between the articulation of this intention and the intended time at which the contract comes to an end therefore constitutes the term or period of notice. Both the employer and the employee alike enjoy equal and absolute rights to end or initiate the ending of a labour contract, as construed from the principle of freedom of labour and freedom of trade. However, the obligation is also incumbent upon the parties, whether at common law or by virtue of the Employment Ordinance, to respect a term of notice whose function is, *inter alia*, to mitigate the disruptive or negative implications of such a unilateral decision for the other party. This 'cushioning' interval affords, for example, the employee a chance to look for a new job while still in his existing employment and reciprocally, the employer to find a new employee as a replacement for the position before it is vacated.

III. Duration of Contracts

441. Given the above definitions, a key factor determining the appropriate term of notice in order to dissolve or terminate a contract of employment is the concept of the duration of a labour contract, which is in turn associated with whether it is continuous or not.

442. An important rule embodied in the Employment Ordinance in this connection is that a contract of employment, if it has become a continuous one, is assumed to be a contract for one month renewable from month to month in the absence of express agreement to the contrary. Such a presumption of a monthly continuous contract cannot be displaced unless it could be established that there was an express agreement to the contrary that it was not a monthly one. Such an agreement purporting to establish a contract other than a monthly one must be a clear and express one, although it need not be in writing.

443. On the other hand, it is legally possible for a contract of employment to be concluded for a period in excess of one month, whether or not it is a continuous contract. However, such an agreement must be produced in writing signed by each party, or else it will still be deemed to be a monthly contract renewable from month to month. Moreover, as stated earlier, if a contract of employment is entered into by a manual worker for a period of six months or more or for an equivalent number of working days, the contract, whether evidenced in writing or not, will still be deemed to be a monthly contract renewable from month to month. This is a protective measure which, in conformity with the International Labour Convention on Contracts of Employment (Indigenous Workers), serves to shield a manual worker from being tied to one particular employer for unduly long periods with liability to pay a substantial sum in damages should he leave the latter's employ in breach of the contract.

IV. Manner of Termination by Means of Notice

444. Either party to a contract of employment may at any time terminate the contract by giving to the other party the appropriate notice, either oral or in writing, of his intention to do so. Preferably the notice should be given and served in writing.

V. The Term of Notice

A. Commencement

445. The term of notice for dissolving or terminating a labour contract under the Employment Ordinance can be served and take effect from any time. It is not necessary to synchronize it with the ending of a wage period, a week or a month.

B. Length

446. The length of notice required to terminate an individual contract of employment under the Employment Ordinance is governed by and dependent upon the following criteria:

(i) whether or not the contract is a 'continuous' one;
(ii) whether or not the contract, if a 'continuous' one, is deemed by law as a monthly contract; otherwise, whether or not there is express provision by contract to the contrary;
(iii) whether or not the contract incorporates a provision or an agreed and valid period of notice; and
(iv) whether or not the employment regulated by the contract has been expressly defined by agreement as on probation.

447. These rules governing the term of notice are, however, independent of the employee's length of service or the relative difficulty of those affected in finding an alternative employment or a replacement in the relevant trade or industry. Specially, the salient provisions in the law prescribe that:

(i) where the contract is or is deemed by law as a contract for one month renewable from month to month and where the term of notice has not been expressly agreed, the reasonable period is normally not less than a month;
(ii) where the contract is or is deemed by law as a contract for one month renewable from month or month and where the term of notice has been expressly agreed, the agreed period which cannot be less than seven days. If the agreed term was less than seven days, it would be deemed null and void, in which instance the preceding rule (i) would instead apply;
(iii) where the contract is a continuous one but which is other than a monthly contract according to mutual agreement and where the term of notice is also laid down under express agreement, the agreed period cannot be less than seven days. If the agreed period was less than seven days, such an agreement would be null and void but the same rule as the foregoing (i) and (ii) would apply;
(iv) where the contract is a continuous one other than a monthly one as agreed mutually between the parties, but where the term of notice has not been yet agreed expressly upon, the reasonable period cannot be less than seven days;
(v) where the contract is not a continuous contract and where the term of notice has been expressly agreed, the period as it has been agreed upon between the parties;
(vi) where the contract is not a continuous contract and where the term of notice has not been expressly agreed, the reasonable period as determined according to common law principles;
(vii) where the contract is on probation as it has been expressly agreed upon, the agreed upon period if the term of notice has been expressly agreed upon. Otherwise, as the Employment Ordinance prescribes in the absence of such an agreement, no notice is required in the first month but during the succeeding second and third months, the term of notice is for a reasonable period which cannot be less than seven days.

A ‘month’ in the above context of giving notice is to begin on the day when the notice of dissolution is given and to end at the end of the day before the corresponding date in the following month. The term of notice to be respected by the party who terminates the contract unilaterally is the same or symmetrical for both the employer and the employee.

VI. Term of Notice for Employees at Retirement Age

448. There is no statutory regulation on retirement age and the law does not specifically define the term of notice expected to be served upon the employer or the employee upon retirement. Accordingly, it can be assumed that in the case of retirement the general rules on notice as given in the foregoing apply.

VII. Waiver of the Right to Notice

449. Either party to a contract of employment may, at the time when notice is to be given, waive his right to notice or the payment in lieu of such a notice. In this connection, an employer entitled to receive a term of notice from his employee on resignation can agree to release him immediately. Reciprocally, an employee being served with a notice of discharge can waive his right to notice, either in part or in full, in order that he can leave his employment earlier, before the notice period expires. However, it would constitute a case of 'contracting out' if such a waiver were built into the individual contract of employment at the time of its formation in anticipation of its possible dissolution at a later date in the future. According to the Employment Ordinance, 'contracting out' occurs when any term of labour contract purports to extinguish or to reduce any rights, benefits or protection which the Ordinance affords. In such instances, the contractual clause curtailing these protected rights at issue will be deemed null and void.

VIII. Suspension of the Term of Notice

450. The law does not specify the conditions and rules governing the suspension of the term of notice. However, it is generally assumed that the incidence of such temporary breaks as those caused by lay-off, sick leave, maternity leave, statutory holidays and annual leave should serve to suspend, where these occur, the term of notice. In the instance of a rest day break, however, the situation is more ambiguous. For a one-week term of notice, the norm requiring seven days' wages as payment in lieu of notice is suggestive of the suspension of the notice term. For a one-month notice term, on the other hand, the corresponding payment in lieu of notice is for one full month or 30/31 days in the case of a monthly rated employee, but only 26 days in the instance of a piece-rated or daily rated employee. The latter practice, in having excluded the four weekly rest days in a month from reckoning, seems to imply the reverse – i.e. the principle of the non-suspension of term of notice on rest days.

IX. Rights and Duties of the Parties During the Term of Notice

451. The individual contract of employment is to be maintained during and throughout the term of notice, so that all the legal obligations and duties attending employment are still effective and binding on the parties during the term of notice. Basically, the employer is required to continue furnishing work for the employee at the same level of remuneration and under the same conditions. Reciprocally, the employee is obliged to continue working and serving the employer – that is continuing to perform his normal duties at work.

452. Given the above status quo rule, any substantial and unilateral alteration in the essential conditions of the contract is hence liable to be held as constituting a wrongful breaking of the contract. Such breaking can, in turn, be a cause for compensation to be effected in the form of payment in lieu of notice. For example, an employer's act in inducing or coercing an employee to leave earlier than the expiry of the period of notice which he has served to the latter may be held liable for an act of 'constructive dismissal'. This notwithstanding, it is permissible for the employer to relieve the employee of his obligation to work yet continue to pay him in the period while the term of notice is being served out. During the period of notice, the law as it now stands does not provide for any contingencies whereby the employee can be allowed occasional intervals of absence from work while being retained on normal payroll in order to look for a new job elsewhere. In practice, it is not uncommon for the employers to grant affected employees such leave concession in the event of redundancy. In other cases, the employer may opt to give the retrenched employees payment in lieu and release the latter earlier rather than having the notice term served out.

§8. Compensation: Payment in Lieu of Notice

453. At common law, the mandatory obligation to observe the appropriate notice in order to dissolve a contract unilaterally by either party is notional, because the law enables, in practice, either side to avoid the onus of a notice requirement by allowing its substitution by the alternative of paying the other party wages in lieu of notice. This principle has been incorporated into the Employment Ordinance and as such, is symmetrical in general between the employer and the employee. The common interpretation now prevails that technically neither party can refuse to accept being paid the appropriate wage equivalent in lieu of notice and insist upon the corresponding notice being worked out.

454. In this connection, either party to a labour contract can, at law, terminate the contract unilaterally without notice if there is an agreement to pay the other party a sum in lieu of notice as equal to the remuneration that would have accrued from work during the notice term. By extension of this logic, either party, albeit having given proper notice in the first instance, may also terminate the contract unilaterally at any time during the term of notice, inasmuch as he agrees to pay the other party the amount equal to the wages otherwise payable for the remaining part of the term of notice not yet served. Such a sum in lieu of notice has to be paid as soon as practicable and not later then seven days after termination. This obligation to effect prompt payment is, however, applicable expressly to the employer at law since there is no specific provision of a similar obligation placed upon the employee although any such payments, if due from the resigning employee, are deductible from the wages otherwise payable to him.

455. In the above context, 'wages' refers to all remuneration, earnings or allowance including pay for habitual overtime work (see the legal definition of 'wages' in Chapter 4), however designated or calculated, which are capable of being expressed in monetary terms and payable to an employee in respect of work done or to be done under the performance of the labour contract. The value of accommodation, education, food and welfare contingencies provided by the employer in kind, any contribution by the employer to any pension fund or provident fund, and payments covering expenses (e.g. travelling) and liberalities (e.g. annual bonus or gratuity payable at the discretion of the employer) are, however, not considered as wages. If the employee is remunerated by the piece or task, the amount of pay in lieu of notice shall be denominated in terms of the average daily wages earned by the employee for the period of twelve months preceding the notice. If this is not practicable, reference should be made to an employee in the same trade or occupation who is engaged for similar work in the same district over the comparable period.

§9. The Breaking of the Individual Labour Contract

I. The Notion of Breaking

456. It has not been common in Hong Kong to invoke the notion of 'breaking' which is the act by which either the employer or the employee puts an end immediately to a labour contract for a 'just cause' – that is, as a consequence of a shortcoming or default in the other party's performance of his legal or contractual obligations which is so serious and detrimental that any further collaboration between the two parties is rendered definitely and immediately impossible. However, at common law, a more or less analogous situation is that of summary dismissal, which is the unilateral act of dissolving a labour contract by the employer without either notice or payment in lieu and is hence ordinarily held to constitute a breach of contract unless there are ample grounds to justify such an act of 'breaking' (for instance, on the ground of the discharged employee's dishonesty, misconduct or consistent negligence). Similarly, the employee is also entitled to the symmetrical right of 'breaking' the contract with 'justifiable cause' and quitting the job in a proper manner without warranting notice or payment in lieu. The Employment Ordinance has, in this connection, prescribed the following conditions permitting what is equivalent to the rightful 'breaking' of the labour contract.

II. Breaking by the Employer

457. The employer may extinguish a contract of employment without prior notice or payment in lieu of notice:

(a) if the employee, in relation to his employment:
  - (i) wilfully disobeys a lawful and reasonable order;
  - (ii) conducts himself in a manner inconsistent with the due and faithful discharge of his duties;
  - (iii) is guilty of fraud or dishonesty;
  - (iv) is habitually neglectful in his duties; or

(b) on any other ground which would entitle him to terminate the contract without notice at common law.

As a sequel to the amendment of the Employment Ordinance in 2000, a strike has been explicitly precluded as a legitimate cause which may enable an employer to discharge an employee on strike summarily, without advance notice.

458. These legally sanctioned causes pertain to and cover the more plausible conditions under which summary dismissal is held justifiable under common law. To justify summary dismissal, the employee's breach of the contract, whether it is an alleged case of disobedience, misconduct or neglect of duty, must be substantial and sufficiently serious to vindicate an intention of the employer to repudiate or abrogate the contract. A single act of a trivial nature committed by the employed is hence insufficient to warrant a justifiable decision to terminate the employment as a lawful 'break' or sanction. The onus of proving that an act of summary dismissal is justifiable rests with the employer who, in principle, should inform the employee of the ground(s) causing the dismissal and allow him an opportunity to be heard in his defence, as provided by a proper set of in-house disciplinary procedures. These procedures are, as advised by the Labour Department, to entail an escalating mechanism with intervening steps of oral and written warnings prior to discharge. This latter practice, however, is not always followed in the real-life context, especially among the small and medium-sized firms.

The legislative amendment of 2000 of placing an embargo upon a strike as a legitimate cause of summary dismissal confers upon the Hong Kong employee a quasi-right to strike – a statutory provision added to the Employment Ordinance of putting into legal effects the 'constitutional' guarantee prescribed by the Basic Law on the civic rights of an employee to strike. However, the striker can still be deemed to have breached his contract if the work stoppage ruptures the 'continuity' of the employment contract.

III. Breaking by the Employee

459. The employee may extinguish his contract of employment without prior notice or payment in lieu of notice:

(a) if he fears with reasonable grounds physical danger of violence or disease as was not contemplated under the contract, whether the danger has been stated expressly or is implied from the nature of such employment;
(b) if the employer ill-treats him; or
(c) on any other ground(s) which would entitle him to terminate his contract summarily.

460. Again, these statutes recognize causes which correspond in general with those otherwise normally tenable under common law. However, they also require, as the case may be, that the element of fear of danger or of ill-treatment has to be of sufficient gravity as to justify the construing of a basic breach of the employer's obligations in order to warrant the employee's breaking with valid causes in a summary mode without involving notice of any period.

In addition to above listed conditions of 'breaking' with just cause, an employee is able to terminate his contract of employment unilaterally and summarily if he is suspended by his employer, provided that the termination takes place during the period of his suspension. A 1997 amendment of the Employment Ordinance also enables an employee who is owed wages in arrears to consider and deem his labour contract as 'broken' by his employer in wage default, if these outstanding wages are not paid within one month. In such instances, the employee is entitled to claim wages in lieu of notice as compensatory payment.

IV. The Remedy for Improper Breaking of the Labour Contract

461. The principal remedy available to the aggrieved party for a breach of contract or its 'wrongful and unreasonable breaking' is an action for claiming damages – i.e. to seek financial compensation for the loss sustained or suffered by the wronged. Even if the Labour Tribunal, or a civil court, rules subsequently that the reasons invoked by the initiating party were not serious enough to justify the summary act of terminating the contract with valid reasons, it is not possible, at least in common law and in spite of the provisions on employment protection introduced as an explicit notion in 1997 by an amendment of the Employment Ordinance, to order reinstatement as a remedy other than on a voluntary basis at the parties' mutual consent. In brief, the breaking of a labour contract is always definitive, inasmuch as it has been the legal premise given by the common law heritage that the employer cannot be compelled to continue hiring a particular person in his employ and nor can an employee be coerced to go on working for an employer against his free will. The logic is analogous to the rationale behind freedom of trade and freedom of labour. Moreover, either party is at liberty to terminate the contract unilaterally and immediately by opting to compensate the other party with payment in lieu of notice and/ or retributory payment.

462. At law, it is noticeable that the damages payable for wrongful 'breaking' of the contract of employment are literally the same as if no notice has been given: that is, it is equal to the amount of wages that would have accrued to the employee during the notice term which should have been respected in order to dissolve the contract properly. In the instance of a contract for a fixed term or for a precisely indicated piece or task, the injured party may be awarded an indemnity equal to the remuneration for the remaining term of the contract or for the time needed to complete the task. It is hence for this reason and in order to shield manual workers from the burden of formidable financial obligations otherwise implied that they are prevented by the law, as noted in an earlier section, from entering into a labour contract for a duration exceeding the six-month period. Where the proper term of notice has been served to dissolve a labour contract, both parties need to respect the notice period which should be worked out. Otherwise, if either party terminates the labour contract prematurely before the expiry of the notice term, it will also constitute a case of wrongful termination, in which instance the indemnification payable will be equal to the remuneration that would have accrued for the interval between the actual 'breaking' of the contract and the time when the notice given would have expired.

463. The court in Hong Kong used to rule, before 1975, that the damages arising from the wrongful dissolution of a contract of employment constituted a form of unliquidated (that is, unascertainable) damages at common law. As such, the real damages are subject to mitigation. There was hence an implied obligation of the aggrieved party to mitigate his loss by finding alternative employment (in the case of an employee) or an alternative replacement (in the case of an employer) as soon as possible. Under such circumstances, the actual damages sustained and awarded were not necessarily equivalent to the wages corresponding to the period between the actual dissolution of the contract and the expiry of the legal notice.

464. Such court decisions, conceivably contradicting the legislative intent to provide better protection of job security, led to a statutory amendment introduced to the Employment Ordinance in 1975. It added to the Ordinance a new Section 8(A) which prescribes unequivocal rights to liquidated damages in the event of wrongful termination. Such a piece of legislative innovation hence served to neutralize the 'common law' obligation incumbent upon the aggrieved party to mitigate his damages.

V. Suspension of an Employee from Employment

465. The conditions under which such a form of disciplinary sanction, a unilateral right of the employer *vis-à-vis* the employed, are reminiscent of those which sanction the summary breaking of the labour contract with just cause. However, the latter was not invoked because in its place 'suspension' serves:

(i) as a disciplinary measure for reasons which would have justified summary dismissal;
(ii) as an interim measure pending a decision by the employer as to whether or not he will exercise his right to dismiss summarily; or
(iii) as an interim measure pending the outcome of criminal proceedings against the employee arising out of, or in connection with his employment.

466. By 'suspension', the Employment Ordinance supersedes the principle of common law and permits the temporary cessation of the employer's basic obligation to provide the employee with work and pay him wages.

467. If the suspended employee is eventually cleared after the completion of the relevant criminal proceedings, as in situation (iii), it is not clear, given the silence of the law, whether the affected employee is entitled or not to 'back pay' or other forms of 'compensation' which would have accrued during and from the 'suspension' period.

§10. Special Protection in the Case of Pregnancy, Maternity, Accidents, Jury Service and Union Participation

468. The employer is prevented at law from dismissing certain categories of employee, so that contravention of such statutory proscriptions gives rise to sanctions such as compensatory indemnification to the employee and, in certain cases, criminal liabilities as well. These are labelled by the law as 'unlawful and unreasonable dismissals'.

I. Pregnancy and Maternity

469. Under the Employment Ordinance and its provisions on unlawful and unreasonable dismissal, the employer is not allowed to terminate his contract with a pregnant employee during the period from the date on which the latter gives notice of her intention to take such leave to the date on which she is due to return to work. As noted in Chapter 5, the employee is required to inform her employer although a medical certificate is not invariably necessary unless so required by the employer. The law does not specify whether summary dismissal for just cause is permissible or not during the relevant period. However, in the absence of any express statutory stipulations sanctioning such an act, it is generally assumed to be proscribed. If there is an unlawful discharge of the female employee taking or about to take her maternity leave, the employer is required to pay her an indemnity or to offer her reinstatement, as the court may order. In addition, the employer guilty of such an illegal break is liable to conviction for an offence punishable by fines. These apart, the period of maternity leave cannot be taken to interrupt the continuity of employment of the pregnant employee.

II. Accidents

470. If the employee is incapacitated due to injury or illness arising from and in the course of employment and is hence entitled to the receipt of employees' compensation, the law prevents his employer from terminating the relevant labour contract until either (i) the employee has been certified by a medical practitioner as fit to resume work or (ii) the compensation for permanent incapacity has become payable to the employee, normally after medical assessment. Such proscriptions are provided in parallel by both the Employees' Compensation Ordinance and the security clause against unlawful dismissal of the Employment Ordinance. If unlawful termination of the labour contract by the employer occurs, he is liable, by virtue of the Employees' Compensation Ordinance, to criminal prosecution and a fine upon conviction. And the injured employee is entitled to the appropriate payment in lieu for being deprived of the proper notice needed to be served, as well as an award of compensation or reinstatement of employment as ordered by the court.

471. In the event of ordinary sick leave taken by the employee, the Employment Ordinance also deems it as unlawful and unreasonable dismissal if the employer terminates the employee's labour contract during the period of the sick leave. Similar compensation is available to the affected employee as in the case of 'maternity' and 'accidents' noted above.

III. Jury Service

472. The Jury Ordinance prohibits an employer from discriminating against his employee for performing jury service. In other words, the employee cannot be dismissed for absence from work which is to enable him to attend such public duties as to serve as a juror. Unlawful discharge of this nature will render the employer liable to criminal prosecution and a fine if convicted of the offence.

473. This enactment against unlawful dismissal under the Employment Ordinance has now extended similar protection for employees in the exercise of their citizens' right as voters in public elections, or to give evidence before a public authority.

IV. Protection Against Anti-union Discrimination

474. Under the Employment Ordinance, every employee is given the right to become a member or an officer of a trade union, to take part in the union's activities at an appropriate time, and to form or apply for registration of a new trade union. Neither the employer nor any person acting in his delegated authority is allowed to prevent, deter or induce an employee from exercising such rights. Should the employer dismiss, penalize or discriminate against an employee in attempts to interfere with the exercise of these rights, or should the proscription against union membership be incorporated into the labour contract as a condition of employment, the employer is liable to prosecution and penal sanctions if convicted.

§11. Redundancy and Severance Pay

475. The Employment Ordinance was amended in 1974 introducing statutory provisions for severance pay indemnifiable to employees under specified conditions of redundancy or lay-off. These severance payment liabilities are due to dismissal by reason of redundancy which the law defines to be contingent upon the following conditions:

(a) the employer has ceased, or intends to cease, carrying on his business in the place where the employee was employed; or
(b) the employer closes or intends to close his business; or

(c) there is a reduction in demand for the employee's particular kind of work (that is, when the requirement of the business for employees to carry out work of a particular kind, ceases or diminishes or is expected to cease or diminish).

476. The legislation provides a liberal definition of dismissal by reason of redundancy, with the qualification that any dismissal will be presumed at law to be dismissal by reason of redundancy unless proof to the contrary is provided by the employer. Besides, prolonged lay-off, by rendering the continuous performance of the labour contract problematic or even untenable, also entitles the employees affected to severance pay. The law hence made severance pay claimable when the 'lay-off' has attained the following scale:

(a) an employee is not provided with work and pay for more than half of the total number of normal working days in any period of four consecutive weeks; or
(b) the non-provision of work and pay exceeds one-third of the total number of working days in any period of 26 consecutive weeks (for reckoning purposes, the days of lock-out, rest days, annual leave days and statutory holidays are not recognized as normal working days in determining whether or not a lay-off interval has exceeded the legally permissible level).

477. Before 1992, severance pay was also claimable where the employer relocated his plant or business across the harbour – that is, from Hong Kong Island northwards to either Kowloon or the New Territories, or vice versa. The presumption behind such a provision, that an employee's dismissal could be deemed to be 'wholly or mainly attributable to the moving of the workplace across the harbour', was found to be increasingly anachronistic in Hong Kong's business and work context – inasmuch as advances in the city's transport infrastructure now enable people to commute between the two sides of the harbour with little difficulty.

478. In other words, it is no longer sufficient to construe at law that the mere factor of the physical change in the place of work (notably, in the classic case of its re-location across the harbour) will render the performance of the contract technically non-tenable or impractical. Instead, where the change of workplace, even if limited in spatial distance, has caused undue hardship to the employee, it is now held to be sufficiently serious to establish a case of 'constructive dismissal' under common law if the employee has to waive his job and as such, will justify a claim for severance pay by reason of discharge due to redundancy.

479. According to the official interpretation published by the Labour Department in its advisory guide, a change in the workplace location is not an *ipso facto* condition sufficient to rupture an employment relationship. In order to establish a case of 'constructive dismissal', it is necessary to submit the claim for severance pay to the test of such criteria as

(i) whether there is an express term in the labour contract entitling the employer to require his employee to work at different places;

(ii) whether the nature of work and the scope of employment activities of the employee make it necessary for him to work at different places;
(iii) whether after the change of workplace, the employee's postion and other terms and conditions remain the same or are no less favourable than before;
(iv) whether the extent of hardship faced by the employee as a result of the change of workplace is significant (for instance, the extra commuting time and expenses spent on travel to and from the new location of work); and
(v) whether the employer has provided a suitable arrangement to alleviate the hardship encountered by the employees, such as the provision of shuttle bus, travelling allowance or re-adjustment of working hours, etc.[20]

I. Calculation of Severance Pay

480. To be eligible for severance payment, the employee has to be employed under a continuous contract of not less than 24 months immediately preceding his dismissal by reason of redundancy or lay-off. For every year of service performed, a monthly rated employee is entitled to two-thirds of his last full month's wages or two-thirds of HK$22,500, whichever is less. Correspondingly, a piece-rated employee or a time-rated other than a monthly rated employee (who can be hourly, daily or weekly rated) is entitled to 18 days' wages based upon any 18 full working days chosen by the employee from his last month of employment,[21] or two-thirds of HK$22,500, whichever is less.

481. The amount of severance payment accruing to the employee is subject to the ceiling of:

(i) the total amount of wages earned during the period of twelve months immediately preceding the redundancy; or
(ii) HK$180,000, whichever is less. However, since 1995, the fixed ceiling rule has been rescinded and replaced by a maximum which is adjusted annually until it attains the threshold of HK$390,000 by the year 2003; and
(iii) a maximum length of service of 25 years for full-rate calculation and beyond that, any years of service are to be reckoned at half-rate. Such a maximum length is, however, extended progressively according to a sliding scale if the redundancy occurs after the 1995 dateline. However, if the redundancy occurs after October 2004, all years of service can be reckoned, with the amount of total payment also subject to a ceiling of HK$390,000. Such a formula of determining severance pay also applies to the computation of long service payment.

---

20. Labour Department, Hong Kong Government, *Explanatory Note on the Eligibility to Severance Payment upon a Change of Workplace under the Employment (Amendment) (No. 4) Ordinance 1992*, Hong Kong: Labour Department, Hong Kong Government, 1992, p. 2.
21. However, if the employee elects, the base of computation can be determined by averaging wages over the latest period of 12 months. For any incomplete year of service, the calculation of severance pay for that period will be pro-rated in terms of a year's complete service.

II. Procedure for Claim and Disbursement of Severance Pay

482. An employee discharged from employment on account of redundancy or prolonged lay-off has to, within the next month on such extended period approved by the Commissioner for Labour, lodge a claim for severance payment by giving notice to the employer. Of course, such a procedural step is not necessary if the payment has already been agreed upon or if the employee has already filed a claim for the payment with the Labour Tribunal. Upon receipt of such a written claim, the employer is obliged to effect payment ot the employee within the next two months, unless the claim is to be determined at the Labour Tribunal. A written statement indicating the manner of calculation of the amount disbursed by the employee has to accompany the payment, which has to be effected in cash – otherwise by cheque, money order, postal order or directly credited to the employee's bank account subject to the latter's consent.

§12. Severance Pay and Transfer of Ownership

483. In the event of change of ownership of the enterprise, an employee cannot lodge a claim for severance pay by reason of dismissal due to redundancy or lay-off if he declines unreasonably the offer by the (new) employer to renew his contract of employment or to re-engage him under a new contract on terms not less favourable than the previous one. This rule applies, however, if:

(i) the offer has not been made less than seven days before the date of transfer and the renewal or re-engagement will take effect on or before that date; and
(ii) the period of employment preceding the transfer is recognized as a period of employment with the new employer and the change does not break the continuity of employment.

484. An unreasonable refusal on the part of the employee of the offer is normally established if he capitalizes merely upon the issue of business transfer as a ground for repudiating the offer.

485. By symmetry, if an offer of renewing the contract or of a new and not less favourable contract has not been forthcoming, it can be construed as a default enabling the employee to claim severance payment from the old employer by reason of dismissal due to redundancy stemming from the changeover of ownership.

§13. Business Failure and Insolvency

486. The financial collapse and business failure of an enterprise leads to the dissolution of the individual contract of employment in a situation which is often a collective experience of trauma and dislocation to its workforce. In Hong Kong, business can take the structural form of constituting themselves as either (i) a limited liability company or (ii) a sole proprietorship or partnership (of unlimited liability).

487. Each of the above is governed by different sets of legislation whose pur view covers as well the exigencies of insolvency and financial breakdown. Limited companies are subject to the statutory prescription of the Companies Ordinance, enacted in 1933, while partnership and proprietorship are regulated by the Bankruptcy Ordinance of 1932.

488. Under the Companies Ordinance, the company is held as a corporate or legal person and only its assets are available for liquidation to obtain the cash for paying off the creditors. However, its shareholders and directors are not personally liable for meeting the debts of the limited company except in the event of fraud or malfeasance committed by an individual member of staff. In the event of an insolvency, any creditors or any contributory parties, including employees who are owed wages, can petition the High Court for a winding-up order, so that the Official Receiver may be appointed to appropriate, realize and administer the assets of the company for liquidation in order to enable him to disburse the proceeds of realized cash for payment of its debts. On the other hand, if an employer of the second category (i.e. a partnership or proprietorship) becomes insolvent, any creditor may petition under the Bankruptcy Ordinance to the High Court for a receiving order enabling the Official Receiver to be appointed over the estates and assets of the employer. This action has the effect of depriving the indebted of possession and control over his assets so that it can be preserved and liquidated for distribution among the creditors.

I. Claims of the Employee in Business Failures and Insolvency

489. An employer is legally obliged to pay the employee the wages due upon the expiry of the wage period or the dissolution of the labour contract. Failure to do so without reasonable excuse is hence a punishable offence. The employer is also legally obliged to terminate the labour contract with the employee in the proper manner if he believes that he has lost his ability to pay wages. Since non-payment of wages constitutes, in Hong Kong's employment context, a serious breach of the employer's obligations, it is generally deemed that such a breach is sufficient to imply a repudiation of the contract by the employer. It follows that where the employer is in default of wage and other payments due, the employees affected are entitled to interpret that their individual labour contracts have been terminated without just cause. Employees' claims arising then tend to cover the following:

(i) arrears of wages for work done;
(ii) compensation for the wrongful break of the labour contract due to the employer's breach of his basic contractual duty – that is, payment in lieu of notice; and

(iii) severance payment, inasmuch as such dissolution of the employment relationship consequential to business failure or insolvency is generally taken as, prima facie, a genuine case of dismissal by reason of redundancy.

II. Insolvency and Priority of Employee's Claims *vis-à-vis* Those of Other Creditors

490. Both the Companies Ordinance and Bankruptcy Ordinance place, under a winding up or official receivership order, certain items of the employee's claims against a business on equal priority level with government debts and in preference to most other debts owed by the company to other creditors. These preferential items include, for each employee:

(i) wages or salaries (including ascertainable commission due) up to a stipulated ceiling;
(ii) wages in lieu of notice which are not to exceed one month's wages or a stipulated ceiling, whichever is less;
(iii) severance pay not exceeding a stipulated ceiling; and
(iv) employees' compensation, if any, for industrial injury and occupational disease.

491. By implication, it is understood that any employee's claims falling outside the above categories and exceeding the prescribed ceiling are not accorded any preference at law over the other debts owed by the insolvent employer. As claimants for the non-preferential debts, the employees only stand as ordinary creditors ranking equally with the other ordinary creditors of the employer.

III. Protection of Wages in Insolvency Fund

492. Wages security is now, however, made available to the workforce of the insolvent employer who has defaulted in his obligation to effect wage and associated payment to his employees by the inception and the availability of the 'Protection of Wages in Insovency Fund'. Correspondingly, the importance of attaching priority over debts owed to employees in the winding-up process has become less important.

Chapter 7. Laws of Anti-discrimination and Equal Opportunities

§1. INTRODUCTION

493. Hong Kong began to legislate against various forms of social discrimination in the mid-1990s. This official initiative was partly due to the rise in awareness in society on women's rights and in part because of the government's intention to benchmark with other developed nations in providing Hong Kong with analogous legislative standards on protection against discrimination and equal opportunities. Strictly speaking, legal censure against employers' acts of anti-union discrimination has been on the statute book since the 1970s, but a systematic approach to this kind of 'rights' legislation did not appear until the 1990s.This body of legal codes, essentially of a retributory rather than a punitive nature, has significant implications for employment and workplace labour relations.[22]

494. The first was the Sex Discrimination Ordinance enacted in 1995, followed later by the inception of the Disabilities Discrimination Ordinance and the Family Status Discrimination Ordinance, all having been placed on the statute book already before the reversion of Hong Kong back to China in 1997. Later, in face of the growing plurality in the ethnic mix of the local population, the SAR government introduced the Race Discrimination Ordinance in 2008.so as to provide safeguards for the racial minorities against discriminatory treatment. Besides, there have been recent clues to suggest that a 'progressive' piece of legislation to rule against 'sex-orientation discrimination' is now in the pipeline. However, such a legislative motion is likely to be greeted by strong qualms in the more conservative sector of the community, inasmuch as traditional Chinese Confucian values are still deeply embedded in this society. Moreover, Hong Kong has not yet made any stride forward in legislating against other kinds of social discrimination, such as those on grounds of age, religious or political affiliation.

§2. SEX DISCRIMINATION ORDINANCE AND ITS MAIN PROVISIONS

495. This Ordinance, introduced in 1995, proscribes against any prejudicial acts, on ground of gender, marital status and pregnancy, to the detriment of the victims. It also creates the Equal Opportunities Commission and puports to correct sterotyed attitutdes and behaviour ingrained within the community pivoted around the nexus of the 'gender' divide. Its provisions largely emulate analogous legal codes in Britain and the European Union. They are also congruent with the normative framework laid down by the United Nations'pertinent instrument which safeguards women's rights adopted in 1979, namely, the Convention on the Elimination of All Forms of Discrimination Against Women (CEDAW). Its enactment was preceded by the convening of an intra-government Working Group on the application of

22. Ng Sek-Hong, Sally Stewart and Chan Fun-Ting, *Current Issues of Workplace Relations and Management in Hong Kong*, Hong Kong: Centre of Asian Studies, The University of Hong Kong, 1997, pp. 153–167.

CEDAW in 1992 and the subsequent publication by the government of a 'Green Paper on Equal Opportunities for Women and Men' in 1993. While the Working Group was conservative in its report the Green Paper espoused euphoria about the establishment of equal rights for women and men in Hong Kong. The latter consultative document hence canvassed a distinct possibility for Hong Kong to adopt the provisions of the CEDAW and eventually introduce 'equal pay' legislation, which would call for a series of far-reaching reforms. However, the Green Paper was sceptical about an undesirable drift towards an over dosage of 'legalism' and institutional inflexibilities if new legislation modelled upon the UK Equal Pay Act were to be introduced.[23]

The persistent and vociferous lobby by the female pressure groups in vindication of women's rights led to a resolution adopted by the Legislative Council in late 1992 calling on the Hong Kong government to extend the provisions of the CEDAW to Hong Kong. In the wake of this mounting socio-political pressure, a sex discrimination law was enacted in 1995, with far-reaching implications for employment at the workplace.[24]

496. Section 11 of the Sex Discrimination Ordinance provides for protection of a woman against discrimination at employment. It is unlawful for a prospective employer to lay down conditions of selection which are prejudicial against a female applicant. Nor is it lawful for an employer to discriminate against her in the employment terms which are offered to her because she is a woman. By the same token, she cannot be denied employment on the ground of sex. After entry into employment, it will not be permissible for the employer to discriminate against a female employee in 'the way he affords her access to opportunities for promotion, transfer or training, or to any benefits, facilities or services' rendered to her. Any treatment to her detriment or discharge for the prima facie reason of sex are also censured by the Ordinance.

497. Being the pioneering piece of anti-discrimination legislation in Hong Kong, the SDO provides for a grace period for small enterprises. Firms with an employment size of five or fewer than five persons are exempt from the exigency of the above provisions for three years after the inception of the ordinance. Where the 'gender' criterion is a genuine occupational qualification for the job, such as in health care services, hospitals and schools, it will not constitute a discriminatory act if a female or a male worker has to be selected for employment.

498. In the case of a contract for services, analogous provisions apply to the dealings between a principal and his/her contract worker. It is hence unlawful for the principal to differentiate the terms of engagement for a female contract worker

---

23. *Ibid.*
24. *Ibid.*

from those for her male counterpart or her access to any benefits, facilities or services which the principal provides, except where the 'gender' criterion is a genuine ground for selection (section 13).

499. The SDO lays down that the ground of discrimination at employment is not limited just to the criterion of gender but also on the basis of marital status and pregnancy (section 5). Hence, it is unlawful to treat an employee or job applicant less favourably because she is a woman, or she is married or she is pregnant. Such a proscription applies also when:

(i) deciding on the admission of a person into a trade union or professional body;
(ii) granting a qualification or accreditation which is needed for a partuclar trade or occupation;
(iii) making available training at employment;
(iv) providing services by an employment agency to a client;
(v) when selecting a partner in a fim of not less than six partners; and
(vi) when hiring a contract worker or a commissioned agent.

500. Under the SDO, sexual harassment at employment is also unlawful (section 6). Such behaviour is defined by law to include:

(i) unlawful sexual advances (for example, leeing and lewed gestures, touching, grabbing or deliberately brushing up against another person);
(ii) unlawful requests for sexual favours (for example, suggestions that sexual co-operation or the toleration of sexual advances may further a person's career within an organization);
(iii) unwelcome verbal, non-verbal or physical conduct of a sexual nature (for example, sexually derogatory or sterotyped remarks, persistent questioning about a person's life); and
(iv) conduct of a sexual nature which creates hostile or intimidating work environment (for example, sexual or obscene jokes around the workplace or display at it of sexist or other sexually offensive pictures or posters).

501. Based upon the above definition of this form of censured behaviour, it is hence unlawful for an employer or his/her agent to sexually harass an employee, a job applicant or an appointee. Reciprocally, it is unlawful for an employee to sexually harass his/her employer or prospective employer. By the same token, it is unlawful for a principal to sexually harass his/her contract worker or a commissioned agent. Concordantly, it is unlawful for a contract worker or agent to sexually harass his/her fellow contract worker or his/her fellow commissioned agent.

502. Section (16) of the SDO is a clause whch deals specifically with discrimination by trade unions, on ground of sex, marital status and pregnancy.

It covers the following treatment of the victim:

(i) terms of admission;
(ii) denial or omission of admission;
(iii) denying a female member access to any benefits, facilities or services otherwise available to a male member;
(iv) rescinding her membership or varying the terms of her memberhip; and
(v) subjecting her to any detriment.

503. The SDO also makes explicit its proscription against sex discrimination by a qualifying body which grants credentials for employment. In this connection, it is unlawful for either a professional body or a trade union which can qualify admission into a particular profession or trade to discriminate against a female applicant or member:

(i) in the terms on which it is prepared to confer upon her that qualification or authorization;
(ii) by denying her admission; or
(iii) by rescinding her credential or varying the terms on which she holds it.

504. The SDO creates the Equal Opportunities Commission which is the competent authority for enforcing the Sex Discrimination Ordinance and other anti-discrimination legal codes which are to come to the statue book later. It also organizes community and education work in propagating the notion of equal opportunities, both at work and in society. It receives complaints on alleged acts of discrimination and provides mediation services to the two parties.

505. The SDO and its ancillary Code of Practice on Employment published by the Equal Opportunities Commission shed a pervasive impact upon human resource management policies and practices among enterprises in Hong Kong. An important implication is that many sex implicated job titles have to be changed into gender-neutral ones. Obvious examples are the renaming of firemen as fire-persons or fire-fighters and air hostesses as flight attendants. Besides, employers have to be cautious about writing their application forms and job advertisement in order to eradicate any possible implications of gender biases in their job descriptions and job requirements.

506. The Code of Practice on Employment elaborates on the ramifications of the SDO for employment practices and policies at the workplace. The more important directives provided by the Code are listed below.

507. It will be discriminatory for the employer to hire or not hire a person on the ground of gender unless sex is a genuine occupational qualification for the job concerned. Such a condition applies where:

(i) the essential nature of the job calls for a man or woman for reasons of physiology or authenticity in dramatic performance;
(ii) the job calls for a man or woman in order to preserve decency or privacy;

(iii) the employee works or lives in a house where he/her has frequent physical or social contacts with its household members;
(iv) the nature or location of the establishment makes it impracticable for the employee to live outside the employer's premises, like a resident janitor at a single sex school where there is no separate accommodation or sanitary facilities for the other sex;
(v) the employing organization is an institution where sex is a genuine requirement for the job-holder in dealing with the inmates; and
(vi) the job holder provides welfare or educational personal services which can be most effectively performed if the person is of a specific sex, like a female counsellor at a sheltered home for women.

508. It is essential for an employer to adopt consistent selection criteria in recruitment, promotion and transfer which mirror the incumbent's capabilities to perform the job, without any prior assumption that a person of a specific sex is able to do the job or to do it better. The same principle applies to discrimination by marital status and pregnancy. Hence, any decisions in recruitment by advertising, and through employment agencies or career offices of educational institutions should be free from such biases. Those staff who handle recruitment, promotion and transfer have to be instructed or trained not to practise any discriminatory acts.

509. In order to conform to the provisions of the SDO, job advertisements and any accompanying literature have to written free from presenting men and women in stereotyed roles. Job titles, headlines and illustrations have to be free from any sex implications. The wordings need to be gender-neutral or jobs have to be paired with sex equivalent, like waiter and waitress. The same rule applies to the design of the application forms. These forms should not be intrusive, for example, in probing the marital status and private life of the applicant. To be specific, they should not solicit information about the applicant's spouse, children, and child-bearing plans. By the same token, the conduct of interviews, psychological and proficiency test and after hiring, promotion, transfer and training should not be amenable to any sex biases. Records on how and why these personnel decisions are arrived have to be kept for at least a year in order to address any complaints on discrimination.

510. The Code also propagates the principle of 'equal pay for equal work' and where practicable the more sophisticated dictum of 'equal pay for work of equal value'. The first one is operationalized by the notion of 'like work', which pertains to work of a broadly similar nature, as gauged by the tye of work performed, skill and knowledge required. The second one can in principle be instituted by objective and professional job evaluation to establish a system of internal relativity within an establishment. This notion purports that jobs can be equated in their value or worth to the organization even where jobs are different yet entailing comparable efforts and responsibilities, skills and knowlege and analogous working conditions.

511. Nevertheless, differences in pay for equal work or work of equal value between employees are permissible provided that they are in line with justifiable differences in performance, or length of service, or work location or because the jobs have been 'red-circled' *vis-à-vis* other jobs after being reclassified to a lower tier as a result of job evaluation.

512. Part-time employees are to be awarded pro-rated pay and benefits, especially if they are disproportionately made up of women. Besides, dress code has to even and balanced between the two sexes although it can be tailored to gender specificities.

513. There was in the past, as provided by the Employment Regulations of the Employment Ordinance, statutory protection of women workers in industry in their rest days, working hours and rest pause as well as night work. However, these restrictive controls to safeguard the health of female workers have been viewed as paternalistic and incongruent with modern values of sex equality. They have hence been abrogated since the late 1990s.

§3. Disability Discrimination Ordinance and Its Main Provisions

514. The second piece of discrimination legislation, the Disability Discrimination Ordinance, was introduced later in the same year, 1995. This Ordinance makes it unlawful for an employer to discriminate against a person with a disability in the selection procedures, in the choice of the successful candidate, in the terms of employment. It is also unlawful for the employer to decline an appointment because the applicant is a disabled person.

515. In parallel, it is unlawful for an employer to discriminate against a person with disabilities in providng access to opportunities for promotion, transfer or training, as well as entitlement to benefits, services or facilities or deliberately denying such a person access to these concessions. It is also unlawful for an employer to dismiss a disabled person or subject the latter to any other detriments at employment without any reasonable excuse.

516. A grace period of exemption from the exigencies of this legislative piece was provided for a small enterprise or employing unit with less than five employees. Such a grace period lasted for three years.

517. The Disability Discrimination Ordinance also provides that anti-discrimination sanctions do not apply under a number of prescribed conditions. The first is where the employer has to hire a person without disability because of the genuine occupational requirement for the job concerned. At law, such a criterion is named 'genuine occupational qualification' (GOQ) for the job. By extension, such an exemption also applies to the provision of opportunities for promotion or transfer or training in such a calling.

Second, it will not constitute a case of discrimination where the employment of a person without disability is justified not because his/her physiological conditions but by consideration of his/her performance, or past training, qualifications and experience which are relevant to the job.

Third, it will not be discriminatory if a disabled person is not hired for a particular job because his/her disability will preclude him/her from meeting the inherent requirements of the job. It will not be discriminatory either if it will require an employer to furnish special services and facilities which are not required by an able person, given that such provision would have imposed undue hardship upon the employer.

518. The test of the 'GOQ' criterion above-mentioned is stringent. It will apply only where the essential nature of the job calls for a person without disability in dramatic performance or other entertainment acts for reason of authenticity. It will also be applicable where the employee has to reside in the employer's premises which are not equipped with accommodation and facilities tailored for a disabled person, provided that an alternation of these premises to suit such a person would have imposed undue hardship upon the employer.

519. Analogous prescriptions are extended to the hiring of a contract worker by a principal, or a contractor or a subcontractor. The Disability Discrimination Ordinance is also competent in regulating employment on a ship or an aircraft registered in Hong Kong. Unlike the cases in many countries, this Ordinance does not lay down any provisions on affirmative actions in favour of disabled persons at employment.

520. Section (16) of the Disability Discrimination Ordinance governs the admission of a person with disability into a trade union, a professional body or an employers' association.

It will hence be unlawful for such a body to discriminate against a disabled person by denying the latter admission into its membership.It is neither permissible to discriminate him/her in the terms of admission into its membership. It will also be unlawful for such a body to discriminate against an existing member with a disability in abrogating his/her membership or varying the terms of his/her membership without justifiable reasons. It is also against the law if there is discriminatory treatment of a disabled member in the access to any benefits, services or facilities which it provides for members.

521. Section (17) of the Disability Discrimination Ordinance pertains to any discriminatory acts against a disabled person by a licensing, qualifying or an authorization body. It will hence be unlawful for such an institution to deny a person with disability the conferment of such a credential or withdrawing from him/her such a credential. It will neither be lawful if there is discriminatory treatment of a disabled person in the terms and conditions of conferring such a qualicatiion. However, it will not be deemed to be discriminatory if there is differential treatment of a disabled person yet such differences can be justified *vis-à-vis* the person's past training, qualification and experience in the trade, occupation or profession concerned.

522. Section (18) of the Ordiance applies to discrimination against a disabled person in the provision of vocational training. It is unlawful for a training institution to discriminate against a disabled person who seeks training helpful to his/her employment. It is discriminatory if it denies him/her access to such training or in the terms of providing such training, or subjecting him/her to any detriments in the course of suc training. It is also discriminatory for such an institution to terminate a disabled person's training without reasonable jusficatioins.

523. The Disability Discrimination Ordinance also censures discriminatory acts of an employment agency. It will be unlawful for such an agency to discriminate against a disabled person in the provision of placement service and career guidance. It will be discriminatory for an employment agency to deny a disabled person in the access to the above facilities, or in the terms of such provision. However, it will not be discriminatory if there is differentiated treatment of a disabled person who seeks such services provided it is justified with consideration of his/her past training, qualification and experiences in the relevant trade, occupation or profession.

524. Besides, this Ordinance makes it unlawful for an employer to advertise job openings with wordings which favour a person without disability unless it is a genuine occupational qualification for the job to be peformed by an able person.

525. A disabled person is also protected at law against harassment in the course of employment, as prescribed by section (22) of the Disability Discrimination Ordinance. It will hence be unlawful for an employer to harass an employee who is disabled. By extension, it will also be unlawful for a principal to harass a contract worker or a commissioned agent who is disabled. Concomitantly, it is against the law for an employee to harass a disabled fellow employee. By the same token, a contract worker who harasses his/her fellow contract worker with a disability also commits an offence.

526. Harassment against a disabled person in other context associated with employment is also outlawed under section (23) of the Disability Discrimination Ordinance. Such proscription applies when harassment occurs when a disabled person applies for membership in a trade union, professional body or an employers' association. In parallel, it is unlawful for a member of a qualifying or accreditating authority to harass an applicant with a disability seeking a credential conferred by the authority. It is also unlawful for a training institution or its agent to harass a disabled person under training. Neither it is permissible for an employment agency to harass a disabled person seeking its services.

§4. Main Provisons of the Family Status Discrimination Ordinance and Employment

527. The third piece of anti-discrimination legislation enacted in Hong Kong is the Family Status Discrimination Ordinance passed in 1997. The Ordinance makes it unlawful to discriminate against a person with family status, which means having family duties. The notion of 'family status' is defined as the status of a person having responsibilities for looking after and taking care of an immediate family member. As a person who is related by blood, marriage, adoption or affinity, an immediate family member covers the following relations:

(i) the parent(s);
(ii) the spouse;
(iii) a parent of the spouse;
(iv) a child or the spouse of a child;
(v) a sibling, either brother or sister, full-blood or half-blood, and his/her spouse;
(vi) a grandparent or a grandparent of a person's spouse; or
(vii) a grandchild or the spouse of a grandchild.

528. By virtue of section (8) of the Family Status Discrimination Ordinance, it is not permissible at law for an employer to discriminate against a person with family duties in selecting an appointee and in the arrangements pertaining to the selection process. It is also against the law for such a candidate to be discriminated against in the terms he/she is offered for employment. Neither it is lawful for the employer to decline deliberately such a person the offer of employment because of his/her family status. After entry, it will be unlawful for an employer to discriminate an employee with family duties in affording the latter access to promotion, transfer or training or to any benefits, facilities or services otherwise available to others. It is also discriminatory and hence an infringement of the law for the employer to dismiss purposively an employee with family status or subjecting him/her to any detriments. The Ordinance caters to the special needs of the small enterprises by granting a grace period of three years' exemption to an employer who hires five or fewer employees from the exigency of the legislation.

529. Section (9) of the Ordinance lays down analogous provisions on discrimination against a contract worker with family responsibilities. It is hence a censured act for a principal to discriminate against a contract worker with family status either: (a) in the terms of hiring; (b) in declining to hire or dissolving the continuous hiring of such a worker; (c) in denying him/her access to any benefits, facilities or services otherwise available to other workers; or (d) by subjecting him/her to any detriments.

530. Section (10) of the Ordinance extends its jurisdiction to cover employment on board any ship which is registered in Hong Kong. Correspondingly, any employment on an aircraft owned by a Hong Kong resident also comes under the purview of the Ordinance.

531. This law also applies to discrimination against a person with family status by a trade union, a professional body or an employers' association. It is hence a proscribed act for such an organization to discriminate against a person applying for admission to membership in the terms of entry or denying his/her application because of the latter's family duties (section 12). It will also not be lawful for such a body to discriminate against a member with family status either: (a) in denying the latter access to any benefits, facilities or services otherwise attainable by other members; (b) by depriving the latter of his/her membership or varying deliberately the terms of his/her membership; or (c) subjecting the latter to any detriment within the organization.

532. Discrimination against an applicant with family duties who seeks recognition by a qualifying, accreditation, authorization or licensing body is made unlawful by section (13) of the ordinance. It is therefore not approved for such an institution which can license or confer a credential needed for engagement in a particular profession or trade to discriminate against such an applicant in the terms on which it is prepared to confer such an endorsement. Neither it is permissible for it to deny the grant of such a credential to an applicant because he/she has family duties. It is also not allowed if such a body withdraws from a qualified person his/her qualification or varies the terms on which it is held becaused the latter has family duties.

533. Under the same law, an employment agency is prohibited from discriminating against a job-seeker with family status in providing the latter with placement services and career guidance. In addition, job advertisements cannot be written so as discriminate against any persons who have responsibilities.

§5. Race Discrimination Ordinance

534. The most recent piece of anti-discrimination enacted in Hong Kong is that against racial biases. This is the Race Discrimination Ordinance passed in 2008 and put into effect from 2009 onwards. Section (8) provides a generic definition of 'race' to include 'race, colour, descent or national or ethnic origin of a person'. Racial discrimination may take the form of discrimination against members of communities based upon serotyped stratification of society such as by the caste system or any analgous systems of rectifying inherited status. An ethnicity biased class system has the adverse effects of nullifying or impairing its members' equal entitlement to human rights. Hence discrimination of such a nature is declared unlawful under this Ordinance. By extension, a 'racial group' refers to a group of persons belonging to a specific race, colour, descent or national or ethnical origin. However, this Ordinance does not extend protection to any person of a specific race or ethnic origin who is not a Hong Kong citizen or has not the right of abode or the right to land in Hong Kong, or who is subject to restriction of stay in Hong Kong under the Immigration Ordinance.

535. Section (10) of the Ordinance governs against racial discrimination at employment. It is hence unlawful for an employer to discriminate, on the ground of race, against a job applicant in the arrangements which lead to selection; or in the terms offered to the latter for employment or in declining employment. After entry, it is against the law for an employer to discriminate against an employee, on the ground of race, in his/her terms of employment or in his/her access to promotion, transfer, training or any other benefits, facilities or services otherwise available to other employees who are of different ethnic background. It is also unlawful for an employer to discriminate against an employee who belongs to a specific ethnic group by purposively discharging the latter or subjecting him/her to any detriments. Analogous provisions apply to the hiring by a principal of a contract worker (section 15) or a commissioned agent.

536. There are limits to the ambit of application of the Race Discrimination Ordinance. First, a grace period of three years is provided for small enterprises with five or less employees, exempting them from the exigencies of the Ordinance during this period. Besides, this law does not apply to employment for domestic household work perfomed on the employer's premises (section 10). However, section (16) places employment of a person of a specific ethnic group on board a ship registered in Hong Kong or on an aircraft registered in Hong Kong and operated by a local resident within the jurisdiction of this law.

537. It will not constitute an unlawful act of race discrimination if the hiring of a member of a specific racial or ethnic group can be justified as a genuine occupational qualification (GOQ) for the job at issue. By the same logic, the allocation of opportunities of promotion, transfer or job training to a member of a specific racial or ethnic group can be justified if such ethnic status is a genuine occupational qualification for the job concerned (section 11). The same section stipulates that the genuine occupational qualification (GOQ) dictum can be applied only when:

(a) the job involves participation in a dramatic performance or other entertainment activities in a capacity for which a person of that racial group is required for reason of authenticity;
(b) the job involves participation as an artist or photographic model in producing a work of art for which a person of a specific racial or ethnic group is needed for reason of authenticity;
(c) the job involves working in a place where food or drink is provided to and consumed in a particular setting such that the job has to be performed by a person of a specific race or ethnic group is required for reason of authenticity;
(d) the job has to be performed by a member of a specific race or ethnic group because the personal services catering to the welfare of such a group can be most effectively delivered by a person belonging to such a group;
(e) the personal services provided are of such a nature as to require familiarity with the language, culture and customs as well as sensitivity to the needs of that racial group, so that these services can be most effectively performed by a person belonging to such a group.

538. However, paradoxically, the above provision has the adverse effects of perpepuating the inclusivity of a specific ethnic group. Such parochialism contradicts the rationale of the Race Discrimination Ordinance which purports to promote the equality of and not isolation of such an ethnic group.

539. It is against the law for a trade union, or a professional body or an employer association to discriminate against a person belonging to a specific racial or ethnic group in denying him/her admission into membership. It is also unlawful for such a body to discriminate against a member of a specific ethnic group in the terms of his/her membership or in discharging him/her purposively from membership (section (18)).

540. It is a contravention of the Race Discrimination Ordinance for a qualifying, authorization, licensing or registering institution to differentiate the treatment of a candidate belonging to a specific race or ethnic group by denying the latter of such conferment. It is also discriminatory for such a body to vary the nature of a credential already granted to a qualified person who belongs to a specific race or ethnic group. It is also unlawful for such a body to deprive a qualified person belonging to a specific race or ethnic group of a credential which he/she has been granted.

541. An employment agent is not permitted to discriminate against a job seeker who belongs to a specific race or ethnic group in providing the latter with its placement service and career guidance. By the same token, it is not lawful for an employment agent to deny a job seeker of a specific race or ethnic group access to its service.

542. Section (16) extends the jurisdiction of the Race Discrimination Ordinance to (i) employment on board a ship registered in Hong Kong and (ii) employment on an aircraft registered in Hong Kong and operated by a Hong Kong resident.

543. It appears that the Race Discrimination Ordinance is largely tailored to protect the rights and interests of a large contingent of the minority races living in Hong Kong, which is essentially a Chinese community. In particular, there has always been a sizable pocket of immigrants from the Indian sub-continent. However, it is doubted to what extent this law is able to nurture a multi-racial and multi-cultural society in Hong Kong, since the South Asians'community in this city has always been an 'enclave' with its members always preferring to associate among themselves. The main effect of the ordinance is to enable the latter to pursue their creed for better employment and economic opportunities in Hong Kong. Unlike many American cities in the United States, this city has been able to preserve much of its Anglo-Chinese heritage and is not a bizarre 'melting pot' of different races and ethnic groups.

544. In Hong Kong, there is absent from the statute book an 'equal pay' law. Such a law will have enshrined the principle of 'equal pay for equal work' or that 'equal pay for equal worth or equal value'. The main reason is that the application of such a principle will have called for the installation of elaborate procedures of 'job evaluation' by the employing units. However, given that the bulk of the enterprises are made up of the small and medium-sized firms which may lack the resources to implement such practices, it is evidently premature for Hong Kong to introduce a generic piece of legislation on 'equal pay'. Moreover, the government is apparently reluctant to extend too obstrusive a 'visble hand'in intervening into the reputedly 'free wage market' of Hong Kong.

545. However, the government is studying the prospect of introducing another new anti-discrimination law on 'sex orientation' for protecting those who are of bi-sexual and trans-gender tendencies in their psychological and physiological conditions. However, such a legislative motion is likely to provoke criticism or even resentment and protests from the religious denomations and more conservative sector of society. There has been assiduous lobby from this trans-gender community seeking leverage from the government against their social disadvantages and disabilities. Moreover, the government hopes to benchmark Hong Kong against most Western industrial societies in this sphere. Yet there is a potential risk that such an enactment will prove to be unpopular within this Chinese community. Virtually, this form of publicly sanctioned behaviour had always existed or even been tolerated within traditional Chinese society, provided that it was in covert form and not open and notorious.

546. As narrated earlier, Hong Kong has already introduced in the 1980s an anti-union discrimination provision within the purview of the Employment Ordinance. In spite of penal sanctions leviable on an offending employer or his/her representative, it has not been easy to launch successful prosecution because an act of discriminating against a unionized employee, such as discharge,can always be disguised under other excuses, which attribute the fault to the employee.

547. Apart from the above battery of anti-discrimination legislation, Hong Kong has also in place a 'Personal Data' Privacy Ordinance. As a sequel, employers have to discrete in eliciting and keeping in custody the personal information of the employee. It is also obligatory for the employer not to disclose and to cease holding personal information pertaining to an employee after he/her has left employment. This law also entitles an employee to inspect his personal record which is in the employer's custody.

548. In retrospect, the 1990s were the watershed years in the gestation and development of an embryonic code of civil and human rights in Hong Kong.

Chapter 8. Covenant of Non-competition

§1. Non-competition with the Employer During the Lifetime of the Individual Labour Contract

549. It is a basic duty of the employee, that he should not enter into competition with his employer in the course of performing his duties implied and given by his labour contract. In general, it appears that, even in the absence of any express contractual provision, the employee may not work or 'moonlight' in his spare time for a competitor to his employer. Obviously, there is an ethical dimension to such a requirement, as it would otherwise be inconsistent with the employee's fundamental duty of fidelity. It follows that if the employee takes up a spare-time or concurrent job which conflicts clearly with the interests of his employer (notably, in not engaging himself in work for his rival), he may be held to have acted in breach of his fidelity – an obligation which is fundamental to the employment relationship. On the other hand, it is much less tenable to argue for the case of restraining an employee from working in a different business in his spare time which does not compete with his employer's business, subject to the general principle that this does not interfere with his normal work and his ability to discharge it faithfully. Such a liberal notion has in particular been popularized in today's mood of work flexibility which cherishes flexi-career, fractional and part-time employment as well manpower dispatch/secondment.

§2. Covenants in Restraint of Trade after Employment

550. By the principle of common law exalting the freedom of, and against the restraint of, trade, any contract of employment which purports to restrict the employee's freedom of labour after employment to work at any time, in any specific business or service, in any particular place, may be deemed unlawful. This is because in general, all restraints of trade are prima facie void at law and unenforceable. Nevertheless, it is permissible for the employee to submit himself to a covenant (say, at the commencement of employment) limiting his post-employment activities to a reasonable ambit, if it is held as reasonable in the interests of the parties to the covenant, as well as reasonable in terms of public interest.

I. Competition

551. A covenant which purports to protect the employer generically against any prospect of a future threat of potential competition from the employee is generally unacceptable at law *per se*. A primary reason is that it precludes the exercise of the employee's skill, experience and knowledge – qualities which are considered to be the employee's own property. Such a ban is deemed undesirable for denying their utilization which can be otherwise beneficial to public interest. In this connection, such knowledge belonging to the employee may not be subject to restraint levied by any covenant.

552. On the other hand, the employer is entitled to protection under a covenant concluded with his employee in respect of certain interests, even if it may have the effects of curtailing or preventing competition or free trade. These interests, in essence, relate to the employee's knowledge of his employer's:

(i) trade secrets, processes of production, etc.; and
(ii) customers and connections tie – that is, that body of networking information and knowledge which is considered to belong to the employer.

II. Limits of Covenants

553. A covenant restraining the employee in his employment activities in the future is upheld to protect the employer's interests only within the ambit of reasonable and proper limits. Any restrictions exceeding these boundaries may hence be deemed void. Factors normally important for defining these limits are:

- Time: a lifetime covenant or one which is unlimited in time may be held as invalid. Indeed, it is imperative normally to examine both the 'time' and 'space' variables together for determining the validity of a covenant. In principle, it is plausible to conclude, theoretically, a lifetime covenant provided that the censured area is so confined as to enable him to work quite freely outside the stipulated spatial limits. However, in most cases the duration of restraint should be of a reasonable period.
- Space: is often a corollary to the 'time' factor just discussed above. The validity of a covenant is less likely to be recognized at law if it specifies no spatial limit to the distance or area within which the employee is restrained. Even where the area is limited, the covenant can still be nullified if the space thus embraced is too wide, having taken into consideration what is reasonable in the context of the type of employment concerned as well as the employer's interests.

III. Connection Between Employment under Restraint and Actual Hiring

554. The restriction in the covenant cannot be invoked in order to prevent the employee from entering into an employment relationship which is non-competing in nature. If the intention is to enable the employer to secure an embargo on competition *per se*, the covenant may be deemed *ultra vires* and hence invalid if the restraint is designed to cover trades or businesses with which the employer is not actually concerned. Similarly, the covenant is problematic if the restraint is intended just to force the employee to conceal, in a fictional sense, trade secrets which could not have been learnt and acquired in the course of employment.

IV. Others

555. It is held generally unacceptable for employers to conclude among themselves a covenant to the effect that any of them will not employ the former employees of the others. Such an industry-wide embargo, which is symptomatic of an employers' cartel, is not recognized at law because of its connotation of restraint of trade – let alone being prejudicial to the individual's freedom of labour. In other words, an anti-raiding agreement among employers in the same industry can be deemed non-enforceable at law.

§3. Severance or Partial Enforcement

556. If a covenant is too restrictive and severe, it may be held invalid in totality and no parts of it are legally enforceable. However, if the covenant contains some terms which are reasonable and valid, in spite of other excessively restrictive and stringent terms, it is plausible for the valid terms to be separated and severed from the invalid clauses and be made enforceable in their own right.

§4. Enforcement of a Covenant

557. In general, the covenant is interpreted very strictly in order to establish a case of its breach. It is normally necessary to substantiate the claim, if it is advanced, that the employee has committed an unequivocal breach of the covenant in its precise and exact terms.

558. The retribution for a breach of a binding covenant can be an injunction restraining the employee from breaking it. However, it is normative that such an injunction may not be commuted and rescinded just by the employee's surrender of the agreed pecuniary penalty as provided in the covenant. The defaulting act has to be halted. On the other hand, if the covenant provides for the payment of liquidated damages upon the breach of the covenant, the employer has to choose between the alternative of either (i) claiming such damages; or (ii) obtaining a court injunction, as the appropriate remedy.

559. However, a covenant attached to a labour contract is only enforceable for an employer who is not himself in breach of the contract. In this connection, an employee who is dismissed wrongfully may be relieved of his obligation to observe the restrictive covenant associated with his labour contract, since the act of wrongful dismissal by the employer would imply repudiation of the entire contract, including the covenant itself.

Chapter 9. Inventions by Employees

560. There are no original grants of patent rights in Hong Kong. However, the Registration of United Kingdom Patents Ordinance provides that any person who is the grantee of a United Kingdom patent may, within five years from the date of its issue, apply for registration in Hong Kong. Such registration confers upon the grantee the same privileges and rights as in the United Kingdom. These protective rights commence from the date of the relevant patent registration in Britain, and continue as long as the patent remains in force. However, since Hong Kong reverted back to China in 1997 as an SAR, it has assumed independent jurisdiction in registering patent rights.

561. By British common law, any service inventions (that is, those invented, in the course of performing the individual labour contracts, by employees who are engaged for such purposes, using the employer's time, as well as his materials and equipment) generally belong to the employer. For instance, if the author of a written work is employed under a contract of employment and the work is written in the course of employment, the employer is normally deemed to possess claims to the first ownership of the copyright. In the second instance, where dependent inventions are involved (that is, those which are not invented in the course of performing the labour contract but are in any way related to it or related to the activity of the enterprise), it is held generally possible for the benefits of any such invention to be apportioned between the employer and the employee. Thirdly, the ownership of any free invention (that is, those which are invented by the employee in his own time and with his own materials, without involving help and support from his employer, and not related to the activity of the enterprise) may be held to belong to the employee himself.

562. However, in individual cases of contested claims, it may require a specific ruling in court in order to determine whether the employer, or the employee, should be either entitled exclusively to or to share between them benefits of the invention at issue.

563. In Hong Kong the protection of copyright and intellectual property rights has been recently enhanced under the deliberate efforts of the government to safeguard inventors' interests in the context of rising global consciousness about the importance of enshrining and conserving intellectual property. The Copyright Ordinance and the Trade Descriptions Ordinance are administered by the Customs and Excise Department of the Hong Kong SAR government, which also liaises closely with trademark and copyright owners, the legal profession, intellectual property rights organizations as well as its foreign counterparts. The Copyright Ordinance was last amended in 1993 to update and rationalize its provisions, in light of current worldwide concern and importance now attached to the protective norms of safeguarding intellectual property and associated rights. It is that competent piece of legislation which protects literary, dramatic, musical and artistic and typographic works and their ownership due to the authors, covering publications, sound recording, film production, broadcasting and stage performance regardless of the domicile of the copyright owners. In line with the international norm, registration of copyright is not practised in Hong Kong. In parallel, the Patents Ordinance provides for the grant of standard patents based on patents granted by the State Intellectual Patent Office of China, the United Kingdom Patent Office or the European Patent Office. It also provides for the grant of short-term patents. The Patent Registry records a total of 12,988 applications for standard patents and 645 applications for short-term patents in the year 2012. Altogether 5,035 standard patents and 515 short-term patents were granted, a size almost comparable to that of 2011.

564. The principal organ now responsible for steering technological and product innovations and development is the Innovation and Technology Commission belonging to the Commerce and Economic Development Bureau of the Government Secretariat. There has existed a stable and developed regime for protecting intellectual property rights. With a comprehensive body of legislation, an easily accessible system of registration procedures and a supportive educational infrastructure, Hong Kong has been able to provide an effective mechanism for protecting intellectual property.

565. Registration of intellectual property rights, like those of patents, registered designs and trade-marks, is administered by the Intellectual Property Department. The registers are maintained in electronic format, with the data retrievable in Chinese or English through the internet at any time without any charges of fee. The filing system also provides a secure and user friendly fixture for intellectual owners or agents to file their applications at any time. The Intellectual Property Department also takes part in a variety of international forums, like the conferences organized by the World Trade Organization (WTO) on Trade-related Aspects of Intellectual Property Rights and the World Intellectual Property Organization.

566. Besides, there are a plurality of programmes with which the government sponsors the development of technology and innovations, especially in the tertary service sector. These include the Innovation and Technology Fund (ITF) and its subsidiary spin-off, the Small Entrepreneur Research Assistance Programme and the Research and the Professional Services Development Assistance Scheme. The government also runs an array of five research and development centres, the Hong Kong Applied Science and Technology Research Institute and a Science and Technology Park for grooming the high-value adding industries and the contingent know-how.

567. There have been established a number of consultative bodies and public agencies in this domain of advancing the technological frontier of Hong Kong industry. These are, apart frpm the Innovation and Technlogy Commission, the Mainland/Hong Kong Science and Technology Co-operation Committee, the Business Facilitation Advisory Committee, the Trade Development Council, the Productivity Council, the Council for Testing and Certification and the Standard and Calibration Services.

Chapter 10. Settlement of Industrial Disputes and the Statute of Limitations

§1. Introduction

568. In Hong Kong, individual disputes relating to the labour contract and its performance are on the whole settled by way of either (i) direct negotiation between the disputant parties or (ii) intervention by official agencies such as the Labour Relations Service of the Labour Department or the Labour Tribunal. On the other hand, the extent of intervention by trade unions is not as common as in other industrially advanced nations. Instead, the union's role is typically relatively limited because in general, the unions here are not highly organized at the workplace level and there is little or no institution of well-developed shop steward systems. Where union intervention is found, it takes the typical form whereby the union officials make representation to the employer on behalf of the aggrieved employees, collectively or individually. In other cases, the union official may accompany the disputant employee(s) in official conciliation or adjudication proceedings.

§2. Claims as Disputes of Right and Settlement

569. Disputes over individual claims not resolved directly at the workplace have to be settled by way of external procedures involving official intervention. Such a process is normally initiated in the form of conciliation with the assistance of conciliation officers from the Labour Relations Service of the Labour Department. However, if no settlement is achieved, the claim can be referred to the Labour Tribunal by the Labour Relations Service for judicial determination. Yet such a procedure is not the invariable or prescribed arrangement, inasmuch as the disputants can lodge their complaints and claims directly with the Labour Tribunal, although references by the Labour Department to the Tribunal are far more common in practice. Moreover, since 1994 as a sequel to the enactment of the Minor Employment Claims Adjudication Board Ordinance, small claims involving claimants of a number smaller than a stipulated size and an amount not exceeding a prescribed ceiling for each person can be referred to the Labour Department for determination.

570. Such individual claims arising from the individual labour contracts generally belong to that class of labour–management conflict or discords known as 'disputes over rights'. These are cases which involve alleged violations of rights already established and enshrined in such instruments as the contracts of employment, labour law, customs and practice and collective agreements. In other words, such disputes pertain to the interpretation of these established rules and norms as to whether they should be applied and invoked in a specific situation.[25] In Hong Kong, these 'rights' disputes, formerly classified by the administration as 'grievances' or

25. For definition of disputes of right and disputes of interests, see Allan Flanders (ed.), *Collective Bargaining*, Harmondsworth: Penguin, 1971, Chapter 1.

'grievance disputes', have been relabelled and categorized officially now as 'claims'.[26] The labelling is streamlined in order to better reflect the phenomenon that any alleged defaults or breaches of obligations, whether contractual or statutory, usually give rise to monetary claims by the damaged party, as an indemnity or compensation.

§3. LABOUR RELATIONS SERVICE (CONCILIATION)

571. Voluntary conciliation by the Labour Relations Service of the Labour Department is normally the first-line facility in the officially sponsored procedures for the settlement of claims, or disputes of rights. Conciliation, by its nature, is pervaded by the nexus of 'voluntarism', inasmuch as the conciliator cannot summon the disputants to attend the proceedings as a mandatory order, nor can he dictate the terms of settlement and impose his suggested ideas upon the parties. His primary task is to endeavour to get the parties together to meet, negotiate and eventually help settle the dispute with an amicable settlement by way of a suasive dialogue. During the conciliation proceedings, it is common practice for the conciliator to explain the relevant provisions of the law to provide a framework of basic understanding between the parties and help them to locate plausible areas of mutual compromise for narrowing and even bridging the initial gap between the contesting parties.

572. The proceedings of the conciliation sessions are informal: typically the meeting is conducted by a conciliation officer of the Labour Relations Service using Chinese (normally, the Cantonese dialect) as the common medium.

573. Official statistics have consistently indicated that the conciliation work pursued by the Labour Relations Service has been instrumental in resolving a significant proportion of the 'claims' disputes. Generalizing longitudinally over the last few decades, it may be observed that more than half of these 'claims' brought before the Labour Relations Service have been resolved under conciliation, without recourse to judicial determination by the Labour Tribunal or adjudication procedures for minor claims.

§4. LABOUR TRIBUNAL (ADJUDICATION)

574. If conciliation is not able to settle a claim amicably, the disputed case may be referred by the conciliation officer of the Labour Relations Service, under a certificate of conciliation, to the Labour Tribunal for legal determination. In essence, the Labour Tribunal is only competent to hear disputes over rights, having in this capacity jurisdiction over claims which arise from a breach of the terms of the contract of employment – whether for local performance, or pertaining to an overseas

26. As a sequel to the enactment of the Labour Tribunal Ordinance in 1972, which later established the Labour Tribunal in 1973.

contract – or of statutory prescriptions of the Employment Ordinance. The Tribunal, however, is not competent to hear any disputes of interest (which pertain to such issues as demands for wage improvements and improvements in other conditions of employment, about which there are not yet any established legal or contractual norms themselves subject to negotiation between the parties). Also falling outside the realm of its jurisdiction are employees' compensation claims, as well as any claims for damages in tort arising from a breach of contract, or a breach of a duty at common law or sanctioned by any other statutory enactments.

575. It was the express intention of the Labour Tribunal Ordinance, when enacted in 1972, to establish the Labour Tribunal as a quick, inexpensive and informal mechanism for the adjudication of claims arising from the individual labour contracts. These claims are hence heard by a Presiding Officer (himself a career judge) who sits alone in an informal manner, normally in public. The informality of such proceedings is noticeable for the following features:

(i) a conscious and deliberate effort to reduce overt legalism as in the ordinary courts of law by disallowing any professional legal representatives to appear on behalf of the disputants;[27] and
(ii) the discretion available to the Presiding Officer to conduct the proceedings in either English or Chinese.

576. Inasmuch as all incumbent Presiding Officers are at present Chinese speaking, it is natural and common for Chinese to be used. Besides, it is necessary at law for the claim to be heard within 30 days after it has been lodged with the Registrar of the Labour Tribunal, unless the parties involved have consented to a delay. In practice, the waiting period for a claim hence filed to be heard in the Tribunal has been extended much longer – producing a queue which probably suggests the popularity of such a 'labour court'. An excessive lead period in clearing the Tribunal's backlog of accumulated cases in the 1990s hence led to the creation of not only additional 'courts' in the Tribunal but also the Minor Employment Claims Adjudication Board as a part of the labour administration within the domain of the Labour Department.

577. Investigation into the background of a claim lodged with the Tribunal is normally conducted by the Tribunal Officers, during the period which intervenes between the registration and hearing of the claim.

578. As a judicial institution, the Labour Tribunal is also a court of record belonging to the judiciary. It is not answerable in such a capacity to the administration of the SAR government, but independent of its decisions.

579. However, when appeals from the Tribunal's decisions, permissible on points of law, are available, they can go to the District Court, High Court or Court

27. Where the Tribunal grants leave, however, an official of a registered trade union may represent the parties at the Tribunal hearing, if so authorized by the disputing party.

of Appeal. An award given by the Tribunal is, furthermore, registrable as a judgment of the District Court. Concomitantly, the Presiding Officer possesses similar judicial power as a court judge – including abilities such as to summon evidence and witnesses, as well as to sentence summarily anyone guilty of wilful contempt of the Tribunal at its hearing.

§5. Statute of Limitations

580. The Labour Tribunal Ordinance places a longitudinal limit to the Tribunal's jurisdiction over claims arising from the individual labour contracts. It is competent to hear within a six-month time limit which follows the incidence of the wrongful act allegedly committed and giving rise to the claims. If the time limit has already lapsed, the case of the claim is actionable in the Tribunal only when the mutual consent of the parties are given. Alternatively, the case can be instituted at the higher level of the District Court or the High Court, as a civil claim. In the latter situation, civil claims over a contract are actionable within the purview of the District Court within six years from the time of the alleged breach.

581. Conversely, those cases pertaining to labour statues which carry penal sanctions and are prosecuted by the Attorney General as criminal offences are instituted normally at the level of the magistracies. Under the Magistracy Ordinance, cases within its purview will become out of date six months after the alleged commission of the legally censured acts.

§6. Minor Employment Claims Adjudication Board

582. The Adjudication Board is an organ created in the 1990s in order to furnish an ancillary supplement to the judiciary machinery of the Labour Tribunal which has become overloaded with outstanding 'claim' disputes. By virtue of the Minor Employment Claims Adjudication Board Ordinance of 1994, the government introduced a board of simplified administrative procedures, as staffed by labour officials within the Labour Department, for adjudicating minor employment claims. As a sequel, a significant proportion of grievance claims at employment, otherwise shouldered by the overburdened Tribunal, is hence now handled and decided by way of an adjudicating mechanism which is, however, outside the purview of the judiciary but incorporated into the jurisdiction of the labour administration.

583. Belonging to the Labour Department, the Board's jurisdiction is yet limited, as it is only competent to deal with those minor claims:

(i) arising from disputes of statutory or contractual rights of employment;
(ii) involving not more than ten claimants; and
(iii) not exceeding HK$8,000 by each claimant.

584. The above notwithstanding, the Adjudication Board offers the essential advantage of a simple, inexpensive and independent, albeit officially sponsored, procedure for settling claims and grievances outside the workplace. Its primary appeal is that its less judicial auspices enable it to work at a faster pace than the core institution of the Labour Tribunal. It is necessary, however, for the voluntary conciliation proceedings to be exhausted before any claims can be entertained by the Board which is hence, unlike the Labour Tribunal, not directly accessible to the disputing parties, unless with referral from the conciliation officer in the Labour Department.

585. Its jurisdiction is analogous to the Labour Tribunal in nature, and as such it is not competent to hear a claim for tortuous damages or one which has to be submitted to proof in a bankruptcy and winding-up proceeding application. The statutory time limit allowed to lapse between the filing of the claim and the incidence of the alleged default giving rise to the claim is 12 months and not 6 months as in the instance of the Labour Tribunal proceedings.

586. Otherwise, the judicial ability of the Adjudication Board broadly emulates that of the Labour Tribunal. The adjudication officer is vested with almost comparable authority as the Presiding Officer in the Labour Tribunal. He is, for instance, endowed with the same privileges and immunities as a High Court judge in civil proceedings. Besides, any failure of the parties and witnesses to submit information and evidence summoned by the Board is held as tantamount to contempt of court, which is a punishable offence. Like the case of a Tribunal decision, an award or order of the Board may be registered in the District Court and enforceable as a judgment of the latter.

587. Appeals from the decision of the Board are entertainable at the level of the High Court, provided that (i) the appeal is lodged within seven days after the order of the award and (ii) it is justified on grounds that the award is wrong on points of law or is outside the valid jurisdiction of the Board.

588. As a sequel to the enactment of the Employment (Amendment) Ordinance in 2012, an employer who defaults in the payment of the sum as awarded or ordered by the Labour Tribunal or the Minor Employment Claims Adjudication Board is guilty of an offence and liable to penal sanctions. Unless otherwise specified, the awarded sum is due within 14 days after the award is made. An employer who does not effect payment within 14 days after the due day, wilfully and without reasonable excuse, is liable to prosecution as a criminal offence and upon conviction, a maximum sanction of HK$350,000 and three-year imprisonment.

In the case of a limited company which defaults on payment, the consent or connivance of its director or any responsible person or the latter's negligence causing the offence will also render him liable to a maximum fine of HK$350,000 and imprisonment for three years.

Chapter 11. Anti-corruption Control and Implications for Employment Rights and Freedom

§1. Introduction

589. In the 1970s a dedicated campaign was launched by the government with a view to curtailing and eradicating malpractices and the vice of corruption in Hong Kong. This problem was considered by both the administration to have been so injurious to Hong Kong society and tarnished it with such a notorious image, especially following the interdiction of two senior police officers in 1973, that it considered that the perversion of social justice and the impediments caused to the efficiency of the official bureaucracy would have been immensely costly to the territory. Accordingly, it was resolved to institute measures to eradicate this form of vice.

590. Emanating from the landmark reports of two successive commissions of enquiry on corruption, both conducted by Sir Alistair Blair-Kerr (then a senior Puisne Judge at the Supreme Court) in 1973, profound innovations have been introduced to the legislative framework governing the definition, control and censure of activities involving bribery and corruption. These statutory reforms, together with the creation in 1974 of a specialized agency (vested with extensive powers of investigation and arrest), known as the Independent Commission against Corruption, today puts in place a pervasive machinery of control which, in spite of its proven efficacy in demolishing, curbing and deterring the vice of corruption, has implied a substantial degree of state-sponsored intervention with an employee's freedom, especially impinging upon the security and privacy of those who are engaged in the public and civil service.

§2. Statutory Provisions

591. In essence, the penal codes for controlling and proscribing bribery and corruption are contained in three sets of interrelated legislation, viz. the Prevention of Bribery Ordinance, the Corrupt and Illegal Practices Ordinance and the Independent Commission Against Corruption Ordinance. In addition, parallel administrative rules may also be found in the Civil Service Regulations and Government Regulations, the sanctioning effects of which are, however, limited to the civil service. While the Independent Commission Against Corruption Ordinance is primarily the enabling legislation which creates the Commission as the investigatory and law-enforcing agency in this area, the Corrupt and Illegal Practices Ordinance has remained relatively dormant in recent years, leaving the Prevention of Bribery Ordinance, enacted as the principal statutory instrument which deals with this type of criminal offence.

592. The Prevention of Bribery Ordinance repealed and replaced its predecessor, the former Prevention of Corruption Ordinance of 1948. While both pieces of legislation were coined largely in the British tradition, the more recent ordinance introduces an element of local adaptation while incorporating selected references to the parallel legislation in Ceylon (Sri Lanka) and Singapore. The law now declares it as an offence, by virtue of its Section 3, for a crown servant[28] to solicit or accept any advantages without the special or general permission of the Governor or the Chief Executive. The law places an express prohibition on any person to obtain benefits other than his own official emoluments by making use of his employment in the civil service. However, exceptions are given for 'entertainment' and specified items of 'advantages' as sanctioned specifically under the Acceptance of Advantages Regulations.

593. Even more restrictive a control in regulating the individual's freedom is that provision, by virtue of Section 10 of the said ordinance, which precludes a crown servant,[29] past or serving, from maintaining a standard of living above that commensurate with his present or past level of official emoluments. Nor is it permissible for him to control pecuniary resources or property disproportionately high *vis-à-vis* his income levels. The clause does not necessitate any material proof of the Commission of any specific act of graft and malpractice – which is often difficult to substantiate technically at law. Instead, it will be sufficient for the prosecution to demonstrate the existence of an excessive standard of living or control of disproportionate financial means in order to establish a prima facie case for indictment.

594. In order to defend one's innocence and to nullify the foregoing presumption, it is incumbent upon the employee himself to submit to the court a satisfactory explanation, which details the reason(s) leading to such incongruence between his income and affluent spending. These legal measures, together with the wide powers of investigation, search and seizure extended by Sections 13, 14, 15, 16, 17 and 18 of the Independent Commission Against Corruption Ordinance, to the Commission's enforcement agents, introduce a relatively coercive flavour of legalistic intervention into the lifestyles and personal finance of those investigated. The investigation of the suspect, inasmuch as the court proceedings are also heard openly, may subject him to public humiliation and the risk of long-term career impairment. The infliction of such damages, has invited a considerable degree of disquiet and scepticism, both within the civil service as well as in the legal profession, that such arbitrary powers are excessive. By enabling the government to intervene readily in the individual's private life, these powers often tamper unduly with the latter's human rights and individual liberty, which are important norms featuring a modern civil society.

595. In spite of its innovative character, the Prevention of Bribery Ordinance kept a relatively low profile in the statute book in the first three years after its inception. It was not activated extensively until 1973, which saw a community-wide movement against corruption, especially directed to scrutinize the police force and other government departments suspected to be corruption prone. Such an anti-graft euphoria in public opinion culminated in the rather dramatic trials of two senior police officers in 1973. Intense pressure represented in the mass media led to the

28. As from 1997 onwards, crown servants are civil servants of the new SAR government.
29. The authority is now the Chief Executive, in place of the Governor.

appointment of the Blair-Kerr Commission of Enquiry in the same year and later, the inception of the Independent Commission against Corruption in 1974.

596. The enhanced application of the legislation in 1973 elucidated the need for its improved amendments in order to reinforce its effectiveness as a cardinal weapon against corruption. By virtue of the subsequent amendments introduced in the same year (1973), the rights of the accused to make representations to the Attorney General prior to court proceedings were rescinded – for the purported rationale to minimize any unwarranted delays caused to the institution of the relevant legal actions. And to forestall any absconding attempts, the amended legislation also empowers the enforcement agent to demand a suspect to surrender his travel documents, thereby circumscribing temporarily the latter's freedom of movement before his indictment was clarified or otherwise.

597. More strenuous prerogative of public intervention into the individual's freedom was yet to be introduced later, under the 1974 amendments to the law. These latter changes introduced a presumption, contrary to the spirit of British common law, which deems the accused to have been in control of pecuniary resources or property held by another person where a court is satisfied, having regard to the such other person's relationship to the accused and other related factors and conditions, that it is reasonable to believe that such a person was holding this property on behalf of the accused. The implication of such a construction is hence to broaden the legally ascertainable and examinable scope of the individual's control of finance and property beyond the prima facie criterion of direct ownership to include as well the wealth of others related to him. Such an extension is legally justifiable, so long as there is a reasonable suspicion of a trusteeship or a transfer in the form of gifts. The legal intent is evidently to make the appraisal of the employee's financial position more realistic and thorough. However, in so doing, the expanded provision is liable to pose a nuisance to or harassment of the rights of the spouse of the suspect, or of his relatives and friends, whose assets have to be subject to protracted official investigation by virtue of their relationship to the suspected public service employee.

598. Concomitantly, it is now an offence as well if the suspect neglects or fails to comply with the investigator's notice requiring him to specify how and when he acquired his property. A civil servant[30] convicted of an offence under the ordinance is, in addition, liable to court orders of confiscation either to pay to the SAR government [31] the amount of value of the advantage received, or alternatively, to indemnify the SAR government a sum tantamount to that part of his property or pecuniary resources the acquisition of which has not been explained to the satisfaction of the Court.

30. See note 39.
31. It is now the SAR government in place of the Crown.

§3. The Independent Commission Against Corruption (ICAC)

599. Prior to 1974, the jurisdiction to investigate an act of bribery and corruption cases rested with the police force which was, paradoxically, one of those government departments considered to be most notoriously afflicted by corrupt practices. The police force had endeavoured to clean its house by several campaigns which were, however, almost invariably futile. The stalemate, as noted in the findings of the Blair-Kerr Commission, finally led to removal of such powers from the police force and their transfer to a newly created agency under statute in 1974. It has hitherto been an 'independent organization, standing apart from any department of the government, and answering directly to the Governor',[32] named as the Independent Commission against Corruption (ICAC). The enabling piece of legislation is the Independent Commission against Corruption Ordinance, introduced and enacted in 1974. Deriving its prerogative directly from the Governor and the Chief Executive after 1997, the ICAC enjoys almost complete autonomy from the administration. The Commission is headed by the Commissioner and Deputy Commissioner, both of whom are appointed by the Governor and the Chief Executive after 1997 on such terms and conditions as he may deem suitable, without being subjected to the normal administrative exigencies of civil service appointments and the associated procedural rules.

600. The Commission, comprising three functional departments (namely, Operations, Corruption Prevention and Community Relations) is empowered, by virtue of Section 12 of the enabling ordinance, to:

(i) receive and consider complaints alleging corruption practices and investigate those complaints warranting investigating actions;
(ii) investigate any alleged or suspected offences under the Prevention of Bribery Ordinance or the Corrupt and Illegal Practices Ordinance;
(iii) investigate any conduct of a civil servant who, in the opinion of the Commissioner, is connected with or vulnerable to corrupt practices and to report thereof to the Chief Executive; and
(iv) examine the practices and procedures of government departments and of private sector businesses in order to ascertain possible areas of corruptive practices and to secure the revision and abrogation of work methods or procedures which in the opinion of the Commissioner, are conducive to corrupt practices;
(v) instruct, advise and assist any person, upon the latter's request, on ways in which to curb or even eliminate corrupt practices;
(vi) advise heads of government departments, public bodies, private enterprises and business and trade associations of changes in practices or procedures which are compatible with the effective discharge of the functions and duties of such organizations which the Commissioner considers to be necessary to reduce the likelihood of any corrupt practices;

32. See note 29.

(vii) educate the public against the evils of corruption; and
(viii) enlist and foster public support in combating corruption.

601. Given the above purview of the Commission's jurisdiction, an employee of the government or any other public bodies or any private companies is hence subject to the special powers of investigation, apprehension and detention by the Commission's officers (including, for instance, extensive powers of search, inspection and seizure of accounts as well as whatever documents in connection with the performance of his employment duties). The Commissioner is, moreover, empowered to impose restrictions on the disposal of the suspect's property or that of any other related third parties during the period of his investigation. In an even more coercive approach, the Commission may even apply *ex parte* for a 'restraining order' from the court seeking to freeze literally all financial transactions relating to the suspect except in accordance with the court's directions. If given a liberal interpretation, these powers could be construed to include a curtailment of the individual's rights of access to his salary and other resources which would normally enable him to meet his living expenses and other standing commitments and obligations. Theoretically, such restraints could apply notwithstanding that these rights are within the ambit of his legitimate employment activities, even where they engender little or no connection at all with the suspected act of corruption.

§4. Implications for Employment and Work

602. The overt success of the ICAC and its effective challenge to the police and its power not only in unveiling police corruption but also posing as an inroad to police authority on account of the 'comparable character' of the two agencies – has bred a substantial amount of discontent and apprehension within the police force. In 1977, unrest erupted among the heavily demoralized and alienated police officers, as manifest in such militant actions as demonstrations and siege of the ICAC headquarters. When the protest threatened to escalate into a full-scale and force-wide police strike, the Governor conceded by granting an amnesty pardoning all the old offenders, thereby averting an imminent police strike (or even 'mutiny', according to some observers).

603. Nevertheless, as its secondary effects, the police upheaval has been instrumental for a major development in policemen's consciousness of their right to organize collectively. In spite of the hitherto proscription under the Police Ordinance on the organization of trade unions in the police force, the rank-and-file members were given the official approval, as a sequel to the 1977 incident, to combine to form a staff association, under the title of the Junior Police Officers Association (JPOA), registered as a society and outside the formal ambit of the Trade Unions Ordinance. However, this association has henceforth assumed a number of quasi-union functions and activities.

604. As another important implication of these developments, the official efforts to eradicate the relatively entrenched social ills of corruption and bribery in Hong

Kong have not only served to repair steadily, since the mid-1970s, the image of the civil service but have also penetrated the private economy in weeding out creepingly various embedded improper and notorious customs and practices there. There were customs once endemic in a profession, a trade, a vocation or an occupation which permitted or, at least, tolerated the employees' tacit (and sometimes unwarranted) expectation for and acceptance of gratuities from their clients/customers in appreciation of their lawful services. These practices were and still are prevalent in service trades like hotels and restaurants, tourism and hair-dressing. However, it appears that such transfers (unless they are simply limited to the form of a token gift) are liable to fall within the definition of improperly acquired 'advantages', now given its extended interpretation under the post-1974 anti-corruption regulatory framework. Yet they are deemed legitimate, provided with the consent of the employer.

605. Since the tightening up of counter-corruption measures, what may free these benefits being offered and received in both the public and private sectors from incrimination as ethically and legally censured acts is only when the advantage is offered and/or received by the employee or hired agent in the knowledge of and with the approval of his employer. A classic example of such a dependence upon the employer's consent or approval to legitimate these transfers between the server (i.e., the employee) and the served (i.e., the customer or client) is in the restaurant, catering and hotel industries for accommodating the enshrined practice of giving 'tips' and their receipt. The employer's acknowledgement or sanction is hence a key factor to determining whether or not a case 'with lawful authority or reasonable excuse' can be established. In any case, it is not permissible for these advantages or benefits to be solicited, directly or indirectly, by the recipient. Even where an advantage has been acquired purportedly in conformity with established custom in a profession, trade, vocation or occupation, the act is still held as unlawful if without the employers' consent. In fact, Section 12 of the Prevention of Bribery Ordinance expressly rules out the admissibility of using reference to trade custom alone as a legitimate and acceptable defence in court.

606. The widened interpretation and application of these legal sanctions *vis-à-vis* the notion of 'advantages' – initially directed at the civil service, extended subsequently to the public bodies and organizations and later, broadened generically to embrace as well the private sector – has won territory-wide approval throughout society as an innovative pointer to enhancing both morality and ethical standards, at work as well as in business. Of course, it has also levied heavily upon Hong Kong's society, in the last two decades, and led to a painful process of transition and adjustments in having these notorious and abhorrent practices rescinded, especially in those industries where these types of transaction have been rooted in traditions considered more or less customary, or 'normative' and even 'irrevocable'.

607. Concomitantly, these revamped and enhanced statutory devices have also devolved to the individual employer, in a vicarious manner, a new measure of discretionary power over his employees. The former's extension or withholding of his consent is now seen as cardinal in legitimating, or otherwise, the latter's receipt of 'advantages' in connection with their employment. Conspicuous and, often, contentious examples of these deeds are 'kick-backs', rebates, gifts, commission or even tips.

608. However, that far-reaching piece of legislative reform which has led to the legality of construing the commission of corruption from the individual's maintenance of an affluent lifestyle or of financial resources, beyond what is tenable under one's official emoluments, has been restricted, almost exclusively, up to the present to the civil service in its application.

609. In the wake of the community's growing awareness about the imperative nature of business ethics and corporate social responsibility, the ICAC as the competent law-enforcing as well as promotion agency, has intensified both its investigatory and publicity-cum-educational activities in private sector business. Its recent endeavours oriented to upgrading the ethical image of the territory's private business are reflected in (i) the increasing number of complaints received by and coming under the agency's investigation (for instance, in the year 2007, the agency received 3,600 reports alleging corruption, of which 66 per cent involved the private sector while the number of cases implicating public sector employees dropped by 9 per cent compared with 2006);[33] and (ii) the inception since 1994, and continuation of an intensive promotion exercise on business ethics, aimed at encouraging the business sector to adopted corporate codes of conduct, a strategy which is seen as crucial for buttressing the city's image as a leading international business centre of high repute.[34]

610. Also, in recognition of the growing and consolidating economic integration (in terms of trade, capital, labour and investment, etc.) between the Chinese and Hong Kong economies, there has emerged a conspicuous increase in the volume and intensity of cross-border cooperation and joint actions between the ICAC and its counterparts in southern China – noticeably in the Guangdong Province. The ICAC collaborates with the anti-corruption authorities in Guangdong and Macao in the authorship of a guide book on the cross-border legislative regulation of corruption. In addition, an anti-corruption publicity campaign was launched in the year 2012 to propagate the core value of integrity at work and in business transactions and dealings. There have been consistent efforts by the ICAC in educating the public against greed and exhortation. Fraud-free election activities are also promoted via various channels of the mass media.

611. At the end of 2012, altogether 2,470 cases were investigated by the Commission. A salient proportion of them were associated with election. A total of 2,413 complaints attributed to election were recorded by the Commission in the same year, emanating largely from the District Council election of the previous year. Such a

33. Hong Kong Government, *Hong Kong 2007*, Hong Kong Government Printer, 2008.
34. Hong Kong Government, *Hong Kong 1995: A Review of 1994*, Hong Kong: Government Printer, 1995, p. 325.

high share of scandalous election behaviour is probably typical of elected democracies. From a more critical perspective, it is also symptomatic of the immature culture of representative election in Hong Kong, which is still in an infant stage of development.

612. As a mechanism of checks and balances on the power of the Commission, there exist four independent commissions which oversee and scrutinize its work. They are the Advisory Committee on Corruption, the Operations Review Committee the Corruption Prevention Advisory Committee and the Citizens Advisory Committee on Community Relations. In addition, an independent ICAC Complaints Committee appointed by the Chief Executive monitors and handles all non-criminal complaints against the Commission and its staff.

613. Notwithstanding the esteem which Hong Kong has enjoyed over the last two decades as one of the world's most corruption-free societies, this image has been recently clouded by the indictment resolution passed by the Legislative Council in 2013 against the out-going Commissioner Against Corruption for his malpractices and lavish spending during his term of office. The episode has led to the initiation of disciplinary procedures against several senior staff members of the Commission. At the same time, public scepticism against the efficacy of the Commission increased.

Chapter 12. Migrant Workers and Labour Importation

§1. Background

614. Hong Kong society and its population have always been in a hybrid state affected importantly by migration into and out of the territory. Historically, the 'visiting' and transient mentality of its 'dwellers', typical before the Second World War, was documented officially in such dossiers as the *Butters Report on Labour and Labour Conditions in Hong Kong*. Mr Butters, the then Labour Officer (equivalent to the Commissioner for Labour today), made reference to the 'Kiu Kong' fluidity of the Hong Kong residents because of their Chinese ethnicity and identity, as he reported in 1939 as below:

> Certain local associations instead of employing the words 'Hong Kong' in their names stills use 'Kiu Kong' meaning that their members regard themselves as only temporarily resident in Hong Kong. Here they have no abiding home. And by Chinese law based on the *jus sanguine*, persons of Chinese race, even if born in Hong Kong, are regarded as Chinese subjects. Such persons have therefore dual nationality [35]

615. Nor has Hong Kong been immune, in its postwar drama of spectacular industrial development, from the influence of migration waves arriving from China which were both conducive to as well as constraining upon its growth. In retrospect, economists agree that the unheralded experience of its industrial take-off in the 1950s and 1960s (it has become a model of 'late-development' for the neoclassical economists, given the economic success Hong Kong has achieved as one of East Asia's leading newly industrialized economies, NIEs, was made possible basically because of the migration push from mainland China in the wake of politico-social upheavals that climaxed in the 1949 Liberation and change of government. There was a 'refugee' stampede, alongside the inflow of industrial capital, entrepreneurship, technological knowhow, technical manpower and semi-skilled/unskilled labour in cheap and abundant supply. The spirit of 'migrant capitalism' and the half-insecure and half-neurotic labouring psychology of a predominantly 'refugee' workforce have hitherto given Hong Kong an efficacious local ethos of 'industrialism' – pragmatic, sensitive, adaptive, flexible and yet instrumental with a yearning for a high degree of market freedom. As narrated by Chen:

> The civil war ended with the establishment of a Comminist regime in China in 1949. Under the pressure of these political events, a huge inflow of labour, capital and entrepreneurial skill from China to Hong Kong occurred during the period 1948–51. Those taking refuge in Hong Kong included young and energetic people who were intelligent and willing to work hard, people with much money capital, and skilled entrepreneurs who were mostly Shanghainese industrialists engaged in the textile industry. The huge inflow of human and

35. H.R. Butters, *Report by the Labour Officer on Labour and Labour Conditions in Hong Kong*, Sessional Paper No. 3, Hong Kong Government Printer, 1939, para. 6, p.108; also see para. 47, p. 116.

capital resources from China formed the basis of subsequent industrialization.[36]

616. The Mainland stampede of immigrants into Hong Kong subsided as cross-border control was later instituted by both the Chinese and Hong Kong authorities in the 1950s. The demographic 'fluidity' of the territory steadily drained away as its society became henceforth increasingly detached from the mainland 'enclave' and its population consolidated as these refugees settled in Hong Kong and became the first-generation belongers to the territory. It has been hence observed:

> Prior to 1941 Hong Kong had always attracted a high proportion of migrant male workers from the neighbouring Guangdong province.... Since 1950, however, the vast majority of the population ceased to be transients. Most people who work in Hong Kong are now also permanent residents in the colony.[37]

617. Notwithstanding the ban on immigration at the Sino-British border which has effectively pre-empted any large-scale influx of mainland Chinese arrivals at Hong Kong, there have been sporadic spurts, during the last several decades, in their entry into the territory, which mirrored the shifting politico-economic mood inside China. The 'stampede' was, for example, 'resumed for only a brief period in 1962 when the Chinese authorities suddenly removed the restrictions' – leading to a peak six-week period in which 'over 600,000 illegal immigrants were arrested and returned to China, while a similar number probably evaded arrest'.

618. Otherwise, Hong Kong society has remained in a virtual state of 'enclave' which depends primarily upon the natural growth of its population. In spite of its transient nature before the 1950s and its refugee background, a 'native' home consciousness began to emerge and take root in the locally born postwar generations whose 'migrant' mentality has steadily subsided.

619. As Hong Kong hastened its industrial growth after the 1960s, its demographic structure steadily matured with declining birth rate and labour shortage began to emerge. Gradually uplifting itself from the low-income 'trap' of a surplus labour economy, Hong Kong's income and wage differentials *vis-à-vis* its hinterland across the border have widened to such a glaring gap that it would have served as a powerful pulling force attracting mainland labour to migrate in search of the lucrative economic and job opportunities available in the territory, were it not for the tight 'iron grip' of bureaucratic controls owed to the 'household registration' system on the mainland and the 'cross-border' immigration checks and barriers which the Sino-British authorities enforced.

---

36. Edward K.Y. Chen, 'The Economic Setting', in Ng Sek-Hong and David Lethbridge (eds.), *The Business Environment in Hong Kong*, Hong Kong: Oxford University Press, 4th edn, 2000, p.4.
37. David Lethbridge and Ng Sek-Hong, 'The Business Environment and Employment', David Lethbridge (eds.), *The Business Environment in Hong Kong*: Oxford University Press, 2nd edn with A Postscript in the 1990s, 1993, p. 80.

620. Such administrative and institutional controls did appear to ease at the dawn of China's modernization as it began to open the country to foreign trade, commerce and capital. The euphoria of the embryonic reform mood in the Mainland instigated a creeping inflow of unauthorized (i.e. illegal) mainland immigrants. They were not seeking political asylum but searching for gainful economic opportunities. These unlawful entries were for a brief interval tolerated by the Hong Kong government, provided that such arrivals were able to make for and reach the urban areas – by a practice generally described as the 'touch-base' policy. Such a 'hiatus' in Hong Kong's immigration history has been documented as follows:

> Coinciding with the inflow of Vietnamese refugees was the pressure of immigrant movements from China around the turn of the decade. The bulk of the Chinese immigrants arriving during this period were illegal entrants without proper official documentation – largely aspiring to the materialistic affluence of life-style in Hong Kong and encouraged by the relative tolerance of the 'touch-base' policy of the Hong Kong Government.[38]

However, the magnitude of the stampede soon grew to such a level that the Hong Kong government was later forced to rescind its 'touch-base' policy.

621. The 'touch-base' policy norm, by which illegal Chinese immigrants who succeeded in evading arrest at the border and countryside and who secured urban accommodation would be allowed *de facto* right of stay, was hence merely a 'stopgap' measure in nature. After October 1980, illegal immigrants were no longer privileged by administrative clemency from apprehension even after arriving at the 'base'. Rather, they were equally liable to arrest and repatriation to China. In order to facilitate detection, the Immigration Ordinance was amended to require all adult residents in Hong Kong to carry their identity cards or equivalent documents, and produce them for inspection upon demand by police, immigration or other authorized officers.

622. In any case, the stampede during this transient interval of liberal admission, as well as the subsequent intake, under an agreed quota jointly administered by the Chinese and Hong Kong authorities, of legal immigrants from the mainland, have given rise to a peripheral and yet significant segment of lesser skilled and lesser paid employment in the Hong Kong labour market. As a territory-wide labour study concludes in its review of the 'immigration drama' at the beginning of the 1990s, 'it appears likely that over 40 per cent of new entrants into the labour market between our two surveys (1975 and 1985) came from this source'.[39] Given 'that immigrant workers, or their counterparts in the imported labour force, are lower

38. Ng Sek-Hong, Hong Kong, a monograph in the series, R. Blanpain (ed.), *International Encyclopaedia for Labour Law and Industrial Relations*, The Netherlands: Kluwer, 1990, Supplement 109, para. 262, p. 165.

39. H. A. Turner, Patricia Fosh and Ng Sek-hong, *Between Two Societies: Hong Kong Labour in Transition*, Hong Kong: Centre of Asian Studies, University of Hong Kong, 1991, p.38.

paid ... and liable to occupy jobs of lesser status and skills than the average member of the labour force',[40] a secondary labour market appears to be consolidating in Hong Kong, where these socially disadvantaged workers are clustered. Their economic deprivation, insecurity and vulnerabilities suggest a local syndrome of 'urban poverty', in spite of the relative industrial affluence and prosperity that Hong Kong society has achieved in these years. Such a 'stratifying' phenomenon has been represented in these terms:

> Openings of lesser jobs in the manufacturing industry provide, instead, tangible opportunities in the secondary labour market for marginal workers like recent immigrants, women workers or part-time employment, or homeworkers in 'putting-out' arrangements.[41]

623. Although in Hong Kong, the buoyant labour market has continued to be 'sufficiently attractive to draw pockets of illegal immigrants from the mainland, especially for work at building and construction sites',[42] the rescinding of the 'touch-base' policy since the early 1980s has stemmed an important source of non-authorized migration and cheap labour supply to the territory – which has served beforehand as an important 'safety-valve' for its manpower economy. Instead, it is now increasingly beset by 'labour scarcity' due to both sustained upsurge in industrial demand and withering natural growth of its population. Compounded by the territory's economic re-structuring process touched off, *inter alia*, by the 'China' factor, labour and land scarcity coalesced, at the turn of the decade, into an upward cost spiral due to rapidly escalating inflation.

§2. The Pre-1997 Syndrome

624. The creeping syndrome of intensifying inflationary pressure which began to build up towards the turn of the decade triggered a vociferous lobby in the business sector demanding that the government, in spite of its initial reluctance,to liberalize its hitherto stringent policy of not admitting any foreign guest workers of a general nature, at the semi-skilled and unskilled levels. Of course, such a policy norm of non-admission of alien labour had never been total and comprehensive, inasmuch as (i) a liberal stance had consistently been maintained enabling expatriate managerial, administrative and professional personnel to enter the top echelon of the territory's manpower hierarchy, justified on the ground that they represented a beneficial factor of skill/know-how/capital transfer to Hong Kong;[43] and (ii) since 1973, foreign domestic helpers have been admitted in large numbers to work in households, to release housewives in many middle-income households for gainful employment in the full-time labour market.

---

40. David G. Lethbridge and Ng Sek-Hong, 'Labour and Employment', in Ng Sek Hong and David G. Lethbridge (eds.), *The Business Environment in Hong Kong*, Hong Kong: Oxford University Press, 3rd edn, 1995, pp. 69-71.
41. *Ibid.*, p. 68.
42. *Ibid.*, p. 67.
43. *Ibid.*, p. 65.

625. The government's concession to industry's demands for labour importation led to the inception of a regulated intake, intended as a 'stop-gap' arrangement in coping with the economy's inflation and bottlenecks stemming from labour shortage, of general guest workers at the semi-skilled and unskilled levels. Such labour importation eventually consolidated, at the beginning of the 1990s, into two administratively distinct *ad hoc* schemes. The first, titled as the General Labour Importation Scheme, prescribed the hiring of alien guest workers, based upon a two-year standard contract which stipulated the payment of at least the median wage in the trade and industry concerned, according to an industrially differentiated quota determined and adjusted by the government with reference to criteria such as the nature of the industry and the skills where shortage lay, the expected size of local supply and the industry's vacancy level. This scheme of general intake, subject to a maximum of not more than 25,000 in number for the entire exercise, also emulated the Singaporean system in following the ILO standards which made it mandatory for the employer to provide accommodation and repatriation facilities for the guest workers. The second, with a regulatory regime broadly analogous to the first, catered specifically to the new airport construction and associated infrastructural projects. As such, the admission quota was assigned basically to employers who were the building and construction contractors who were allowed to recruit semi-skilled labour from overseas – up to a ceiling not exceeding 17,000 in size.

626. The above enlargement of expatriate and alien guest labour in Hong Kong was hence an unprecedented measure in labour market deregulation. Its implications had been essentially twofold in affecting labour and employment in Hong Kong, which used to be conserved in an 'enclave' at the lower-reach of its skill market, among the semi-skilled and unskilled personnel, both manual and non-manual.

627. The first had been the strong and persistent hostility articulated by the labour movement – apparently antagonized by the lack of adequate official consultation since such advisory bodies as the Labour Advisory Board on which organized labour was represented was by-passed before the relevant policy decision was made. Organized labour's disquiet has since then been laden with an overtone of 'protectionism', which appealed to the 'grassroots' sentiments in the currency of the 'electoral' contests. Candidates sponsored by the labour unions were keen in bidding for the workers' votes. They canvassed assiduously a parochial perspective, blaming the newly imported guest workers for blocking the transfer to job openings available and re-employment in the new tertiary service sector of the mid-career industrial workers who were hived off from the quickly shrinking manufacturing sector. The drift of a growing casualty of industrial unemployment was hence symptomatic of the territory's economic restructuing around this period, due to the *en masse* immigration northwards of Hong Kong factories, pushed away by soaring and formidable costs of land and labour and in search for their cheaper and more ample supply in the Mainland.

The visiting alien worker was hence 'castigated' widely in the labour sector as the culprit responsible for perpetuating Hong Kong's agony of its unemployment problem. Worse still, in spite of the government's widely publicized 're-training' efforts, the low transferability of the hard-core industrially unemployed (due to their middle or old age) to the service industries has rendered ineffective any corrective to the intersectoral imbalances in the skill market caused by reasons as noted above. In this context, the labour movement perceived as its mission to 'crusade' for the abolition of general labour importation, perceived as the key lever to the unemployment phenomenon that began to beset the territory in the mid 1990s.

628. The second ramification pertains to the vulnerabilities of the 'guest' workers, by virtue of their alien status and social marginality, to workplace abuse and exploitation as 'sweat shop' labour. These problems have been attested by the disclosure, in a number of labour grievance disputes affecting both mainland Chinese and Thai imported workers hired at the airport and associated construction and building sites, that these imported workers were susceptible to excessive wage deductions or other devious squeezes levied by either the employer, or the intermediary acting as the recruitment agency. Substantial assistance was provided by the local unions which intervened actively in helping these deprived visiting labour to recover their wages and legal entitlements in employment. Ironically, the same union organizations have also been the principal social agencies having instigated the public to 'arm' against labour importation. Their inhospitable or even hostile reception of the guest workers was a key factor which explains the widespread and lingering social prejudices and discrimination against these workers.

629. The industrial drama spearheaded by organized labour's 'crusade' waged against imported labour began to subside, when the government yielded to the pressure and announced in September 1996 its decision to phase out the General Labour Importation Scheme with a substituting but much diminished Supplementary Labour Scheme, whose scale was trimmed down to a nominal size of 3,000. Paradoxically, the labour unions have been pretentiously silent about the existing, and rather sizable, population of expatriate professionals, corporate managers and executives as well as the foreign domestic helpers. This society's silent consent on their entry contrasts sharply with the offensively high intolerance articulated by its unions towards the semi-skilled and unskilled 'alien' workers, especially those from the Mainland.

630. The irony of the official decision to deregulate the hiring of guest workers has been concomitantly a meticulous concern by the authorities to regulate and control strenuously the intake of these foreign workers. Essentially, this regime of formalized rules was designed to safeguard guest workers' rights and to contain their competitive threats to locals. The cornerstone instrument was a fixed-term standard contract of two years' duration. While such contracts had the intrinsic appeal of delimiting the parties' commitments, the provisions also helped to enhance the parties' certainty during the contract duration. Guest workers were guaranteed a secure job for two years and vice versa for employers. The contract also served to limit the parties' commitment to the prescribed period. Besides, it helped assure apprehensive locals that such guest hiring was of a nature and did not impede their job opportunities in the longer-run.

Parallel to these advantages of certainty was a formidable rigidity due to the rules against any lateral or vertical transfer of the guest workers from the jobs for which they were designated. Guest workers' 'life chances' were frozen with assignments as given in the contract's job title. These provisions were intended to be protective against employer's abuse but in practice had the effect of demarcating and enveloping guest workers as an 'enclave' segregated and detached from the wider labour market or even company-based internal labour markets.

Other important regulations governing guest workers included employer obligations to provide board and lodging and repatriation upon contract expiry. These rules are based primarily upon humanitarian considerations of the moral duty of the host (at both national and company levels). However, the practical implications of these hospitality rules have been to restrict the freedom of guest workers and place them in the custody of employers. Such roles were probably consistent with a paternalistic imagery of the employers. Yet, it was also a practice liable to place guest workers totally dependent upon, and at the mercy of, employers, which could breed servile labour (as alleged in many of the complaints by guest domestic helpers).

Another set of rules emanating from the guest workers' scheme was a levy placed on per capita entry (largely in emulation of Singaporean practice). It was intended to help regulate numbers by serving as a rationing device. Such a tax would also dissuade employers from drifting into this type of hiring at the expense of locals. Interestingly, this tax went into a fund to help finance retraining of the unemployed, although the government maintained its equivocal attitude in not publicizing the rationale. Whether this was a tacit acknowledgement that there existed an association between labour importation and unemployment of locals (a perspective canvassed relentlessly by unions but formally denied by the authorities) was left unclear because of official silence. However, this levy has been now rescinded.

However, the hallmark feature of official regulation on guest workers admission has been in the domain of wage control. Departing from the enshrined norm of free wage policy, the government has been compelled to extend its interventionist lever of promulgating a standard wage floor (since the 1970s) for guest domestic household helpers and later prescribing analogous measures for all guest workers. In the latter instance, the government made it mandatory for employers not to pay less than the median wage in the relevant industry to guest workers. Such an official prescription on the wage level 'floor' was tantamount to declaring a sectoral minimum wage, although its application was explicitly limited to guest workers. Official acts of intervention into wages were to protect not only against low pay and sweatshop conditions, but also the interests of locals fearful of cut-throat cheap labour. The irony is that by liberalizing its guest worker ban, the government has inadvertently stepped into an area of minimum wage regulation which represents a radical departure from its celebrated tradition of a free and self-adjusting market left to the parties' own choice.

631. Although the entry of general imported labour was later scaled down to a skeleton supplementary labour scheme of guest workers on the eve of Hong Kong's reversion back to China, the post-1997 SAR government has been engaged in a long-drawn process of consultation with industry and organized labour about the prospect of reviving the *en masse* recruitment of guest workers as a lever of revitalizing the textile and garment industries with incentives to attract Hong Kong capital deployed in the mainland back for re-investing in Hong Kong. The government is likely, were the plan to materialize, to offer organized labour major concessions (such as by stipulating prescribed ratios of guest workers to their local counterparts at the workplace) in order to secure their consent and partnership in this exercise of industry renewal.

632. Compounding the issue of migrant workers in the last decade was the 'brain drain' or emigration syndrome in the wake of the imminent 1997 'changeover'. The exodus has strained Hong Kong's manpower heavily in the earlier years of the 1990s, especially in the upper echelon of executive and professional personnel. The drain has in turn beset corporate employers and caused the territory to 'internationalize' its managerial-cum-professional markets. However, as the local 'fever' of a 'foreign passport' quest subsided, especially as the status quo pledge by China was attested by Hong Kong's stability as an SAR sustained after the 1997 'dateline', the emigration flood slowed down, coupled with a reverse flow of the emigrants returning to Hong Kong in search for the relatively buoyant opportunities it offered. Again the prosperity and sustained stability of this society, in spite of the psychological insecurity which clouded earlier over its dramatic experience of socio-political transition in anticipation of 1997, has proved to be the main pulling force – for both the 'returnees' as well as expatriates from abroad aimed at the white-collar professional and executive job market. Indeed, the territory's creeping unemployment problem has been attributed in part by the government to the accelerated growth in Hong Kong population and labour supply at the turn of the decade. In this context, the liberal admission of expatriates – let alone the returning tide of emigrants – can be problematic in adding a new dimension to the current policy debate about unemployment and alien labour. A manpower glut of over-supply of university graduates has become increasingly evident because of the proliferation of local universities (the 'brain drain' syndrome has caused the government to adopt a liberal policy of upgrading post-secondary tertiary institutions to the status of universities). Before 1995, Hong Kong housed only three universities but now the number has grown to eight, plus a fringe of degree-giving institutions. Such a drift can hence pose a potential challenge, if not addressed effectively, of intellectual unemployment which breeds the 'diploma disease'. The recession sustained over the first half of this decade attests to such an experience, as unemployment besetted the upper strata of the local labour market for the professional and managerial white-collar workers. The glut led to intense bidding for these jobs and vulnerable white-collar executives, especially in the finance sector, were known to work long and extended hours voluntarily as they strove to retain their employment.

633. And still posing a hiatus on the policy agenda of the SAR government is the status of a sizable population of foreign domestic helpers, initially almost entirely from the Philippines but now increasingly pluralistic and covering a spectrum of Asian nationalities. The local labour unions here have been remarkably quiescent about their stay in Hong Kong. However, a question of 'equity' has always remained unanswered: that is, why mainland China has consistently been denied as a source from which these domestic helpers can be recruited? The perpetuated practice of privileging intakes drawn from the Philippines, Thailand, Indonesia and other

East Asian societies to the exclusion of the mainland is hardly laudable. At December 2012, there were altogether 312,395 foreign domestic helpers in Hong Kong. Filipino maids comprised almost 50 per cent of this population while those from Indonesia made up 47.8 per cent.

634. Ironically, the mainland has, instead, been targeted by the SAR government for recruiting white-collar guest workers at the managerial and professional level. A twin scheme has been instituted since the earlier part of this decade for serving such a purpose. The first, entitled 'Admission Scheme for Mainland Talents and Professionals' was launched in 2003 with the policy aim of attracting talented people and professionals from the mainland to work in Hong Kong to meet local manpower needs, facilitate local economic and other development, and enhance Hong Kong's competitiveness in the globalized market. Successful entrants may also apply for the right of abode after having resided in Hong Kong for a continuous period of not less than seven years. The scheme prescribes no sectoral restriction or quota and vets admission using criteria as those stipulated by the General Employment Policy (by virtue of which, foreigners may work or invest in Hong Kong if they possess special skills, knowledge or experience of value to and not readily available in Hong Kong and receives salaries broadly commensurate with those on the market, or who can make a substantial contribution to the economy). By 2006, 14,155 entry applications have been approved.

The other scheme, named Employment of Mainland Graduates with Hong Kong Degrees and launched since 2001, enables mainland students who are trained and have graduated from Hong Kong universities (as funded, specifically, by the University Grants Committee, UGC) since 1990 to enter Hong Kong for employment, subject to the general qualifying condition that they should also possess special skills or knowledge of value to but not readily available in Hong Kong. This scheme was extended in 2005 to those who studied at non-UGC-funded institutions during the academic year 2005–6 and thereafter, and who obtained degrees or higher accreditations from local institutions where they studied full-time. The policy aim of this arrangement is to attract outstanding mainland students who have completed full-time degree or higher level courses to re-enter Hong Kong for employment. During the year 2006, the immigration authority extended approval to 405 mainland students to enter Hong Kong for work and employment within the purview of this scheme.

635. Hong Kong society has always been permissible and pluralistic. And for that reason, it has also been known for its 'openness' and yet 'fluidity'. A great deal of this historical character is due to the factor of migration, the effects of which is always felt on the labour and employment market. It will be a testing task ahead for the SAR government to continue to keep these diverse influences of the 'migration' phenomenon under rein, in order that the delicate equilibrium of the economy, the demography and the society can be sustained in support of Hong Kong's prosperity and stability in the future.

Part II. Collective Labour Relations

Chapter 1. Trade Union Legislation and Its Background

636. A brief survey of the evolution of the trade union law in Hong Kong is useful to give the normative-cum-institutional context to the understanding of the trade union movement and collective industrial relations in Hong Kong.

§1. Introduction

637. Two exogenous factors and their influences are in particular worth noting in tracing the development of the legal framework governing trade unions in Hong Kong. The first is almost endemic, the 'China' factor, especially given its contemporary history of socio-political upheavals. Within the mainland, a perennial state of bitter internal strife and instability has been perpetuated since the overthrow of the Imperial Manchu reign in the 1911 Revolution, through the days of the Republic, the War-lords and the Communist-Nationalist tussle, until the 1949 Liberation establishing the People's Republic. Even beyond 1949, the trauma of embattled political struggle has not completely subsided, as evident in the upheavals of the Cultural Revolution in the 1960s and early 1970s as well as the Beijing Episode of 1989. Because of the territory's geographical proximity and ethnic links with the mainland, it has been impossible to isolate Hong Kong as an 'enclave' on its own and immune from the influences of politico-social crises inside China. Compounding such a connection has been the reciprocal role of Hong Kong serving as the 'gateway' for the diffusion of Western culture, ideas and influences, both materialistic and normative, to China.

Inasmuch as a politically inspired labour movement might cause social tumult inside China and inspire unrest and disturbances in Hong Kong, the government of this territory, both before and after 1997, has carefully adapted the legal framework in order to hold trade unionism within the 'rings'.

638. The second source of influence shaping trade unionism in Hong Kong has been the legacies of the British legal system, the imprints of which are readily identifiable in all aspects of Hong Kong's legal-cum-administrative framework – including that aspect governing the trade union and associated labour legislation. It follows that its legal infrastructure is heavily reminiscent of the British tradition, such as in mirror of the 'non-interventionist' theme of the British 'voluntarist' doctrine. In essence, this is the celebrated principle that trade unions will thrive best if provided with immunity from any illegality that might be attached to the act of union combination, and that it is not necessary or even undesirable to confer upon them any unequivocally positive rights – such as a requirement, as in the USA, upon the employer to bargain with the recognized trade union in good faith.

§2. The Early Years Before 1919

639. Just as in China, unions in Hong Kong can be traced back in history to a mixed origin comprising a constellation of craft guilds, clan and regional associations, or even (criminal) secret societies. The Chinese traditional guilds were in many ways analogous to the trade societies and medieval guilds which tradesmen (including both the journeymen and masters) organized in various European states prior to the Industrial Revolution. Often featuring elaborate rituals, custom and practices, these guilds, both East and West, were engaged essentially in economic rather than political activities. They were hence primarily concerned with maintaining a localized monopolistic control over the trade (as a 'cartel') and to organize in common both the workingmen and employers alike in the trade. However, secret societies were far less apolitical and many, especially the Triad Society, were known for having indulged in notorious criminal enterprises and evolved from political fraternities aimed to foment rebellions in China during the imperial era.

640. By the turn of the century, the domestic political turmoil and the embryonic advent of industrialization precipitated the birth of the modern Chinese labour movement. Still reminiscent of the traditional Chinese guild system, this labour movement has been from the onset laden by a pervasive politico-ideological theme and allied closely with the obscure activities of the 'secret societies'. In Hong Kong, the criminal threats posed by these secret societies to its internal law and order, as well as the diplomatic embarrassment inherent in the deposition of these societies to foment upheavals and disorder in China had induced a relatively reluctant colonial government to enact against their operations (both covert and overt), as early as in 1845 – just five years after British 'colonization'. This piece of legislation, aimed principally at containing their unlawful and notorious activities, was soon consolidated into the Triad and Unlawful Societies Ordinance in 1887, re-cast in 1911 into the Societies Ordinance which controlled, *inter alia*, the political activities of voluntary and fraternal associations in Hong Kong. All societies, including guild and labour oganizations, were hence required to register or obtain exemption from registration under the Ordinance.

641. By virtue of the Boycott Prevention Ordinance, no. 41 of 1912, a 'society' was defined as including any company, corporation, club, guild, or any combination or association of any kind whatsoever, consisting of more than two persons, whether such combination or association be known or designated by any distinctive name or not. There were a number of quasi unions and/or guild associations exempted from registration under the 1911 Societies Ordinance. These included, *inter alia*, two general merchants' associations; 34 masters' trade guilds and societies, three of which were mixed combinations which included workmen; as well as seven guilds of workmen. By 1919, there were exempted 36 masters' trade guilds and societies (five of which included the workmen), 35 workmen's guilds – plus another 24 trade guilds or societies which were listed on the registration list just like other registrable and registered associations. Save for the restriction levied by this statute, there was general freedom in Hong Kong for workmen to associate and organize collectively, either on their own or in alliance with their employers. However, with the post-imperial development of Chinese politics polities, labour organizations were vulnerable to stricter government control in China and strikes were often suppressed with a dosage of overt coercion.

642. In parallel, the Boycott Prevention Ordinance of 1912 made it an offence for anyone who was a member of or took part in a 'society' using violence, threat, intimidation against any person(s) with the view to causing them to do any act which they had a legal right to abstain from. The same ordinance also laid down a wide definition of acts deemed to be 'boycotting'. This piece of legislation, enacted in 1912 following the boycott of the Hong Kong Tramway (a local tramway monopoly) which insisted upon fare payment in Hong Kong currency, lasted for only a brief duration. It was suspended in 1913 by Proclamation no. 13 of 1913 and since then, it has not been reactivated, even during the turbulent years of the general strikes between 1922 and 1926.

643. In the wake of the spill-over of the May Fourth upheavals to Hong Kong, the administration abolished the registration requirement under the revamped Societies Ordinance in 1920 – largely in recognition of the administrative difficulties in securing reliable information and control over the societies. Apart from prohibiting the Triad Society and all societies which used a Triad emblem or practised associated rituals, the revised legislation also outlawed all societies which had among their objectives any unlawful purposes or purpose incompatible with the peace and good order of Hong Kong. It hence enabled the Governor-in-Council to declare as unlawful any such society, if it was believed to be used, or likely to be used, for unlawful purposes or for purposes incompatible with the 'peace and good order' or 'by reason of its actions or proceedings calculated to excite persons to crime in China'. Thereafter, trade unions and labour organizations were relieved in this context of the obligation to register, provided that they were not declared illegal at law.

§3. General Strikes of the 1920s: 1922 and 1925

644. Echoing the May Fourth Movement on the mainland, a flood of industrial strife erupted in Hong Kong in the early 1920s, peaking in the 'landmarking' seamen's strike of 1922 which was in pursuit of their pay dispute with the shipping owners. The strike resulted in the employers' concession to most of the seamen's demands and the victory conferred upon the Chinese Seamen's Union considerable power and glory. The euphoria of its 1922 industrial success provided an important impetus to the labour movement, both in Hong Kong and the mainland, blended with a strong politico-ideological flavour.

645. In this currency, the Hong Kong Federation of Labour was formed from over 70 unions, pleading its struggle against 'imperialism' and 'capitalism' as the movement's primary goals. With the Chinese seamen constituting the most powerful wing, the leaders of these unions were political 'vanguards' who were not, in many instances, *bona fide* members of those particular trades which the unions purportedly represented. Thus, economic amelioration of the workers' vicissitudes in industry was frequently subordinated to the wider objectives of fomenting and furthering a consciousness of revolutionary nationalism in the working class.

Given such an orientation, the unions often channelled their funds and resources into political actions and ends. These political propensities eventually caused the 'neurotic' Hong Kong government to introduce more stringent controls over the local unions, lest their association with covert political and criminal activities would pervert the delicate stability of the territory.

646. In 1925, the historically famous General Strike (the second in close succession after the seamen's strike, in the turbulent decade of the 1920s) broke out, orchestrated by the Chinese Seamen's Union and the General Labour Association of Hong Kong (a union federation also formed in the 1920s).

647. The character of this strike was essentially political, organized in sympathy with 'parallel' industrial actions waged by unions in Canton (Guangzhou) and Shanghai on the mainland. The strikers' demands were manifold, ranging from complete freedom of speech, association and publication in Hong Kong, through that for equal treatment of Chinese *vis-à-vis* foreigners, to a package deal for labour's betterment comprising an eight-hour day, workers' insurance, minimum wage and collective bargaining arrangements. A general strike-cum-boycott, named in history as the 'Canton-Hong Kong Strike Boycott' was declared by the strikers' fraternities in the mainland and lasted until 1926. The upheaval and its apparent collapse, coinciding with the rise to power of the conservative Nationalist government and the beginning of systematic curtailment of union power in China, led to the censure of the General Labour Association under the Emergency Regulations, as well as the outlawing of the Chinese Seamen's Union under the new Societies Ordinance – both instruments being enacted in 1927.

§4. ILLEGAL STRIKES AND LOCK-OUTS ORDINANCE (1927)

648. An immediate offshoot of the abortive Canton-Hong Kong Strike Boycott was the enactment in 1927 of the Illegal Strikes and Lock-outs Ordinance in Hong Kong – a year after the Canton-Hong Kong General Strike. Based upon the Trade Disputes and Trade Unions Act, 1927 of the United Kingdom, this piece of legislation reflected both the influence of the British legal tradition in industrial relations as well as the response of the Hong Kong government, beset by the lessons of the earlier industrial strife, to adapt to the local political exigencies due to the territory's mutuality with China. As the pioneering enactment in Hong Kong dealing specifically with the trade unions, its approach was overtly restrictive with the purpose to 'suppress the illegal activities of unions (rather) than to encourage their legal ones'.[44] The Ordinance declared any strike as illegal if it had any object other than, or in addition to, the furtherance of a trade dispute within the trade or industry in which the strikers were engaged, and was a strike designed or calculated to coerce the Hong Kong Government, either directly or by inflicting hardship upon the community or any substantial portion of the community. It became an offence under the Ordinance for any employees in the civil service or in certain essential public services to break, as by way of a strike, an agreement of services if the probable consequences were to hinder or prevent the discharge of the government's functions.

649. The 1927 legislation also outlawed the control of any Hong Kong union by any trade union or organization outside the territory, as well as the use of union funds for political purposes, within or outside it. In fact, the ordinance was conspicuous in having incorporated features which were reminiscent of the 'restrictive' British codes of (i) the Trade Disputes and Trade Unions Act of 1927, which declared as illegal any sympathetic strikes and strikes against the government;[45] and (ii)to a lesser extent, the Conspiracy and Protection of Property Act of 1875, which made it a criminal offence for employees in essential services like the gas, water and electricity workers to break their contracts knowing that the probable consequence would be to deprive persons dependent upon these services of their supply.

§5. The Years 1927–1930

650. In the aftermath of the 1925–6 Canton-Hong Kong Strike Boycott and its collapse, there was a sharp retreat in the territory's level of union activity and its 'revolutionary' militancy after 1927, especially following the passage of the Illegal Strikes and Lock-outs Ordinance and the enforcement of the 1920 Societies Ordinance, which had the effect of casting a dubious legal status upon the trade union combinations. Since then, there have been no major labour disputes until the Second World War and the unions were so docile that they were described as 'little more than friendly societies concerned more with the provision of funeral expenses for the dead than the improvement of the conditions of the living'.[46] Reinforcing the effacing withdrawal of the local labour movement were other external factors: noticeably in the repercussions of the worldwide economic depression and the 'spill-overs' from the repressive containment of the mainland's workers' movement by an inhospitable Nationalist government. During the period, a total of about 15 labour associations or trade societies were officially outlawed under the Societies Ordinance or the Emergency Regulations.

44. Butters Report, p. 120, para. 113
45. The Trade Disputes and Trade Unions Act was introduced to Britain in 1927, after the General Strike of 1926 and reputed to be one of the most coercive and interventionist pieces of collective labour law ever enacted in history in Britain.
46. Butters Report, p. 117, para. 55.

§6. THE BUTTERS REPORT (1939)

651. By the turn of the decade into the 1930s, however, there began active and global initiatives organized by the British Government to foster the development of 'responsible' trade unionism based on the home model in its dependent territories. Such a commonwealth (or empire)-wide drive emanated largely from two interrelated sources. The first was the lobby waged by the British Trade Union Congress seeking to diffuse and transfer to the colonies the parent British home institution in industrial relations and the second was the appointment of Sidney Webb (Lord Passfield) to the office of Secretary of State for the Colonies under the Labour Government of 1929. A directive was issued to all colonial governments advising them to introduce trade union legislation which should (i) require compulsory registration and (ii) grant immunities from criminal and civil liabilities similar to the 'negative rights' conferred by the Trade Union Act of 1871 upon unions in Britain. It was in this context, given the then depressed state of local unionism and its growing vulnerability to the criminal influences of the Triad Societies, that the Hong Kong Government adopted a major review of its trade union policy. In a report published in 1939 by the Labour Officer (whose office was equivalent ot that of the Commissioner for Labour today), H.R. Butters, important reforms were hence canvassed as he analysed and questioned the restrictive effects of a battery of emergency laws and advocated in their place a more liberal approach by abrogating the majority of them.[47] The report was also critical of the abolition of the registration procedure of societies under the Societies Ordinance of 1920 – arguing on the ground that 'genuine trade unions of workingmen lost the status afforded by official recognition or exemption and became merely not unlawful societies'.[48]

652. To encourage legal and responsible unionism, a new Trade Union Bill was drafted by Butters, 'based on the law of England, to define the status and powers of trade unions and to provide for their registration'. The intention was 'to bring the position of trade unions in Hong Kong into alignment with that of English trade union'.[49] The 'blueprint' legislation envisaged the introduction of voluntary registration for trade unions which would have, contrary to the assumption of the Societies Ordinance, given 'genuine trade unions a certain amount of "face: and inculcate a certain degree of responsibility'.[50] The primary criterion of 'responsible' unionism was stated explicitly as being 'the improvement of the working and living conditions of the workers' – and not participation in Chinese politics and their self-aggrandizement which the government apparently did not endorse and felt embarrassed about.[51]

---

47. That body of law applicable to emergency situations included the Offences against the Person Ordinance, no. 2 of 1865, the Peace Preservation Ordinance, no. 10 of 1886; the Boycott Prevention Ordinance, no. 41 of 1912; and regulations under the Emergency Regulations Ordinance, no. 5 of 1922.
48. Butters Report, p. 166, para. 232.
49. *Ibid.*, p. 166, para. 230.
50. *Ibid.*, p. 166, para. 232.
51. *Ibid.*

§7. Second World War

653. Echoing these official strategies on trade union reforms was the territory's labour movement renewal initiatives on the eve of the Second World War. The renewal endeavours were inspired to a large extent by the political developments in mainland China, where the Nationalists and Communists abandoned temporarily their mutual hostilities to establish a common front in face of accentuated Japanese aggression. Backing such a revival of the mainland labour movement, the Chinese workers and their unions in Hong Kong began to rediscover and revitalize their activities in nationalist solidarity with their mainland compatriots. This union recovery, chiefly inspired by its nationalist and political yearning, was further reinforced by the arrival of refugee labour from Shanghai and other places who bought along with them their unionization and agitation propensities. By the late 1930s, there were about 300 associations in Hong Kong organizing the workplaces, claiming a nominal membership of 11,400. Among these were 28 merchants' guilds; 28 craft guilds or guilds with mixed masters and workmen membership; 84 labour unions; 89 pseudo-labour unions and 31 seamen's clubs, lodging houses and employment agencies.

654. Such a favourable climate for trade union renewal and reform was, however, swamped by the outbreak of hostilities around the Second World War. The plan of the Hong Kong Government for laying down a new set of trade union legislation did not progress beyond the embryonic blueprint drafted by Mr Butters, the Labour Officer – when the colony was occupied by the Japanese in 1941. During the occupation until 1945, trade unions were banned but the Triads as secret societies remained active underground.

§8. Postwar Recovery

655. Political and economic forces in the immediate postwar years operated to re-kindle the activism of the local trade union movement and instilled into it fragments of its hallmark today. In the first place, the shortage of the craft and semi-skilled labour had enhanced sizably the bargaining power of these two groups. Second, the general labour force was conversely distressed and trapped in hardship due to the rapid pace of postwar recovery and inflation – in particular, by the spiral of soaring prices of food and other essentials. These led to widespread labour protests, wage demands and industrial strife, especially in the public utilities. Parallel to the challenge of these economic vicissitudes was third: the resurgence of organized labour solidarity, inspired on one hand by the war stimulated patriotic sentiments of Chinese labour and spurred, on the other hand, by the resumption and escalation of the Communist-Nationalist confrontation on the mainland.

656. In this highly politicized context, the emergence of rival trade unions with opposing political sympathies in the industry, trade, occupation or enterprise became almost a commonplace feature of the labour movement in the territory. From this time onwards, the left–right polarization of Hong Kong trade unionism has hence crystallized into an entrenched character of the territory's industrial relations terrain. Also adding to the stalemate was the persistent and notorious presence of the Triads and other criminal societies, which continued to contaminate the union movement by virtue of their vicious control of the unskilled labour market.

§9. THE FIRST TRADE UNION LEGISLATION (1948)

657. It was against this volatile socio-economic background that the Hong Kong government was prompted to revive the prewar (Butters') blueprint on the first comprehensive set of trade union legislation, in order to contain the various potentially disruptive forces in the labour movement and to regulate and nurture its development in the desired direction of 'responsible' unionism. The first piece of trade union law was hence introduced in 1948, enacted under the name of the Trade Unions and Trade Disputes Ordinance (1948), itself based upon the model Trade Union Ordinance circulated earlier by the home British Government to its overseas dependencies in 1941. This model Ordinance provided for, *inter alia*, the compulsory registration of trade unions, the legitimation of peaceful picketing and removal of any legal liability otherwise levied upon union combinations for interfering with the business of others; a declaration that trade unions were not in restraint of trade, and provision of immunity to them from actions on grounds of conspiracy of inducement of breach of contract.[52] The application of the model Ordinance was nevertheless adapted in order to deal with and contain the overtly political character of the Hong Kong labour movement at that time. There were, accordingly, careful modifications made in respect of political funds, in harmonizing the new ordinance with the Illegal Strikes and Lock-outs Ordinance, 1927 and in adopting some features of Ceylon's Trade Union Ordinance, 1935. Thus, the 1948 legislation may be seen to lay the foundation of the legal framework that confers legality upon the trade unions in Hong Kong. The enactment also epitomized the official intent that 'it was necessary and reasonable to expect from trade unions, duly registered, a high sense of responsibility and a measure of administrative regularity'.[53]

658. Concomitantly, the Societies Ordinance was revamped in 1949, requiring the mandatory registration of every club, company, partnership or association of persons, except for (i) those specifically exempted,[54] or (ii) trade unions or trade union federations registered under the Trade Unions and Trade Disputes Ordinance. By implication, a union not registered is hence unlawful unless it seeks registration as a society under the Societies Ordinance. By the end of 1948, altogether 180 labour unions were registered or in the process of seeking registration. In 1949, the two politically polarized trade union centres in Hong Kong, the Communist Hong Kong Federation of Trade Unions (FTU) and the Nationalist Hong Kong and

52. B.C. Roberts, *Labour in the Tropical Territories of the Commonwealth*, London: The London School of Economics and Political Science (G. Bell and Sons), 1964, p. 261.
53. Second Reading Speech pertaining to the introduction of the Trade Union Registration Bill, 1961, in the Hong Kong Legislative Council. See *Hong Kong Hansard*, 1961, p. 289.
54. For instance, exemption from the purview of the Societies Ordinance is available to companies registered, instead, under the Companies Ordinance.

Kowloon Trades Union Council (TUC), were both registered. Yet both chose to register as societies under the Societies Ordinance and not as unions *per se*.

§10. Revision of Trade Union Legislation (1961)

659. By the early 1960s it became evident that the trade union registration law was in need of a major overhaul, since the 1948 legislation could no longer cope with the challenge and experience of the industrial advances in the economy and society. Moreover, the application of the 1948 Ordinance had also revealed gaps of its inadequacies, notably such problems as those of control over mismanagement and abuse of union funds, the restrictive effect on the appointment of union executives, union amalgamation and the absence of judicial remedies for the unions to appeal against the administrative decision of the Registrar of Trade Unions. Legislative renovations took place accordingly in 1961, when the Trade Unions and Trade Disputes Ordinance was repealed and replaced by the Trade Union Registration Ordinance 1961. The new legislation hence (i) granted trade unions corporate status so that they could handle transactions independently; (ii) strengthened the control and protection of union funds; (iii) reinforced the power of the Registrar of Trade Unions with regard to internal union administration; (iv) removed at the same time from the Registrar his power to refuse registering a new union on the ground of its duplication with existing ones; (v) relaxed the conditions for unions to amalgamate and to appoint their officials; and (vi) placed the jurisdiction of hearing appeals against actions by the Registrar with the Full Court instead of the Governor-in-Council. Moreover, the streamlined legislation would from then onwards concentrate upon the regulation of trade unions, and that part of the 1948 Ordinance dealing with trade disputes and their settlement machinery was retained and re-titled as the Trade Disputes Ordinance, Chapter 64 of the Laws of Hong Kong.

§11. Revision of Trade Union Legislation (1971 and 1977)

660. The Trade Union Registration Ordinance was amended ten years later, in 1971, and renamed the Trade Unions Ordinance, the intent being to contribute towards the more effective administration of the affairs of trade unions so as to help rationalize and foster the reforms of the internal management of unions and redefine the power of the Registrar of Trade Unions as well as buttress the rights of union officers and members to appeal against his decision.

661. By a subsequent amendment in 1977, the Trade Unions Ordinance was liberalized again in respect of the qualification to become a union executive or official. This piece of legislative reform apparently emanated from the government's endeavours to promote the quality of trade union leadership and government.

662. However, in terms of freedom of association, the legal protection of the individual employee to join or not join a union and participate in its activities did not come into the statute book of Hong Kong until 1974. Such statutory safeguards were incorporated, however, into the Employment Ordinance, instead of under the auspices of the Trade Unions Ordinance. The amendment legislation lays down an 'anti-union discrimination' provision which extends the protection on the freedom to associate to all employees in Hong Kong and makes violation by the employer a punishable offence.

§12. The 1997 Political Reversion, the SAR Government and Trade Union Law

663. Prior to the 1997 'dateline' of Hong Kong's reversion to China, the pro-democratic wing of the labour movement expressed anxiety that the post-1997 SAR administration would, in order to tighten its grip of political control, adopt a more restrictive or even a coercive approach to the trade union legislation. Apprehension was articulated, for example, over the likelihood that the trade union law would be amended to curtail and interfere with labour unions' freedom to associate with their fraternities overseas.

664. Some of these fears proved, however, to be inflated, inasmuch as the trade union law has been maintained by and large as the status quo, without experiencing any major overhaul after 1997, which would have restrained trade union freedom or enhanced the SAR government's control of the labour movement. In fact, shortly after the change of government, the Trade Unions Ordinance was amended, in 1997, to liberalize unions' ability to mobilize their funds for electoral activities as well as the conditions by which they can combine forming union federations. However, in the domain of overseas affiliations with labour unions and organizations outside Hong Kong, the new governing regime retains essentially a similar measure of control to that which has been levied upon local unions during British rule. Specifically, the consent of the Chief Executive has to be sought in order for such affiliation to become legitimate. Such control was later liberalized by a 1998 amendment which exempts unions seeking overseas affiliation from such a requirement, provided that such a motion has been authorized by secret ballot by a majority of the voting members of the union present at a general meeting. Besides, it was made explicit by the 1998 amendment that the nature of these overseas organizations need to be either trade unions or professional associations. The same provision, section (45) of the Trade Unions Ordinance, declares that such a liberalized measure shall not be 'construed as allowing or providing for a registered trade union to be or become a member of a political organization or body established in a foreign country' (Subsection 6(b)).

665. Prior to 1997, unions in Hong Kong were permitted to federate provided that they were from the same industry, trade or occupation. In other words, it has not been permissible for unions to federate across industries, trades or occupations. Such a restriction was, however, rescinded by the 1997 amendment, enabling a union federation to be formed and constituted by unions organizing divergent industries, trade or occupations. The liberalization measure equips the SAR government with a rejoinder in answering the criticism that the former restriction placed upon union federation across industries epitomized an official design to pre-empt the emergence and development of large and powerful trade unions which could pose an alternative power centre challenging the authority of the government.

666 By virtue of the Trade Unions Ordinance amended in 1998, it has become permissible for a trade union, if authorized by secret ballot of a majority of its membership, to establish an electoral fund to cater to expenditure on electoral activities listed by the law to include:

(i) expenses incurred directly or indirectly by a candidate for election to a District Council or the Legislative Council;
(ii) expenses for meetings or preparation and distribution of literature or documents in support of a candidate for election to a District Council or the Legislative Council; and
(iii) expenses related to the registration of electors or the selection of a candidate for election to a District Council or the Legislative Council (Section 33A(i)).

In the absence of such a standing electoral fund, it is also permissible for the union to mobilize its funds for those electoral activities as prescribed, provided that such expenditures are authorized by secret ballot by a majority of its voting members present at a general meeting or of a majority of members' representatives present at a general meeting.

However, apart from these electoral activities as specified above, the law remains unequivocal in proscribing the use of union fund for any political activities and purposes. Hence, section 34 of the Trade Union Ordinance precludes expressly the use of any unions' fund 'to be applied either directly or indirectly for any political purposes or be paid or transferred to any person or body of persons in furtherance of any political purposes'.

Chapter 2. The Protection of Trade Union Freedom

§1. The Effects of International Labour Conventions

I. Hong Kong and International Labour Conventions

667. Hong Kong is affiliated to the International Labour Organization (ILO), not as a full Member State but as a non-metropolitan territory of the United Kingdom prior to July 1997 and since then, as an SAR of the People's Republic of China, after its sovereignty reversion to and reunification with the latter.

668. Previously under British rule and as a non-metropolitan territory, Hong Kong was not called upon to ratify international labour conventions promulgated by the ILO. However, declarations in respect of the Hong Kong position on the application of those conventions already ratified by the UK were made by the British government on behalf of the Hong Kong government after full consultation between the two. In making a declaration for Hong Kong, the relevant convention could be:

(i) applied without modification (i.e. with all its provisions accepted and followed);
(ii) applied with modification (i.e. with some and not all its provisions accepted and followed); and
(iii) accorded the notification of 'decision reserved' (i.e. not accepting the relevant Convention for the time being since many of its provisions cannot be implemented by legislative or administrative measures in the foreseeable future).

Since Hong Kong became an SAR of China after the change of government in 1997, its status as a non-metropolitan territory has been rescinded but the practice of Hong Kong in applying appropriate and commensurate ILO conventions continues. As at the end of 2006, 41 ILO conventions were applied to the Hong Kong SAR, with or without modification. It has been the policy norm of the government, both before and after 1997, to maintain within the SAR a level of labour standards broadly equivalent to those of neighbouring countries with similar economic development as well as social and cultural background, to be achieved through continuous improvements to labour legislation and administrative measures designed to implement the ILO conventions and other internationally accepted labour standards.[55]

II. ILO Conventions Applied in Hong Kong Pertaining to Trade Union Freedom and Protection

669. Convention No. 11 on Right of Association (Agricultural) guarantees to employees in agriculture the same right of association and combination as that to

55. Labour Department, *Annual Report 2006*, Hong Kong: Labour Department, Hong Kong SAR Government, 2007, paras. 7.1 and 7.2.

industrial workers and provides for the repeal of any statutory or other provisions that restrict such rights for the agricultural workers. However, in Hong Kong, the agricultural sector is simply rudimentary, since full-time wage-earning agricultural workers are nominal in number, accounting for hardly more than 1 per cent of the aggregate labour force. This notwithstanding, agricultural workers in Hong Kong enjoy the same rights of association and combination as any workers in other economic sectors by virtue of the Trade Unions Ordinance and its provisions.

670. Convention No. 84 on Right of Association (Non-Metropolitan Territories) applies to non-metropolitan territories for the purpose of guaranteeing the rights of employers and workers to associate for all lawful purposes. It also safeguards the rights of trade unions to conclude collective agreements, to enter into joint consultation with employers' organizations and to have access to simple and expeditious means of settling disputes by conciliation and with the assistance of public officers, if necessary.

In Hong Kong, the right of association is hence safeguarded and regulated by the Trade Unions Ordinance of 1971 and its subsidiary Trade Unions Registration Regulations while the official machinery for settling labour–management disputes is provided under the respective provisions of the Labour Relations Ordinance of 1975, the Labour Tribunal Ordinance of 1972 and the Minor Employment Claims Adjudication Board Ordinance of 1994, backed by the voluntary conciliation facilities administered by the Labour Relations Service of the Labour Department.

The legality of association of employers and of employees is conferred, provided that the association is registered with the government, by the Trade Unions Ordinance which also grants such a registered trade union certain rights and privileges, including immunity from civil suits on such grounds as restraint of trade, conspiracy, intimidation, inducing the breach of contracts, etc., as well as shelter from actions in tort pursued in connection with the contemplation or furtherance of a trade dispute. In principle, workers' unions and employers' associations are free to conclude collective agreements, without being subject to any administrative or legalistic constraints. Enterprise-specific joint consultation has been actively promoted by the Labour Department although its implementation, voluntary in nature, has not yet been widespread.

671. The voluntary conciliation service of the Labour Department provides the 'front-line' mechanism for official intervention to help settle labour–management disputes in Hong Kong. Should conciliation be unable to yield a settlement, the dispute will be referred to either of three legally sanctioned methods of settlement according to its nature. If the conflict is a claim (i.e. a dispute of right arising from a breach of contract or of statutory standards), it can be processed subsequently either at (i) the Minor Employment Claims Adjudication Board for awards if the claims involves not more than ten claimants for a sum not exceeding HK$8,000 per claimant or (ii) otherwise, the Labour Tribunal for judicial determination. If, however, the dispute is one over interests as in the instance of pay negotiation, it is likely to be handled in the context of the Labour Relations Ordinance which may authorize official intervention in the form of escalating procedures of authorized conciliation, special conciliation or beyond that, as ordered by the Chief Executive in

Council, voluntary arbitration, appointment of an enquiry board or whatever appropriate actions deemed appropriate in order to facilitate the settlement of the dispute.

672. Convention no. 98 on Right to Organize and Collective Bargaining lays down the principle that the workers shall enjoy protection against acts of anti-union discrimination in the context of their employment, especially against acts which are contemplated to gear the employment of a worker to the condition that he shall not join a union or relinquish trade union membership; or those acts causing the dismissal of a worker by reason of his union membership or because of his participation in union activities. This basic principle guaranteeing the individual's freedom to associate is given effect in Hong Kong by the 'anti-union discrimination' statutory safeguards provided under the Employment Ordinance.

The same ILO Convention no. 98 declares, in addition, an obligation to protect workers' and employers' organizations against any act of interference by each other or each others' agents or members in their establishments. The Convention also notes the importance of voluntary negotiation between unions and employers or employers' organizations with a view to regulating the terms and conditions of employment – such as by way of collective bargaining. In Hong Kong the right to associate and organize unions, both of the employees and employers, is generally guaranteed by the Trade Unions Ordinance. The principal exceptions are members of the armed forces who are governed by the regulations and etiquette appropriate to their specific services; as well as of the police force in which disciplined staff are prohibited from taking up union membership under the Police Force Ordinance, Chapter 232 although it is permissible for them to join one of the three policemen staff associations having, as registered societies, some of the properties of a trade union and vested with a *de facto* role in pay negotiation.

III. Other International Labour Conventions Relevant to Hong Kong

673. Other than having applied in full the above ILO conventions, Hong Kong has also applied with modification an important instrument of international labour standard governing trade union freedoms. This is International Labour Convention no. 87 on Freedom of Association and Protection of the Rights to Organize.

In essence, the above ILO instrument proclaims the right of the employers and workers to establish and join an organization of their choice without the requirement to seek prior authorization or consent from the other side.

These combinations are also entitled to:

(i) draw up their own constitutions and rules, elect freely their representatives, organize their internal administration and formulate their own programme of activities;
(ii) the right that the organization cannot be suspended or dissolved by the state's administrative authorities;
(iii) establish and join federations and confederations, and any such organization, federation or confederation also has the right to affiliate itself with international workers' organizations; and

(iv) the right that its attainment of legal status cannot be made subject to such conditions or requirements which would impede the exercise of the freedom of association.

This convention has been applied in Hong Kong by virtue of the Trade Unions Ordinance and its subsidiary legislation, save with the following modifications:

(i) that the manner of expenditure of trade union fund is circumscribed by the Trade Unions Ordinance;
(ii) that the administrative authority may intervene to supervise the accounts of trade unions and ensure the enforcement and observation of the union rules;
(iii) that union amalgamation has to be sanctioned by the administrative authority according to statutory procedures prescribed by the Trade Unions Ordinance; and consent of the administrative authority is necessary for local trade unions to seek affiliation with an international organization unless the proposed affiliation has been endorsed at a general meeting of the union by a majority of the members by secret ballot; and
(iv) that federations of trade unions are allowed only for trade unions engaged in organizing the same trade, occupation or industry. Yet such a restriction has been liberalized by the SAR legislature in 1997 shortly after the new government came to power.

674. The SAR government, however, has been criticized by the ILO Committee on Freedom of Association for repealing and rescinding a liberal piece of legislation, entitled the Right of Collective Bargaining and Consultation and ushered successfully to the statute book as a private Members' Bill by the liberal and pro-labour wing of the pre-1997 Legislative Council on the eve of the territory's reversion back to China. This statute, modelled extensively on the American procedures of granting exclusive rights of collective bargaining representation to a trade union elected to be the bargaining agent by its constituency in the bargaining unit, introduced to the Hong Kong workplace analogous balloting procedures, which would have extended similar rights on collective bargaining and collective consultation to the trade union elected and certified to be the most representative organization to deputize for the employees as the electorate at the workplace level. This aborted legislative instrument, strongly contested and denounced by the business sector, was considered as incommensurate with the Hong Kong environment lacking allegedly a mature collective bargaining culture and where small and medium-sized enterprises (SME) proliferated. It was abrogated by the SAR Provisional Legislative Council shortly after the changeover of government. There were subsequent attempts by trade union leaders sitting on the SAR legislature to reinstate the law on collective bargaining rights but these attempts were effectively pre-empted by a conservative and pro-business SAR legislative assembly.

675. It is also worth noting that International Labour Convention no. 135 on Workers' Representatives is another important instrument extending protection to workers' representatives in an enterprise against any acts prejudicial to them, based upon their status or activities as workers' representatives and insofar as they act in conformity with existing laws, collective agreements or other jointly agreed arrangements. However, since the present 'anti-union discrimination' provisions of the Employment Ordinance do not afford safeguards to those workers' representatives who are not union officials or members (for instance, those sitting on staff councils and joint consultative committees), it has not been possible for Hong Kong to apply this convention but to register instead a 'decision reserved' position against it. Another problem is that Hong Kong has not made it mandatory for employers to make available facilities for workers' representatives in their establishments enabling them to perform their functions effectively, which this IL Convention has also called upon as an obligation incumbent upon the employer.

§2. Trade Union Freedom and the State

I. Trade Unions' Freedom as a Legal Right and Its Limits

676. Trade unions in Hong Kong can be described generally as being independent of the government insofar as their organization, objectives and activities are concerned. There are no legal impediments on individual employees in associating and organizing for collective bargaining purposes, provided that the relevant trade union has registered with the Registrar of Trade Unions. The latter's discretion to refuse registration is limited, invokable only where:

- there are contraventions of the ordinance;
- the purpose of the union is unlawful; and
- the proposed name of the union is the same or so similar to that of another union as to be misleading.

677. In essence, registration with the Registrar of Trade Unions as a procedure serves to confer upon the union its corporate status, immunity from actions in tort, protection of persons acting in furtherance of trade disputes, and freedom from liability to criminal prosecution for conspiracy. Although unions are required to submit their rules, expenditure and accounts to the supervisory control of the Registrar, unions in Hong Kong enjoy virtually unlimited freedom to determine their leadership, administrative structure, policy and programme of activities. Unions are generally free to amalgamate and are permitted to federate, now even across trades, industries or occupations. At the international level, unions must gain the prior consent of the Chief Executive unless there is a majority support of the union membership attested by secret ballot, before they can affiliate with any trade union or other labour organisaton established outside Hong Kong. The commission of any union fund directly or indirectly to any political purposes outside or inside Hong Kong is expressly proscribed but the application of union funds for electoral activities within the territory (at the dualistic tiers of the District Council and Legislative Council) is permissible and legitimate.

678. Conceivably, the rationale of the above stated legal limits has now become historical. These control measures were largely symptomatic of the government's primary concern to ameliorate the penetration and image of the territory as an extended arena of Chinese domestic politics, rather than an authoritarian intent to restrain the development of bona fide unionism in Hong Kong.

II. Union Participation in the Government

679. The government of the territory, both before and after the transfer of sovereignty and reversion back to China from British rule in 1997, can be described as a tolerant and permissive one, highly responsive *vis-à-vis* the people it governs, especially now that democratic reforms have been well under way since these were instituted more than three decades ago. It is a sacrosanct policy norm pledged by the SAR government to evolve a political infrastructure of representative government which will feature direct electoral arrangements for both the Chief Executive and the Legislative Council, to be introduced towards the turn of the decade.

680. Purportedly in practice of the 'open' government approach by 'consensus', the Hong Kong SAR government emulates its predecessor and continues to maintain the tradition of administration by consultation with as wide as possible a diversity of representative opinions in society. While incumbency in the top-level consultative organ, the Executive Council, still remains exclusively 'appointed', the law-making legislature has been 'democratized' as a sequel to successive stages of electoral reform. The Legislative Council has hence become a fully elected assembly based upon the dualistic 'functional' constituency and 'geographical' constituency since the general election of September 1995. Given the programme of electoral reforms mandated by the Basic Law, direct election to the district-based 'geographical' constituency has now been instituted, as the indirect election system which returns candidates on the 'functional' constituency is eventually phased out.

681. Trade union and employee representatives have always been involved in the consultative machinery over matters affecting labour, employment and training, etc. The most notable examples are the Labour Advisory Board, a tripartite advisory committee to the government on labour policy and labour legislation; the Vocational Training Council (a tripartite statutory organ to help design and monitor the official manpower and training policy) and the Employee Retraining Board, which assists employees in job transfers because of redundancies caused by technological displacement and economic restructuring process, which entails intersectoral readjustment of the workforce.

682. The officially sponsored political and electoral reforms in the territory, which transcended the 1997 dateline, have made the trade unions a key beneficiary as they are now designated as the representative organizations on the 'labour' functional constituency, besides acting as quasi-political parties in articulating the grassroots workers' interests in the contests for seats in the legislative assembly by way of direct election. An offshoot of the rapid escalation of the vanguard unions into the rank of Hong Kong's new class of political *nouveau riche* has been the augmented participation of union and labour leaders in the consultative system of the

SAR administration as noted above. However, this process has also led unwittingly to the intensified polarization between the pro-China bloc (led by the Hong Kong Federation of Trade Unions, FTU) and the pro-democratic camp (spearheaded by the Hong Kong Confederation of Trade Unions, CTU) in a politico-industrial arena fringed by other lesser union federal bodies like the pro-Taiwan Hong Kong and Kowloon Trades Union Council and the (purportedly) neutral Federation of Hong Kong and Kowloon Labour Unions. Their leaderships have successfully enshrined themselves as political activists, with a sizeable number from their ranks co-opted now into the establishment as elected members of the legislature, the law-making Legislative Council.

683. Interaction between the government and the labour movement has intensified and widened as a sequel to the above developments, in part because of the official anxiety to elicit labour's support in the newly institutionalized arrangement of popular electoral politics and in part because of organized labour's enhanced capacity to articulate workers' interests by way of these representation avenues now available because of such reform initiatives.

684. Although falling short of a socio-political alliance between the union movement and the administration, these shifting trends and emerging new terrain are therefore suggestive of a broadened labour voice in the sphere of public policy making and a rising horizon of union articulateness, which may need to be accommodated not only at the wider level of union–government–employer tripartite dialogue but also in the enterprise with an improved system of workplace representation and labour–management dialogue. This issue will be discussed further below.

685. Persistent lobbying by organized labour at the turn of the decade into the 2010s for the enhanced protection of the low-paid workers eventually led to the enactment of a minimum wage law in 2011, when private businesses and their associations succumbed to the pressure of the labour movement and extended consent to the legislation. To begin with, the law prescribed an economy-wide statutory wage floor of HK$28 an hour. The union sector continued to canvass for upgrading this level which was revised to HK$30 an hour in 2013.

§3. Trade Union Freedom and the Relations Between Trade Unions

I. Multi-unionism and Trade Union Law

686. The right of freedom of association implies the possibility of creating different unions or associations to represent the same group of employees or employers, although the proliferation of multiple unions inherent in such a 'drift' of freely pursued combinations can be incompatible with the enshrined principle of union solidarity which deplores union fragmentation and inter-union rivalry.

687. It has been argued that the Hong Kong legislation has given greater effect to the first of these two conflicting tendencies, especially since the 1961 overhaul of the trade union registration law, whereby the Registrar of Trade Unions lost his former power to refuse registration of a new union because of duplication with existing unions in terms of the relevant objects and/or trade or industry. It was, until this legislative amendment, considered reasonable and legitimate 'to refuse registration on such grounds, in disregard of differences of dialect, or cherished distinction in trade or craft, or when the applicants were discontented with the administration or political leaning of an existing union, but it was also (held) incompatible with the right of freedom of association'.[56]

688. Within the existing framework of the territory's industrial relations, however, there are no legal provisions for recognition procedures and the extension of such rights to the relevant unions at the plant or company level, as are available in the United States and elsewhere. An emulative piece of legislation was ushered to the statute book on the eve of the 1997 political handover but was repealed as too progressive and potentially disruptive to industrial relations stability by the SAR government shortly after it came into office. The problematic nature of multi-unionism and its implications for the local labour movement will be further discussed below.

II. The Association of Trade Unions

689. Parallel to their freedom on the formation and registration of a new union, trade union organizations in Hong Kong enjoy more or less the same degree of freedom if they wish to amalgamate with each other. In this connection, they are free to amalgamate across trade or industry or occupation, provided the amalgamation is supported by a 20 per cent majority of the membership of each of the constituent union in a secret ballot cast by at least 50 per cent of the voting members. Previously, the right was not symmetrical or analogous in the associated case of union federation, inasmuch as the unions seeking to federate had to come from the same trade, or industry or occupation. However, such a restrictive prescription was rescinded when these provisions on union federation were liberalized in 1997. Concomitantly, the freedom for a trade union to seek affiliation outside Hong Kong – that is, to become a member of any kind of trade union or other organization outside Hong Kong – was a right more circumscribed and was allowed only with the consent of the Governor, as it was the situation prior to 1997. Again, such an exigency has been liberalized since 1997. Consequently, the consent of the Chief Executive (equivalent to the Governor when Hong Kong was under British rule) is now no longer necessary where the overseas organization with which affiliation is sought is specifically a trade union or a professional body. By implication, if the overseas organization is not of such a nature as prescribed, the consent of the Chief

56. Registrar of Trade Unions, *Annual Departmental Report*, Hong Kong, 1961–2.

Executive is still a prerequisite. And the 1997 amendment to the Trade Unions Ordinance makes explicit that the law will continue to preclude any such affiliation with a political organization abroad established outside Hong Kong.

690. Historically the rationale behind the above restrictions has been to preempt penetration of the local unions as a vehicle which might prove detrimental to Hong Kong's fragile or delicate equilibrium of political stability. Similar constraints could have helped explain those statutory limitations placed upon the unions' ability to federate across industrial or occupational boundaries. That is, for fear of political aggrandizement if these freedoms, if left unlimited, might become conducive to 'big unions' potentially provocative and posing a threat to the governments in Hong Kong and China were they in pursuance of political objectives. Yet such a containment notion has been interpreted sceptically in some quarters of organized labour as a negative factor which has stifled and even impeded the 'native' development of union organizations in Hong Kong. But evidence has been sparse to authenticate the official apprehension, as pointed out by Professor Turner and his investigatory team in their landmark labour study of the territory, first in the late 1970s and again, in the late 1980s.[57] Today, such official neurosis about unions as a vehicle of foreign political infiltration and as an inhospitable alternative power centre to the authority has largely subsided. It has to await the incumbency of the new SAR administration for the trade union law to be liberalized to rescind the restrictions hitherto placed upon unions' ability to federate and augment their freedom to associate with labour organizations overseas.

III. Trade Unions and Employers

691. A union as a legal collectivity in Hong Kong is not just confined to a workers' combination but in line with the British legal tradition and the 'guild' background of trade unionism in Hong Kong, its statutory definition has been generic in embracing not only workers' unions, but also employers' associations as well as the mixed organizations having both worker and employer membership. However, as expected, the number of such mixed associations has become sparse today. By the end of 2012, there were 31 mixed associations of employers and employees and 18 employers' associations, as against a total of 800 employee unions, making up altogether 849 unions listed on the Registry of Trade Unions. The declared union population has been stagnant around a total figure of 740,000. This represents a union density of about 22 per cent for the economy.

692. Today, vestiges of the guild tradition have largely withered away, so that the employer–employee demarcation is far less blurred and the principle of mutual noninterference is generally observed between the unions and the employers and the latters' associations. Besides, financial contribution by employers to trade union

57. See H.A. Turner *et al.*, *The Last Colony: But Whose?* Cambridge: Cambridge University Press, 1980; also H.A. Turner, Patricia Fosh and Ng Sek-Hong, *Between Two Societies: Hong Kong Labour in Transition*, Hong Kong: Centre of Asian Studies, University of Hong Kong, 1991.

funds such as for the purpose of education is rarely known, although this type of practice is not specifically proscribed under the law. There is no legal codification on any principle and etiquette of equality governing the mutual relations between trade unions. However, it has been a commonplace in Hong Kong that they have enjoyed equal and uniform status at law, without being subject to any inter union discrimination.

§4. Individual Trade Union Freedom

I. Legal Right to Join and Participate in Trade Unions

693. In Hong Kong, the Employment Ordinance has, since 1974, provided an explicit statutory safeguard for the exercise of trade union freedom by individual employees in respect of their membership and activities in trade unions. Every employee has hence the right to become a member or an officer of a trade union, to take part in its activities at any appropriate time (that is, the time which is either outside normal working hours or within, provided that it has been agreed with the employer with his consent). The same right applies if the individual organizes, together with other persons, a new trade union and applies for its registration with the Registrar of Trade Unions in accordance with the Trade Unions Ordinance.

694. Such legal protection of the individual's ability to join and participate in a union at his own 'free will' gives effect to the international norms of labour standards as promulgated under International Labour Convention 87 and Convention 98. Moreover, these rights are backed by legal sanctions inasmuch as the Employment Ordinance prohibits the employer from interfering with and compromising the exercise of these rights. It declares it a punishable offence if an employer, or his agent, acts so as to prevent or deter an employee from exercising these sanctioned rights. Nor is it permissible for the employer to dismiss, penalize or discriminate in whatever way against an employee for having pursued or sought to exercise such statutory rights. By implication, it is also declared illegal for the employer or his agent to compromise the individual's union freedom by making employment or the offer of it conditional upon the employee having to relinquish his union membership or office, or not becoming a trade union member or officer, or not associating with other persons to form and apply for registration of a new trade union in conformity with legal procedures.

695. Violation of these anti-union discrimination clauses constitutes a criminal offence punishable by fines. However, it has to be conceded that it is exceedingly difficult at law to establish that an unequivocal act of anti-union discrimination has been committed by an employer or his agent. Since a covert intent to discriminate can always be disguised under other manifest cause(s), especially since there are absent from the territory any statutory norms on 'unfair dismissal' which may provide, as in the British situation, a protective shield of a vicarious and indirect nature. Such constraints notwithstanding, the law has still served the symbolic function of declaring a clear message of moral disapproval against such censured acts of discrimination, thereby reinforcing the legitimacy of union membership and participation by the individual employee.

Unions and employees are now more articulate in lodging complaints against employers for violating these anti-union discriminatory norms but up to now no successful prosecutions have been brought before the court by the Labour Department – even after the legal proceedings have been amended placing the onus of proof upon the accused employer allegedly having committed the act of victimization.

II. Union Membership

696. Unions in Hong Kong admit members in accordance with the criteria laid down in their union rules, the registration of which with the government is mandatory. In general, it is imperative for these admission rules to specify the industrial, occupational or trade basis for demarcating membership. During the period of pre-industrial guilds, the organization of unions in terms of ethnic and dialect divides was common. However, as unions become less parochial and administratively rationalized, it is now less likely for them to sustain such 'closedness' and exclude members on account of these particularistic considerations. On the other hand, although it is rare for unions to discriminate overtly against entry by reason of the ideological affiliation of the applicant, it appears that political conviction and sympathy may still be crucial in influencing whether or not the individual employee will join a trade union and if so, which specific union. Such a psychological disposition is easily understood, given the traditional politico-ideological split in the local labour movement. Moreover, the degree of involvement of the individual member in the union may be subject to constraints due to his age as well. By virtue of the present Trade Unions Ordinance, trade unions may admit minor members, that is, members under the age of 21, unless the rules provide to the contrary. However, no minor can hold office as a union executive and cannot be a voting member of the union if under the age of 16. Likewise, members who retire from their employment because of age or ill health cannot be voting members either, even though they may retain their union membership. Under the existing trade union law, no legal redress is available to an individual employee if he is refused membership by a union, unless it is, prima facie, a case of sex, disability, family status or race discrimination. However, unions in Hong Kong are generally known to maintain an open and liberal policy on membership recruitment, insofar as the applicant is able to satisfy the basic criteria qualifying for membership as the law or the union's specific rules may prescribe.

III. Right of the Individual Member *vis-à-vis* the Union

697. Apart from safeguarding the general ability of the individual members to participate in the election, government, leadership and other activities of the union, the Trade Unions Ordinance also confers upon the individual a battery of rights for protecting his interest *vis-à-vis* the union. Under these legally sanctioned rights, the individual member is entitled:

(i) to have delivered to him a copy of the rules of the union on demand, on payment of a sum not exceeding HK$2.00;
(ii) to receive, free of charge, a copy of the union's annual statement of account as submitted to the Registrar of Trade Unions;
(iii) to inspect personally or by means of his authorized agent, the union's account books and registers of members;
(iv) to inspect, free of charge, at the Registry of Trade Unions, any documents which the union or the federation to which the union belongs is required to file with the Registrar;
(v) as a voting member, to sue, in any court, any treasurer or other union officer who, on being relieved of office, fails to hand over any balance of union funds, moneys, securities, effects, papers and property;
(vi) as a voting member, to apply to the District Court for an injunction restraining a trade union officer from holding office or controlling union funds; and
(vii) as a voting member, to apply to the District Court for an order for the return of union funds, property, etc. wrongfully withheld or misapplied.

IV. Anti-union Discrimination and Union Security Instruments

698. The 'yellow-dog' contract is a document which is a signed undertaking by the individual worker whereby he is required, as a condition of employment, to waive his right of trade union participation – that is, to cease belonging to or not to join a trade union. Such a waiver, however, is not recognized in Hong Kong, since it is not only void but also illegal as it makes the employer liable to prosecution and criminal sanctions by virtue of the anti-union discrimination provisions under the Employment Ordinance.

699. Conversely, it is generally tenable to lay down virtually any voluntarily agreed union-security clauses since the existing trade union law does not place any restrictions limiting the institution of such 'security' practices as the agency shop or other arrangements on the maintenance of union's membership. However, such union-security clauses, reminiscent of the British industrial relations tradition of 'voluntarism', are in fact not commonly known to be in practice in Hong Kong. By virtue of the anti-union discrimination clause in the Employment Ordinance, a 'closed shop' agreement which the employer concludes with a union can be deemed as illegal and void because it makes the employment of a person conditional upon his membership in the union.

700. Legally speaking, it is also permissible for a trade union to conclude with management a 'check-off' agreement, which is an arrangement enabling the employer to act on behalf of the union to collect its union dues by way of withholding the relevant amount from the payroll of its members who are in its employ. The legality of such provisions is, however, subject to the prior consent of both the Commissioner for Labour as well as the individual employee who is the union member concerned. Otherwise, such unauthorized wage deductions may constitute an offence under the Employment Ordinance. In Hong Kong, the 'check-off' practice is again rare and exceptional, hardly known to exist save, during the 1970s and 1980s, in a lead tele-communication corporation whose workforce had a tradition of solidaristic organization by its company-based union.

Chapter 3. Organization and Structure of the Trade Unions

§1. Union Membership Strength in General

701. The trade union movement in Hong Kong was traditionally split along politico-ideological lines of cleavage, clustering into two rival divisions: on the left led by the pro-Communist Hong Kong Federation of Trade Unions (FTU) and its allies while on the right headed by the pro-Nationalist Hong Kong and Kowloon Trades Union Council (TUC) and its associates. Such a pattern of dichotomous polarization within the labour movement started to take root in 1949, when the two rival trade union centres, FTU and TUC, were created and registered, for convenience, as societies under the Societies Ordinance. The impasse of schism persisted until the late 1960s, when this uneasy equilibrium was disturbed by the eruption of 1967 civil disturbance in Hong Kong. Such an internal upheaval, generally considered as a spill-over from the Cultural Revolution in mainland China, cast a general political strigma on the whole labour movement. Union membership in 1967 therefore took a sharp dip, especially within the FTU bloc. In 1967, the aggregate number of unionized workers shrank from 171,620 to 165,579 and the declared strength of the FTU dropped from 96,735 to 95,408. This phenomenon was, however, merely transient since by the turn of the decade most of the major unions, notably the left-wing ones, began to recoup their membership strength again.

702. The upturn coincided with the changing posture of China after the Cultural Revolution. China's improving international status induced many of the local workers to identify with the mainland and to join unions for expressing their patriotic sentiments and attachment to the PRC. Another structural factor contributing to the rise of aggregate union membership during the early and mid1970s was the bureaucratization of large workplaces which stimulated the growth of the white-collar 'service' workers and their unionization. Such an organizational trend was conspicuous in the civil service and public sector involving occupations like the teachers, nurses, social workers, technicians and even office clerks. This third sector of the labour movement comprising the independent group of unions, notably the civil service staff unions, had since the mid-1970s overtaken the right-wing union bloc as the second largest wing of the labour movement, with a growth pace which outstripped that of the FTU group in the late 1990s and early 2000s.

703. At the turn of the decade into the 1980s, unions affiliated to or friendly with the pro-China Hong Kong Federation of Trade Unions accounted for about 67 per cent of the total union population. On the other hand, the independent or politically non-affiliated unions organized about 23 per cent of the unionized workers whereas the right-wing unions (affiliated to or friendly with the Nationalist Hong Kong and Kowloon Trades Union Council) took up a mere 10 per cent of the aggregate union membership.

704. However, the rather significant growth of the territory's union density in the mid-1970s began to subside towards the turn of the decade. Indeed, there was, beginning from1978, a sustained decline in the size of the unionized sector in both absolute and relative terms. Some observers have suggested that, while pointing to the almost universal trend of union decline in other industrial economies, such a receding membership was hardly surprising and by no means unique to the Hong Kong situation.

705. There were other concomitant factors of a more intrinsic character that might have helped explain the membership decline among unions during this period. Their declining membership, especially for the traditional manual unions, attests to their own organizational fragility and the ambivalent attitude held by the younger members of the workforce as they became more educated and sophisticated in expectations. It has been noted, in this connection, that these unions were more acting as 'locally specific combination(s) of friendly society and socio-political organization(s)' and less as labour's representative agents in 'economic bargaining and political pressure'. One important reason was that these unions often lacked the organization capabilities, leadership and power resources for sustaining a viable programme of their ' activities. Their feeble capacity to meet the needs and rising aspirations among the workers in Hong Kong hence posed growing challenge to unions on their missions and agendas.

706. Two other developments since the late 1970s had further emasculated the popular appeal of these 'veteran' labour organizations. These pertained, first, to the usurping effects implied by the government's enhanced programme of legislative intervention and welfare provisions and second, the zealous attempts of labour 'pressure group' (the more articulate ones being the church-denominated but non-union voluntary organizations) to represent the voice and interest of the labouring mass. Recent official sponsorship of labour reforms and the augmented provision of social wages (government funded) in public housing, medical care, education and social security payment increased, paradoxically, the working people's dependence upon the government, instead of their own self-organization, to achieve betterment in their conditions of employment and quality of working life.

707. The rise of these labour pressure groups operating outside the purview of the Trade Unions Ordinance was viewed with apprehension by the traditional union sector for eroding their grassroots base of popular support. The ability of these labour-oriented pressure groups in articulating the workers' interests could have impeded organized labour's endeavour to canvass support from the labouring mass, especially since these voluntary bodies did not charge any union dues for rendering the almost equivalent of the latters' services.

708. The decline in the unionized population during the 1980s could have, in addition, reflected a fundamental problem of trade union government, endemic in such strategic aspects as leadership, administration and organization. Given the amateur nature of administration in most Hong Kong trade unions, their membership base could easily be eroded when their members moved their homes, changed jobs or if their employers relocated their enterprises and restructured their businesses. Literally, as will be discussed later, it has posed a global challenge to trade unionism inasmuch as the average workplace has been emasculated as the basis for membership organization and mobilization.

§2. Political Changes and Membership Surge: the '1997 Syndrome'

709. However, the labour movement during the late 20th century and early 21st century was patently affected by its process of political transition. By virtue of the Sino-British Joint Declaration of 1985, Hong Kong was destined to be a highly autonomous Special Adminstrative Region (SAR) able to conserve its capitalist lifestyle and institutions after reversion back to China's sovereignty from British rule. The transition, which lasted for a prolonged 13-year period, featured, *inter alia*, the paradox of its simultaneous propensities to 'depoliticize' as well as to 'politicize'. The following narrative helps to elucidate such a dilemma:

> Ironically, the distillation of the vanguard image of the local labour movement that emanates from the politico-ideological polemics between Communist China and Nationalist Taiwan has not emasculated or diminished the 'political activity' of trade unions in Hong Kong. Instead, with the gradual transition of the 'civil service' type of colonial administration to a popularly elected government for the territory, the effective role of trade unions as the representative organizations and spokesmen of the labour sector is likely to be enhanced. The 'particular' status of the unions in electoral politics has been given recognition in the official White Paper, published in 1984, entitled *The Future Development of Representative Government in Hong Kong*. 'Specifically … together with other so-called "functional constituencies", … organized labour has been enshrined in a strategic partnership … within this reformed framework of Hong Kong's present and future political institution'.[58]

710. There were signs, albeit implicit, during the extended years of political transition since the signing of the Sino-British Joint Declaration in 1984, that organized labour in the territory had been increasingly embraced in a slow yet steady process of 'social partnership' building with the government and employers in the domain of labour policy and law-making. In addition to the three seats designated for the labour constituency in the Legislative Council, popular trade union leaders were able to win several directly elected seats in the district-based geographical constituencies as well as retain control of the teachers' and nurses' seats in the corresponding functional constituencies during recent elections. At the same time, two of the leading trade union centres, the Hong Kong Federation of Trade Unions (FTU) and the pro-democratic Hong Kong Confederation of Trade Unions (CTU),[59] appear to have each evolved a quasi-ally relationship with the two most powerful 'political parties' in Hong Kong. The FTU is close to the pro-China

58. Ng Sek-Hong, 'Labour' in Joseph Y. S. Cheng (ed.), *Hong Kong in Transition*, Hong Kong: Oxford University Press, 1986.
59. The 'independent' groups of trade unions, organizing preponderantly the white-collar occupations clustered in the civil service and public (subverted) sector, amalgamated to form themselves into, at

Democratic Alliance for the Betterment of Hong Kong, while the CTU is friendly with the 'progressive' Democratic Party.

Compounding the making of such a 'partnership' was, however, a series of episodes emanating from, around the turn of the decade into the 1990s, the 'growth' syndrome of the territory featuring both an acute labour shortage and an incessant inflation spiral. The government conceded to the employers' restless lobby in approving the large-scale admission of guest workers from outside into Hong Kong as a 'stop-gap' anti-inflation measure to dampen the 'heated' skill market. Such a policy decision evidently departed from its established stance of not allowing the entry of imported workers *en masse*. Such a policy shift also defied organized labour's relentless opposition to the government's policy decision in liberalizing such an entry. Paradoxically, the qualms of the embattled union movement, acting concertedly across its segmented factions, were audible enough in spurring a reluctant administration to offer a seemingly compensatory deal for the territory's working class – in a piece of labour policy innovation which was reminiscent of a 'social contract' found popularly in Western Europe in the 1960s and 1970s. Such an official intent led the government's initiative to institutionalize the retirement protection of the workforce on a territory-wide basis, which precipitated a fundamental public policy debate dissecting the community, especially between business and labour organizations, as to the appropriate form that such protective arrangement should adopt (namely, the choice between the options of an old-age social pension, or a central provident fund or a comprehensive yet privately administered provident fund under official supervision).

711. All these developments had the effects of enhancing the popular image of trade union associations in Hong Kong as small quasi-political parties for the 'grassroots' working people. The shifting character of trade unionism was noticeable, inasmuch as

> performance of these voluntary bodies will no longer be measured by what they might have accomplished for their membership as specific interest groupings, but how successful they are in canvassing electoral support and campaigning for an elected seat in the Legislative Council. ... What claims precedence on the union's platform ceases to be the commitment to 'deliver the goods' wanted by their membership, but instead becomes the question of how best to appeal to the votes ...[60]

712. In summary, during the era of political transition towards the 1997 'dateline', the 'politicization' of labour-cum-employment issues and the concomitant fashioning of trade union organizations into pseudo-political collectivities with an augmented role in electoral politics, have rekindled and spurred mildly the propensity of the local workforce to join trade unions. Mirroring these tendencies, there

---

the beginning of the 1990s, the second largest trade union centre after the FTU. This is named the Hong Kong Confederation of Trade Unions (CTU), conceived in 1990.

60. Ng Sek-Hong, 'Labour', *op. cit.*, pp. 283–285.

has been a creeping yet steady rise in the territory's union density, its size of unionized population as well as the number of employee unions registered, as the following statistics indicate:

Table 2 Union density

Year	*1990*	*1991*	*1992*	*1993*	*1994*
Number of employee unions	452	469	481	491	506
Size of unionized population (declared union membership)	468,746	486,961	525,538	543,800	562,285
Trade union participation rate (i.e., union density)	18.84%	19.98%	21.16%	20.91%	20.90%

Source: Hong Kong Government, Report of the Commissioner for Labour, 1994, Figs. 18 and 19, pp. 42– 43.

§3. Political Division of the Labour Movement and Multi-unionism

713. A consistent feature of the local labour movement and its membership since the Second World War has been its internal fragmentation caused by union proliferation along ideological, political, ethnic and other parochial lines, leading to multi-unionism at all levels of the enterprise, industry and economy. This pluralistic syndrome has always emasculated the internal solidarity and industrial strength of the local labour movement. The historical polarization between the left-wing FTU and the right-wing TUC, with their political sympathies owed respectively to the mainland and Taiwan, started to wither away gradually from the mid-1980s onwards. There were growing signs of mutual accommodation, dialogue or even *ad hoc* collaboration between the two trade union centres. However, since the turn of decade into the 1990s, the terrain of union pluralism has been compounded by the presence and increasing influence of the new white-collar unions, mostly concentrated in the public service and posing as a third independent force outside the FTU/ TUC ambits. Partly inspired by the euphoria stemming from the officially sponsored electoral reforms, and partly as a strategic response to the territory's political transition, these new unions coalesced by forming a third trade union centre, the Hong Kong Confederation of Trade Unions (CTU) in 1990. Allied with Hong Kong's main liberal political party, the Democratic Party, the CTU has gained quickly in popularity and membership, dislodging the TUC as the second leading trade union centre after the FTU. The emergent tripartite state of union pluralism makes the Hong Kong labour movement even more fragmented than before, in spite of nominal and sporadic demonstrations of inter-union solidarity over such 'core' issues as imported labour and retirement security.

§4. THE TRADE UNION CENTRES AND THEIR RENEWAL

I. The Hong Kong Federation of Trade Unions (FTU)

714. The FTU supports the policies of the government of the People's Republic of China now that it has resumed sovereignty of Hong Kong after its reversion back to the 'motherland' in 1997. The trade union centre espouses a strong sentiment of nationalism, mobilizing its membership to support the implementation of PRC's political model of 'one country, two systems' in Hong Kong. In spite of its endeavours to harmonize its policies and activities with the governance of the SAR government, the FTU purports to maintain its independent posture in protecting and bettering the employment interests and rights of the labouring mass at the 'grassroots' level. As illustrated by the past 16 years of Hong Kong's experience as an SAR of China after the 1997 political reintegration with China, this era has been punctuated by the FTU's challenges to the labour policy of the administration. This government has been wavering or even lukewarm in pursuing fundamental labour reforms like introducing a minimum wage law (a law prescribing a general minimum wage was, however, eventually enacted in 2011) and conferring collective bargaining rights upon unions – inasmuch as it has to 'rope-dance' between a powerful business lobby on one hand and an occasionally recalcitrant labour movement on the other.

715. The above notwithstanding, the FTU has continued to function like a pseudo-representative of China in Hong Kong aimed at cultivating the support from and a dialogue with the labouring mass, in addition to its nature and role as a trade union centre. In 2006, the FTU had altogether 174 unions affiliated to it (the Registrar of Trade Unions used to identify in his annual report those unions appearing to him as friendly with the FTU, other than those formally affiliated with it, but no longer now). While annual contributions are normally paid by its affiliate unions, the FTU is in law not a union federation of its affiliates which are registered under the Trade Unions Ordinance. As a friendly society, instead, it has by implication no direct authority *vis-à-vis* its individual member unions as a national union congress would have. This by no means, however, suggests the inability of the FTU to exercise a strong influence on the policies and activities of its affiliates. That this has in fact been the case is evident from the high level of inter-union solidarity and of structural harmonization among the affiliates in their membership organization and policy platform.

716. Nor has the FTU been conspicuous in planting a strong ideological 'nexus' in the labour movement. And industrial militancy was and has been remarkable for its absence from the trade union centre's action programme. Hong Kong can be said to have enjoyed general industrial peace over the last four decades, sustained here since the mid-1970s. Strikes occurring within this period are comparatively few and the scale of working days lost as a result is relatively low, *vis-à-vis* those in other newly industrialized economies (NIEs) or industrially advanced nations. Such a stable state of industrial harmony and peace is attributable, to a large extent, to the restrained, moderate and non-belligerent posture which the FTU has adopted during these years since the post-socialist reforms began in mainland China.

717. For instance, it has been suggested that during the 1974–5 recession, the relative freedom of the territory from any massive labour protests and unrest (when the economy was beset by such vicissitudes as unemployment, short-time working, lay-off and wage-cut) owed a great deal to the strategic moderating role played by the FTU. Such a conciliatory gesture was symptomatic also in the disbursement by the FTU of redundancy gratuities and unemployment relief, as well as its organization of consolation visits to the dismissed workers. These 'stop-gap' measures helped ameliorate the vicissitudes of the recession for the labouring mass. The FTU was not keen in supporting or orchestrating strikes or other militant actions to register the workers' agitation and dissatisfaction with their impoverishment due to the economy caught in doldrums.

718. Since the turn of the 1980s the FTU has also steadily moved away from its former stance of abstaining from any dialogue with and involvement in the labour administration's public policy deliberation and consultation in the field of labour, wage and employment. Its increasing presence on these public policy forums and organs emerged in the late 1970s when it successfully fielded a candidate for the election of employee representatives on the Labour Advisory Board, consolidated later when it accepted official appointment of its representatives to such consultative organs as the Vocational Training Council, the Occupational Safety and Health Council and the Employee Re-training Board. The newly discovered mission of the FTU to lobby and partner with the 'establishment' on labour and workers affairs was probably attested by the enthusiasm and interests shown by the FTU and its affiliates in mobilizing support for and participating in electoral activities for the legislature, the Legislative Council, and at lower levels, in the elections for the District Councils.

719. The shifting nature of the FTU's labour agenda in response to a rapidly changing political milieu, both domestically as well as externally, is hence noticeable. In addition, these changes can also be interpreted as a rational strategy of self-modernization and reform after thirty years of its organizational stagnation and conservatism (which persisted from the late 1940s until the second half of the 1970s). These reforms were hence intended to enable the FTU to cope better with the challenges of a new era with the turn of the millennium after the 20th century. In its context, such an initiative of policy revitalization and organizational rationalization of the FTU witnessed since the late 1970s has also a three-fold significance as follows. First, its comparative passivity earlier has allowed the development of private sector industrial conflict to evolve outside its control, leaving a vacuum filled by the new 'independent' unions which consolidated themselves into the third power centre in the union movement, the Confederation of Trade Unions (CTU). And the FTU's reforms are in part a response and in part a pro-active measure in order to neutralize this strategic disadvantage in their mutual bid for leadership. Second is the increasing composition in the labour force of the postwar second and third generations whose members, as they are young, educated, inquisitive and relatively free from the early-day refugee mentality, now expect a more effective and less docile collective voice articulated by the labour movement. The FTU is naturally keen, as the territory's largest labour centre, to canvass and capture the 'grassroots' support by harmonizing its activities and platform more closely with these newly arising expectations. The third consideration is perhaps more endemic in nature, as its reforms are symptomatic of the Federation's desire to align itself with the policy orientation of China, which has always been directed to the nation's modernization and the preservation of prosperity and stability in Hong Kong.

720. Up to the present, the FTU has retained its 'lead' position in having the largest membership strength among all trade union centres in Hong Kong. The division between an industrial wing and a political wing within its organization has also become more conspicuous. Its leaders are lay politicians, one being appointed to the Executive Council while several participating actively in the largest pro-China political party, the Democratic Party for the Betterment of Hong Kong. The latter are often able to secure seats in the Legislative Council by direct election. Moreover, the FTU returns successful candidates to the labour 'functional constituency' in the Legislative Council. This union centre also files and sponsors candidates in running for elections for the District Councils at the lower level of the representative system. However, unlike the case of the British TUC, this political division has not splintered off to form a separate political party.

As the largest centre of organized labour, the FTU purports to be the most dedicated custodian of the interests and well-being of the labouring mass. It was the chief driving force in having successfully brought to the statue book an economy-wide minimum wage law in 2011, against the celebrated heritage of a 'free wage' market in Hong Kong. It has continued to lobby for the enactment of standard work hours, although the stern resistance of business does not make its realization too prospective in the near future. The government is now on the verge of succumbing to the labour movement's demand to liberalize further the qualification for 'continuous employment' in order to include more part-time employees in the safety-net of entitlement to statutory benefits. In addition, the FTU is still the vanguard in pressurizing the government against any resumption of importing guest workers on a large-scale.

The FTU is still caught in keen competition with its rival, the Hong Kong Confederation of Trade Unions (CTU), in bidding for membership for its affiliates. It has an upper hand in organizing blue-collar workers while the CTU appears to have more appeal to white-collar office and service workers. The two trade union centres also differ in their strategy in intervening in trade disputes and industrial conflict. The CTU's posture is always more militant, playing the role of the 'avant garde' in calling for and organizing strikes in order to force the employers to terms. By contrast, the FTU adopts more moderate methods, often employing more subtle tactics and working through networks of social ties and personal connections.

II. Hong Kong and Kowloon Trades Union Council (TUC)

721. The right-wing counterpart of the FTU is the TUC, which is ideologically committed to an anti-communist stance with strong leaning towards the government in Taiwan. The ebbing influence of Taiwan as the bastion of the Nationalists, let alone the reversion of Hong Kong from British rule to China's sovereignty in 1997, has emasculated the popular basis of the TUC. There has consequently been a creeping but sustained decline in membership of the TUC and its affiliates. The pro-Taiwan Council has responded to these adversities by consolidating itself and its activities on a narrower front. Although the TUC has inherited an image which is conservative and 'veteran' (inasmuch as a significant number of its affiliates are traditional guild-fashioned craft unions), it has shifted to adopt a more versatile union strategy in harmonizing it with members' labour market needs. As a sequel, it succeeded in consolidating a foothold in a few key industries, notably in the restaurant, hotels and catering trades. However, its influence has evidently withered among the major public utility enterprises, where there used to a balance of power between the rival right-wing and left-wing workplace unions. Moreover, the TUC and its affiliate members have always been keen to participate in the consultative arrangements of the Hong Kong government and involve themselves in labour policy formulation. On this basis, it has always remained articulate in the representation of labour's interests in the political arena. Prior to the SAR days, the TUC was able to return successfully a candidate each in the electoral campaigns for (i) the Labour Advisory Board and (ii) the 'labour' functional constituency in the Legislative Council. However, the TUC was on longer able to retain its elected seat on the 'labour' functional constituency, which it has held since 1984, in the 1995 Legislative Council elections and thereafter.

III. Hong Kong Confederation of Trade Unions (CTU)

722. The Confederation of Trade Unions was formed in 1990, largely as a coalition of the 'independent' and 'politically' unaffiliated union organizations, most of which are new white-collar unions organizing the civil service and professional/service employees in the public and subvented sectors. Noticeable examples are the Professional Teachers Union, the Social Workers General Union, as well as a postal workers' union and the union organizing train drivers and other staff members of the Operations Department of the public enterprise which used to run the territory's underground rail system, the Mass Transit Railway Corporation before its merger with the Kowloon-Canton Railway to form the Hong Kong Railway Corporation.

723. The mission and policy orientation of the CTU are heavily rooted in the backing and involvement of a church-sponsored labour organization, celebrated for its labour 'pressure group' activities in the 1970s and 1980s. This is the Hong Kong Christian Industrial Committee (CIC), which has been consistently critical of and occasionally hostile towards the official administration, as it defined its position *vis-à-vis* the government in such terms:

> Both as a Christian group and a worker organization we hold to the basic belief that a colonial government, by its very nature, is untrustworthy and therefore must be watched, scrutinized and criticized until ... on specific issues it demonstrates to the people otherwise.

724. The platform of the CIC, laden with a mild dosage of radicalism, has therefore betrayed a 'quasi-socialist' orientation which owes its inspiration to the 'welfare state' philosophy of the labour movements in some European nations. For this reason, the Confederation of Trade Unions, of which the CIC is the chief proponent and sponsor, has also inherited such a 'vanguard' image and is now considered popularly as the more liberal sector in the territory's pluralistic union movement. The CTU has nurtured an 'allied' or 'partnership' link which with one of the largest of Hong Kong's political parties mushrooming in the late 1980s – the Democratic Party which is known for its liberal platform highly critical of China's policies and those of the SAR government.

725. The 'vanguard' role of the CIC in the 1970s and 1980s was manifest not only in its activities on worker education and involvement in industrial disputes; but it has also been a leading voice in the grassroots movements yearning for legislative enactments or improvements in the labour and employment field. Moreover, it lobbied vociferously for official intervention in transport, housing, general price levels and other aspects of bettering the working people's quality of life and standard of living. However, much of this role of 'frontline' union participation has now been taken up by the Confederation under the auspices of a trade union centre (which similar to the older centres like the FTU and TUC, is registered under the Societies Ordinance as a friendly society), while the CIC has retreated to the background as a 'resource' agency specializing in worker education and labour related social research activities.

726. The CTU is tilted towards organizing the public sector employees and civil servants in the membership and nature of its affiliate unions. It has under its umbrella the largest union in Hong Kong, the Professional Teachers Union, alongside with the nominal affiliation of the politically more independent Hong Kong Federation of Labour Unions (FLU). It has hitherto enjoyed an edge over the FTU in bidding for membership from such sources as the air transport (like the flight attendants), the mass transit railway, the postal and clerical workers in the civil service, as well as professions like the teachers and social workers. Its organization strategy has been to intervene in labour strife and help the workers locked in disputes to form new unions under its mentorship. Examples are the unions organizing the rank-and-file employees of the leading supermarkets and super-stores as well as those organizing the delivery workers of bottled drinks suppliers. It has also penetrated the public bus companies and the public utility enterprises. However, its affiliate unions which enrolled the bus drivers are always at loggerheads with their counterparts belonging to the FTU in negotiations for wage increases. The CTU have also helped its affiliate members to lodge their claims in several pioneering cases on anti-union discrimination. The Confederation has been known for its propensity towards industrial militancy in handling industrial disputes, *vis-à-vis* the more moderate and cautious orientation of the FTU. Its presence in industrial strife has always been deplored or even detested by employers.

727. Keen rivalry between the CTU and FTU was witnessed in several landmark industrial disputes in the 2010s. One was the strike of the bar-benders in the building and construction industry in 2011 over wage hikes in the industry. In spite of the tussle between the two trade union centres, the strike led to substantial wage concessions by the contractor association in the trade. Another was the demand for pay rise of the pilots and the flight attendants of Hong Kong's flagship airline, Cathay Pacific Airways. The CTU had an upper hand in organizing the flight attendants and orchestrating their maneuver, while the FTU continued to enjoy stronger influence in the building and construction trades. In 2012, the wharf workers in the largest container port handler went to strike in protest against their wages and work hours. The CTU was vociferous in backing the strikers. The strike lasted for almost a month and at its height almost paralysed the imports and exports of the SAR. Many traders relocated their connecting port from Hong Kong to those in the Mainland, Singapore and elsewhere. International union solidarity was also demonstrated as trade union leaders overseas, notably those from the maritime worker unions in Australia, were ushered to Hong Kong to articulate their sympathetic support for the striking workers. The vanguard role of the CTU in this dispute apparently eclipsed that of the FTU, which played a waiting game. In spite of the industrial militancy manifested in this dispute and its high medium exposure, the government remained lukewarm and was reluctant to invoke the mechanism of intervention provided by the Labour Relations Ordinance. A 'cooling-off' period could have been decreed but it was not. The dispute was eventually settled when the company conceded and instructed its contractors to grant a wage increase to the satisfaction of the striking workers.

728. The CTU has also been active in participating in the domain of international labour movement and labour affairs. It has several times lodged complaints with the Committee on Rights of Organization of the International Labour Organization (ILO) against the SAR government for breaches of the relevant Convention. Besides, it is also affiliated to a variety of international trade union centres and trade secretariats. It is linked, alongside with the right-way TUC, with the International Confederation of Free Trade Unions (ICFTU). The postal union owes an affiliation to the International Federation of Postal Workers. The transport worker unions belonging to the FLU have a tradition of belonging to the International Federation of Transport Workers (ITF).

729. As the industrial 'partner' of the leading Democratic Party, the presence of the Confederation in the elected law-making assembly (the Legislative Council) is highly visible, both before and now during the SAR days. At least five of the officials of the CTU and its affiliates have been elected to the Council in recent general elections, enabling the CTU to claim more or less the equivalent strength of political representation in the legislature as the FTU. The CTU has also sponsored the inception of a Labour Party, with a platform to champion for the interests of the working class. Concomitantly, the CTU and the Labour Party has become more detached from the Democratic Party in their action programme. The leader of the CTU has at the time of writing been elected to be the president of the United Front for Democracy in China. Such developments imply to a certain degree the re-politiciation of the labour movement in Hong Kong.

§5. Unionism in the Post-transitional Period and the SAR Era: An Emerging New 'Paradigm'?

730. As earlier noted, there have been assiduous efforts by the ideologically enmeshed trade unions centres to depoliticize their programmes of work. With such a strategy of 'pragmatizing' their agendas, trade unions under their respective leadership have attempted to adapt their policies in order 'to meet the needs and know the problems of the young workers'. They modernize their previous image as welfare-oriented friendly societies by converting themselves into service organizations to appeal to the membership as agencies of 'collective instrumentalism'. The unions' renewal agenda is oriented towards renovating and updating the basket of membership benefits provided. Instead of supplying philanthropic wage supplements to those who are in need, they offer services which will appeal better to the average wage-earner as both a privatized affluent consumer and a receptive young worker yearning for after-work education and association activities. In this connection, the FTU and its large affiliates, which were relatively resourceful in providing space within their premises, emerged as one of the best-known agencies organizing the private equivalents to the university fixtures of extra-mural educational activities. Concomitantly, many of the bigger labour unions, whether affiliated to the FTU, CTU, TUC or 'independent' bodies such as the civil service staff unions, have stepped up their cooperative enterprises by providing their members with retail outlets dealing in a variety of popular merchandise items at concessionary prices, often extended to include catering and travel agency services, as well as credit card facilities. Other popular services/amenities addressing their members' leisure past-time needs cover, for example, recreational activities, sports and outings, as well as extra-mural programmes or a variety of fixtures for adult education and vocational skill training. In this connection, it has been a commonplace for the leading trade union centres to each institute a worker education centre as an annex to the union administrative organ.

731. In spite of their political ascendancy since the mid-1980s, there has been not been any noticeable advance of the unions in improving their workplace status. Trade unions have remained feeble in penetrating the workplace, inasmuch as any structured shop steward arrangements similar to those in Britain were little known. This feebleness has also been attested by the persisting failure of Hong Kong labour unions to make any progress in negotiating for voluntary union recognition for collective bargaining by the 'lead' private corporate employers. Concomitantly, sporadic incidents of union militancy have appeared but invariably collapsed, as illustrated by the 'landmark' industrial episode of the famous air stewardess strike waged against Cathay Pacific Airways in 1993, which failed. Union feebleness to levy defensive industrial action was also demonstrated, about a decade later, by other examples of organized labour's collective acquiescence. A benchmark case was the mass lay-offs by Hong Kong Telecom (later taken over by and re-named as Pacific Century Cyberworks Ltd., PCCW) and its subsequent 'downsizing' exercises. This was later ensued by other incidents of corporate reorganization in the public utility and banking industries. In spite of the qualms voiced by the affected workers about their precarious job security, these exercises have not touched off any militant acts of union protests and labour agitation.

732. The docility of Hong Kong unions as documented above are explicable to a large extent by the de-industrialization-cum-re-commercialization process which this society experienced during the last three and half decades as it evolved into a postindustrial economy. This process took place across a time horizon transcending both the late transitional and early SAR periods.

The deindustrialization attrition process occurred due to the migration of factories away from Hong Kong in the 1990s. Paradoxically, this took place because of mainland China's industrial take-off. The PRC, in its reform euphoria since the mid-1980s, has liberalized admission of foreign and overseas investment. It provided a lucrative outlet for Hong Kong capital with an expanded market, a supply of cheap labour, land and production goods. Hence it has afforded this city economy a low-cost 'hinterland' (of cheap land and labour) to which the latter's manufacturing activities could be decanted and relocated. The migration *en masse* of Hong Kong-based factories across the border, pushed away by escalating production costs (of land and labour prices), led to a dramatic 'withering away' of Hong Kong's manufacturing sector. Deindustrialization has also drastically curtailed the size of Hong Kong industrial employment causing a sizable group of middle-aged and redundant blue-collar workers to be hived off from their workplaces.

Concomitantly, Hong Kong has evolved to enshrine itself as a leading business and financial centre of East Asia vested with an efficient infrastructure of transportation, telecommunications and banking services, plus a stable government and convertible currency regime (let alone an enshrined system of 'rule by law'). Hong Kong has been recycled swiftly back to its commercial role as an entrepôt, especially as the gateway to China. It used to serve for China in this capacity before the Korea War embargo. Instead of concentrating on such traditional maritime industries as shipbuilding and repairs, wharf and godown storage, and waterfront stevedoring, as it did before the war, Hong Kong has advanced and diversified its core tertiary activities into new areas such as container port handling and trucking, air cargo transport, logistics, stock and currency trading, banking and telecommunications.

733. The above economic processes engender a twofold implication which has affected the development of trade unionism in Hong Kong. First, there was a drain of the blue-collar veteran members from the older and established trade unions as the size of the production workers shrank rapidly because of de-industrialization. Some unions, in particular those belonging to the FTU and CTU blocs, responded with an enhanced endeavour to recruit white-collar union members from the newer service occupations like those located within the finance and banking sector. However, the industrial basis and the working class solidarity of the entire labour movement were noticeably emasculated. Second, the factories became less and less tenable as the basis at the workplace level for unions to liaise with and organize their members, largely as a sequel to their *en masse* migration northwards across the border to the mainland. Indeed, the changing configuration of the labour market due to the growth of atypical employment, flexi-career, and foreign migrant labour has made the workplace increasingly marginal as the recruiting ground for trade unions and for them to consolidate and cement their membership. In this context, it appears that Hong Kong trade unions, in spite of their newly discovered political status and influence in the domain of electoral politics, are eclipsed increasingly in their industrial agenda as workers' combinations which are purged of an industrial basis because of the transient nature of the workplace for work and employment, which has become less secure and stable.

734. The advent of the East Asian financial crisis and the recession afterwards, ensued in 2003 by the epidemic and its depressing impact upon the Hong Kong economy, have exposed the vulnerability of the labouring mass and the incapacity of the trade unions. The latter were almost helpless and resourceless as workers' defensive organizations to shield the Hong Kong employees at perils from the vicissitudes of capital and predicaments of widespread job losses and dislocation due to a retreating economy. Downsizing, business closures, lay-offs and wage cuts, as well as the creeping growth of a recasualized labour market (largely due to part-time and short-term contract hiring practised increasingly among employing organizations) bred a new urban sub-class of the unemployed and low waged peripheral workers. However, lacking an infrastructure of established collective bargaining practices, Hong Kong trade unions were powerless and characteristically docile about the syndrome of labour market squeeze, with the exception of sporadic industrial militancy in the retail and aircraft engineering trades.

735. Ironically, such union docility at workplace level organization and the absence of an entrenched collective bargaining tradition among enterprises have bred an element of resilience actually enjoyed by the Hong Kong labour unions. This is because of a strategic flexibility they apparently possessed, inasmuch as they were able to avert and bypass the thorny task of having to defend what has always been viewed as the orthodox function of Western-styled business unionism, which was the role as a collective bargaining agent. The embattled contest between management and labour in many Western industrially advanced economies has been centred upon the adversarial collective bargaining system and by default, Hong Kong unions may have, even unwittingly, enjoyed a strategic gain by not having to defend their continued existence, because of their relative absence.

736. Paradoxically, a feeble tradition of collective bargaining has made it possible to advance a thesis that trade unions in Hong Kong have a propensity to develop and evolve into 'community unionism' as a new form of 'third sector' organization. This is because of the pre-1997 political reforms sponsored by the government which led to a process of democratization and growing mass participation in election activities. The continuation of this process has been guaranteed by the Basic Law for the Hong Kong SAR after 1997. Trade unions in Hong Kong are encouraged by such a process of electoral reforms to evolve a strategic role of organizing the neighbourhood community in partnership with the political parties and for mutual assistance among the residents, many of whom are wage-earners.

737. The euphoria of Hong Kong's reunification with China stimulated the growth of the union population. In the wake of transfer of sovereignty organized labour had gained in membership, sustaining a continuous increase in number of declared members for the successive years of 1997, 1998 and 1999 (*see* Table 3). Unsurprisingly, the bulk of the membership growth during these inaugural years of the SAR accrued to the pro-China bloc of the Hong Kong Federation of Trade Unions. Such membership growth during this three-year period nullified the fear articulated earlier by the sceptics and pessimists that the new administration would place an 'iron grip' on the grassroots popular associations like the trade unions. Union density stayed at the relatively stable level of 21 to 22 per cent during these early years of the SAR. Such stability in unionization suggests that the labouring psychology of the working people has been perpetuated – with hardly any drastic adjustments after crossing the 1997 dateline.

738. Subsequently, at the turn of the millennium, the size of the unionized population consolidated mildly, taking a slight dip successively for the years 2000 and 2001, probably as a sequel to the recession which attended the global retreat of the bubble boom of the information technology based new economy. However, union membership recovered swiftly in 2002, when it actually peaked at the level of almost 690,300. Correspondingly, union density of the general workforce also reached a new height of 22.15 per cent for the post-1997 period, sustained possibly by the brief interlude of recovery in 2002. Yet the euphoria soon gave way to the 'doldrums' of 2003 in the advents of the epidemic. Mirroring a psychology of employee restraint and pessimism in expenditure, alongside sustained high levels of unemployment due to business closures and re-structuring, the union population declined quite sharply in both years of 2003 and 2004 to just above 670,000. The union population continued to recede in 2005, in spite of signs of abatement in its downward trend. For the same year, union density also ebbed, registering a 'low' level of 20.6 per cent.

Table 3 Union membership

Year	*Size of unionized population (declared union membership)*	*Trade union participation rate (i.e. union density)*
1997	663,814	21.85
1998	672,577	21.46
1999	689,717	21.45
2000	686,970	22.08
2001	683,483	22.10
2002	690,256	22.15

Year	*Size of unionized population (declared union membership)*	*Trade union participation rate (i.e. union density)*
2003	681,127	21.80
2004	670,750	21.04
2005	667,503	20.60

Source: *Labour Department Annual Report*, Hong Kong SAR government, for various years.

739. In retrospect, organized labour in Hong Kong has not been subject to any vicissitudes of political handicaps or disabilities due to intervention from the mainland government on their freedom to associate. However, the varying level of membership size and density during these years suggests the latter's sensitivity to cyclical fluctuations, given the politico-economic context of the SAR since its inception. Besides, the Hong Kong labour movement has been confronted, before and after 1997, with the secular problem of membership attrition due to retirement of ageing members, as well as the drain of blue-collar unionists displaced from their industrial jobs because of deindustrialization. Also besetting the labour movement was the shifting composition of the general labour force stemming from the restructuring of the labour market. Due to the process of labour market 'recasualization' and the subsequent growth of the self-employed, seasonal workers and part-time employees and those employed in other forms of atypical employment arising from the labour market flexibility 'creed', the workplace has retreated into an eclipsed position and become less the 'bastion' for labour unions to enlist and organize their membership.

740. In response, the labour movement appears to have adopted a threefold strategy in addressing the membership crisis. The first has been the growing attention paid by the major trade union centres to organizing white-collar workers now that these occupations are proliferating in such new tertiary industries as financial and business services, information technology, logistics, telecommunications, banking, stock and share trading as well as property deals. The vanguard trade union centre, the Hong Kong Confederation of Trade Unions, has always catered to the organization of these trades. Even the FTU, traditionally the 'mainstream' basis of the blue-collar union movement, has penetrated a number of new service and professional (and quasi-professional) occupations in recognition of the potential potency of white-collar unionism. .

741. A second strategy, especially pursued with zeal by the FTU, has been the gestation of general unions along industrial lines by way of either amalgamation or federation. During the ten-year post-handover SAR period, four general unions each catering to a major industry have been created within the FTU umbrella. Such union mergers, purportedly innovative in the organizational history of FTU, were aimed at restructuring and rationalizing the organizational structure of the FTU in search for enhanced solidarity of its membership. . An associated intention of these union structural reforms was to help address the perennial problem of multi-unionism which had contributed to the 'syndrome' of union fragmentation which weakened the labour movement. Moreover, a more consolidated system of industrial general unions was assumed to be able to mobilize resources more effectively – in say, organizing membership recruiting exercises.

742. Thirdly, as a union strategy of far-reaching implications noted earlier, there was a propensity for Hong Kong's trade unions to develop and evolve into 'community unionism' as a new form of 'third sector' organizations. Besides performing a quasi-political role of organizing the grassroots neighbourhood community in partnership with the political parties, many trade unions in Hong Kong are equipped with the organizational experience and resources to perform an 'agency' role in penetrating and assisting the neighbourhood community for mutual aid and insurance. And as a sequel to the emasculation of the workplace for employment , the unions are paying equal attention to the residential community for maintaining contacts with their members.

743. This 'lay' approach is also consistent with the legacy of Hong Kong unions, which have never been strong at the workplace level. Given their feeble industrial strength, some 'vanguard' unions now act as the spokespersons of workers across all trades in the neighbourhood on employment, wages and labour market issues. The labour grievances which some unions articulate are even generic and not specific to employment affairs. These issues can pertain, instead, to housing, transport, general price level and cost of living, pollution and environment, as well as associated ecological problems which can affect the wage-earners' common well-being either as employees, contingent workers or self-employed. The agenda for these unions is to cater for the 'working-life' betterment and 'quality of life' of working people, whether they are workplace or neighbourhood-based. They also lobby extensively for official leverage against the industrial vicissitudes of 'postmodern urbanism', as labour pressure groups belonging to the 'third sector' domain at a time when these agencies are expected to have a widened scope in Hong Kong.

§6. THE CONTESTED TERRAIN: RIVAL TRADE UNION CENTRES AND PERSISTING UNION PLURALISM

744. The FTU has been the most advanced among labour organizations in the SAR in evolving and developing 'community unionism'. A number of policy themes were evident in the FTU's agenda of post-1997 adjustments. First, the trade union centre began entering the 'corridor of power' of the establishment and assuming the 'transmission belt' function as a quasi-political party of the working class. Penetration into the neighbourhood community is perceived as one of the key approaches to gaining access to the labouring mass. Second, there is a conspicuous attempt by the labour federation to organize the local community in order to address the drain of membership caused by the *en masse* migration of Hong Kong factories north across the border. Such an exodus of Hong Kong's manufacturing plants and their relocation in the mainland, almost epidemic after the mid-1980s, disrupted and purged the FTU of its traditional base of shopfloor organization. The FTU is hence anxious to compensate for this membership attrition by opening up new avenues of enlisting new members, such as contacting and organizing the wage earners at the neighbourhood level.

745. The steady shift of the Federation's attention in its membership maintenance and liaison work, away form the workplace level to that of the residential neighbourhood, was also explicable by the factor of changing labour market and employment structure. There were the growing size and importance of the white-collar service workers in constituting the local working population. And yet, they were less amenable to organization at the workplace level because of the nature of their work and labouring psychology. And the recasualization of an enlarging segment of the labour force, made up of the self-employed, temporary and contingent workers and even part-timers without a full-time regular job and a stable place of work, posed an analogous problem inasmuch as they lack any permanent attachment to any specific workplace.

746. Indeed, neghbourhood programmes were not an entirely new development for the FTU. The Federation formalized its agenda of community participation in 1994 together with the inception of service provision. The Department of Community and District Services, with a network of ten district offices, appeared to perform a 'start-up' role as a 'transmission-belt' organ largely in pursuance of China's 'one country two systems' policy. For instance, the department mobilized, through its district offices, both the members of the Federation's affiliate unions as well as their families in support of electoral activities for the Legislative Council and the district councils at the local government level. These activities embraced actions such as encouraging and persuading the grassroots workers to turn out at election (to a certain extent, the SAR government has viewed the voters' turn-out rate as a vicarious indicator of its level of legitimacy and popularity), as well as campaigning for candidates either nominated directly or sponsored by the Federation. The ascendancy of the Federation in political status has placed it in a 'transmission belt' role to liaise with the Hong Kong working class for their 'compatriot' support and ensure the success of the 'one country two systems' experiment.

747. Given such an orientation towards 'community-based' unionism, the trade union centre has also restructured the delivery of membership services, notably those of worker education (especially pertaining to labour law and occupation-specific knowledge and skill) as well as grievance advice, consultation on labour legislation and employment protection, which has now been devolved to the level of the neighbourhood community. Where these services become available at the district offices, it is no longer necessary for union members to commute to the union offices at either the headquarters or the branches for consultation.

748. An allied task of these district offices, usurping virtually the role of the shop steward system, has been to cultivate and recruit new members. In this connection, the Community and District Services Department pursues its organizing work which is increasingly instrumental for the intake of new members. Concomitantly, these community offices also act as the liaison points with the rank-and-file members, acting in a shop-steward like capacity and collecting dues from the union members. The Federation has initially created altogether 14 district services offices and two district liaison offices. In 2006 it established an additional new district office, enabling the network to cover altogether 17 districts. This number has been now increased to a total of 18 district services/liaison offices, each to cater to every district designated under the auspices of the government prescribed electoral geographical constituencies.

749. The tussle between the Hong Kong Federation of Trade Unions (as the 'mainstream' of the labour movement) and the Hong Kong Confederation of Trade Unions (as the progressive 'vanguard' of the union movement) has been sustained up to the present. The contest for membership between these trade union centres has always been keen. Both have been assiduous in penetrating the new white-collar occupations of knowledge and service workers in replenishing and expanding their membership number. Their rivalry, especially in intervening in trade disputes and wrestling recognition from employers to their affiliate unions as bargaining partners, almost re-created the 'syndrome' of multi-union bidding which featured the terrain of workplace labour relations in the 1950s and 1960, when the competition at that time was between the left-wing pro-mainland Federation of Trade Unions and the right-wing pro-Taiwan Hong Kong and Kowloon Trades Union Council.

750. On the periphery of these two contesting trade union centres in the labour movement, there continues to exist a fringe of lesser federated union bodies like

(i) the pro-Taiwan Hong Kong and Kowloon Trades Union Council; and
(ii) the nominally neutral union groupings such as the Federation of Hong Kong and Kowloon Labour Unions and the federal-like Civil Service General Unions – the biggest of which is the Chinese Civil Servants Association (the union now with the second largest membership in Hong Kong, after the Professional Teachers' Union). A number of key personalities in their leadership echelon have successfully enshrined themselves as political leaders during the transition period and post-transitional era of the SAR regime, with a few of them being co-opted into the establishment as elected members of the law-making Legislative Council.

751. The enhanced activism of the Hong Kong Confederation of Trade Unions (CTU) since the 1997 'watershed' probably attests to the accommodating policy and tolerance of the SAR administration *vis-à-vis* the workers' movement as a potentially alternative power base. In particular, the CTU has been a purportedly 'independent' body yet appearing essentially as a democratic, anti-China and curiously, a quasi-socialist (anti-capital) grassroots organization of the labouring mass. As the vanguard of progressive (and occasionally militant) unionism in Hong Kong, the CTU has posed the heaviest challenge to the FTU in contending for leadership in the labour movement and representing labour's political influence on the governance of Hong Kong. The CTU's agenda is even more ambitious – not only to serve as the standard-bearer of the alternative movement to the FTU 'mainstreaam', but also to introduce into the legislative infrastructure a number of hastily assembled pro-labour legislative motions (like the 1997 law providing for collective bargaining and consultation rights to trade unions at enterprises, which was later repealed by the newly incumbent SAR government). There is still noticeable a professed endeavour by the CTU to erect a 'pro-active' institutional system of 'rule by law' within Hong Kong. Besides, the CTU has also been keen to nurture and consolidate a web of international hedging with friendly overseas organizations in an attempt apparently to pre-empt any excessive intervention and coercive control by the PRC on trade union freedom and rights of association in Hong Kong after 1997. Given such an avant-garde orientation and posture, it has represented the 'core' voice of organized labour's apprehension about the central government's intention to legislate on Article 23 of the Basic Law on national security, which might curtail individual freedoms in Hong Kong. Besides, it spearheaded, prior to the enactment of a general minimum wage law in 2011, recalcitrant labour's protests against the government's evasive attitude to introducing such a piece of legislation. By contrast, constrained by its pro-establishment position, the FTU articulated a stance of more moderate opposition towards the indecision of the SAR government and its lukewarm attitude on minimum wage and standard work hour legislation.

752. For the present, the labour movement has remained pluralistic and fragmented, with a proliferation of small unions having overlapping bases of organization. In the year 2012, registered trade unions totaled 849, comprising 800 employee unions, 18 employers' associations and 31 mixed organizations of employees and employers, alongside eight trade union federations. During the last five-year period, the size of the union population has stabilized around the level of 740,000 menbers. Union density, as measured by the percentage of salaried employees and waged earners who belong to trade unions, varies around the level of 22 per cent during this period. The labour movement is still polarized between the pro-China Federatiion of Trade Unions (FTU) and its more vociferous counterpart, the Confederation of Trade Unions (CTU). There were altogether, in 2012, 184 employee unions affiliated to the FTU and 80 unions affiliated directly to the CTU. However, within the CTU umbrella was the Federation of the Hong Kong and Kowloon Labour Unions (FLO), to which 74 unions owed their affiliation. When aggregated together, the CTU had altogether 154 unions affiliated to it. The right-wing pro-Taiwan veteran trade union centre, the Hong Kong and Kowloon Trades Union Council (TUC), increasingly eclipsed in its influence since 1997, had a relatively small number of only 28 affiliate unions.[61]

Organized labour has succeeded in wresting from the SAR government and the business sector their concession in introducing a statutory minimum wage level for the working population. A Minimum Wage Ordinance was enacted in the year 2011, which places a statutory floor to the general wage level, with a Minimum Wage Commission appointed for the fixation of the minimum wage level. This was first fixed at the hourly rate of HK $28 and subsequently upgraded to HK $30. In addition, the labour movement continues to lobby for the liberalization of the criteria

61. *Hong Kong 2012* (Annual Report for the Year 2012), Hong Kong: Information Services Department, Hong Kong SAR Government, 2013: p.112.

for defining the 'continuity of employment' in order to extend the cover of statutory employment benefits to include more part-time and temporary employees. It also canvasses for official leverage to redress the malaise of urban poverty and the incessant problem of income and wealth inequality, as well as enactment on standard work hour. However, because of strong employers' resistance and the technical complexity of enforcement, the regulation of general working hours in Hong Kong is not prospective.

The CTU was able to sponsor the creation of a Labour Party. However, this party has been perceived as too radical in its action programme. Being embryonic, it still lacks a wide basis of popular appeal. In counterpoise, the FTU continues to function as a quasi-political party, fielding candidates for elections at various levels of representative government. The two major trade union centres are still at loggerheads with each other in competing for membership and intervening in labour disputes. The industrially deprived and refractory section of the labouring mass tends to look to the CTU for assistance and support, often manifesting militancy in industrial strife. A landmark dispute in the year 2013 was the strike of the container port workers over wage disagrements. Apparently, the CTU overshadowed the FTU in the series of industrial actions waged against the principal employer and its contractors. This industrial episode will be discussed in further detail in a later chapter on industrial conflict.

§7. Union Dues

753. The amount of union dues and the manner of collection may vary from union to union, as stipulated under these unions' respective rules. However, since 'check-off' arrangements negotiated with the employers are relatively uncommon (they are known to have been practised, in the past, only by a leading enterprise union organizing the staff members of a public utility corporation in the territory's telecommunication services before the deregulation of this monopolistic industry), the majority of the local unions seemed to have relied upon a system of lay 'workplace' or 'unit' representatives for liaising with its rank-and-file members, including the collection of union subscriptions. The basic organization of most FTU unions appears to remain that of the old revolutionary 'cell', with around a dozen members and based upon the workplace. They elect a representative whose principal function is to liaise between this unit and the union leadership. These representatives will usually collect subscriptions, may act as shop-stewards, and in the larger unions will generally be either the delegates to the annual or biennial general meeting or the potential candidates from which such delegates are elected.

754. Paid-up membership of the union, as determined by the number of members who have paid up their membership subscription, constitutes the basis of the qualified membership strength according to official usage. As such it is distinguished from the union's declared membership – that is, the strength which it claims, yet embracing those members who have paid up their dues as well as those who have not. The Registrar of Trade Unions publishes statistics on union strength only on the basis of declared membership; he also used to produce estimates of paid-up membership belonging to the three sectors of FTU, TUC and CTU groups of unions but no longer does so.

755. On the whole, trade unions in Hong Kong are known to have levied a relatively low fee charged upon their members for subscription. Estimates ascertained on the basis of the Trade Unions Registrar's report in the mid-1980s (precisely, his 1985/86 report on the average of the unions' receipts from their paid-up members) indicates that the annual due payment subscribed by the unionized population averaged about HK$80 (equivalent to about US$10 or UK £7) only – about less than 0.2 per cent of average employee earnings around this period.[62] Such a meagre level, of course, has been interpreted as an important factor explaining the relatively limited resources and financial capabilities that unions are able to mobilize in Hong Kong. However, the proliferation of unions in number could have exerted a strong competitive pressure among unions not to charge a fee above the 'market' norm,[63] or simply to adjust its level in line with inflation – unless it was absolutely necessary.

§8. Union Branches

756. The locational or spatial pattern of the unions in Hong Kong is generally different from that found in larger Western countries such as Britain or the United States, where the national unions are normally constituted by a hierarchical organizational structure featuring the national, provincial (state), district (regional) and local tiers of operation. Because of the territory's compact geographical size and the concentration of its urban population, the preponderance of unions here have a single office, without administering any branches or locals. Only the bigger unions operated branches on a district basis, but the latters were sparse, seldom autonomous but often acted as subsidiaries under the central administrative control of the headquarters. However, as pointed out in an earlier section, such a paucity of union activities at the district neighbourhood level has now been compounded by the emergence of 'community unionism' which is nurtured at a swift pace by the 'mainstream' labour movement led by the FTU for addressing the gap left by the retreat of the workplace as the basic unit of organizing members at the grassroots level.

757. Virtually, what has persisted from the past has been the weak and feeble organization of the union at the workplace level. In essence, the shop-steward system is conspicuous for its absence from the average enterprise in Hong Kong. In a sample study of 34 trade unions and employee associations in the late 1980s, an impoverished pattern of union 'branch' organizations was uncovered by the researchers:

> ... at least in the old Hong Kong unions, the branch does not mean the basic or workplace organization (to one of which all members are allocated) of the

62. *Ibid.*, p. 153.
63. *Ibid.*

western type, but generally a sub-office of the union, often with a canteen and social facilities attached. In fact, only four of our respondent unions reported having such branches: and they had only 8 branch offices – of which 7 were operated by 3 large FTU affiliates.[64]

§9. INTER-UNION RELATIONSHIP

758. The state of multi-unionism in Hong Kong has meant a contested terrain of inter-union competition in the same industry or enterprise for membership. Unions tend to proliferate not only by virtue of political cleavages but also because of their historical origins, ethnic and linguistic (in terms of dialect diversities) affiliations – let alone traditional craft boundaries. Indeed, the left-wing and right-wing unions have been known over the earlier years for their mutual bidding for membership in such industries as textiles, restaurants and catering, stevedoring and inland transport, as well as 'in-house' within the major public utility enterprises. It appears, at least in the past, that the utility enterprises have preferred to enter into regular dialogue (which was tantamount to an informal manner of voluntary union recognition) with the right-wing unions and less with their left-wing counterparts, in spite of the latters' better positions in membership and organizational strength. Such practices have been permissible in Hong Kong, where the law does not prescribe any compulsory recognition procedures by means of popular balloting.

759. Multi-unionism had, however, not resulted in any major inter-union jurisdictional or demarcational disputes, given that the practice of collective bargaining had not been widespread in Hong Kong. Yet industrial strife is still liable to be compounded by the rivalry between the FTU and the CTU and their affiliate unions in bidding for control over the terms of settlement.

760. The intense polemics once dividing the left-wing and right-wing sectors of the labour movement have now subsided. Both sides are ideologically less polarized and have shown increasing flexibility and pragmatism at mutual accommodation. And either is even amenable to *ad hoc* cooperation with its former adversary in approaching specific issues on the public policy forum (like that of labour importation). Yet the withering away of the left-wing versus right-wing confrontation within the labour movement coincides with the escalation of rivalry between the pro-China FTU and the pro-democratic CTU in bidding for leadership of trade unionism. Their struggle for power has actually intensified in the post-1997 SAR days. In a number of recent disputes, the two trade union centres openly fought for the right to represent employees in dispute. Such contests are reminiscent of jurisdictional disputes.

761. Apart from the FTU and the CTU blocs, a third sector of the labour movement is made up the civil service trade unions. The leading one is the veteran Chinese Civil Service Union, the second largest union after the Professional Teachers

64. *Ibid.*, p.156.

Union. Moreover, the Federation of Labour Unions (FLU) appears to have dissociated increasingly from the CTU and to be steering a more independent position in articulating its members' interests and participating in local electoral politics.

§10. Trade Union Government and Leadership

I. Union Constitution

762. Subject to the legal perimeters defined by the Trade Unions Ordinance, individual unions, provided that they are registered, are free to choose and determine the structure of their internal government. Such an organizational form is normally specified under the union rules or constitution of the union concerned, the provision of which is mandatory at law. It is also obligatory for the union, in writing its constitution for registration, to ensure that its provisions would list:

(i) the name of the trade union and the address of its registered office;
(ii) the whole of the objects of the trade union which must include, *inter alia*, distinct provisions for regulating the relations between employees and employers or between employees and employees, or between employers and employers, etc.;
(iii) the conditions under which members may enjoy voting rights, the conditions under which non-voting membership is available and the provisions for maintaining a register of the union's members;
(iv) the maintenance of discipline within the trade union, including the provision for appeal to the general meeting of its members against any decision of the union's executives and leaders;
(v) the procedures for convening and conducting annual general meetings and the matters to present to the membership thereof. These matters must include, the presentation of audited accounts;
(vi) the appointment and replacement of the union's officers, and the power of the voting members to vote in deciding such appointments ;
(vii) the amount and manner of payment of subscriptions, fees and contributions payable by members of the union and the purposes to which its funds may be appointed;
(viii) the creation, administration, protection, disbursement and disposal of welfare funds and the conditions under which any union member or his family may become entitled to any such benefits;
(ix) the custody and investment of the union's funds, the designation of the officer(s) responsible for such functions and the keeping and auditing of accounts;
(x) the commencement and closure of the union's financial year;
(xi) the power of the members to inspect the union rules, its account books and the register of its members' names;
(xii) the making, altering, amending and rescinding of the union's rules;
(xiii) the method of dissolving the trade union and the manner in which its funds shall be disposed upon its dissolution; and
(xiv) the safe custody of the union's common seal.

II. Machinery of Union Government

763. Typically, the ultimate authority of decision-making in a union rests with the general meeting of the members which, in Hong Kong, normally elects the executive committee and in some cases, the supervisory committee as well. The executive committee, usually headed by the union chairman, is responsible for the day-to-day administration of the union although for major decision-making (such as involving any amendments to the constitution, proposals on mergers or changes in policy), reference has to be made to the general meetings. In many of the older unions, especially the traditional craft associations, the union governance system also includes a supervisory committee. The role of such a supervisory organ is chiefly to oversee, supervise and criticize the work of the executive body and the individual functionaries under it.

764. Such a union structure has been described as simple, , although in the civil service the larger white-collar unions organizing different departmental grades have adopted 'a quasi-federal form through the affiliation of smaller ones or the formation of specialist (grade or department specific) units'.[65] On top of these basic structural features, a three-fold organizational trend in the labour movement has been identifiable since the 1980s, namely:

> One is a multiplication of executive sub-committees, to deal both with the increased variety of union services now offered to members, and with the public and community issues in which many unions are now involved. The second reflects the FTU's attempt – having failed to move any further towards amalgamation of its minor affiliates than the merger of three craft print workers' unions previously linked in a federation – to regroup its unions as industry federations … .And the third – and probably most important – trend is an increase number of full-time officers themselves.[66]

III. Union Leadership

765. Historically, most of the 'mainstream' unions in Hong Kong emerged as an outgrowth from the wider political movement inside China and as such, it has been customary in the past for the majority of the vanguard union leaders to be recruited from the echelon of political/revolutionary ideologues. Correspondingly, union consciousness of the labouring mass at the grassroots level has been weak and feeble. In this connection, most unions are organized from the top downwards, normally lacking the basis of a strong and spontaneous shopfloor movement at the bottom. Such a tradition has not been conducive to the grooming of union leaders from among the working class itself.

65. *Ibid.*, p. 156.
66. *Ibid.*, p. 159.

766. Compounding the problem in the past, until the law was liberalized in 1977, had been the legislative insistence upon staffing unions only with lay officials. Before 1977, the Trade Unions Ordinance prescribed that no person could be an officer of a trade union unless he is (was) 'habitually engaged in a trade, industry, or occupation, with which the trade union is (was) directly concerned'. However, it was problematic inasmuch as many of these lay officials 'habitually' hired in their trades were found wanting in their education, professional knowledge and competence in union administration. Recognizing the restrictive effects of these provisions and in order to enable the local unions to rationalize their internal administrative structure, the government amended the Trade Unions Ordinance in 1977 rescinding the above constraints so as to make possible the election or appointment of capable persons who used to have been engaged in the relevant trade, though not hired in a habitual manner or at present, to become the leader or official of the union.

Paid clerks were and are still, probably the most common type of salaried full-time officials employed by the unions in Hong Kong. However, their quality is also dubious since most of them were found to be conservative, elderly and amateur in an earlier study.[67] The law has been improved since the Trade Union (Amendment) Ordinance of 1977 which aims to encourage upgrading in the quality of these paid union officials.[68]

767. As a sequel to the 1977 amendments to the Trade Unions Ordinance, the legal prohibition against an individual holding office in more than one union has been liberalized as well. However, to preclude the penetration of unions by the criminal influence of the Triad and other secret societies, the legal censure against any individuals who have been convicted of an offence which involves fraud, dishonesty, extortion or membership in a Triad society to serve as an officer of a trade union has been kept on the statute book. Such a ban is applicable within five years from the date of conviction or discharge from imprisonment.

768. In spite of its history of weakness in its unions' leadership, Hong Kong witnessed in the 1980's the rise of a crop of articulate leaders groomed by and working for the major trade unions and trade union centres like the Hong Kong Federation of Trade Unions, the Hong Kong Confederation of Trade Unions, the Federation of Hong Kong and Kowloon Labour Unions, the Hong Kong and Kowloon Trades Union Council and the Chinese Civil Servants Association. Mostly self-made and of working-class background, these union officials (many of whom were lay officials) have been active in electoral politics, posing themselves as authentic spokesmen for the labouring mass at the grass-roots level of society. Their ascending social image and popularity were attested amply by their widened success in the

67. For details of this study's findings and conclusions, see Joe England and John Rear, *Chinese Labour Under British Rule*, Hong Kong: Oxford University Press 1975, p. 100.
68. The paid clerks have become re-defined as paid staff – that is, as a clerk or person appointed by, and acting under instruction of the executive thereof as well as paid from the funds of the trade union or the branch of the trade union or the trade union federation, as the case may be.

post-1997 SAR days in winning direct elections for seats in the law-making assembly, the Legislative Council. Organized labour also constituted one of the core functional blocs in the Legislative Council. However, these union leaders have now become veterans or retired, leaving a vaccum of succession because of the sparse number of younger union members who are interested in or aspire for incumbency of trade union offices.

IV. Rank-and-File Union Membership

769. By virtue of the present Trade Unions Ordinance, membership in a union is restricted only to those persons who are ordinarily resident in Hong Kong and are hired in the trade, industry or occupation with which the trade union is directly concerned. Members who have retired from the trade due to age or ill health are normally allowed to retain their union membership although they cease to be voting members. In addition, those under the age 21 can be minor members but cannot be union officials, while those under 16 cannot be voting members. The rank-and-file members, whose involvement in the internal affairs, government and activities of their unions can vary widely between unions in nature and intensity, are guaranteed certain legal rights by the present trade union law. These legal abilities pertain to, *inter alia*, safeguards on the individual's access to the union's rules, power to inspect, at the Registry of Trade Unions, any document which the union is required by law to file with the Registrar, as well as the abilities to take legal proceedings so as to restrain a trade union officer from holding office or controlling union funds – or to sanction the return of union funds or property wrongfully withheld or misapplied in connection with the union and its activities.

V. International Union Affiliation

770. At the international level, both the TUC and the CTU are the local trade union centres which are affiliated to the International Confederation of Free Trade Unions (ICFTU). They are, however, registered as societies outside the purview of the Trade Unions Ordinance and are hence free from the restraints placed by the Ordinance on overseas affiliations of local unions. Yet, there are a number of trade unions registered under the Ordinance which are also known to be affiliated to international trade secretariats belonging to the ICFTU umbrella or other union organizations of their respective trades. For instance, the right-wing Cotton Industry Workers' General Union of Hong Kong is affiliated to the Textile Workers Asian Regional Organization of the ICFTU; the Hong Kong Chinese Civil Servants' Association, a public sector staff union, is affiliated to the Public Services International, also of the ICFTU. The international affiliation of the registered trade unions used to need the prior approval of the Governor by virtue of the Trade Unions Ordinance in the pre-1997 era. However, such a requirement was rescinded by the SAR government when these provisions were liberalized shortly after it came to power.

VI. Union Activities

771. The pervading theme of political unionism, the weakness of workers' union consciousness at the grassroots level as well as their relatively feeble organization and leadership in the average workplace have not been conducive to the development of collective bargaining in the way that it has been a central function of Western trade unionism in advancing the common and job-based economic and occupational interests of their members. Nor have most unions in Hong Kong purported to pursue a radical or revolutionary programme of political activities in their agendas and pledged a mission to reform or restructure the existing social order. Instead, given the legally prescribed constraints circumscribing the political activities of trade unions rooted in Hong Kong's labour history as well as the internal limitations of the union's resources and organization, most of Hong Kong's labour unions – especially the older ones which emerged tamed from the early years of embattled political strife in the 1920s, – have adapted themselves to function and behave in a restrained style more as welfare unions and friendly societies than as bona fide unions emulating the Western model in activities and purposes. To a large extent, these roles are reminiscent of the indigenous nature of the traditional pre-industrial craft guilds in China. It has been a popular method for trade unions to attract new members with the offer of concessionary merchandise to members at a discount comparable to a cooperative. In addition, many unions also serve as a kind of mutual aid or insurance agency for their members via pay-outs of cash benefits from members' subscription or welfare contributions to cover unemployment, sickness and injuries, as well as marriage, maternity and childbirth. Besides, some of the large unions provide in their office premises an equivalent to a club house for their members to associate and socialize after work. As the workers' fraternities or friendly societies, these unions facilitate the building of occupational communities, which contribute hence indirectly to the workers' mutual solidarity and sociability. It has been customary in the older craft trades for the unions' members to exchange job and wage information – and sometimes to introduce each other for job placement via the occupational contact networks built and sustained among members. Today, with the development of geographically based electoral activities and the emasculation of the workplace for recruiting and liaising with members, it has been suggested that unions may start to penetrate the neighbourhood community and act as a 'third sector' agency for the residential wage earners to better their quality of working life. The FTU, for instance, in erecting a network of district and community offices, apparently envisages an agenda of evolving a system of 'community unionism' as a strategy of union organization now and in future.

On the other hand, the rise of the new independent and essentially white-collar oriented unions since the late 1970s and beginning of the 1980s has epitomized a new spirit and approach in local unionism, which is visibly more concerned with Western-style collective bargaining activities as well as the articulation of labour interests in influencing the government's legislation and public policies in manpower and employment (especially in light of the accentuated participation of union representatives in the law-making assembly, the Legislative Council). Many of these unions are within the civil service and are affiliated to the CTU, either as individual unions or union federations. They waged a sequel of industrial strife against the government as the employer over pay relativity in the 1970s and early 1980s. Teachers, social workers, nurses and postal workers were among the most vocal occupational groups during this period. These waves subsided eventually as the government yielded to most of the demands. For rationalizing and the more effective administration of civil service pay, a Standing Commission on Civil Service Salaries and Pay Structure was established in the late 1970s. The government has also been conducting pay consultation as a quasi-form of collective negotiation (apparently modelled upon the Whitley system) on service-wide annual salary adjustment percentages with the major civil service unions which it recognizes. These activities are multi-tiered, involving the Senior Civil Service Council, the Junior Civil Service Council, the Disciplinary Staff Council and the Police Staff Council.

§11. Legal Status of Trade Unions

772. The Trade Unions Ordinance imposes a legal duty upon trade unions in Hong Kong to register with the Registrar of Trade Unions of the government. In essence, the act of compulsory registration has such implications as the following for the unions concerned:

(i) conferring upon them a legal status;
(ii) making them corporate bodies; and
(iii) bestowing upon them specific rights and obligations.

These aspects are each discussed briefly in turn.

I. Legal Capacity

773. A chief effect of union registration is to legalize any such association or combination whose principal objects are liable to render its nature being deemed at common law as 'an unlawful combination by reason of some one or more of its purposes being in restraint of trade', inasmuch as it is oriented to the 'regulating of relations between employers and employees, or between employees and employees, or between employers and employers'.[69] As such, any person who acts as an officer or participates in the administration of an unregistered union is punishable by legal sanctions. Registration under the Trade Unions Ordinance, in addition, removes such a combination from the exigencies of the 1949 Societies Ordinance. The latter is Hong Kong's principal legislative instrument governing societies as voluntary associations in the SAR; it declares any club, company, partnership or association as unlawful unless it has been either registered with the Registrar of Societies (who is the Commissioner of Police) or is specifically exempted from registration – as in the case of companies registered under the Companies Ordinance as religious,

69. Trade Unions Ordnance, 1971, Section 2.

charitable or recreational societies.[70] However, it is also specifically declared by the Societies Ordinance that it does not apply to trade unions or their federations, provided that they are registered under the Trade Unions Ordinance.

II. Body Corporate

774. A trade union is incorporated by virtue of its registration under the Trade Unions Ordinance. As a corporate body for all purposes, the union is entitled to hold property without further formality and without the expense of trust deeds. It also implies the capacity of the union to enter into contracts, to sue and be sued in suits and pursue other legal proceedings. Unions can conclude with employers or with each other collective agreements, whether they are employees' unions or employers' associations. Nevertheless, following the British tradition, the general presumption here is that these collective agreements are not legally enforceable in court.

III. Trade Union Rights and Obligations

775. Besides its lawful and corporate status, a registered trade union is vested, by virtue of the Trade Unions Ordinance, with a battery of rights concerning union protection and freedom. These rights, which are largely inherited from the British tradition, include, *inter alia*, immunity from either civil actions or criminal liability for conspiracy, or because the purposes of union are in restraint of trade. They also enjoy exemption from actions in respect of torts for any acts done in contemplation of furtherance of a trade dispute. Moreover, the liberty of peaceful picketing at or near the workplace is also safeguarded by the same legislation although it censures any associated activities involving violence, intimidation and 'watching and besetting' the employer.

776. Reciprocally, there are certain obligations which are incumbent upon a registered union pertaining to its registration and its internal administration. Basically, a union is required to register with the Registrar of Trade Unions and to register with him its constitution, which has to incorporate a series of 'prescribed' provisions to safeguard members' rights and its administration in a constitutional and proper manner. The contents of the constitution (plus any ancillary rules) as well as any subsequent amendments to it have to be submitted to the Registrar for his scrutiny. The Registrar may not register them unless he is satisfied that these union rules are consistent with the legally prescribed standards, and that they are not imprecise, incomprehensible or mutually contradictory. In addition, it is a legal duty for registered unions to submit to the Registrar for examination at annual intervals their returns of membership, as well as their audited accounts after the closing of the union's financial year. The union is also legally obliged to notify the Registrar about

70. This, however, has been liberalized under amendments in the nineties to the Societies Ordinance which substitutes the registration system with a notification procedure instead.

any change in its name in order to have the latter's consent for purpose of registration. Notification is also mandatory on the establishment of every branch by the union, including any subsequent changes in its address, as well as the variety of the union's business, charitable, cultural, medical and educational undertakings.

IV. Registration

777. Generally speaking, the Trade Unions Ordinance stipulates liberal procedural rules for trade unions to seek registration. For the inception of a new union, it needs only seven voting members to sign the application for registration, to be submitted to the Registrar for Trade Unions. The submission has to include, *inter alia*, the proposed constitution of the union, the offices and the names of the officers on its preparatory committee as well.

778. The administrative discretion of the Registrar to refuse the application for registration is highly circumscribed. It is limited to such legally specified grounds as:

(i) non-compliance with the Ordinance or its regulations;
(ii) the purposes of the union being unlawful;
(iii) the proposed name of the union being the same as or similar to that of another union so as to cause confusion; or
(iv) the union being substantially one whose registration has been previously and lawfully cancelled.

779. Upon approving the application, the Registrar has to certify the registration in writing by issuing a certificate of registration to the new union.

780. The Registrar is also vested with the symmetrical power to cancel an existing union's registration. Again, such a power is highly restricted and applied only either in response to the voluntary request of the union, or where the union has ceased to exist, or as a measure of censuring the union for breach of the law. Specifically, the conditions which enable the Registrar to invoke cancellation as a sanctioning measure against an existing union are limited to default situations where:

(i) registration has been found to have been obtained by fraud or mistake;
(ii) registration is void because any of its purposes is unlawful;
(iii) the union has been used for any unlawful purpose or for any purpose incompatible with its objects and rules;
(iv) the Trade Unions Ordinance has been contravened;
(v) the union's funds have been spent on an unlawful or unauthorized purpose (for example, a political purpose other than for electoral activities) or in an unlawful manner; and
(vi) the accounts have not been properly kept.

V. Amalgamation

781. The Registrar's consent is necessary for an amalgamation of registered trade unions to come into effect. It may be sought provided that a majority of the officers of the unions involved have voted in the first instance in favour of making an application to the Registrar for his consent. As in the case of initiating union registration, the Registrar may refuse to give his consent only for delimited reasons. He can withhold consent where the name of the amalgamated union is not distinctive, if any of its purposes are unlawful or if there has been a failure to comply with the relevant legal provisions.

782. It is necessary for the amalgamation proposal to be endorsed by the membership in the respective unions involved. Each of these unions seeking to amalgamate has to conduct a secret ballot among its members in order to ascertain their approval or otherwise. The voting criterion is twofold. First, the balloting is not effective unless at least 50 per cent of the union's voting members vote. Second, whether the proposed amalgamation can proceed or not depends upon the condition that the votes cast in favour have to exceed those against the motion by a margin of at least 20 per cent.

783. Such a voting principle is adopted basically after the model of the British Trade Unions (Amalgamation) Act of 1917. However, in 1964, the comparable legislation was amended in Britain to liberalize the conditions governing amalgamation, making it possible for such merger to be sanctioned by a simple majority without any stipulation on the relative size of the polling base.

784. In Hong Kong, before 1961, unions seeking to amalgamate had to be within the same trade or industry. However, such a restriction was rescinded as a result of the 1961 amendments to the Trade Unions Ordinance. In the event of a union proposing to amalgamate with a trade union or other organization established outside Hong Kong, the prior consent of the Chief Executive has to be obtained.

VI. Federation

785. Prior to 1997(8) and under British rule, the freedom for trade unions to federate, however, was more circumscribed than in the case of amalgamation. Unions in Hong Kong were allowed to form a union federation and seek registration thereof, provided that their members were all engaged in the same trade, industry or occupation. It was hence in part because of this reason that the major trade union centres like the FTU, TUC and CTU, had to register themselves outside the purview of the Trade Unions Ordinance by virtue of their 'cross-industry' nature. Instead, they have been registered as societies under the Societies Ordinance. Similar to the case of amalgamation, the support of membership of the constituent unions is necessary for federation to proceed, to be determined also by way of secret ballot. However, there is no legal stipulation as to the size of the voting base, and it is presumed a simple majority of the votes obtained in each union in support of the proposal is sufficient.

The SAR government liberalized the legal condition that unions could federate only within the same trade, industry or occupation by rescinding this provision from the Trade Unions Ordinance in 1997(8). However, in spite of the law's liberalization, the trade union centres have opted to remain registered as societies because of the freedom they enjoy as societies by operating outside the jurisdiction of the Trade Unions Ordinance.

786. The registration of a proposed union federation follows more or less the same procedures as those for the registration of a new trade union, save with modifications. Probably, the single and benchmark case of unions combining into a federation in Hong Kong's labour history was the inception in 1975 of the Federation of Hong Kong Printing Trade Workers' Union, constituted of the Hong Kong Lithographic Workers' Union, the Hong Kong and Kowloon Printing Trade Workmen's Union, the Commercial Press Workers' Union and the Hong Kong Chung Hua Book Co. Workers' Industrial Union. However, in 1985, this union federation, which owed its affiliation to the FTU, was again re-organized into an amalgamated union.

787. Since the 1970s, there has been a movement within the civil service sector seeking to form a service-wide federation among a number of occupation-specific public service unions, under the sponsorship of international trade secretariats like the Public Service International (PSI) and such British white-collar general unions as the Association of Scientific, Technical and Managerial Staffs (ASTMS). Such an endeavour to organize, however, has not successfully materialized into any registered civil service union federation. Instead, it has provoked debates and controversies within the labour movement as to whether the existing trade union law acts as an impediment constraining the unions' solidaristic development in this direction. One line of argument has been that the civil service is too diversified as to be able to qualify for the description of a simple and unitary 'trade, industry or occupation' – so that the Trade Unions Ordinance would have technically precluded the federation of these occupationally distinctive unions within the civil service under its provisions before 1997(8). Conversely, opinions which favoured a less restrictive interpretation of the notion of 'trade, industry or occupation' argued that it was fictional and even deceptive to construe any substantial legal obstacles implied by the then trade union law against any federated move of civil service unions. This was because the civil service could be seen, at least in notional terms, to comprise a single industry or a unified economic sector. If the problem was merely a judicial issue of interpretation of the letters and spirit of the law (that is, as to whether a liberal interpretation or a restrictive one should prevail), the debate could have been resolved around that time either by submitting a test case of application to register a proposed civil service union federation to the High Court for ruling or via legislative amendments to clarify the ambiguities clouding the definition of a trade, industry or occupation under the Trade Unions Ordinance. However, the debate has become nostalgic, now that the SAR administration has removed the 'single industry' restriction placed upon the ability of Hong Kong unions to combine into federations.

788. Virtually, it has been observed that quasi-federal union bodies have been always existent within the civil service. For instance, the second largest union in Hong Kong which is also the leading general union in the civil service, the Chinese Civil Servants' Association (CCSA), has since its inception taken a federal form that entails an umbrella of more than fifty semi-autonomous units, each catering to the specific (sectional) interests of separate occupational groups. The CCSA, in addition, accepts affiliation to it by other civil service unions, besides its own basis of individual membership. In parallel, the Civil Servants' General Union, created in 1978 in counterpoise to the CCSA, has also operated on the basis of broadly similar organizational logic. Besides, the Federation of Civil Service Unions, founded in 1984, and the Joint Organization of Unions, re-structured in 1984 from the Liaison Office of Public Service Unions, each performs as a quasi- union federation in terms of their roles, structure and activities.[71] They are registered as societies.

VII. Union Affiliation (Overseas)

789. Prior to the SAR regime when Hong Kong was under British rule, it was necessary for unions in the territory to secure the prior consent of the Governor before they could become affiliated as a member of any kind of trade union or other organizations established outside Hong Kong. Such a legal prescription by the Trade Unions Ordinance has been widely interpreted among local trade unions as a preventive one – designed to check any tendency of a union to be indulged in political strife linked with the upheavals in mainland China. A sequel to this provision has been to outlaw any close association between union organizations in Hong Kong and their counterparts in mainland China, although these links were common before the Second World War – notably in the key role the latters played in instigating a large-scale labour challenge to the authority of the Hong Kong administration in the 1925 Canton-Hong Kong Boycott Strike. However, the Hong Kong Federation of Trade Unions (FTU), registered as a society outside the purview of the Trade Unions Ordinance, has maintained close yet informal links with the All-China Federation of Trade Unions (ACFTU) and its trade union councils in various localities. The Confederation of Trade Unions (CTU) was known to have canvassed vigorously for the liberalization of this provision,given its and its affiliate unions' persistent search for widened freedom to seek international affiliation with such international labour bodies as the International Confederation of Free Trade Unions (ICFTU) and its International Trade Secretariat (ITS). The lobby succeeded to induce, at least partly, the SAR government to rescind such a requirement (provided that the overseas body with which affiliation is sought is a labour organization and not otherwise) shortly after it came into office in 1997. This legislative amendment epitomizes an advance in trade unions' freedom to associate with their overseas counterparts without subject to the surveillance of the incumbent government.

---

71. For an authoritative discussions on these propensities for civil service unions to associate and combine into federal bodies, see H.A. Turner *et al.*, *The Last Colony: But Whose?* Cambridge: Cambridge University Press, 1980, pp. 29–30.

However, affiliation with political organizations and the donation of union funds to its overseas affiliates still need the prior approval of the Chief Executive.

VIII. Union Funds

790. The manner in which unions may spend and dispose of their funds has been strenuously defined by the Trade Unions Ordinance, given that it has been a historical concern of the Hong Kong Government to eradicate and neutralize any covert activities in the organized labour sector to mobilize unions' resources for Triad and other criminal and unlawful 'enterprises', or in support of political espionage.

In this connection, the legislation specifically prohibits the application of any union funds, direct or indirect, for any political purposes within or outside Hong Kong, in spite of its limited liberalization, now in the currency of the territory-wide electoral reforms, enabling a trade union to spend its money in support of election to the Legislative Council and the District Councils. The law also declares that the union's welfare funds may only be collected and expended for its members' welfare benefits as specified in the union's rules and as such, cannot be used for other purposes. Technically, it is not permissible for a trade union to spend its union funds outside the specified items as listed below:

(i) payment of salaries, allowances and expenses to officers and paid staff of the trade union;
(ii) expenses of administration, prosecution or defence in legal proceedings for securing or protecting the rights of the union or of any member in his dealings with his employer or employee;
(iii) the conduct of trade disputes and compensation of members for loss arising out of trade disputes;
(iv) purchase of land, securities or property;
(v) payment to other lawful organizations established in Hong Kong;
(vi) promotion, entertainment and contribution or donations to similar organizations established outside Hong Kong;
(vii) payment of fines being imposed on the trade union for any offence on which it is convicted; and
(viii) provision and maintenance of a welfare fund.

IX. Individual Liability of Union Officers

791. A trade union registered in Hong Kong is a legal entity which can be fined, upon prosecutions, for offences and contraventions of the Trade Unions Ordinance. However, as a corporate body, it cannot be imprisoned. On the other hand, every individual officer belonging to a trade union which has committed an offence is vicariously liable at law for the same offence and as such, is hence also punishable by penal sanctions, unless it can be established in court that the offence occurred without his knowledge or consent.

Chapter 4. Employers' Associations

§1. General Situation of Employers' Associations in Hong Kong

792. It has already been noted in an earlier section that the employers' associations in Hong Kong are also regulated and registerable as trade unions under the law. In 2007, there were 21 such employers' associations registered with the Registrar of Trade Unions. In addition, there were 23 mixed organizations of employers and employees, also registered officially as trade unions. In 2012, the comparable figures were 18 employers' associations and 31 mixed organizations of employers abd employees (this 'hybrid' combination type is actually reminiscent of the pre-industrial system of traditional Chinese guilds). Apart from the Employers' Federation of Hong Kong, whose organizational ambit cuts across industrial boundaries, these employers' unions are mostly based upon a specific industry, sector or trade. Some of them are still anachronistic in internal structure, having organizational elements carried over from the Chinese traditional craft and merchant guilds. While some associations perform as a mutual fraternity (that is, like a 'friendly' society), others tend to emphasize more instrumental activities of industrial cooperation such as mutual coordination among their members on wage rates, price levels and conditions of employment. Often there is also a tacit agreement among them against raiding each other for members.

793. In Hong Kong, there are other organizations catering to the representation of business interests, as distinct from the registered employers' trade unions. These non-union trade or business associations also perform industrial relations functions with varying degree of vigour. For example, most of the major industries, especially the modern ones like hotels, tourism and retails, are each organized by a single or multiple trade or manufacturers' associations which are registered as societies or companies. Their primary concern is largely the promotion of members' common business and trade interests, which often include industrial relations and labour matters as a 'core' issue. Due to ethnic, dialect and historical reasons, multiple trade associations are often recognizable in many industries and trades.

794. In addition, a third type is the non-union association of employers, whose nature is also trans-industrial like the Employers' Federation of Hong Kong. There are five major general employers' and business bodies of such a nature, namely: the Hong Kong General Chamber of Commerce, the Chinese Manufacturers' Association, the Federation of Hong Kong Industries, the Chinese General Chamber of Commerce and the American Chamber of Commerce. These general employers' organizations, in spite of their non-union legal status, are actively involved in the articulation of the business sector's interests in areas of labour legislation and associated labour matters. Occasionally, they may extend their activities by assisting their members in handling labour–management issues at the workplace.

§2. The Employers' Federation of Hong Kong (EFHK)

795. The Employers' Federation of Hong Kong, established in 1945 as a sub-committee of the Hong Kong General Chamber of Commerce, has since August 1948 become an independent general union of employers registered under the Trade Unions Ordinance. Its principal objective has been to organize employers in all kinds of businesses in Hong Kong and in such a capacity, to assist them in attaining harmonious relationships with employees, using such methods as representation, consultation and dissemination of information. It also seeks to articulate its members' interests in lobbying the government in its public policy formulation, especially in relation to labour legislation and labour market regulation (for instance, on minimum wage legislation and standard work hour regulation and earlier, about intakes of foreign guest workers imported into Hong Kong for trades and industries where labour shortage exists). As the principal employers' association, it is represented in such official advisory bodies as the Labour Advisory Board, the Vocational Training Council and the Employees Re-training Board.

796. In 2007, the Federation registered a membership of about 450 companies, organized into ten groups according to the nature of their trade or industry (namely, the Trading and Distribution Group, Shipping and Port Operations Group, Industrial and Manufacturing Group, Professional and Business Group, Insurance Group, Banking and Financial Services Group, Public Utilities Group, Transportation Group, Property and Construction Group, and Hotel and Catering Group). Each group elects its chairman, who sits in turn on the Council which is the governing body of the Federation.

797. It has been observed that since its inception, the Federation has been engaged in comparatively few instances of collective bargaining with employees and or their unions. This is understandable, as it has been the Federation's declared policy to leave actual industrial negotiation to its individual members rather than to involve itself directly in bargaining activities. Instead, it has consistently preferred to provide background information and advice to its members to facilitate negotiation. However, it could negotiate with unions directly if warranted by circumstances (as in the instance of standard wage negotiations in the stevedoring industry). In the wake of recessions afflicting Hong Kong in the earlier half of the 2000s, the Federation has begun publishing economy-wide wage guidelines and norms advising its members on their annual pay adjustments.

798. In summary, the functions of the Employers' Federation are more conspicuous outside the arena of open intervention in industrial negotiations at the workplace level. Instead, it has performed its role more in terms of the influence it can bring to bear indirectly upon the shaping of labour-management relations practices, *vis-à-vis* both public policy as well as the policy of individual members. In performing such a role, the Federation has commented widely and often on labour legislation and employment policies of the government, as well as furnished its members with information about prevailing wages, fringe benefits, welfare and various standards in labour practices.

799. In the international sphere, this employers' general union is also represented in the Asian Regional Conferences of the International Labour Organization (ILO), which are tripartite, as well as on the Committee of the Organization of Employers' Federations and Employers in Developing Countries, of which it is a member.

§3. The General Chamber of Commerce (GCC)

800. The Chamber, founded as early as in 1861, is the oldest and perhaps most established organization of business and employers' interests in Hong Kong. It is incorporated as a limited company under the Companies Ordinance, with a current membership which exceeds 4,000 companies. It identifies as its fundamental aims the promotion and protection of the members' interests in trade, commerce and industry – the scope of which covers as well employee-employer relationships. The Chamber is consulted closely by the government on these subject-matters. The shift in its attitude towards the motion of an economy-wide minimum wage from that of opposition to that of consent was a key factor behind the success of the SAR government in introducing a general minimum wage law in 2011. At present, it represents probably the most powerful and articulate voice in representing the interests and views of Hong Kong employers on labour and employment matters. The Chamber is closely associated with the Liberal Party which is always in partnership with the establishment and often supports the policy decision of the SAR administration. Besides, its membership has been enfranchised, under the officially sponsored political reforms, as the electorate to return an elected representative to sit on the law-making assembly, the Legislative Council, as a designated functional constituency in the 'business and commerce' sector.

§4. The Chinese Manufacturers' Association (CMA)

801. In contrast to the General Chamber of Commerce and the Employers' Federation of Hong Kong, which are dominated by Western capital and modern corporations, the Chinese Manufacturers' Association preponderantly organizes the smaller and local Chinese enterprises, of which there are more than 3,700 on its membership. Incorporated under the Companies Ordinance in 1934, the Chinese Manufacturers' Association has been active in the spheres of trade promotion, industrial development and representation of the interests and concerns of small industry and business in public policy decisions of the government. It has also been enfranchised as the electorate for a seat in the Legislative Council, with its members enrolled as the competent voters under the 'functional' constituency arrangement, again in the 'business, commerce and industry' sector.

§5. The Federation of Hong Kong Industries (FHKI)

802. The Federation was created by statute in 1960, essentially to facilitate the technical development of the local industries in Hong Kong. However, this body has also been audible on manpower, labour relations and other matters pertaining to the economy, society and employment of the territory. . Now having a membership of more than 2,800 industrial and commercial concerns, the Federation provides a variety of industrial support services to its members, including the issue of certificates of origin, the Hong Kong Quality Mark Scheme, insurance policy, consultancy work on quality assurance, trade marks and copyrights, trade enquiries and economic research. Similar to the General Chamber of Commerce and the Chinese manufacturers' Association, its membership are designated as one of the functional constituencies in the business sector to elect its representative to sit in the Legislative Council.

803. These four leading employers' bodies are articulate in expressing their views on various government policies on labour and employment in Hong Kong. For example, the Hong Kong Employers' Federation, the Hong Kong General Chamber of Commerce and the Hong Kong Federation of Industries jointly published in 1994 a voluntary guideline on equal opportunities in the workplace. They have also represented their comments on the 2013 Policy Document on Population issued recently by the SAR government, which devotes an important part of its contents to the implications of anticipated demographic changes for the manpower conditions of Hong Kong. These associations are in favour of augmenting the present intakes of imported guest workers for redressing the expected shortage of skills but meet with the ardent opposition of organized labour. Due to their concession, the government was able to introduce a minimum wage law for the economy in 2011, after almost thirty years of extended tussle and haggling which they had with the labour movement. However, it is not likely that they will to give their consent to organized labour's quest for standard work hour legislation and that for collective bargaining rights.

§6. The Joint Associations Committee of Employer/Employee Relations (JACEER)

804. It is worth noting an endeavour by these employers and trade associations to cooperate and work collectively in advancing the common interests which they share when dealing with labour–management relations. The impact of the 1967 civil disturbance and its aftermath led the Employers' Federation of Hong Kong, the General Chamber of Commerce, the Chinese Manufacturers' Association and the Federation of Hong Kong Industries, to form together in late 1967 a joint forum for mutual consultation specifically on labour relations matters, known as the Joint Associations Committee on Employer/Employee Relations. The primary function of this organ is to provide a common employer front and platform, basically in connection with labour legislation and other social issues of relevance to labour, so as to 'protect the realistic interests of both the employer and the employee'. However, it is only a consultative body, lacking any delegated prerogative to represent any of the member organizations in any collective bargaining activities or decision making. Literally, the Committee has been docile and even dormant during the 13 years of political transition before the transfer of sovereignty and also after, when Hong Kong becomes an SAR of the People's Republic. It has continued to remain inactive in the last few years.

§7. Collective Power of Employers and Their Organizations

805. The collective power of employers as an organized interest group is probably loose but can be audible over issues like those as documented above. Perhaps, the general ineffectiveness of the labour unions has posed little of a collective challenge to the employers. Union docility hence implies the relative absence of any industrial pressure upon the Hong Kong employers to organize *visà-vis* the labour movement for such activities as collective bargaining. The number of employers' associations registered with the Registrar of Trade Unions has been hitherto low and declining: in 1976 there were 44 associations representing 4,848 enterprises and by 1985 these dropped to 33 associations with a total membership of 3,133. In 1995, the comparable figures were 26 associations, altogether having a membership of 2,604. These numbers further receded in 2007, when there were 21 associations organizing 1,782 employers. In 2012, there were only 18 employers' associations and 31 mixed organizations of employers and employees on the Trade Union Register.

806. With the exception of the Federation of Employers (HKFE), the majority of these employers' unions operate in the lesser and older industries. Many of them are, like their counterparts in the organized labour sector, more 'mutual aid' or friendly societies than bona fide industrial organizations specializing in labour–management matters.

807. However, as noted in the preceding paragraphs, there exists, outside the purview of the Trade Unions Ordinance, a host of trade, business or industrial associations whose activities include, *inter alia*, acting as the spokesmen for the employers' interests on various consultative public organs as well as the law-making assembly, and even as vehicles for the coordination of wage information, whether territory-wide or at industry level. These business and quasi-employers' bodies (registered under the Societies or the Companies Ordinance), together with the registered employers' unions, was estimated in the early 1980s in a labour study to cover a very sizable sector of the economy, responsible for about four-fifths of its private sector employment.[72]

72. H.A. Turner *et al.*, *The Last Colony: But Whose?* Cambridge: Cambridge University Press, 1980, pp. 36–37. Also see H.A. Turner *et al.*, 'A Summary Account of an Enquiry: Labour Organisations, the Labour Market and Labour Relations in Hong Kong', Faculty of Economic, Cambridge University, cyclostyled, 1980, p. 6.

808. Such employers, trade and business interest groups are effective and articulate in lobbying the government, both before and after 1997, in the labour and employement domain. This influence has become even more conspicuous, since the designation of the three leading associations (namely, the General Chamber of Commerce, the Chinese Manufacturers' Association and the Federation of Hong Kong Industries) as functional constituencies to elect each a representative sitting on the Legislative Council, alongside the cooptation of their leaders into the Executive Council during the SAR administration. However, these employers' bodies are not known to be doctrinally antagonistic towards any statutory or administrative provisions and initiatives to improve labour standards in Hong Kong. The resilience of the territory to achieve labour–management understanding, cooperation or even consensus on labour enactments and other public policies of mutual interests has been partly attributed to the stability and efficacy of a 'tripartite' dialogue (namely, among the three parties of the government, organized labour and organized business-cum-employers) consistently entailed by the Labour Advisory Board. The Board has been established since the 1920s as the principal consultative organ representing labour and employers to advise the government on its labour policy, labour legislation and labour administration.

809. Ironically, such a celebrated and time-honoured institution of 'tripartite' consultation on public policy determination in the labour and employment area is being challenged and eroded by a more powerful and vocal Legislative Council as the latter becomes increasingly 'democratized'. This is because some elected deputies on the Legislative Council, who are pro-democratic union leaders anxious to assert their elected mandate and authority in law-making, start to initiate legislative motions seeking to compromise, over-rule, and even reverse the recommendations submitted by the Labour Advisory Board to the government on labour legislation proposals. These acts of 'politicizing' public policy decisions on labour and employment matters have the effects of emasculating the efficacy of the Board in helping employers and the employed in working out a workable consensus. It appears that the aggrandizement in power of the elected Legislative Council has unwittingly perverted the working 'trust' which has been sustained in the Labour Advisory Board between organized labour and organized business.

810. Notwithstanding such development, it has been observed that the practice of 'information consulation' and 'information exchange' as a common method which these trade associations adopt for promoting their members' interests appears to have worked to facilitate a mild measure of coordination or tacit understanding among companies in the same industry or trade, especially on such employment and manpower issues as recruitment, wages and other labour market matters. However, such 'information network' generally falls short of any concerted policy collusion among employers. Yet, these informal norms are still instrumental in enabling Hong Kong employers to take wages and recruitment out of the arena of mutual 'cut throat' competition – especially when the territory experienced cyclical waves of labour shortage. Otherwise, it has been the exception rather than the rule that these employers/trade associations are entrusted with substantive power by their membership to prescribe any industry-wide wage standards, payment system, negotiations and grievance procedures, or other industrial relations norms.

§8. Professional Institutes

811. An institutional corollary to the employers' organizations in industrial or postindustrial societies is the development of professional bodies in the area of personnel management, now retitled under the highly popularized label of 'human resource management'. Such a 'professionalizing' trend is symptomatic of the growing specialization and sophistication in management resources that deal with human relations in employment.

812. In the Hong Kong context, several background factors have given significant impetus to the professionalization of the knowledge, skill and practice of human resource (personnel) management in the workplace, especially among the medium-sized and large modern corporations. The first source was the challenge and aspirations espoused by a general labour force of growing sophistication. The Hong Kong workforce is drawn increasingly from the second and subsequent generations of settlers, who are hence less affected by the 'refugee mentality' in which their parents used to be trapped. At the same time, they are also better educated and informed – and are hence more articulate and aspiring in yearning for betterment in labour conditions and quality of working life. In the second instance, sustained labour shortage and hikes in labour wages due to the territory's rapid economic development and industrial/business restructuring since the late 1970s have also lifted substantially the premium of manpower as a key factor of production, so that it is increasingly imperative for enterprises to rationalize their acquisition, utilization, commitment and conservation of their human resources. Thirdly, the arrival of the American and other foreign multinationals, conspicuous since the late 1960s, has also been conducive to these 'professional' developments in human resource management as an external stimulus or catalyst, inasmuch as their role is not only that of overseas investors but also that of carriers of advanced technology and 'software' practices including modern managerial skills and organizational techniques. In the fourth instance, the development of labour administration and the growing involvement of public policy on labour and social issues, noticeable in its 'heavy' programme of labour legislation and education, manpower training and re-training, are also conducive to the higher importance and priority which most Hong Kong enterprises now place upon human resource and its development. Fifth, de-casualization in the 1970s and 1980s and the subsequent popularization of atypical employment and outsourcing have also led to a growing demand for experienced and qualified personnel in human resource management.

The movement to organize among professionals and practitioners in human resource activities has led to the inception of several bodies which are addressed to a more or less common basis of potential membership. Such a a pluralistic situation of multiple organizations in this field of practice is reminiscent of the fragmentation typical of employers/trade associations as well as labour unions in Hong Kong.

813. The leading one is the Hong Kong Institute of Human Resource Management, founded on the model of its British counterpart in 1977 (that is, the UK Institute of Personnel Management), under its old name 'the Hong Kong Institute of Personnel Management'. It was retitled to its present name in 1994 in order to mirror better the latest development in this field of practice. Achieving by 2009 a membership of 4,000, plus a contingent of 40 student members, the Institute aims at developing and maintaining the professional standard of human resource management in Hong Kong, to contribute to the promotion of harmonious industrial relations and to advance labour productivity and manpower development in business enterprises as well as organizations of other nature in Hong Kong. At the end of 2014, the institute registered a membership of more than 5,300, among whom about 600 were corporate members. Approximately 60 per cent of the members were at managerial or director level, while 9 per cent were students.

Chapter 5. Institutionalized Workplace Relations Between Employers and Employees

§1. Introduction

814. In Hong Kong, the average workplace is characterized by a low level of institutionalization of labour–management relations. Invariably, workplace labour relations have been informal and lightly regulated by any established machinery for regular and sustained joint labour–management dialogue.

815. Since the early 1970s, it has been part of the government's industrial relations policy to promote the notion of joint consultation as a way of strengthening labour relations at the workplace. Such an official endeavour was largely inspired by the industrial upheavals and militancy which featured the civil disturbance in 1967. As a sequel, the administration started to launch a promotion campaign on such practices, aimed at encouraging the larger enterprises (with 100 employees and above) to establish joint consultative committees as a means of institutionalizing enterprise-specific labour–management relations. The system of joint consultative arrangement inculcated is, however, voluntary in nature and modelled essentially upon the British system developed since the war years in the earlier half of the last century for enhancing productivity.

816. Up to the present, there has been no statutory regulation of the actual conduct and pattern of workplace labour relations in Hong Kong, apart from the Labour Relations Ordinance of 1975 and the legislation on collective bargaining rights enacted on the eve of the 1997 political handover but rescinded subsequently by the SAR government. Nor is it popular for unions to institute locally here a shop-steward system in organizing the workplace although a quasi-system of workplace representatives is not entirely unknown in the internal administrative structure of some large industrial or occupational unions.

§2. Joint Consultation (JCC)

817. The essential features of joint consultation in its orthodox form, as of the voluntary type promulgated by the Labour Department, are portrayed as follows.

Joint consultation as an industrial notion is defined as the process of discussion between management and the employees (i.e. the workforce) on matters of mutual concern and interest, yet subject to the express qualification that 'it is not a negotiating body, for the purpose of collective bargaining'. It is to facilitate a two-way communication and a spirit of genuine cooperation between labour and management at the workplace level.

Joint consultation in practice is hence carefully designed to avert any infringement upon managerial prerogative. There is an aversion to introducing any degree of worker participation in the decision-making process of the enterprise.

The Labour Department has in its advisory pamphlet declared the importance, when practising joint consultation, 'of ensuring that management retains the right to manage' and proposes that a JCC be made competent, by its constitution, to discuss issues including:

(i) all matters affecting the well-being of the employees at the workplace level, which pertain to for example, cleanliness, ventilation, lighting, rest pause and their sitting posture;
(ii) suggestions for improvements in methods and organization of work;
(iii) suggestions for the revision or amendments of work rules; the interpretation of instructions, orders or notices, the prevention of accidents as well as the prevention of waste of time, materials and other resources;
(iv) investigation of any impediments which may reduce efficiency or in any way interfere with the satisfactory working of the establishment.

The structure of a joint consultative committee should be two-sided and defined by a written constitution. Such rules of governance should prescribe, *inter alia*, the appointment of representatives from both the employee and management sides, with the latter normally assuming chairpersonship. Joint secretaryship nominated by either side is nevertheless advocated. In addition, it is considered that to ensure that the employees' needs can be effectively articulated in the consultative activities, employee representatives should be best chosen by and from the employees, selected by election, preferably by secret ballot.

818. The formal type of joint consultation as portrayed above has proved so far not popular in the labour and employment domain of Hong Kong. Its application has not been widespread as the responses of both the employers and the employed have been lukewarm or apathetic. Three decades ago, in the mid-1980s, a senior labour official conceded to a local vaccum of workplace institutional arrangements lacking 'any established machinery for labour–management dialogue or communication'.[73] He disclosed that as few as 32 industrial and service establishments were known to the Labour Department to have set up formal joint consultative committees (JCC) in emulation of the British model.[74] In effect, the active practitioners of the orthodox JCC in Hong Kong have been essentially limited to the British enterprises, public utilities and government departments. In other words, they are likely to be work organizations sharing a British heritage.

819. A host of factors can probably be cited to help explain the lack of success of the JCC prescription in Hong Kong. These include, for example, (i) the highly circumscribed role and authority of the JCC system, having little more than a ritualistic function for communication; (ii) the preponderance, in the Hong Kong context, of the small and medium-sized enterprises, which are evidently more suited to the simple and informal means of labour–management communication, as

73. Yeung Chi-Kin, 'Joint Consultation, Collective Bargaining and Trade Union Recognition: status and prospect', in Y. C. Jao, David A. Levin, Ng Sek-Hong and Elizabeth Sin (eds.), *Labour Movement in a Changing Society: The Experience of Hong Kong*, Hong Kong: Centre of Asian Studies, University of Hong Kong, 1988, p.54.
74. *Ibid.*

compared with the more structured arrangement epitomized by the JCC model; and (iii) an overt dearth of any faith or commitment from both sides of employment in the institution of the JCC for workplace integration. Management tends to harbour a stern suspicion towards the JCC system as an extension of workers' power and refrains from extending to it any power beyond window-dressing. Correspondingly, employees are also sceptical about its efficacy. Either because of sheer apathy or for fear of being castigated as siding with the employers, employees are inclined to decline nomination for election or appointment to deputize for the workforce on the JCC.

§3. Workplace Delegates and Workplace Labour and Employment Relations

I. Workplace Permissiveness

820. The average workplace in Hong Kong is not organized for the representation of the views and interests of the rank-and-file members of the workforce on the shop-floor. Specifically, there is absent from most plants and workplaces a shop steward structure or any system of union representation. These union deputies would have been able, as in many European nations, first, to represent the union *vis-à-vis* its members or potential members at the workplace level and secondly, to act on behalf of its members or other (non-unionized) employees in the enterprises *vis-à-vis* management on grievances, discipline, job allocation, demarcation, working environment, custom and practice, work hours, overtime, pay and other issues pertaining to employment conditions and labour relations, individual or collective.

821. Nevertheless, employees' aspirations for improved and better employee representation at the workplace might gain stronger momentum as (i) the Hong Kong workers become more articulate and educated; and (ii) Hong Kong's society is now in the process of evolving an increasingly mature culture and system of representative government and electoral politics.

822. Such shifts in labour attitudes were actually evidenced by the Turner series of industrial studies dated as early as from the mid-1970s. In particular, the second survey by Professor Turner and his associates on workers' attitude in 1985 suggests interesting clues to the shifting Hong Kong workers' expectations in Hong Kong as how to achieve improvements in their labouring conditions. These changes in worker attitudes are elucidated by the authors as follows:

> We noted in comparing employee preferences between methods of improving labour conditions that in our surveys of the 1980s 'joint consultation' had displaced 'action by the administration' in popularity among our respondents, compared with our results in 1976. And we also noted that our respondents clearly conceived this as involving a formal right to consultation through employee-elected representatives – not merely on the narrower questions of welfare, physical conditions and the like which concerned the UK-derived

> from of joint consultation ... but also upon the broader issues of pay, fringe benefits or related matters and of workplace grievances procedures.[75]

However, such a prediction appears now to be over-stated. Up to the present, there are still few signs to suggest that the new generation of Hong Kong employees espouses a strong yearning for workplace collective consultation and negotiation. Conspicuous by their absence are any work councils from among enterprises in Hong Kong of the type that can be found in many European nations.

II. Workplace System of Communication

823. At the workplace level, the institutional linkage is hence weak between labour and management on a collective basis. In the small enterprises, labour and industrial relations are reminiscent of the traditional paternalism of Chinese management which placed an emphasis upon personalized contacts, interactions and informal ties between the employer and the individual employees. In the larger establishments, where the scale of operation precludes direct face-to-face contacts between management and the rank-and-file workforce, a latitude of shopfloor labour– management issues have to be handled by either the work group itself or the line supervisor in consultation with the personnel or human resource or staff department. The importance of the 'staff' support functions of the human resource department is probably made more important by the absence of any widespread 'shop steward' or 'employee delegate' system in Hong Kong.

Given the problems experienced in propagating the joint consultation prescription, the Labour Department adopts a less technocratic approach in promoting workplace labour relations among enterprises in the private sector by appealing to employers to enhance their communications arrangements and to benchmark with each other and emulate arrangements elected as the 'best practices' in people management by the practising firms.

824. However, these official measures are probably intended as correctives to the general image that personnel or human resource management has always been weak as a professional practice in Hong Kong. Concomitantly, among most workplaces disciplinary and grievance procedures are always unilaterally determined by management, often without any employee participation in their application. However, as it matures the Hong Kong Institute of Human Resource Management has contributed a new dynamism to the professional upgrading of this field which helps, in turn, promote stable and harmonious workplace labour relations in Hong Kong.

---

75. H.A. Turner, Patricia Fosh and Ng Sek Hong, *Between Two Societies: Hong Kong Labour in Transition*, Hong Kong: Centre of Asian Studies, 1991, p. 108.

III. Workplace Labour Relations and Personnel Practices

825. The actual conduct of labour–management communication and personnel practices tends to assume varied forms among different workplaces in Hong Kong. A sample survey by the Hong Kong Institute of Personnel Management on Management/Employees Communication, Consultation and Negotiation in the Private Sector in 1980 indicates that the use of written notices and circulars was most prevalent among enterprises, although the large and service establishments seemed to have relied rather extensively upon the publication of house journals or news bulletins as well. Other collective means of face-to-face labour–management dialogue, propagated by the Labour Department and aimed at reaching the grass-roots, include such practices as informal discussion groups, on-the-spot briefing sessions, production on service unit meetings or even quality control circles (QCC) or work excellence groups. The application of such collective communication practices has now widened but the scale still remains limited today, after three and a half decades.

826. In 1989, a comparable study of workplace practices commissioned by the Asian Productivity Organization elucidated by and large a similar pattern in terms of the relative density of a variety of communication methods, as adopted by a sample of 45 firms presented in Table 4.

Table 4 Communication methods

Means of communication	*Number of firms which reported its practice*	*Percentage of sample (N = 45)*
i Company newsletter/bulletin	30	66.7
ii Suggestion system	25	55.6
iii Shopfloor meeting	22	48.9
iv Grievance machinery	21	46.7
v Shopfloor small group	11	24.4
vi Labour-management Consultation	11	24.4
vii Worker director	4	8.9
viii Collective bargaining	2	4.4

Source: Ng Sek-Hong, 'Workplace Industrial Relations in Hong Kong', in International Labour Organization (ed.), *The Development of Sound Labour Relations*, Bangkok: International Labour Organization, 1991, p. 39.

827. Ten years later, a study was conducted by the Workplace Study Group of the Chinese Management Centre of the University of Hong Kong on workplace communication and human resource activities among Hong Kong enterprises in the wake of the 1998–9 recession, under the sponsorship of the Labour Department. The study illustrated both continuities as well as discontinuities *vis-à-vis* the earlier pattern of the 1980s. On a few workplace labour relations features, the study suggested that Hong Kong was on its way to converging with Western practices, while retaining its distinctiveness.

828. The findings also disclosed that some enterprises allowed a limited degree of negotiation in their dialogue with their staff and employees. This was suggestive of an employer's flexibility, probably owed to a Hong Kong style, on the use and application of a workplace device which is supposedly distinct from the institution of formal union–management collective bargaining. The researchers argued that the eclipsing and usurping of unionism and its bargaining functions, by using joint consultation as an equivalent, could be a purposive personnel strategy, as it 'could have enabled these establishments to hold at arms' length any full-scale collective bargaining with trade unions'. Another concomitant feature was the workplace legacy of Chinese paternalistic benevolence, which was reminiscent of an employment-based 'welfarism', so that 'the firm behaves like an extended family analogous to the notion 'of "commonwealth"'. However, this 'nostalgic' element now appears to be emasculated. The systematic erosion of the permanent hiring norm, because of the fashionable move of modern business enterprises and workplaces towards the 'competitive' model of a 'flexi-organization', has now become more conspicuous. It appears that both globalized competition and emulation of human resource strategy popularized by Euro-American enterprises have worked to reshape the pattern of employment and personnel approach of the Hong Kong workplaces. As the study observes:

> Human relations at work hence became increasingly short-term and transit, centred upon the 'cash' nexus yet at the same time emphasizing performance and its measurement to help ensure a 'fair deal' at work. And yet, such a performance-based approach to building an effective, dedicated, and committed workforce also engenders its own limits and problems.

829. The study also uncovered the equivocal attitude of human resource specialists and practitioners to the workplace protocol on the disclosure of information to the employees on a collective and representative basis. As an enlightened sign of professionalism, such disclosure has always been propagated by scholars in the area of industrial relations and human resources as instrumental in briefing the staff on delicate personnel matters. However, in practice, the human resource managers in most large corporate workplaces elected to withhold information from the staff affected until the eleventh hour. The researchers lamented that 'even apparently liberal managements at enterprises with an established reputation for their enlightened approach toward staff relations were known to curfew and embargo news about who were to be laid off in downsizing exercises because of their neurosis and suspicion that any advanced notification would invite possible acts of sabotage'. What these managerial preferences betrayed was a low-trust workplace syndrome, inasmuch as the firm's human resource calculation and decisions clearly 'put the employing organization's interests above everything else'.

830. The subject enterprises were also found to be lukewarm and equivocal towards erecting any practice of 'bilateral collectivism' on a formal basis. The workplace culture of trade union recognition has remained as feeble as it was in the 1970s and 1980s:

> The practice of workplace labour relations has remained as pluralistic, diversified and even loose, as it was three or four decades ago, except where the growth of modern managerial practices (like human resource prescriptions) and the enlarged scale of business have led to the denser application of communicative devices. However, in an age of globalization and convergence of trade, business and employment standards, a distinctively 'Hong Kong' looseness and diversity can look backward when benchmarked against standards promulgated by the International Labour Organization (ILO) and other international governmental agencies like the WTO. It may hence be desirable for the administration to encourage better standardization of labour–management protocol at the workplace level, rather than leaving an evident 'institutional' gap of 'workplace "normlessness" detrimental to Hong Kong's image in the labour and employment area'.

§4. Joint Industrial Committees

831. It has been increasingly recognized that, therefore, both as an intrinsic right of the employees as well as an important key to securing their faith, trust and commitment to their jobs and organizations, they are entitled to at least a minimum amount of consultation and access to information as to be disclosed by corporate management and employers in modern enterprises. As noted earlier, a formula designed to answer such a need was advanced by Professor Turner and his associates in a longitudinal series of territory-wide labour studies which they conducted in the 1970s and 1980s. The idea was canvassed that the Hong Kong government should initiate, by legislative measures, a scheme of workplace joint industrial committees, to be made mandatory for enterprises above a specified size (say, having 100 employees or more).[76] The proposal envisaged the representation of employees in individual enterprises on in-house joint committees by way of workplace election which permitted, like the works councils in Germany and France, a limited degree of trade union participation. Such an enterprise-specific joint committee was to be vested with the prerogative of being consulted by its management regularly on matters relating to welfare, working conditions and employment. The proposed organ should also be competent to ratify pay scales, wage systems and fringe benefits, as well as to administer a set of grievance procedures where these measures had not been covered otherwise under a collective agreement. The governance of such a committee, including its constitution and electoral rules, should be subject to the Labour Department's supervision and auditing. It was a blueprint of salient insight to restructure workplace industrial relations in Hong Kong and would have implied were it adopted by the government, an innovative corrective to the vacuum

76. Turner *et al.*, *The Last Colony: But Whose? op. cit.*, pp. 163–165.

of territory-wide workplace permissiveness. However, in spite of the reiteration of such an idea again in the author's 'follow-up' study in the late 1980s and 1990s, the official reaction has remained lukewarm and apathetic up to the present.

§5. Labour Advisory Board

832. The Labour Advisory Board, created since the 1930s as a result of the 'model' recommendations dispatched by the British Colonial Office (which is now the British Foreign Office) to its overseas dependent territories, is a consultative public body whose primary role is to advise the government in the conception of labour legislation as well as the formulation of labour and related public policies. The Board is tripartite in its membership, headed by an *ex officio* chairperson who can either be the Commissioner for Labour or his/her deputy and is constituted of parity representation from both the employer and the employee sides – with a secretariat staffed by the Labour Department. At present, there are six members representing each of both sides of the Board, whose detailed composition is as follows:

> Of the six employee representatives, five are nominated from and elected by the registered employees unions in Hong Kong; the remaining one representative is appointed by the Government. On the other hand, the employers' representatives are drawn from the four major employer/business interest organizations in Hong Kong (namely, the Employers' Federation of Hong Kong, the General Chamber of Commerce, the Federation of Hong Kong Industries and the Chinese Manufacturers' Association) which are designated to nominate each a representative to sit on the Board; again the remaining two other employers' members are appointed by the Government.

833. Although it is just an advisory body, the Labour Advisory Board has been a strategic input to the gestational process of formulating labour legislation and related labour policy, especially given its composition of a tripartite representation. Successes in labour reform involving authorship of important legislation achieved in the 1970s and 1980s are attributed importantly to the high instrumentality of a regular employer–employee dialogue which leads to consensus building between the two adversarial sides on this public policy forum. However, there have been emerging signs of the Board's emasculation in its authority and capacity of influencing the government's labour and manpower policy – largely because of its eclipse by the 'politicization' of the democratized Legislative Council as the law-making elected assembly.

Chapter 6. Collective Bargaining

§1. Introduction

834. Collective bargaining may assume different forms. It has always been interpreted, in the context of Western industrialized societies, as embracing that type of activities, often institutionalized as a regular process, the output of which is the conclusion of collective agreements between the two parties, namely, the employers and the employees, or between their representative bodies. By providing for bilateral negotiation on an equal footing, collective bargaining also represents a stable arrangement for joint labour–management regulation on pay, conditions of employment and whatever other issues which may be the subject-matter of collective bargaining activities. In governance terms, collective bargaining also epitomizes an institution of industrial jurisprudence, inasmuch as it generates a body of rules, both procedural and substantive, for regulating the industrial behaviour of the employer and the employed at the workplace level, as well as industry-wide and nation-wide.

§2. Status of Collective Agreements in Hong Kong

835. The local industrial relations system in Hong Kong has inherited a salient British feature, inasmuch as any collective labour–management agreement that results from voluntary collective bargaining is not legally enforceable in any court of law. As in the British situation, any specific terms contained in a collective agreement can be enforced at law provided that they are incorporated, either expressly or by implication, into the individual labour contract between the employer and the employee.

§3. Bargaining Procedures

836. In Hong Kong, there are no statutory provisions on compulsory bargaining procedures involving the definition of the bargaining unit, the bargaining agent and the relevant procedural rules for their determination at the workplace level. The introduction of such measures on a mandatory basis has been deemed undesirable, inasmuch as they might impede the managerial prerogative of the employer, Moreover, its practice within an enterprise could throw into disarray the delicate balance of power within the labour movement by forging ahead a confrontation between the mutually antagonistic pro-China FTU and pro-democracy CTU groups of unions. In any case, the efficacy of such requirements on the employer's obligation to bargain is doubtful, given the organizational vacuum of sparse union membership and strength in the newer industries and services.

837. It is not possible to identify readily the existence of any specialized institutions or official agencies which are responsible for advising and assisting employers and employees alike on the orderly negotiation in Hong Kong about any procedural or substantive norms in activities of collective bargaining. However, the

Labour Department is known to have organized training courses on trade unionism and collective bargaining in earlier attempts, during the 1960s, to promote labour union organizations and their administration. Yet such activities have not been sustained in the subsequent decades – primarily because of the lukewarm or even apathetic responses from the unionists and the unorganized employees.

The Department continues to provide, via its Labour Relations Service, conciliatory service to the disputing parties and advice to enterprises and their employees on the improvement and strengthening of enterprise specific industrial relations. Earlier in 1976, the Department published an advisory document, entitled the 'Code of Labour Relations Practice', which set out a body of voluntary guidelines to workers and their management on the desirable ways and policies to adopt whereby workplace labour relations can be harmonized and improved. However, as it stands now, such a document is not oriented explicitly towards the promotion and encouragement of collective bargaining *per se*. Yet, it still epitomizes a classic document today for instructional advice on the conduct of good labour and employment practices.

§4. Trade Union Recognition and Collective Bargaining Rights

838. It has been a perennial focus of consistent lobbying by organized labour in Hong Kong in search for the legal vindication, by way of statutory enactment, of the unions' rights of collective bargaining. Such a 'collective bargaining' right is tantamount to the introduction of a legal duty obliging the employers to recognize trade unions for collective bargaining purposes. However, the widespread conservatism of employers in Hong Kong and their non-recognition of trade unionism have long been acknowledged as a persistent feature of local industrial relations culture, as it has been noted:

> And trade unions are often not accorded recognition status at the enterprise level. For instance, in the 1981 HKIPM survey, out of the 14 companies reporting the presence of a trade union at the plant, six firms stated that no union recognition was extended in spite of its presence. ... And the prospect for a more positive union-management relationship has remained remote, inasmuch as a later study in 1987 indicated that among the 34 companies in the inquiry which did not have trade unions, a mere four of them showed a willingness to recognize one and such recognition was subject to the condition that the trade unions concerned were able to represent the interest of the majority.[77]

839. Even today, the labour movement is still highly critical of many large corporate employers for their adamant attitudes in withholding voluntary union recognition. For example, the left-wing trade union centre, the Hong Kong Federation of Trade Unions, now in the mainstream of the labour movement, has complained that

77. Ng Sek-Hong, 'Workplace Industrial Relations in Hong Kong', in International Labour Organization (ed.), *The Development of Sound Labour Relations*, Bangkok: International Labour Organization, 1991, pp. 41–42.

in several major enterprises 'management had broken off negotiating relations with their unions after the strikes of 1967 – or even those of 1950/51'.[78]

840. The prospects for the SAR government now in office to introduce new legislation which can otherwise prescribe compulsory union recognition procedures analogous to the American system of workplace election (that is, to elect the most representative union as the sole bargaining agent in the officially demarcated bargaining unit) are likely to remain remote, for several reasons which have been articulated in the official explanation. First, such an enactment could be seen as unduly interventionist and alien to the 'voluntary' tradition of labour policy and logic of labour law assumptions in Hong Kong. Second is the alleged preference of both employers and the employed for retaining their individualized market flexibility and freedom from the 'collective bargaining' type of institutional constraints, given the comparative preponderance of small and medium-sized enterprises in the territory. Third is the official apprehension about the risk of politicizing and destabilizing harmonious industrial relations at the workplace in view of the present state of trade union multiplication in industries and occupations. An electoral system of mandatory bargaining procedures is still strongly suspected for its propensities of inducing the contending unions to take to excessive electoral bidding, competition or even strife in canvassing for 'balloting' support.

841. In summary, any institutional arrangement of joint industrial regulation by way of labour–management collective bargaining – in particular, the full-scale development of adversarial sectional bargaining and industrial negotiation of the Western style – is not likely to crystallize on a large scale in the near future. Its lukewarm status is historical and almost endemic in Hong Kong's society and economy, as Turner and his associates have summarized in their remarks as follows:

> The reliance which has already developed on administrative and legislative protection, the uncertain willingness and ability of the major union group to participate in formal collective bargaining, and the apparent general skepticism among employees of that process as viable route to improvement, seem in themselves to make the imported UK model of 'voluntaristic' sectional collective bargaining an inappropriate one for Hong Kong.[79]

842. Collective bargaining has in the past been inactive and is likely to remain docile now in the 2000s, as 'free competition in a free labour market' is still the

78. H.A. Turner *et al.*, *Between Two Societies: Hong Kong Labour in Transition*, Hong Kong: Centre of Asian Studies, University of Hong Kong, 1991, p. 82. Also See Ng Sek-Hong, 'Strike at Mass Transit Railway Corporation: Its Implications,' *Hong Kong Law Journal*, vol.15, no.1, 1985, pp. 84–85 for discussions of a classic illustration of such managerial conservatism in the public transport sector, where the management's resistance has provoked the train drivers union to organize twice in 1984 a strike against its corporate employer, the Mass Transit Railway Corporation, which was a public enterprise.
79. H.A. Turner *et al.*, *The Last Colony: but Whose?*, Cambridge: Cambridge University Press, 1980. p. 163.

prime lever for fixing employee pay and fringe benefit.[80] It appears that both the official and private employers' attitudes towards any formalized arrangements for the joint regulation of labour–management relations at the workplace have stayed in more or less the same mood as it was four decades ago, 'in spite of Hong Kong's recent industrial and social advancements, the professionalisation of its managerial resources (including those in the area of personnel and human resource management) and the apparent emergence and growth of enlightened managerialism'.[81]

843. Apparently, such a neurotic psychology against collective bargaining rights has persisted beyond 1997 into the SAR era. Anxious to maintain Hong Kong as a capitalist economic regime under the 'one country, two systems' political formula, the SAR administration espouses an antagonistic posture towards sponsoring collective bargaining as an industrial relations practice in the SAR. It acted swiftly, after assuming office in 1997, to repeal those newly gestated pre-handover provisions which introduced workplace collective bargaining and consultation on a mandatory basis in enterprises above a stipulated size, where endorsed by a balloting process conducted for the workforce. In justifying its censure against the law on collective bargaining rights, the SAR administration has openly castigated this piece of law as 'the uncritical and harmful emulation of Western industrial institutions which were costly as these might impede Hong Kong work and business practices'.[82]

844. Yet there are still sporadic cases of collective bargaining or negotiation in this territory. For example, the Cathay Pacific Airways, the flag carrier airline of Hong Kong, has been known for its established practices of collective bargaining with its in-house unions representing its pilots, flight attendants and ground service staff. The Hong Kong Aircraft Engineering Company has channels of regular consultation and pay negotiation with its technicians' union. The public bus companies have to negotiate with their rival enterprise unions in their annual pay adjustments. Industry-wide collective agreements have also existed in such craft trades as printing. In addition, quasi-types of collective bargaining are practiced within the civil service and the Hong Kong Railway Corporation (a public enterprise formed from the merger of the former Mass Transit Railway Corporation and the Hong Kong Kowloon Railway) within the domain of their joint staff consultation councils.[83]

---

80. David G. Lethbridge and Ng Sek-Hong, 'Labour and Employment', in Ng Sek Hong and David G. Lethbridge (eds.), *The Business Environment in Hong Kong*, Hong Kong: Oxford University Press, 3rd edn, 1995, note(29), p. 86.
81. Ng Sek-Hong, 'Workplace Relations in Hong Kong', *op. cit.*, p. 40.
82. Ng Sek-Hong, 'Hong Kong Labour Law in Retrospect', in Lee Pui-Tak (ed.), *Hong Kong Reintegrating With China: Political, Cultural and Social Dimensions*, Hong Kong: Hong Kong University Press, 2001, p. 149.
83. Ng Sek Hong and Carolyn Y. W. Poon, *Business Restructuring in Hong Kong: Strengths and Limits of Post-Industrial Capitalism*, Hong Kong: Oxford University Press, 2004, chapters 2 and 3.

§5. Minimum Wage

845. The system of minimum wage in its rudimentary form has always existed in Hong Kong. For example, a statutory mechanism for minimum wage fixation has been instituted here since 1940 under the auspices of the Trade Boards Ordinance. Yet it has never been invoked in its history.

I. History

846. Hong Kong has legislated upon minimum wages as early as 1932. The Minimum Wage Ordinance, no. 32, of 1932 hence gave the Governor-in-Council the ability to promulgate a minimum wage for any occupation or trade where the wages were considered to be unreasonably low. An inquiry could hence by called, to be conducted by a board of commissioners appointed by the Governor, to be constituted of five members of whom one should be a judge or magistrate who should also chair the board. However, the 1932 legislation had been described as nothing more than 'merely a legislative gesture' because of the terms and scope of the ordinance itself. A notable defect observed was the lack of any provision for an inspectorate 'with the right to require employers to supply information regarding the wages paid to employees, to see that any minimum is (was) adhered to'.[84]

847. Given the problematic nature of the Minimum Wage Ordinance, the then Labour Officer (whose office was tantamount to that of the Commissioner for Labour today), Butters, recommended its abrogation in his report of 1939. The repeal took place subsequently. Yet, during its lifetime no board of inquiry had ever been appointed and no minimum wage fixed. In place of the Minimum Wage Ordinance, Butters advocated that the trade boards be set up or a sectoral basis according to needs as they arose. Such an organ was to be composed of representatives in equal number of workers and employers from the trade concerned, plus a labour leader from a better organized trade and a representative of the employers – sitting in session under the chairmanship of the Labour Officer. Its competence was prescribed as follows:

> The trade boards should have the power and duty of fixing minimum wage, determining normal working hours … and fixed overtime rates in trades where the wage standards are (were) low and where organization of employers and workers is (was) ineffectual.[85]

848. The Butters proposal was largely adopted in the 1940 legislation, named as the Trade Boards Ordinance which has since remained, however, relatively inactive in the statute book. This piece of legislation emulates the British system of wage council and like its predecessor, has never been activated to initiate an inquiry into

84. H. R. Butters, *Report by the Labour Officer (W. H. R. Butters) on Labour and Labour Conditions in Hong Kong*, Hong Kong: Government Printer, 1939, para. 233.
85. *Ibid.*, para. 235.

low pay in any trade or industry. The official explanation advanced is that there has been so far no emergent economic or social need, nor has there been any representation from the public which seeks the setting up of such trade boards.

849. In any case, the 1940 legislation has made available in the statute book a mechanism for fixing minimum wages by means of a trade (sectoral) board on which both employers and workers are represented. This law, as well as the 1932 Minimum Wage Ordinance, have enabled Hong Kong to apply International Labour Convention no. 26 on minimum wage fixation machinery. The Convention lays down the provisions to create and maintain a machinery whereby the minimum rates of wages can be fixed for workers in certain trades or parts of trades where no existing arrangements exist for the effective negotiation and determination of wages or otherwise, where wages are deemed to be too low.

II. The Debate

850. It has always been a perennial issue of public debate as to whether it is desirable or not for the government to introduce a territory-wide minimum wage standard. Ten years after the SAR administration assumed office, the debate escalated into a policy controversy polarizing capital and organized labour.

Proponents of official wage regulation on the issue were sceptical of the low pay and 'sweatshop' labouring conditions reported to have persisted in some of the marginal trades, especially among the older and migrant workers. Minimum wages were hence canvassed as a lever to ameliorate such a workplace malaise. It was argued, moreover, that a statutory wage floor would help to guarantee a basic living standard of average decency to the working people. Nevertheless, while such an argument entailed an admirable element of crusade on behalf of the less privileged, there was also articulated by the employers strong reservations on the merit and practicability of introducing a minimum wage on a territory-wide basis.

851. A common rejoinder advanced earlier against minimum wage legislation cited the sustained trend of improving real wages due to the booming economy which lasted until the eve of the 1997 East Asian financial upheavals, so that the need for a minimum wage did not exist materialistically. Another argument cited the administrative complexities that might accompany its enforcement. There were other, perhaps stronger arguments. For instance, a minimum wage could induce employers to restrict employment below their capacity, thereby indirectly creating more unemployment especially for the marginal workers whom it was designed to protect. A minimum wage level had also been suspected to be perverting because such a standard, once promulgated by the government, might be used by employers as the 'official rate' and cited to counteract any workers' demands for wage increases. Even trade unionists have articulated a fear that any declaration of a statutory general wage 'floor' would serve, inadvertently, to draw a ceiling on wage levels since employers were not likely to concede anything voluntarily above the statutory minima. Adding to this industrial concern was the prospect of its negative implication in having emasculated further the practice of private collective bargaining, inasmuch as it might create an even more passive labour force which could become dependent upon the government not only for labour standards but also for guidelines in wage norms as well.

III. Shifting Terrain

852. However, the steadfast stance of the administration against its active intervention into the wage market in Hong Kong has been modified, now that the government, both before and 1997, has intervened administratively in the wage standards of foreign domestic helpers by requiring their contracts to provide for wages not less than the level stipulated by the government and administered by the Labour Department. Such a measure, later extended to include the employer's obligation to pay all imported labour of a semi-skilled or unskilled nature a standard wage equivalent to the median wage level in the trade, industry or occupation where these workers are engaged, is hence tantamount to a form of minimum wage regulation – yet by administrative control rather than statutory enactment and limited solely to the imported sector of guest workers from outside Hong Kong.

853. Indeed, the official prescription of the standard (minimum) wage for foreign domestic helpers is almost a classic illustration of an 'occupational minimum wage', reminiscent of the intent of the Trade Boards Ordinance but falling short of its institutional auspices. Aimed at safeguarding a socially decent level of earnings for these guest workers, it has also been placed under periodic review for adjustment intended to offset the effects of inflation. However, unlike the cumbersome tasks of administering and servicing the national minimum wage levels in societies like Japan, South Korea and Taiwan, this administrative process in Hong Kong of adjusting wage standards for the foreign domestic helpers is linked essentially with the factor of inflation and does not make any explicit reference to considerations about productivity improvements and economic growth. In such a sense, the 'servicing simplicity' in Hong Kong has rendered such an exercise less vulnerable to public controversy.

IV. The Legislative Impasse

854. In the wake of the post-1997 recession waves, the Hong Kong SAR faced a creeping phenomenon of growth in 'atypical employment', including non-regular hiring under part-time, temporary and short-term employment contracts, which contributed to a low-wage 'trap'. A 1999 study on the Hong Kong labour market and minimum wage legislation, conducted by the Workplace Study Group of the Chinese Management Centre of the University of Hong Kong, for example, identified a corroborative and consistent pattern of association between part-time work and low pay. Literally, the labour market syndrome of low wages and atypical employment helped perpetuate not only the vicissitudes of urban poverty caused by post-industrial capitalism in the Hong Kong SAR but also sustained the pathos of labour and employment in the workplace in several respects. First, the popularization of flexible employment prompted the low paying industries, especially the service ones like the fast-food, catering and retailing, to casualize or recasualize part of their workforce to save on labour costs and associated overheads. Apparently, the part-time work hour norm appealed to employers in concealing low wages as pay became fractionalized and denominated on an hourly basis. Many corporate employers, when streamlining their organization, might hive off their non-core functions to external vendors. Examples were cleansing and security guarding. It was always the case that these subcontractors employed workers at low wages, probably with the exception of the public sector.

The fringe nature of these part-time workers as a peripheral segment of the general labour force was corroborated by their socio-demographic profile as portrayed by the 1999 General Household Survey which the Census and Statistics Department conducted on part-time working. These part-time employees were likely to be female and married persons in the middle-age bracket. A sizable proportion of them were also housewives. The largest employer of such a marginal labouring group was the hybrid service sector of 'wholesale, retail, and import/export trades, restaurants and hotels'. Low skills or lack of skill was a common problem among these workers, of whom one-third were located in occupations graded as elementary in skill status.

855. The emergence and accentuation of the low wage-cum-urban poverty phenomenon subsequently rekindled a public debate on the minimum wage legislation motion, again clouded with heated controversy. However, the administration was still lukewarm about the idea of such an enactment and equivocal in responding to organized labour's concerted demand for a general minimum wage law which would cover the entire workforce. Invoking the celebrated principle of 'voluntarism' as the dictum of designing labour policy, the SAR government continued to lay aside any decision of legislating on a minimum wage level and standard work hours in the territory. Instead, it devolved a power of self-regulation to both sides of industry within the low pay sector and left the issue to the lever of private initiatives. In his annual policy address for 2006–7, the Chief Executive hence declared that the government would launch a 'Wage Protection Movement' for employees in the two industries notorious for low wages – the cleaning and guarding services sector. Corporations and contractors were actively encouraged to join the Movement 'to ensure that employees in these two sectors will receive wages not lower than the average market rates of the relevant industries and occupations' as published in the Quarterly Report of Wage and Payroll Statistics of the Census and Statistics Department.

856. Concurrently, the government declared a pledge that it would set out to prepare for the introduction of legislation for a minimum wage in the cleaning and guarding services sector pending upon a review two years after implementing the movement. Yet such an exercise was viewed by sceptics as a transit, 'stop-gap' and 'half-way house' measure intended to evade and even pre-empt a legislative approach to protect employees trapped in the low-pay syndrome.

857. However, the voluntary appeal to employers in these two industries was not well received. Their response and participation in this Movement proved to be dismal. Upon review, the government in 2008 decided to move ahead with the legislative process on an enactment of an economy-wide minimum wage level. Such a move was intended to benchmark Hong Kong with other industrially advanced countries most of which have promulgated a statutory minimum wage for the working populations. Moreover, there was a political need to answer the increasingly vociferous demands from organized labour for minimum wage protection, especially since pockets of low pay among fast food stores, retail shops and cleaning janitors were exposed more widely in the social media. At the same time, the major employers and industrial associations conceded and waived their hitherto steadfast adherence to the 'free wage market' principle. Such an overture was apparently to testify to their managerial enlightenment as well as viewed as a 'trade-off' with the labour movement for blocking any prospective enactments on standard work hours and collective bargaining rights.[86]

858. In this context, a Minimum Wage Ordinance was brought to the statute book in 2010 and came into force a year after. Its scope of application does not include student interns, work experience students and foreign domestic helpers. A Minimum Wage Commission was appointed for fixing and recommending to the government the minimum wage level, subject to review every two years. The inaugural wage level was HK$28 an hour. This was raised to HK$30 an hour two years later in 2013. At present, the Commission is conducting a review exercise and it is likely for it to be adjusted upwards to HK$32 or $33 an hour next year in 2015. However, such an anticipated extent of minimum wage hike falls short of organized labour's expectations. For example, the Confederation of Trade Unions (CTU) continued to lobby for a higher level of wage adjustment.

859. The implementation of the minimum wage law has not precipitated any significant fall in employment. In general, employers are able to shoulder the burden where they need to adjust their pay in order to conform to the statutory minimum wage level and complaints on defaults have been few. The human resource function of wage computation is compounded by the complexity of pay calculation which has to be denominated in terms of minimum wage level. Low paid workers like cleaning janitors, retail shop assistants and security guards are able to benefit from this piece of enactment. According to the wage survey statistics published by the Census and Statistics Department of the government, the median monthly income for employees ascended from HK$ 11,800 in the second quarter of 2010 to HK$12,800 by mid-2011, largely as a sequel to the statutory minimum wage level. This represents an increase of 8.5 per cent (see 2011 *Report on Annual Earnings and Hours Survey,* Hong Kong Census and Statistics Department, March, 2012).[87]

86. Olivia K.M. Ip and Sek-hong Ng, 'Labour and Employment in the Tsang Administation, in Joseph Y. S. Cheng (ed.), *The Second Chief Executive of Hong Kong SAR: Evaluating the Tsang Years, 2005-2012,* pp. 424-25.
87. *Ibid.*, p. 425.

V. Collective Bargaining and Its Prospects

860. It has been a commonplace phenomenon of the workplace among establishments and enterprises in Hong Kong that collective bargaining has always been marginal and trivialized. In spite of the relative docility of this type of collectivized industrial activity, the debate on the suitability of collective bargaining for this city economy has always been audible. Trade unions are always keen and have lobbied the government, both before and after the 1997 political reversion, for official sponsorship to confer upon them what has been labelled as 'collective bargaining rights'. The notion emulates basically the American system of prescribing at law a set of electoral arrangements and procedures, so that the union elected successfully will be certified as the competent bargaining agent for the employees represented at the works (known as the 'bargaining unit'). In other words, the law will assist the employees associations (unions) by obliging an employer at law to recognize a union which was able to demonstrate its popular representative basis with the ballot box, for purposes of collective bargaining.

861. Literally, Hong Kong labour unions succeeded in soliciting from the colonial government its consent to introduce to the statute book, on the eve of Hong Kong's reversiom back to China in1997, an elaborate piece of legislation which provided for collective bargaining rights to apply to enterprises above a stipulated size. This new law would have altered drastically the nature of workplace labour relations in Hong Kong and stimulated the workplace organization of labour unions yet eroded the hallmark norm of a free wage and labour market in Hong Kong. However, this new law (of collective bargaining rights) was heavily attacked and bitterly resisted by the employers and their associations. Even the new SAR government was sceptical and disconcerted by this piece of legislation and viewed it as detrimental to the economy. Such negative sentiments led to a subsequent review by the Labour Advisory Board which recommended its repeal to the Provisional Legislative Council. As a sequel, this law was abrogated by the Council at the end of the year 1997.

862. Employers have been sternly opposed to any official acts of intervention which could have sponsored the practice of collective bargaining with compulsory procedures of union recognition. Moreover, the official administration has always been lukewarm about such a proposition for a threefold reason as follows.

First, such an enactment can be seen as unduly interventionist and alien to the 'voluntary' tradition of labour policy and logic of labour law assumptions in Hong Kong. Second is the alleged preference of both the employers and the employed for retaining their individualized market flexibility and freedom from the 'collective bargaining' type of institutional constraints, given the preponderance of small and medium-sized enterprises in the territory. Third is the official apprehension about the risk of politicizing and destabilizing harmonious industrial relations at the workplace in view of the present state of trade union multiplication in industries and occupations. The institutionalization of collective bargaining and union recognition procedures would have led to excessive electoral bidding or even strife among competiting unions in canvassing for 'balloting' support.[88]

VI. Legal Status of the Collective Agreement and Quasi-collective Bargaining in the Public Sector

863. Collective bargaining as a labour–management negotiation activity normally yields a collective agreement. It is enforceable at the National Labour Relations Board in the United States and elsewhere at court in many European nations. However, it is not enforceable legally within the British system and is observed and upheld simply in the tradition of a 'voluntarist' (non-coercive) spirit as a 'gentleman's agreement'. The exact legal understanding of such a practice is that 'any specific terms contained in a collective agreement can be enforced at law provided that they are incorporated, either expressly or by implication, into the individual labour contract between the employer and the employee'.[89] Within the civil service, public sector employees are covered by a quasi-process of collective bargaining between the government as the employer and the staff unions, on forums of bilateral dialogue provided by the staff councils, which are basically formal joint consultative bodies emulating the British model of the Whitley Council. These staff councils are standing bodies with ad hoc ability to negotiate annual pay adjustment levels. Such negotiation activities are based typically upon the data yielded from the annual pay trend surveys which the Pay Investigation Unit of the Civil Service Bureau conducted at yearly intervals. There are now altogether five staff councils established at the central level for service-wide consultation on staff relations and pay adjustment negotiation, each to cater to a family of civil service pay grades and classes. They are (i) the Senior Civil Service Council; (ii) the Model Scale I Staff Council; (iii) the Disciplinary Force Staff Council; iv) the Police Council; and (v) the Judiciary Staff Council. The directorate grade staff is, however not represented on these councils because of their managerial capacity and status.[90]

864. Besides, some public enterprises and private corporations are known to have instituted joint consultative committees and made use of these channels for informal exchange and even negotiation with staff representatives on the extent of annual pay adjustments. Such an exercise normally takes into consideration the factors of the inflation rate, the going market pay trend and the productivity and profit gains of the enterprise. Examples are the Hong Kong Railway Corporation and the Link, which was incorporated from the former Housing Department of the government. Another case is the collective agreement which was concluded between Cathay Pacfic Airways Limited and one of its house unions, Cathay Pacific Airways Flight Attendants Union, probably first in 1984 and now subject to annual review. The coverage of the agreement is comprehensive, stipulating, *inter alia*, the salary scales and a variety of fringe benefits like housing, line duty allowances, out-port

88. Ng Sek Hong, *Hong Kong*, pp. 244–5.
89. *Ibid.*, p. 239.
90. *Ibid.*, p. 243.

allowance, retirement benefits, staff travel concessions as well as the rules governing promotion.

865. Collective agreements of an informal nature were formerly known to have existed in such traditional craft trades as furniture making, printing and ivory carving. However, they were archaic and no longer existed as these industries which had either withered away or were re-located to the Mainland. However, multi-union bargaining with management is conducted almost annually at public utility companies like franchised public bus, gas and electricity power supply enterprises.

Chapter 7. Industrial Conflict

§1. Introduction

I. Definition of Industrial Conflict

866. Industrial conflict can be defined as the behaviour and attitudes that express opposition and divergent orientations between industrial owners and managers on the one hand, and working people and their organization on the other.[91] Industrial conflict can assume an overt form, such as in open disputes and stoppages, or it can occur in a covert fashion, as in the form of high labour turnover and absenteeism, or even in industrial accidents and injuries.

867. The offensive in industrial strife can be initiated either by the employees against the employer as in the case of a strike or vice versa, by the employer against his/her employees, as in the instance of a lock-out. The classic industrial weapon available to the workers and their unions in confronting their employers in modern industrial societies today is hence the strike, which has been defined as a concerted 'refusal by employees to continue working, the object usually being to secure an improvement, or to resist a worsening, in the terms and conditions of work of the workers concerned, or to achieve similar results for other workers'.[92] However, other forms of industrial strife involving actions such as go-slow, work-to-rule, (plant) occupation and demonstrations are also known in Hong Kong's labour history in addition to 'strike'. These can be spontaneous shop-floor actions, if not organized by a labour union.

II. Trade Disputes versus Individual Claims

868. In Hong Kong, an official distinction is made between two principal categories of labour–management dispute, namely, 'claims' and 'trade disputes'. 'Claims', otherwise also known as 'grievance disputes' as it was in the past, arise from differences or over the interpretation or defaults (or failures) in the application of an existing provision stipulated under either the private contract of employment (contractual) or the Employment Ordinance (statutory).[93] As such, these claims are actionable in the Labour Tribunal. In essence, 'claims' can be said to correspond generally to the notion of 'disputes over rights' which involve the interpretation of industrial norms already established. It has been the general practice to process 'claims' on an 'individual' basis, rather than collectively, especially where they are settled by way of judicial determination in the Labour Tribunal.

---

91. Arthur Kornhauser, Robert Dubin and Arthur M. Ross (eds.), *Industrial Conflict*, McGraw Hill, 1954, p. 13.
92. Arthur I. Marsh and E.O. Evans, *The Dictionary of Industrial Relations*, London: Hutchison, 1973, p. 297.
93. The legal definition of a 'claim' is given in the Labour Tribunal Ordinance, Laws of Hong Kong.

869. By contrast, trade disputes are collective in nature, pertaining to the parties' differences associated with the employment or non-employment or the terms of employment, or with the conditions of or affecting employment of any person.[94] Such an ambit as given in the official definition is hence consistent with the notions both of 'right disputes' as well as 'interest disputes'. Cases in the latter category, namely those of interest, have as their object the establishment or the alteration of collective norms about wages and other conditions of employment, as they may affect both the mutual relationship as well as interest of the parties.

III. Local Statistics

870. In Hong Kong, statistical information on strikes is denominated by the number and intensity of work stoppages waged by employees in trade disputes, as measured by the indicators of (i) number of these stoppages, (ii) number of workers involved in these stoppages and (iii) number of working days lost through these stoppages. Following basically the British system of compiling 'strike' statistics, the official record on work stoppages here in Hong Kong collates only those of an industrial nature which arise from trade disputes due to the employment and non-employment, as well as terms of such employment. However, due to technical reasons, small strikes involving not more than ten workers in scale or less than one day in duration are not recorded, unless the aggregate number of working days lost exceeds a hundred. Besides, political strikes are not included in these statistics. This will be further discussed in the next section.

§2. Legal Regulation of Industrial Conflict

I. Legal Definition of 'Strikes' and 'Lock-outs'

871. In Hong Kong, a 'strike' is given its legal definition by both the Trade Unions Ordinance and the Labour Relations Ordinance. A strike is hence defined by these laws as:

> the cessation of work by a body of persons employed acting in combination, or a concerted refusal, or a refusal under a common understanding, of any number of persons employed, to continue to work for an employer in consequence of a trade dispute, done as a means of compelling their employer or the employer of any other person or body of persons, or any person or body of persons employed, to accept or not to accept terms or conditions of or affecting employment.[95]

94. The legal definition of a 'trade dispute' is provided by both the Labour Relations Ordinance and the Trade Unions Ordinance
95. The legal text of this definition is adapted mainly from the corresponding UK legislation which includes, namely, the Conditions of Employment and National Arbitration Order (SR 60, 1940, No. 1305) and the Contracts of Employment Act 1963.

872. As noted in the preceding section, such a definition has limited the official cognizance of strikes to those due to economic (and not political) causation. In other words, only those stoppages which are attributed to trade disputes and associated with economic objectives and involving issues of employment are reckoned as 'strikes'.

873. Symmetrically, the legal definition of a 'lock-out' is also indicative of such an economic perspective in the official interpretation of work suspension initiated by the employer:

> the closing of place of employment, or the suspension of work, or the refusal by an employer to continue to employ any number of persons employed by him in consequence of a trade dispute, done with a view to compelling those persons, or to aiding another employer in compelling persons employed by him, to accept terms or conditions affecting employment.

874. These official definitions as adopted in Hong Kong have hence in general excluded from their purview political strikes such as those in support of certain political or ideological causes or aimed against the policy of the domestic administration or of foreign governments. In effect, the now defunct Illegal Strikes and Lock-outs Ordinance and the Trade Disputes Ordinance used to prescribe expressly that the notion of an illegal strike or lock-out, now rescinded, would have covered certain types of political strike as that laden with:

> any object other than or in addition to the furtherance of a trade dispute within the trade or industry in which employers or employees are engaged and is a strike or lockout designed or calculated to coerce the Government either directly or by inflicting hardship upon the community or any substantial portion of the community.

875. However, the legal notion of an illegal strike or lock-out has been dissolved as a result of the repeal and replacement of the Illegal Strikes and Lock-outs Ordinance and the Trade Disputes Ordinance by the Labour Relations Ordinance enacted in 1975. Anyway, it has been commonly interpreted that sympathetic strikes are not inconsistent with the legal definitions of 'strike' and 'trade dispute' in current application – which may embrace, theoretically, therefore a 'secondary' trade dispute involving an employer and employees employed elsewhere. In these instances, employees may strike in sympathy against their own employer in support of their fellow workers employed elsewhere so as to bring pressure upon the latters' employer in order to coerce him into concessions to be made to their demands.[96]

876. The law, strictly speaking, does not address explicitly other forms of industrial actions such as unofficial strikes and unconstitutional strikes (that is, wildcat strikes), 'work-to-rule', 'go-slow', 'sit-in' and 'occupation'. The legal status of such

96. See Labour Department, Hong Kong Government, *Strikes, Strikers and the Law*, Hong Kong: Labour Department, 1976, p. 7.

activities is not unequivocally clear. Presumably, the legality of such actions needs to be submitted to the judicial test of court rulings. However, the Labour Relations Ordinance, in its provisions on the 'cooling off' period, makes reference to the so-called 'irregular industrial actions short of a strike'. This notion covers any concerted actions, other than a strike, by the employees which is intended to prevent or interfere with the production of goods or services. As such, it may be deemed as a breach of contractual duty under common law.

II. Laws of Industrial Conflict

877. As inherited from the British tradition, the law in Hong Kong does not confer any substantial positive rights upon the employees involved in a strike or other forms of industrial action. However, the Basic Law and the Bill of Rights Ordinance both have a rhetorical reference to the right of strike in Hong Kong. Moreover, the strikers, if acting in connection with the contemplation or furtherance of a trade dispute, are protected under the law with a certain degree of immunity or freedom from civil and criminal liabilities at law.

878. Following the model of British trade union laws, the Trade Unions Ordinance in Hong Kong has granted similar immunity to trade unions and the strikers whom they organize from the possible onus of criminal and civil liabilities for conspiracy at common law. Removing the risk of criminal stigma otherwise implied for conspiracy, the Ordinance declares that 'an agreement or combination of two or more persons to do or procure to be done any act in contemplation of furtherance of a trade dispute shall not be triable as a conspiracy if such act committed by one person would not be punishable as a crime'.[97] Secondly, to nullify the possibility of tortious action for the civil wrong of conspiracy, the same statute lays down the rule that 'an act done in pursuance of an agreement or combination by two or more persons shall, if done in contemplation or furtherance of a trade dispute, not be actionable unless the act, if done without any such agreement or combination, would be actionable'.[98] What is hence implied is that such legislative exemptions available to the strikers may not apply where the agreement, albeit in contemplation or furtherance of a trade dispute, is to commit an act of malicious damage or is a conspiracy which is punishable by any enactment in Hong Kong. Similarly, they are not absolved from the legal obligations, as citizens in Hong Kong, to observe any legal norms in the Public Order Ordinance governing demonstrations, public processing, riots, unlawful assemblies, and breach of peace, or sedition or any offence against the State or the sovereign. Nevertheless, the Public Order Ordinance has itself been liberalized substantially in harmonization with the Bill of Rights Ordinance.

879. Generally speaking, in Hong Kong's legal context, the pursuance of a strike, picketing and other industrial actions in respect of a trade dispute is hence subject to the legal prescriptions of the following statutes:

97. Trade Unions Ordinance, *Laws of Hong Kong*, Section 48(1).
98. *Ibid.*, Section 48(2).

(i) the Trade Unions Ordinance;
(ii) the Public Order Ordinance;
(iii) the Labour Relations Ordinance.

III. Trade Unions Ordinance

880. The Ordinance prescribes the legally permissible scope of peaceful picketing, by stating it as 'lawful' for one of more persons, acting on their own behalf or on behalf of a registered trade union or an individual employer or firm, in contemplation or furtherance of a trade dispute, to attend at or near a place where a person works or carries on business, if they so attend merely for the purpose of peacefully persuading any person to work or abstain from working and communicating with the latter.[99]

881. Such a right to picket is, however, qualified by the legal prohibition against the pickets to so attend in such numbers, or otherwise in such manner, as to be calculated to intimidate any person in that place, or to obstruct his/her approach thereto or egress therefrom, or to lead to a breach of the peace.[100]

882. Such an act is punishable as a criminal offence. As illustrated by the Labour Department in its explanatory pamphlet, it may constitute a breach of the 'picketing' provisions if the pickets violently and continually bang on doors, if they shout out, if they obstruct the highway by lying down in front of vehicles, if they make a show of violence, if they obstruct people in the road by standing in their way or catching their arms and compelling them to listen, etc. The statutory limit on the maximum number of pickets is, however, not specified. If more are employed than are reasonably required, the court may infer and hold that the intention is not bona fide and hence censure it.[101]

883. Presumably, the regulation about 'reasonable numbers' has to be read in conjunction with the parallel provisions as given in the Public Order Ordinance.

884. The Trade Unions Ordinance, in addition, outlaws the use of intimidation and annoyance as an acceptable means while picketing in pursuance of a trade dispute. It hence constitutes a summary offence under the Trade Unions Ordinance if anyone who, in order to compel any person to abstain from doing or to do any act that the latter has a legal right to do or abstain from doing, uses violence wrongfully and without legal authority against or intimidates such a (other) person or his wife

99. *Ibid.*, Section 46.
100. *Ibid.*
101. *See* Labour Department, *Strikes, Strikers and the Law*, *op. cit.*, pp. 4–5.

or children;[102] or injures his property;[103] or persistently follows the latter from place to place. The same legal sanction applies if the picket hides any tools, clothes or other property owned or used by the latter; or deprives him of the same or hinders him in the use thereof; or watches or besets the house or other place where the latter resides or works or carries on business or which happens to be on the approach to such house or place; or follows the latter in a disorderly manner in or through any street or road.[104]

885. Earlier reference has been made already to the legal immunities granted by the Trade Unions Ordinance to registered trade unions from civil liabilities for any act, which is otherwise actionable under common law, done in contemplation or furtherance of a trade dispute to which a members(s) of the trade union is a party. Such immunities are specified under Section 42 of the Ordinance, as they pertain to the torts of inducing some other person(s) to break a contract of employment or of interference with the trade, business or employment of some other person or with the right of some other person to dispose of his labour or capital as he wishes. In fact, a comprehensive buffer is provided by Section 43(1) of the same ordinance, which prohibits any court action in tort against a registered trade union for any tortuous act committed in contemplation of furthering a trade dispute. However, whether the individual as an employee, or a union official or member is entitled in his personal capacity to such protection is not specified expressly in the law. Conceivably, the interpretation has to be left to the court for a ruling but up to the present there has not been any industrial conflict which warrants judicial intervention of such a nature.

IV. Public Order Ordinance

886. The ability to strike and picket in Hong Kong is also qualified by the Public Order Ordinance which regulates generally any possible breach of peace in the community. Before the Ordinance was liberalized in 1980, any strikers or pickets wishing to hold a public meeting or procession in the course of industrial actions needed to apply, like all other persons, for a licence from the Commissioner of Police, to be issued not later than seven days in advance.[105] Otherwise, it would have been held to constitute an unlawful assembly and its organizers and participants would have been liable to prosecution and penal sanctions. Under the 1980 amendments to the Public Order Ordinance, the licensing system is now replaced

102. 'Intimidation' is defined under the Trade Unions Ordinance to mean 'causing' in the mind of a person a reasonable apprehension of injury to himself or to any member of his family or to any of his dependants – including apprehension of violence or damage to the person or property.
103. 'Injury' is defined under the Trade Unions Ordinance to include any injury to a person in respect of his business, occupation, employment or other source of income, and include any actionable civil wrongs.
104. Trade Unions Ordinance, Laws of Hong Kong, Section 47.
105. A meeting is defined under the Public Order Ordinance to include any gathering or assembly of people convened or organized for any purpose or, if originally disorganized, over which someone assumes, or attempts to assume leadership or control.

by a simplified notification procedure. A public meeting is now also accorded a more restrictive definition, so that its coverage is limited to those convened to discuss issues or matters of interest or of concern to the general public, but leaving outside its purview those which are held purely for social, educational or religious purposes. The notice of intention to hold such a public meeting has to be served at least seven working days in advance. The presumption now introduced is that the meeting under notice is able to take place unless proscribed specifically by the police. Prohibition as such is justifiable only where:

(i) the notice conflicts with the legal requirements; or
(ii) the publication of advertisements of the meeting is unlawful;
(iii) the meeting, when held, is considered likely to prejudice the maintenance of public order or be exploited for unlawful aims; or
(iv) the organizer of the meeting has been convicted previously of an offence under the Public Order Ordinance[106]

887. When a public meeting, procession or gathering fails to comply with the notification requirements, the offence is now called 'unauthorized assembly', and no longer labelled as 'unlawful assembly'.

V. Labour Relations Ordinance

888. The Labour Relations Ordinance was enacted in 1975. Its Part I, when brought into effect, will empower the Chief Executive in Council, where warranted, to declare a 'cooling-off' period in respect of a trade dispute. Such a 'cooling off' period order will oblige the parties to the dispute, and any third party specified in the order, to discontinue or defer any industrial action – that is, to resume temporarily the status quo and for work to be restored to normal. Otherwise, any defiant party could be held guilty of contempt of the order (deemed equivalent to that of committing contempt of the High Court). The initial period of the 'cooling-off' order is not to exceed 30 days but the Chief Executive in Council is able to extend its duration for another 30 days, provided that the total period does not exceed 60 days.

889. Such an executive power to declare a 'cooling-off' period cannot be applied indiscriminately, lest it would have become an excessive and undesirable coercive weapon for the administration to curb an ordinary strike or industrial action in process. Indeed, specified conditions need to be satisfied for such a power to be exercised, namely, that:

106. These limiting conditions enabling the police to disallow a public processing and/or meeting are liberalized further by a 1995 amendment to the Public Order Ordinance in order to harmonize better with the Bill of Rights Ordinance. By virtue of this amended provision, the Commissioner of Police can only censure a public processing where it conflicts with the public interest (such as where public safety is envisaged at peril, due to overcrowding, incited passion and emotions, and stampeding). However, the SAR government, after assuming office in 1997, later abrogated these legislative amendments held to be too hasty and liberal, for alleged reasons of suggesting a propensity towards 'syndicalism' which may rupture social stability.

(a) It is an industrial action in contemplation or furtherance of a trade dispute, consisting of (i) a strike; (ii) any irregular industrial action short of a strike; or (iii) a lockout which has begun or is likely to begin;
(b) The situation arising out of the trade dispute is of such a nature, or on such a scale, as to be likely to cause an interruption in the supply of goods or in the provision of service which might:
   (i) be gravely injurious to the economy of Hong Kong or seriously affect the livelihood of a substantial number of persons, or create a serious risk of public disorder, or seriously jeopardize the internal security of Hong Kong;
   (ii) endanger the lives of a substantial number of persons to serious risk of disease or personal injury; and
(c) Having regard to all the circumstances of the trade dispute, it would be conducive to settlement of it by negotiation, conciliation, arbitration or the appointment of a board of inquiry if the industrial actions were discontinued or deferred.[107]

§3. Strikes and Security in the Individual Contract of Employment

I. The 'Suspension' Theory

890. It has been acknowledged widely that a strike is, by its nature, a temporary cessation of work. The argument is that the striker has no intention of relinquishing his employment by going on strike. Instead, the normative assumption is that the strikers wish to return to their jobs at the end of their actions.

891. The logic justifying such a thesis, which is popular among European countries, is that the strike is the workers' weapon in industry consisting of the temporary withdrawal of labour in order to apply sanction or pressure *vis-à-vis* the employer. The argument follows that strikes involving no criminal intent would only suspend the individual labour contract, and non-performance of duty in this respect would not be sufficiently serious to justify the breaking of the individual labour contract, even if it were not covered by advance notice or compensation in lieu.

II. The Hong Kong Situation

892. According to the above suspension theory, a strike even where not covered by notice is not to be deemed as a breach of contract or as a default for the purpose of proceedings in tort against the striker(s). It is common, outside the Anglo-American legal system, as in continental Europe and Japan, for a nation's constitution to recognize that 'a strike only "suspends" an employee's obligation pursuant

107. Labour Relations Ordinance, *Laws of Hong Kong*, Section 35.

to his labour contract to work during the period of strike. It does not repudiate it altogether.'[108]

893. Locally, however, such a 'suspension' theory has not been recognized at law or at least, its status is dubious in Hong Kong. Often upheld here, instead, is the traditional and orthodox opinion that at common law and in the absence of the relevant provision in the contract, express or implied, a strike is a breach of contractual duty unless it is preceded by appropriate notice. The interpretation is hence tenable that where a group of employees stop work and fail to give notice thereof, their work stoppage might be construed to constitute a contractual breach of their employment duties.[109]

894. What the above implies seems to be a general position in Hong Kong, following the repeal of the Illegal Strikes and Lockouts Ordinance in 1975, that the notion of an 'illegal strike' has disappeared: 'in as much as strikers have been freed of illegal connotations, workers in Hong Kong are no longer subject to any legal disabilities if they strike'.[110] However, there remains problematic in Hong Kong the ambiguity of the status of a strike at common law, so that such a freedom to strike is not tantamount to 'a positive and unequivocal "right to strike" as enjoyed by workers in Continental Europe and Japan whereby strikers are afforded job protection by the constitution and law'.[111]

895. The above common law ambiguity notwithstanding, the Basic Law bestowed upon the worker a constitutional right to strike after Hong Kong became an SAR of the PRC in the post-1997 era and the Employment Ordinance has been recently amended to give statutory effect to such a right, by making explicit that a strike canmot be held at law as a breach of the labour contract.

§4. Present State of Industrial Conflict

I. Introduction

896. Industrial relations in Hong Kong on the whole have remained stable during recent years. The bulk of industrial conflicts pertain to discords of rights and concerned with individual claims over grievances and breach of the employment ordinance or employment contracts. They are settled either at the workplace level or by conciliation provided by the Labour Department. Otherwise, they are determined by the Labour Tribunal or the Minor Employment Claims Abjudication Board of the Labour Department.

---

108. Ng Sek-Hong, 'Trade Union Organisation and Labour Legislation', in Raymond Wacks (ed.), *Human Rights in Hong Kong*, Hong Kong: Oxford University Press, 1992, p. 452.
109. *Strikes, Strikers and the Law, op. cit.*, paras. 21 and 22, p. 6.
110. Ng Sek-hong, 'Trade Union Organisation and Labour Legislation', *op. cit.*, p. 452.
111. *Ibid.*

897. Hong Kong has always been free from the menace of frequent and widespread collective labour strife. The number of work stoppages due to strike has remained low. Concomitantly, working days lost caused by stoppages are sparse by international standards. The presence of trade unions in these trade disputes has also been conspicuous, often mirroring the rivalry between the pro-government Hong Kong Federation of Trade Unions (FTU) and the pro-democracy Hong Kong Confederation of Trade Unions (CTU). They are prone to intervene in labour disputes in bidding for new members and establishing their competing spheres of influence.

898. Voluntary conciliation by Labour Department officials in these disputes has also been common. In several cases, conciliation was authorized under the Labour Relations Ordinance. However, special conciliation was only known in one case, in an airline labour dispute.

II. Industrial Conflict in the Late 1990s and Early 2000s

899. The East Asian financial-cum-currency upheavals triggered off a sizable number of company insolvency and collapses, especially in the retail and department store sector. Notably, there was a wave of closures of Japanese department stores climaxing in the landmark case of the failure of Yaohoo, which was liquidated at the end of 1997. There was a conspicuous withdrawal of Japanese capital from the retail industry, Examples were Daimaru and Mitshibitsu. These businesses either halted their operation or re-structured themselves into leaner outlets. Lay-offs and retrenchment led to a rise in unemployment.

900. In 1998, Hong Kong Telcom, a franchise corporation in the telecommunications industry, attempted to rescind the provision of year-end double pay and substitute it with a profit-related flexible bonus for its staff. This move, resisted by the house unions, was greeted by workplace labour protests. Subsequent consultation with the apprehensive unions led to the company's offer of stock options to the staff. Such a measure was able to appease its employees and the unions, leading to the settlement of the dispute. Later, the tele communications industry was liberalized, admitting multi-players and intra-industry competition. Hong Kong Telecom was taken over by the Hutchison-Whampoa Group and re-named as the Pacific Century Cyber Works Ltd. (PCCW).[112] The PCCW, no longer covered by franchise and striving to maintain its competitive edge, carried out a number of retrenchment exercises in hiving off several departments. Instead, the work entailed was outsourced to the retrenched staff as external vendors. These acts, dubious in terms of business ethics, helped the company to save substantially on labour overheads.

901. Moreover, labour discord in this period was also inflicted on the air transport sector. Industrial contests were witnessed at two 'lead' enterprises, Cathay Pacific Airways and the Hong Kong Aircraft Engineering Company. Cathay Pacific

112. Ng Sek Hong and Carolyn Y. W. Poon, *Business Restructuring in Hong Kong: Strengths and Limits of Post-Industrial Capitalism*, Hong Kong: Oxford University Press, 2014, p. 41.

was afflicted by its pilot strike in 1999 over a dispute over pay cut. Another pay dispute brewed and erupted in the mid 2000s. The company discharged 49 of the strking pilots. These pilots, who belonged to their pilot union in Britain, took the airline to court on ground of 'unfair dismissal'.

The Flight Attendants' Union organizing the cabin crew has been purged of its militancy since the collapse of the air stewardesses' strike in 1992–993. It was accommodating towards the company's pay freeze and recourse to part-time casual hiring in the aftermath of the East Asian financial upheavals in 1997. However, it was locked in a bitter pay rise dispute in 2012 and the union at one point threatened strike action. Yet it was averted when the dispute was eventually settled with the conciliation assistance of the Labour Department authorized under the Labour Relations Ordinance.[113]

902. In the aftermath of the Asian financial upheavals of 1997 and the ensuing downturn of the economy, the Hong Kong Aircargo Company at the Airport Cargo Terminal attempted to impose a wage cut and trim down its workforce in 1999. The Hong Kong Federation of Trade Unions (FTU) intervened, leading to a process of hard bargain and a strained settlement. The embattled staff had to put up with a pay cut of 10 per cent. Severance pay for those who opted for retrenchment was doubled compared with the initial offer. Work resumed to normal around the end of October in that year. In the following year, 2000, another pay-cum-retrenchment dispute occurred between the Hong Kong Aircraft Engineering Company Limited and its employees. The company planned to hive off 200 of its technicians, leaving a consolidated strength of 2,000 technical personnel. The house union, the Civil Aviation Union and affiliated to the FTU, took a survey among the employees and came up with a wage demand in the range between 4 and 7 per cent. Management, after consulting the senior officials of the FTU, conceded and agreed to a pay hike of seven percent. Retrenchment proceeded in line with the company's plan.

III. Industrial Conflict in Recent Years

903. Industrial conflict has levelled off in recent years as the economy stabilizes and improves. However, there were two landmark disputes which led to prolonged work stoppages. The first one was the bar-benders strike in the building and construction industry in 2007. This trade was among those few traditional industries in Hong Kong where collective negotiation has been conducted on an annual basis between the trade association and the trade union(s) which belonged to the FTU. The agreement between the two sides on pay and work hour standards provided the guideline norm for hiring within this trade.

At the beginning, it was widely rumoured that an upward adjustment to a daily wage of HK$950 and eight-hour day could be expected. However, this was far beyond the capacity of the building contractors and the bar-bender contractors to shoulder because the industry was still trapped in stagnation. The Bar-benders

113. *Ibid.*

Union negotiated a modest formula of a wage hike from HK$800 to $850 and a cut-back in working hours from an eight and a half day to eight and a quarter hour day. Yet it fell far behind the expectations of the bar-benders who waged a strike and occupation in the Central District of Hong Kong. Apparently, the bar-benders' militancy was instigated by the Hong Kong Confederation of Trade Union (CTU) in counterpoise with the FTU. The CTU's intervention led to the escalation of the dispute. Its affiliate, the Building Sites Workers General Union, was a keen rival to the Building Workers General Union in the FTU camp. The CTU mobilized the students and the media in backing the strikers and set up a strike fund but wielded limited support from the public because of the nuisance caused to traffic in Central by the strikers. The staying power of the employers was enhanced by the declaration of the Builders Association and the Developers Association that they would not hold the building contractors liable for delays in the works due to the strike, which paralysed the industry. Under the conciliation by the Commissioner for Labour, a settlement was eventually arrived at in mid-September, whereby the daily wage was fixed at HK$860 and an eight hour day. It was reputed that the barbenders would opt for a lower wage increase in favour for a shorter working day. The barbenders resumed work, after a prolonged strike of more than a month.

As a sequel, the CTU sponsored the establishment of the Barbenders Solidarity Union, which enlisted around 300 new members, out of a total number of more than a thousand strikers. Ironically, the Building Sites Workers General Union suffered a setback in fall of membership size. Conversely, the Barbenders Union belonging to the FTU achieved a modest membership growth, doubling almost in size. Thereafter, in the following years, as the real estate sector recovers and the building and construction industry flares, there have been steady advances in the wage level of the barbenders largely because of a shortage of skill due to the sparsity of new entrants.[114]

904. Industrial harmony appears to have prevailed in Hong Kong for the following years until the container port workers'strike in the spring of 2012. It erupted at the largest terminal owned by Hutchison Whampoa. This container port operator, the Hutchison International Terminal, had the practice of reviewing the pay level for its workforce at annual intervals. It dealt with the Hong Kong Federation of Trade Unions (FTU) and the Hong Kong Federation of Labour Unions (FLO) but refrains to have any dialogue with the Hong Kong Confederation of Trade Unions (CTU). About two-thirds of HIT's 3,500 strong workforce are outsourced to some twenty contractors, which covered three main occupational types, namely, cargo handlers, crane drivers and container lorry drivers. They were organized by two unions, including the Container Transport Workers General Union affiliated to the FTU and the Hong Kong Wharf Staff Association belonging to the CTU. The former organized mainly the inland container truck drivers while the latter drew its members from the cargo handlers and crane drivers. On the other hand, the Hong Kong HIT

114. Chau Ye, *Labour History of Hong Kong*, Hong Kong: Nice News Publishing Co., 2009, pp.527-540. Also see Ng Sek-hong and Grace Lee, 'Workers' Industrial Militancy and Dependency Upon the State Lever: The Paradox of Industrial Relations in Hong Kong', *The Journal of Industrial Relations*, vol.52, no.4, September 2010.

Staff General Union, an affiliate to the FLU, was able to reign in organizing the direct employees of HIT.

905. In March 2012, the Hong Kong Wharf Staff Association moblilized the cargo handlers and the crane drivers working in the HIT Terminal for a strike in demand for pay rise and work hours improvements. Orchestrated by the CTU, the strike was directed at the two contractors who were their employers and the principal, HIT. The employer's initial offer of a 9.5 per cent wage hike was turned down by the strikers. The strike was a manifestation of the discontents harboured by the disgruntled workers, who had to work excessively long hours in appaling conditions and won sympathetic support from the students and overseas wharf workers' union. At its peak, the strikers numbered more than 500 but later withered down to about 350 persons. Because of the key importance of these two kinds of job, the operation of the container port was paralysed for a brief period but Hutchison Whampoa was later able to transfer a large proportion of its container business to its container port at Yantin in Shenzhen across the border in the Mainland. This re-location could have worked to the detriments of Hong Kong as the world's leading centre for container shipment.

906. The Federation of Trade Unions (FTU) attempted to intervene in this dispute but was of no avail since the strikers were the strong hold of the CTU. Appeals were made to the public for donation to a strike fund. Almost unprecedented in the labour history of Hong Kong, a huge strike fund amounting to eight and half a million (HK dollars) was collected and enabled the strikers to stay on. The strike lasted for more than two months and was widely reported in the media around the world. Pickets were held at the container wharf and outside the Hong Kong and Shanghai Bank (HSBC) in Central. It was an episode of overt industrial militancy. Slogans were shouted and banners were waved at the strikers' demonstrations in protest against Hutchison Whampoa and HIT for practising blatant capitalism.

907. In May, the contractors jointly issued a communiqué, offering a pay rise of 9.8 per cent across the board. The offer was repudiated by the strikers at the beginning. However, HIT and its subcontractors made it clear that this was the baseline, beyond which no more concession was tenable. One of the two contractors hiring the strikers also announced its 'closure' decision. As a sequel, its workers on strike were all laid off.

908. The retrenched wharf workers were later eventually absorbed by other contractors. In the meantime, the strikers decided to accept the pay offer and resumed work in early May. Declaring its victory in this industrial warfare, the Hong Kong Wharf Staff Association pledged to continue its battle to wrestle recognition from HIT and its contractors for collective bargaining on behalf of the container wharf workers.[115]

115. Chan Ye, *A Concise History of the Hong Kong Labour Movement*, Hong Kong: Nice News Publishing Co., 2013, pp. 265-269.

909. These two disputes attest to the problematic nature of the outsourcing and contracting system, which has been popularized now in the name of contributing to business flexibility. The contractors are often caught at loggerheads with the workers whom they hire and the liability is often traced back vicariously to the principal company. If backed by their principals, the contractors are often able to wield considerable bargaining power and hold their workers in dispute at bay. Another point worth noting is that if the strike is able to impair or halt the normal operation of the employers, the strikers can command substantial staying power and persist in their fight. However, strikes are often more effective if they are sudden and short in taking the employers by surprise. Otherwise, the employers will be able to adjust their operations to cope with the work stoppages. Moreover, the strikers may be deprived of their means of livelihood because of suspension of pay. In both of these two cases, however, the CTU was able to summon and manage a strike fund in support of the strikers, so that the latters could hold on to their actions. Yet they are probably more of an exception than the rule in the context of Hong Kong.

910. The statistics in Table 5 are indicative of a secular decline in the level of industrial conflict in Hong Kong. This trend coalesces with the earlier observation that workplace labour relations have been stabilizing since the turn of the century. Yet, the volume of industrial discords peaked in the years of 2002 and 2003 when Hong Kong was afflicted by the epidemic.

Table 5 Longitudinal Profile of Industrial Conflict in Hong Kong, 2000-2012

Year	*Number of Claims (disputes of right)*
2000	28,620
2002	34,821
2003	33,689
2006	24,958
2007	21,698
2008	20,623
2009	24,305
2011	18,086
2012	18,920

Year	*Number of labour disputes (including disputes of interests and disputes of rights)*
2000	308
2001	369
2002	433
2003	427

Year	*Number of labour disputes (including disputes of interests and disputes of rights)*
2004	270
2005	237
2006	199
2007	124
2008	120
2009	143
2010	68
2011	86
2012	79

Sources: Annual Reports of the Labour Department, Hong Kong SAR.

Postscript: Where are Labour Law and Labour Policies Headed?

911. Until the time of writing, Hong Kong has been able to sustain its 'capitalist' rubric as a Special Administrative Region (SAR) of China within its ingenious political model of 'one country, two systems' engineered by Chairman Deng Xiaoping. Cultural pluralism and cosmopolitanism continue to thrive. 'The rule of law' has been kept in place. The accelerated post-modernization economic reforms in the Mainland nurture a dual process of deindustrialization and re-commercialization which has converted this city economy into an international financial centre based predominantly upon high-value-adding tertiary and service industries. Its buoyancy is backed by a free currency system, a low tax regime and an efficient infrastructure of banking, human resource, transport and telecommunications.

912. Hong Kong is not entirely free from its domestic problems, which are essentially two-fold. The first is its proneness to social protest by different interest and pressure groups. The second is growing wealth and income inequality, which probably emanates from the vicissitudes of advanced capitalism. Endemic to these twin problems is probably (i) the unarrested fragmentation of society into strata and sub-strata of divergent or even polarized interests and (ii) the growing impotence of a weary administration to reconcile and accommodate these haggling forces.

913. By and large, the SAR administration has on the whole been tolerant towards a free and often obtrusive press, demonstration, public assembly and procession. This permissive posture has been conducive to the gestation of civic protests. Anxious to demonstrate its resolution to implement the cherished policy of 'one country, two systems', the Beijing central government has been prudent in restraining itself against undue intervention in the domestic affairs of Hong Kong, except on a few critical issues like the entry of immigrants from the Mainland into Hong Kong and most recently, the electoral rules on the nomination of candidates for the office of the Chief Executive. Nevertheless, as wealth becomes more concentrated, injustices in the distribution of life chances and economic deprivation, alongside the alienation of sectional interests, have caused waves of demonstration clamouring for various demands. Even within the law-making Legislative Council, factional strife sometimes goes adrift and can be manifest in belligerent acts in defiance of internal house rules and in breach of the orderly conduct of meetings.

914. As early as in 2003, just five years after the handover, Hong Kong was labelled by the *Washington Post* as a 'city of protests' when large-scale protest marches captured exposure in the media worldwide.[116] Demonstrations have been commonplace at weekends. Roads are often blocked by large-scale public assemblies and processions on key public holidays like Labour Day, Foundation Day of the SAR and National Day. The latest episode was the 'Occupy Central' movement

116. Sek-hong Ng and Olivia Ip, 'Labour and Society', in Joseph Y.S. Cheng (ed.), *The Hong Kong Special Administrative Region in Its First Decade*, Hong Kong:City University Press of Hong Kong, 2007, pp.443–493.

spear-headed by the intellectuals and students who yearned for bona fide representation in the nomination of candidates for the general election of the Chief Executive scheduled for 2017. This popular campaign, branded as 'a peaceful war of civic resistance', aimed at paralysing the Central District of the Hong Kong Island, which was the banking centre of the city, in order to bring pressure to bear upon the government. It commenced on 28 September 2014, amidst a thunderstorm, and was widely reported as the 'Umbrella Revolution' in foreign press. Students demonstrating against the official election blueprint took to the streets and halted traffic on various main roads. Schools had to be cancelled and normal life was heavily disrupted. At the time of writing, the SAR government was striving to seek a dialogue with the leaders of the defiant and refractory students in search for a settlement.[117]

915. The advent of the 'Occupy Central' movement soon permeated almost every stratum and walk of life of Hong Kong society. The police at first adopted a 'hard line' but later softened it because of worldwide condemnation of its relentless use of pepper spray and tear gas. Street violence erupted amidst confrontation between the protestors and people who wanted to quell the 'occcupation' because of its impediments on traffic and normal life. This tide of social unrest was unprecedented and not paralleled by the Riot of 1956 and the Civil Disturbance of 1967. This was because the demonstrators were mostly students and workers. Their agitation was not only inspired by their yearning for democracy but also emanated from their grievances about social inequality, deterorating life chances and above all their detestation of an administration which, void of a popular basis, was increasingly drained of its legitimacy. As pointed out by Giddens, 'whether combined with more orthodox democratic institutions or not, dialogic democracy becomes a prime means for the containment or dissolution of violence'.[118] In this latest episode, Hong Kong faced a crisis since student militancy was precipitated by students' dismay over a 'closed' government which failed to respond to their quest for democracy. The protesting students, mostly from the universities but some from secondary schools, began to combine to register their agony and protest when the government announced that the general election scheduled for 2017 would be just nominal rather than bona fide.[119] The official reason given was that the election rules, laid down in the Basic Law, had to be housed within the interpretative framework promulgated by the People's Congress, which was paramount.[120]

117. See, for example, 'The Party v. the People', *The Economist*, 4 October, 2014, p.13, and Hannah Beech, Elizabeth Barber, Rishi Iyengar, Emily Rauhala and David Stout, 'Hong Kong Stands Up: Why the Territory's Fight for Democracy is a Challenge for China', *Time*, vol.184, no.14, 13 October, 2014, pp.10–15.

118. Anthony Giddens, *Beyond Left and Right: The Future of Radical Politics*, Cambridge: Polity Press, 1994, pp. 244-25.

119. Beech *et al.*, *op. cit.* See also 'Hong Kong Protests: The Waiting Game', *The Economist*, 11-17 October, 2014, p. 30.

120. For a pseudo-orthodox interpretation of these electoral procedures as prescribed by the Beijing Central Government, see, for example, Leung Mei-fun, 'HKs Reform Must Follow Constitutional Framework', *China Daily*, 6 October, 2014, p. 5.

916. The 'Occupy Central' drama was later compounded when the livelihood of the grassroots people was at stake because of the blockade of the main roads due to the barricades erected by the protestors. At the beginning, the Professional Teachers' Union, the biggest labour union in Hong Kong, called a general strike of the teachers while the affiliated unions of the Hong Kong Confederation of Trade Unions expressed sympathetic support for the protestors. However, they lost steam as the street demonstrations dragged on. The problems caused by the road blockades incited hatred and vociferous opposition from many workers and petty shopkeepers, who were prevented from making their normal living. There was open hostility to the pro-democracy pickets when they stormed the latter's barricades. Officials and members from the Building and Construction Worker's General Union, the Motor Transport Workers General Union, the Taxi Drivers and Operators Association, the Tramway Workers' Union and an array of other transport workers unions which belonged to the pro-government Hong Kong Federation of Trade Unions, were conspicuous for their presence among these counter-occupation agitators.[121] Apparently, the 'Umbrella Revolution' represents a paradoxical influence on the labouring mass, which was split between those who were sympathetic and those who were antagonistic to the cause of the students.

917. Growing inequality in income and wealth is attested by the secular rise in the Gini ratio.[122] Although Hong Kong proves to be resilient in maintaining its prosperity and stability, wealth has become increasingly concentrated at the top in the hands of a small business elite. A potent problem besetting the grassroots has been the rising cost of living due to inflation and high property price and rental. In spite of the enactment of an economy-wide minimum wage in 2011, low pay still persists within a sizable pocket of the working class, especially among the recent immigrants, many of whom are living below the poverty line. Besides, the 'diploma disease' has been endemic because of over production of university graduates who glut the professional and executive labour market, causing many of them to move down to jobs of lesser status and responsibilies, like clerical posts. Their disillusion and sense of deprivation due to their under-employment could have sowed the seed of the social discontents of the intellectual unemployed and underemployed. Such ripple effects hence help fuel the 'Occupy Central' movement.

918. Industrial unrest in Hong Kong has stayed at a low level by international standards, probably because of a continuously buoyant labour market and the paucity of the strike funds held by the labour unions. However, there were two landmark work stoppages in recent years. As noted earlier, these were the bar-benders' strike and the strike by the wharf workers at the container port in 2012. Each lasted for a long duration and the tussle between the two sides was incensed. In spite of

---

121. For reports on the Counter-Occupation protests, see, for example, 'Police Vow to Restore Public', *China Daily*, 6 October, 2014. Also see *Wen Wei Po*, 16 October, pp. A2-A5; *Headline Daily*, 14 October; 15 October,18 October and 21 October 2014.

122. The Gini coefficient, as published by the government, has been rising consistently over the last three decades, from 0.451 in 1981, through 0.476 in 1991, 0.525 in 2001, to 0.533 in 2006 and 0.537 in 2011. Census and Statistics Department, Hong Kong SAR Government, *Population Census and By-census*, for various years from 1971 to 2011.

the prolonged stalemate in either case, the government refrained from invoking the Labour Relations Ordinance, either to freeze industrial actions or to facilitate negotiation and settlement of the discord. The efficacy of the Ordinance has hence not been tested.

919. Seventeen years after the reversion of Hong Kong back to China, labour law has been conserved within the anglo-saxon system of common law in its interpretation and application. To a certain extent, Hong Kong's labour legislation has also served as a model for reference and even emulation in the Mainland which is building up a modernized body of labour codes. An example is the Employment Ordinance which has inspired the writing of some provisions in China's Labour Contract Law of 2008. At the same time, Hong Kong has kept its low tax regime in order to attract capital and human talent. As such, it has not been an effective corrective to the re-distribution of income in society, which has been sharpened as the reward system is biased in favour of the rich and the cream of the meritocracy.

920. In retrospect, the labour law system has become more polished and interventionist so as to provide a better protective net for the employees, as attested by the enactment of a general minimum wage legislation and an array of anti-discrimination laws. However, there are still important gaps, notably, the absence of any enactments on standard work hours, age discrimination, equal pay and collective bargaining rights.The rationale for this absence is probably to leave a latitutude of flexibility in the economy and for purportedly free trade and business.

921. Formulation of labour policy since the inception of the SAR administration is visibly fashioned by the 'tug of war' between the business sector and the labour movement. Without departing sharply from what it was during the reign of the colonial government, its essence is to place priority upon labour law as the key lever for safeguarding the well-being of the workers and regulating labour–mangement relations. The rationale of the present labour policy is apparently to attain gradual betterment in labouring conditions yet without upsetting a business environment hitherto favourable to capital. In other words, the government has to rope-dance in mitigating between the divergent interests of the workforce and business corporations, which are the key stake-holders in the political economy. Ideologically, the governing elite continues to subscribe to the philosophy of 'free market' and 'neo-liberalism', subject to the overriding dictum of 'one country, two systems' as the political formula of accommodation with a socialist mother country and the sovereign prerogative of the central government in Beijing.

922. The chief advisory organ to the government on labour policy and labour law getation remains the tripartite Labour Advisory Board, with equal representation from oganized labour and business. It is still chaired by the Commissioner for Labour or his deputy.The Labour Department also provides it with secretarial support. The election of workers' representatives on the Board has, since the inception of the SAR, been dominated by the left-wing Hong Kong Federation of Trade Unions. Under its influence, the Hong Kong Confederation of Trade Unions, its arch rival, has been excluded from membership in the Board, in spite of its presence on the Legislative Council. There have been suggestions that the functions and membership of the Board, which have been kept in virtual status quo since its inception in the 1930s, be widened and restructured. For example, the Board can incorporate members from the professional and academic ranks, like lawyers and scholars, who can act as resource persons in advising it from a legal and learned perspective. Up to the present, its present function has been essentially consultative, without any effective power apart from vetting application from employers on importing guest labour. Given its tripartite composition, it is perhaps desirable for the government to vest it with wider prerogative. An example is to bestow upon it a quasi-form of law-making power like the promulgation of subsidiary legislation, that is, regulations annexed to labour ordinances.

923. By its nature, the Labour Tribunal is literally a labour or industrial court except for its informal auspices. Up to the present, the Tribunal's jurisdiction has been limited to adjudication over claims or disputes of rights. By implication, it has not been competent to hear disputes of rights like those over pay rises. Nor can it determine simplified workmen's compensation cases or claims of damages over tort. The administration may wish to consider extending its scope of jurisdiction so that it can provide a judicial procedure for settling disputes of the latter kind.

924. At the time of writing, Hong Kong society is still haunted by the ills of persisting or even increasing inequality in income and wealth. Even the middle-class are emasculated in their economic conditions as wealth becomes increasingly concentrated in the hands of a few rich.[123] As observed by Piketty, '(w)hen the rate of return on capital exceeds the rate of growth of output and income, as it did in the nineteeth century and likely to do again in the twenty-first, capitalism automatically generates arbitrary and unsustainable inequalities that radically undermine the meritocratic values on which democratic societies are based'.[124] In the Hong Kong context, an accelerating trend of wealth inequality is prone to perpetuate social injustice and feed labour protest and social unrest. As it stands now, labour law will by and large remain the status quo and its ameliorating effects upon inequalities and injustice are hence limited. Besides, the 'diploma disease' of intellectual unemployment due to the over-production of university graduates helps explain the radical social actions pursued by a disillusioned and refractory educated mass. Meanwhile, the vicissitudes of job insecurity and the lack of employment benefits will continue to

123. At the beginning of the 2010s, the deepening wealth gap led to 'the creeping rise of an alienated feeling of hatred for the rich' among Hong Kong people. In 2010, Oxfam reported that the number of working poor families has gone up by 12 per cent between the years of 2005 and 2010. See Joseph Y. S. Cheng,'Has He Got the Job Done? An Evaluation of Donald Tsang Administration', in Joseph Cheng (ed.), *The Second Chief Executive of Hong Kong SAR: Evaluating the Tsang Years: 2005-2012*, Hong Kong: City University of Hong Kong Press, pp.10 and 12. Evidently, urban poverty has continued to plague Hong Kong society. In reviewing the 'Occupy Central' movement, *Time* magazine also observes recently that income inequality in Hong Kong 'has surged since 1997 and now ranks as the highest in the developed world'; See Elizabeth Barber, Rishi Iyengar and David Stout, Voice of a Generation: a youthquake that's shaking up Hong Kong, *Time*, vol. 184, no. 15, 20 October 2014, p.20.

124. Thomas Piketty, *Capital in the Twenty-First Century* (translated by Arthur Goldhammer), Cambridge: The Belknap Press of Harvard University Press, 2014, p.1.

'beset those who are casually hired in atypical employment arrangements'.[125] It is expected that the Employment Ordinance will be shortly amended to afford wider flexibility to the definition of a continuous employment contract, so that more part-time employees can be included within its coverage and hence eligible for statutory employment benefits. However, as the business community shifts to a more conservative mood in the wake of the 'Occupy Central' enigma, such a liberalization measure will probably be diluted and less generous than what was contemplated earlier. It is envisaged that the existing prerequisite that there should be at least 18 hours worked for each week will be rescinded, yet the total number of hours which have to be worked to qualify for continuity of employment will be kept intact.

125. Oliva Ip and Sek-hong Ng, 'Labour and Employment in the Tsang Administration', in Joseph Cheng (ed.), *The Second Chied Executive of Hong Kong SAR: Evaluating the Tsang Years: 2001-2012*, op. *cit.*, 429.

Selected Bibliography

Beijing Review, vol. 29, no. 2, 13 January 1986,

Butters, H.R. (1939), *Report by the Labour Officer (W. H. R. Butters) on Labour and Labour Conditions in Hong Kong*, Seasonal Paper No. 3, Hong Kong: Government Printer.

Chen, Edward K.Y. (2000), 'Economic Setting' in Ng Sek Hong and David G. Lethbridge (eds.), *The Business Environment in Hong Kong*, Hong Kong: Oxford University Press, 4th edition.

Chen, Edward K.Y. (1995),'The Economic Setting', in Ng Sek-Hong and David G. Lethbridge (eds.), *The Business Environment in Hong Kong*, Hong Kong: Oxford University Press, 3rd edition.

Clark, John and Wedderburn, Lord (1983), 'Modern Labour Law: Problems, Functions and Policies', in Lord Weddeburn *et al., Labour Law and Industrial Relations: Building on Kahn-Freund*, Oxford: Clarendon Press.

Davis, Paul and Freedland, Mark (1983), *Kahn-Freund's Labour and the Law*, London: Stevens and Sons.

Deng, Xiaoping (1985), *Building Socialism with Chinese Characteristics*, Beijing: Foreign Language Press.

England, Joe and Rear, John (1975), *Chinese Labour Under British Rule*, Hong Kong: Oxford University Press.

Flanders, Allan (ed.) (1971), *Collective Bargaining*, Harmondsworth: Penguin.

Hong Kong Government, *Hong Kong 2007*, Hong Kong Printing Department, 2008.

Hong Kong Government, *Hong Kong 1995: A Review of 1994*, Hong Kong: Government Printer, 1995.

Hong Kong Government, *Report of the Commissioner for Labour*, 1994.

Joint Declaration of the Government of the United Kingdom of Great Britain and Northern Ireland and the Government of the People's Republic of China on the Question of Hong Kong, 1984.

Hong Kong Hansards, for various years.

Haddon-Cave, Philip, (formerly Chief Secretary, Hong Kong Government) (1984), 'The Marketing of Some Aspects of Public Policy in Hong Kong', in David Lethbridge (ed.), *The Business Environment in Hong Kong*, Hong Kong: Oxford University Press, 2nd edition.

Kahn-Freund, Otto (1972), *Labour and Law*, 1st edition, London: Stevens and Sons.

Labour Department, *Annual Report 2007*, Hong Kong: Labour Department, Hong Kong SAR Government, 2008.

Labour Department, *Annual Report 2006*, Hong Kong: Labour Department, Hong Kong SAR Government, 2007.

Labour Department, *Annual Report*, Hong Kong: Labour Department, Hong Kong SAR Government, for various years.

Labour Department, Hong Kong Government, *Explanatory Note on The Eligibility to Severance Payment upon a Change of Workplace under the Employment (Amendment) (No. 4) Ordinance 1992*, Hong Kong: Labour Department, Hong Kong Government, 1992.

Labour Department, Hong Kong Government, *Strikes, Strikers and the Law*, Hong Kong: Labour Department, 1976.

Lethbridge, David G. and Ng Sek-Hong (1995), 'Labour and Employment', in Ng Sek Hong and David G. Lethbridge (eds.), *The Business Environment in Hong Kong*, Hong Kong: Oxford University Press, 3rd edn.

Lethbridge, David G. and Ng Sek-Hong (1993), 'The Business Environment and Employment', in David Lethbridge (ed.), *The Business Environment in Hong Kong*, Hong Kong: Oxford University Press, 2nd edition with a Postscript on Hong Kong in the 1990s.

Marsh, Arthur I. and Evans, E.O. (1973), *The Dictionary of Industrial Relations*, London: Hutchison, 1973.

Ng Sek-Hong and Cheng Soo-may (1994), 'Affluent Migrants as a "Class Phenomenon: The Hong Kong Case"', in Lau Siu-kai, Lee Ming-Kwan, Wan Po-san and Wong Siu-lun (eds.), *Inequalities and Development: Social Stratification in Chinese Societies*, Hong Kong: Hong Kong Institute of Asia-Pacific Studies, The Chinese University of Hong Kong.

Ng Sek-Hong (1990), Hong Kong, a monograph in the series, R. Blanpain (ed.), *International Encyclopaedia for Labour Law and Industrial Relations*, The Netherlands: Kluwer, supplement 109,

Ng Sek-Hong (1986), 'Labour' in Joseph Y.S. Cheng (ed.), *Hong Kong in Transition*, Hong Kong: Oxford University Press.

Ng Sek-Hong (1991), 'Workplace Industrial Relations in Hong Kong', in International Labour Organization (ed.), The Development of Sound Labour Relations, Bangkok: International Labour Organization.

Ng Sek-Hong (1985), 'Strike at Mass Transit Railway Corporation: Its Implications.' *Hong Kong Law Journal*, vol. 15, no. 1.

Ng Sek-Hong (1995), 'Workplace Relations in Hong Kong', in Ng Sek Hong and David G. Lethbridge (eds.), *The Business Environment in Hong Kong*, Hong Kong: Oxford University Press, 3rd edn.

Ng Sek-Hong (2001), 'Hong Kong Labour Law in Retrospect', in Lee Pui-Tak (ed.), *Hong Kong Reintegrating With China: Political, Cultural and Social Dimensions*, Hong Kong: Hong Kong University Press.

Ng Sek-Hong (1992), 'Trade Union Organisation and Labour Legislation', in Raymond Wacks (ed.), Human Rights in Hong Kong, Hong Kong: Oxford University Press.

Registrar of Trade Unions, *Annual Departmental Report*, Hong Kong, 1961–1962.

Roberts, B.C. (1964), *Labour in the Tropical Territories of the Commonwealth*, London: The London School of Economics and Political Science (G. Bell and Sons).

Trade Unions Ordinance, 1971.

Trade Unions Ordinance, *Laws of Hong Kong*.

Turner, H.A., Fosh, Patricia and Ng Sek Hong (1991), *Between Two Societies: Hong Kong Labour in Transition*, Hong Kong: Centre of Asian Studies, University of Hong Kong.

Turner, H.A. *et al.* (1980), *The Last Colony: Best Whose?* Cambridge: Cambridge University Press.

Turner, H.A. *et al.* (1980), *A Summary Account of an Enquiry: Labour Organisations, the Labour Market and Labour Relations in Hong Kong*, Faculty of Economic, Cambridge University, cyclostyled.

Yeung Chi-Kin (1988), 'Joint Consultation, Collective Bargaining and Trade Union Recognition: status and prospect', in Y.C. Jao, David A. Levin, Ng Sek-Hong and Elizabeth Sinor (eds.), *Labour Movement in a Changing Society: The Experience of Hong Kong*, Hong Kong: Centre of Asian Studies, University of Hong Kong.

Selected Bibliography

Index

The numbers given are paragraph numbers

Index

Index

Index

Index

Index

Index

Index

Index

Index

Index

Index